W9-DHM-272

JSOT/ASOR MONOGRAPH SERIES

Number 8

HOUSES AND THEIR FURNISHINGS IN BRONZE AGE PALESTINE
Domestic Activity Areas and Artefact Distribution
in the Middle Ages and Late Bronze Ages

by

P.M. Michèle Daviau

HOUSES AND THEIR FURNISHINGS
IN BRONZE AGE PALESTINE

Domestic Activity Areas and Artefact Distribution
in the Middle and Late Bronze Ages

P.M. Michèle Daviau

DS
111.1
.D29
1993
seal

THE UNITED LIBRARY

Copyright © 1993 Sheffield Academic Press

Published by JSOT Press
JSOT Press is an imprint of
Sheffield Academic Press Ltd
343 Fulwood Road
Sheffield S10 3BP
England

Typeset by Sheffield Academic Press
and
Printed on acid-free paper in Great Britain
by Biddles Limited
Guildford

British Library Cataloguing in Publication Data

Daviau, P.M. Michele
    Houses and Their Furnishings in Bronze
    Age Palestine: Domestic Activity Areas
    and Artefact Distribution in the Middle
    and Late Bronze Ages.— (JSOT/ASOR
    Monographs, ISSN 0267-5684; No. 8)
    I. Title II. Series
    933

ISBN 1-85075-355-5

CONTENTS

PREFACE

The preparation of a major research project is a test of one's courage and the generosity of the scholarly community in which one works. The community provides support and stimulation for the arduous task ahead. In my case, the Department of Near Eastern Studies at the University of Toronto provided the milieu in which I could develop as a research scholar. To all its members, I am indebted. Therefore, I would like to take this opportunity to acknowledge that debt and thank the members of the department who generously shared their expertise and provided moral support. Special mention must be made of Dr John S. Holladay, Jr for his direction and advice during the preparation of this work. Dr Ernest Clark, Dr Nicholas Millet, Dr Joe Seger and Dr Joseph Shaw, members the dissertation committee, also offered constructive comments and suggestions. Dr Gloria London and Dr Bryant Wood made specific suggestions regarding pottery production and use. Information concerning Egyptian iconography was generously supplied by Dr Ronald Leprohon of the University of Toronto. Rosemary Aicher of Kitchener, Ontario and Laurie Cowell of Waterloo, Ontario provided technical assistance. Pride of place goes to my husband, Dr Paul E. Dion, of the University of Toronto, for his unflagging support and encouragement during many long years of study. To him, I dedicate this study, with love and devotion.

LIST OF FIGURES AND CHARTS

The figures for this study have all been redrawn and adapted to a
standard style. Those drawings prepared by me include Figs. 1, 5, 6,
7, 8, 9, 10, 11, 12, 31, 32, 33, 34, 35, 37, 38, 42, 45, 46, 49, 50, 51a,
51b, 52, 53, 54, 59, 61, 62a, 62b, 63, 66, 67, 68a, 68b, 69a, 69b, 74,
76, 77, 79, 86. The remaining plans were drawn by Rosemary Aicher
of Kitchener, Ontario.

A key to architectural features is given below. Functional designations are included on certain plans. The code used to designate various
functions includes:

F = food preparation/consumption
S = storage
T = textile production
P = pottery production
B = business
A = adornment
M = metallurgy

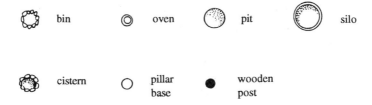

bin   oven   pit   silo

cistern   pillar base   wooden post

Figures

Charts

ABBREVIATIONS

AASOR	Annual of the American Schools of Oriental Research
ADAJ	*Annual of the Department of Antiquities of Jordan*
AJA	*American Journal of Archaeology*
AOAT	Alter Orient und Altes Testament
ARCE	American Research Center in Egypt
BA	*Biblical Archaeologist*
BASOR	*Bulletin of the American Schools of Oriental Research*
BASORSup	*Bulletin of the American Schools of Oriental Research, Supplements*
BSAE	British School of Archaeology in Egypt
CAH	Cambridge Ancient History
CMO	Collection de la maison de l'Orient Méditerranéen ancien
CRAIBL	*Comptes rendus de l'Académie des inscriptions et belles-lettres*
IEJ	*Israel Exploration Journal*
IFAO	Institut français de l'archéologie orientale
IFAPO	Institut français de l'archéologie du proche orient
JEA	*Journal of Egyptian Archaeology*
JSSEA	*Journal of the Society for the Study of Egyptian Antiquities*
PEQ	*Palestine Exploration Quarterly*
QDAP	*Quarterly of the Department of Antiquities in Palestine*
RB	*Revue biblique*
SEÅ	*Svensk exegetisk årsbok*
SIMA	Studies in Mesopotamian Archaeology
VT	*Vetus Testamentum*
ZDPV	*Zeitschrift des deutschen Palästina-Vereins*

INTRODUCTION

The study of modern town planning and community development has generated a renewed interest in the organization and layout of ancient cities and towns.[1] Modern zoning regulations distinguish between commercial zones, parks, domestic and industrial areas. Recognizing that the inhabitants of ancient cities also engaged in a wide variety of activities, archaeologists, in their excavation of urban sites, seek to distinguish areas of public buildings, fortifications and housing. They also identify palaces, temples, houses, workshops and stables. When archaeology was in its infancy, these identifications were based on weak inference, and conditioned by the excavator's learning and experience. For the cities of the Middle East, this knowledge was based essentially on nineteenth century European views of the biblical world.[2]

After the turn of the century, when excavations took place at the major biblical towns of Samaria (1909–1910), Megiddo (1925–1939), Beth-Shan (1921–1933) and Tell Beit Mirsim (1926–1932), archaeologists began to understand the complex process of tell formation, making possible the recovery of superimposed structures dating from the Neolithic to the Roman Period.[3] In the Middle and Late Bronze

1. Interest in the ancient city is seen in two major works: Mumford 1961 and Hammond 1972.
2. L. Woolley's interpretation of the function of house rooms uncovered in his excavations at Ur shows a combination of archaeological analysis and cultural conditioning. His analysis was based on the archaeological finds themselves, his observation of contemporary Iraqi dwellings and on the study of 'house omen texts'. On the other hand, Woolley's own cultural conditioning led him to identify a ground floor bedroom as the servant's quarters in view of his theory that each family had a servant and that the family itself slept on the upper floor (Woolley and Mallowan 1976: 23-25).
3. Unlike the early excavations at Gezer (Macalister), Shechem and Jericho (Sellin), the work of G. Reisner and C. Fisher at Samaria reflected an understanding of tell formation and the superimposition of soil layers that was advanced for its time. For a presentation of the history of excavation methods and the principal scholars involved, see King 1983.

Age strata, residential areas contained house plans which became
prototypes for classifying future discoveries. Albright articulated a
typical plan for Middle and Late Bronze Age Palestinian houses based
on the Stratum D Patrician house at Tell Beit Mirsim (1938: 36-7).

> All these... noble houses consisted of a court and a row or rows of rooms
> communicating with it; living quarters for the patrons were in a second
> story (Albright 1960: 93).

A second type of domestic structure, that of the Late Bronze Age
Amarna style house, was identified at Beth-Shan (Rowe 1930), with
further examples at Tell el Far'ah (S) (Petrie 1930; MacDonald 1932)
and at Mt Gerizim[1] (Albright 1960: 101).

These excavations during the 1920s and 1930s set the standard for
years to come. Archaeologists identified major architectural styles,
established a sound pottery chronology that enabled them to date various occupation layers, and distinguished the cultural and behavioural
characteristics of the inhabitants of ancient Canaan. Subsequent excavations would build on the models established during this classic
period.

After World War II when excavations in Palestine resumed, many
large sites were explored, some for the first time. Most sites, however, were already known from previous excavation, such as Hazor
(Garstang's soundings in 1928), Shechem (Sellin's excavations, 1913–
1914 and 1926–1927), and Jericho (Sellin and Watzinger's excavation
during 1907–1909). With the revival of excavations at these sites,
archaeologists employed new techniques of stratigraphic control,
pottery reading, recording and scientific analysis. These techniques
resulted in the retrieval of an increased amount of information
regarding the function of ancient buildings and the life style of the
inhabitants. Archaeologists recovered many new styles of architecture
and identified additional types of ceramic wares. While these additions
enriched the respective corpora, it also became clear that new methods
were needed for understanding these finds and the human dynamics
involved in their production and use. As an analytical method,
comparison with standard types, supplemented by parallel examples
from other sites of the same period in the ancient Near East, became

---

1. Albright identified the building on Mount Gerizim as a house dating to the
Middle Bronze Age. For a reinterpretation of this house, see the excavation report by
R.G. Boling (Boling 1975).

insufficient. The goal of 'New Archaeology' was to develop a multidisciplinary approach that would explore the total environment of the ancient city and the life ways of its inhabitants.[1]

Some Near Eastern archaeologists also began to employ 'newer' methods of data analysis patterned on the work of prehistorians and New World archaeologists. This development in methodology is under way, both in the area of theoretical approaches to the past, and in the means of analysis. Under the nomenclature of 'Social Archaeology', Renfrew specified five approaches to the past: (1) understanding the growth and decline of population; (2) investigation of social stratification; (3) use of ethnographic analogies; (4) study of exchange mechanisms to reveal social behaviour; and (5) study of social environment in the pattern and hierarchy of settlements (Renfrew 1973: 11-15). By employing these approaches, it is now possible to re-examine the most ordinary archaeological remains and discover a wealth of new insights into the life ways and social organization of ancient peoples.

While this development in archaeological theory has been influential among Near Eastern archaeologists in their field work during the past two decades,[2] an extended scholarly discussion of the theories and methods used to attain the goals of anthropological archaeology has been in process among New World archaeologists during a much longer period.[3] Indeed, there remains a certain gap between those archaeologists who function as anthropologists making use of scientific methods of analysis and those in Near Eastern archaeology who are concerned primarily with ancient history and chronology. New World scholars see the exclusive task of archaeology to be the study of cultural process or change (Binford 1972: 125-32; Flannery 1972: 102-107). This position assumes that the tasks of documenting culture history and understanding ancient life ways is either complete or unable to be realized (Leone 1972: 26).

---

1. A good description of the recent developments in Near Eastern field methods and theory is presented by L.E. Toombs (1982: 89-91), and in a series of articles by W.G. Dever (1980: 40-48; 1981: 15-29; and 1982: 103-107).

2. This development is seen most clearly in the statement of an archaeological project's research design submitted to the American Schools of Oriental Research by its directors prior to an excavation season; for example, the proposals of the Joint Archaeological Expedition to Tell el-Hesi, Israel, and that of the Madaba Plains Project (unpublished materials in the possession of the author).

3. The study most often cited is that of L.R. Binford (1967).

While it is true that the large number of Palestinian mounds, excavated during the past thirty years, has increased our knowledge of the occupation history of individual sites, I. Nicholas contends that our knowledge of the culture history of the Near East is still insufficient. She stresses that studies of cultural process 'must rest on a solid framework of sites that are well-excavated and well-understood in terms of their internal structure and function' (1980: 2).

In this study, my interest is limited to one aspect of that culture history, namely the organization of domestic space and the location of activity areas within that space. The identification of individual activity areas depends on spatial distribution studies and functional analysis of all excavated objects. Such a functionalist approach to the study of artefact distribution and correlated human behaviour patterns should provide the basis for a better understanding of the use of architectural space, room arrangement and house plan in antiquity.[1]

The State of the Question

During the past decade, three major studies of domestic architecture in the Eastern Mediterranean have appeared; F. Braemer, *L'architecture domestique du Levant à l'âge du fer* (1982), J. McEnroe, *Minoan House and Town Arrangement* (1982), both doctoral dissertations, and a three volume work by O. Aurenche, *La maison orientale: L'architecture du Proche Orient des origines au milieu du quatrième millénaire* (1981). These studies gathered together, respectively, the results of numerous excavations in Palestine, Crete and the Levant as a whole, and presented an analysis of room arrangement and house type.

Braemer assembled a catalogue of domestic structures excavated at Syro-Palestinian sites of the Iron Age (1200–586 BC) and compared their architectural plans and construction techniques. In order to distinguish domestic structures from public or official buildings, Braemer established three criteria: (1) the architecture itself, (2) its location in the urban space, and (3) the associated installations. However, in his criteria for determining function, Braemer did not include a discussion of associated artefacts or features except in those cases where a feature altered the architecture (Braemer 1982: 9). As a

---

1. In her own work at Tal-e Malyan, Iran, I. Nicholas undertook a structural and functional analysis of the architectural units and the distribution of finds within those units, identifying the finds according to their functional class.

result, he was unable to elaborate on the life style and activities of the inhabitants. In sum, his study is an architectural comparison of Iron Age house plans and the evolution of those plans within a given cultural horizon.

McEnroe also undertook an architectural study. His method for establishing a typology of Minoan houses of the Neopalatial period (c. 1550–1300 BC) consisted of the identification of room function on the basis of shape, size, location within the house and construction details (McEnroe 1982: 3). House types were then classified according to 'specific combinations and relative frequencies of a number of characteristics' (p. 3). McEnroe examined each house in relation to 32 possible characteristics which fell into four categories: type of room, construction materials, architectural details and total floor space (pp. 18-19). McEnroe himself admitted that this kind of typology is not a comprehensive one; he might have reached more definitive conclusions had he taken pottery and objects into account to identify room function and determine the domestic character of the structures themselves (personal communication).

The most comprehensive work is that by Aurenche which included evidence from all the major countries of the Middle East[1] during the Neolithic Period (7000–3700 BC). Aurenche made use of recent ethnographic studies of village life in his analysis of construction techniques, room arrangement, architectural features and the use of space. His own study of contemporary usage of comparable building materials in a similar environment formed the basis of his hypothesis for testing ancient building methods. Utilizing a large corpus of excavated house remains from published reports, Aurenche developed general principles concerning various architectural elements, their organization, and the location of activity areas in domestic structures. In order to determine principal room function, he depended on the identification of architectural features in the room itself.[2] While this

1. From Egypt, there were excavated remains of domestic architecture dating to this period at the time Aurenche was writing; see Vandier 1952: 117-19. Why Aurenche omits any discussion of Egypt is not clear.

2. See Aurenche 1977. This study of architectural construction techniques and features shows Aurenche's extensive knowledge of Near Eastern architecture, contemporary and ancient. Another useful work is that of G.H.R. Wright (1985). In this work, Wright presents a survey, commentary and bibliography for all structures, public and private, recovered through archaeological excavation.

was a useful method for his study because he drew on evidence from many different sites, each published in a different way, he made no attempt to incorporate the evidence of small finds and ceramic vessels. An analysis of house form as a cultural artefact by architect K. Schaar advanced the study one step further. Schaar studied houses found at Tarsus in Turkey, and at Alambra and Lemba in Cyprus. The presupposition for this study is his view of house form 'as the definition and articulation of interior space with architectural features'. This view is supported by several propositions. First, 'house form is the culturally conditioned partitioning of spaces for activities'. Indeed, 'it is a manifestation of the activities' themselves. Secondly, house form is the common convention of people sharing cultural ideas and symbols, and finally, it 'is an artifact, created and used by the members of the culture that produced it' (Schaar 1983: 1).

Although Schaar moved the discussion of house plan from the purely architectural to the ideological by his interest in the use of space, his functional analysis did not take into account the finds uncovered in each room. This is due not only to his method but also to the fact that the inhabitants of Tarsus apparently swept their floors before installing a new surface. The result was a dearth of sherds and bone fragments.

In 1974 K. Yassine completed a dissertation entitled *Domestic Architecture in the Second Millennium in Palestine*, in which he established a typological classification of Palestinian domestic architecture. In the process, Yassine assembled a corpus of house plan types from earlier periods and used these types to identify discrete housing units and describe their development during the Middle and Late Bronze Age. Yassine's basic method was architectural analysis based on published house plans. His major assumption, derived from the work of Albright (Albright 1938: 36-37), was that the basic plan included a large room, usually a courtyard, with rooms on one or more sides (Yassine 1974: 2).

Yassine supported his thesis regarding courtyard location as an essential element in the distinction of house types by listing the contents of presumed courtyards to show their multifunctional use (Yassine 1974: 106ff.). Although this characteristic multifunctionalism can be verified in some cases, it does not support all of Yassine's identifications of individual housing units. Nor does this characteristic alone eliminate the possibility that some multifunctional areas were roofed rooms instead of courtyards. In some cases there could be more than one such room per house.

Dependence on predetermined types can be severely restrictive. Indeed this method assumes that the identification of a courtyard, characterized by the presence of an oven, distinguishes individual houses. This understanding of Palestinian house plans does not allow for the possibility of seasonal variations, such as a winter oven inside a roofed room and a summer oven outside in a courtyard. Any typology should take into account the impact of climate, topography and available building materials on house plan and construction. Such considerations may help resolve the crux surrounding the identification of large rooms—when was it a roofed hall and when was it an open courtyard?[1]

Allowing for more than one courtyard or large room within a single housing unit could reflect industrial use, or space available in the urban setting, and/or the social structure or status of the family. Recognition of craft areas as an integral, but distinct, part of the domestic structure could expand our understanding of life style, economic status and social organization.[2]

From these considerations it is apparent that before a new typology of domestic architecture can be suggested, a better understanding of the evidence for ancient behaviour and use of space is needed. Whether the archaeological record preserves, in all cases, sufficient evidence to identify activity areas and determine room function and arrangement remains to be tested for each site. The current study investigates the degree to which reports published in the past 75 years present sufficient information to identify domestic activity areas in Palestinian houses of the second millennium BC.

1. Albright distinguished a change in architectural style at Tell Beit Mirsim between Stratum E, where the typical house contained a main hall, and Stratum D where it contained a courtyard (1938: 39).

2. One might hope that further studies based on the results of distribution analysis could determine the wealth, social organization and cultural influences operative within a given society. However, a recent statistical analysis by H. Gopnik has shown that no significant economic differences could be demonstrated on the basis of decorated pottery for inhabitants of the same town (Gopnik 1984: 27). A further test comparing a large town with a small village is needed.

Chapter 1

THEORY AND METHOD

Research Design

Approached as an anthropological discipline, archaeological analysis of ancient housing is more than architectural typology. It concerns itself with the material remains that reflect various types of human behaviour and the meaning of these activities in a cultural system. As Schaar has pointed out, domestic architecture is an important part of any cultural expression (1983: 1). However, architecture alone is not the only useful element of that expression. The distribution of finds, their location in and around the architectural space, and the nature and quantity of the finds themselves all serve as evidence of culturally determined human behaviour. It is this complex of data that the archaeologist seeks to rediscover in order to ask such questions as: what do these data (that is, objects and pottery quantitatively and locationally determined with respect to the architectural components) tell us about room function and the activities taking place in a house? Can we distinguish between primary living areas and secondary areas such as workshops, stables and storage facilities? What does house size tell us about the size and structure of the family? Are there signs of status differentiation reflected in the various modifications of the basic house plan? Is there evidence for social and political organization? Can comparisons between sites show the extent of influence from different cultural traditions? Few of these questions can be addressed in this study. Indeed, in those cases where all artefact and ceramic evidence is lacking or is stratigraphically mixed, these questions can only be addressed by means of analogy with those sites where clear evidence does exist.

The Archaeological Record

The ambiguity of the archaeological record results primarily from the fact that the record itself is only a partial subset of the ancient material remains (Deetz 1967: 8). It is rare to find an ancient house abandoned with all the artefacts related to daily activities left in place. Excavation usually reveals structures that have been abandoned and emptied, looted and burned, or subsequently destroyed by natural or human forces. This means that anything of value has probably been removed, and all items that were perishable have decomposed. The archaeologist is left to piece together the past from a few remnants. To a certain extent, the deposition process itself causes a certain amount of distortion that must be unravelled before the data can be interpreted (Gibbon 1984: 11).

In an attempt to exploit the archaeological record to the fullest, detailed recording systems are in place in most Near Eastern field projects. However, the published results of such projects continue to illustrate ceramic and artefact remains in stylistic groupings[1] rather than in locus groups. This editorial decision reflects the goals of the excavator and the questions asked of the archaeological record in the field and the laboratory. These goals and questions determine the selection of ceramic and artefact remains for publication both in terms of type and number. As a result, it is a painstaking task to assemble functional groupings according to locus in order to distinguish the partially preserved material correlates of specific behaviour patterns.

The organization into locus groups of excavated finds from reports published prior to 1950 and the determination of their location relative to the architectural space is difficult in all but a few cases. Ideally, the scatter of these finds should be able to be plotted to identify the areas of concentration and distribution within each room and in neighbouring rooms. However, due to the great variety of digging methods and reporting techniques employed in excavating Palestinian tells, such extensive analysis is not often possible. In most cases, the precise find spots of objects and ceramic vessels, especially of sherds, have not been published. In the worst of such cases, attempts to identify room function on the basis of contents are completely frustrated. As already

---

1.   See the recent excavation reports from Tell Mevorakh (Stern 1984), Jericho (Kenyon 1981; Kenyon and Holland 1982) and Shechem (Cole 1984).

noted, even with the most careful excavation and documentation, the archaeological record is seldom complete. And the usual delay of the final publication for 20 or 30 years exacerbates the problem. Nevertheless, the employment of new methods of analysis on the published record of domestic architecture, excavated during the past 60 years, may result in a better understanding of domestic behavior patterns.

The present study of Middle and Late Bronze Age houses is a test of published excavation reports to determine their usefulness in a quantitative and functional study of the finds and their spatial distribution. The artefact assemblages from each locus will be analysed, according to function, in order to recognize typical domestic activity sets. The location of these activities will then be plotted within the architectural space to identify behaviour patterns and determine room function and arrangement. Finally, this study will suggest certain practical alternatives for excavation techniques and publication procedures.

Analogy in Archaeology

Recent efforts to interpret more precisely the evidence of archaeological remains and their relationship to behaviour and culture are heavily dependent on ethnographic study. The value and comparability of observed, contemporary behaviour patterns to those of ancient peoples have been the subject of extensive discussions concerning the nature of ethnographic analogy.[1] These discussions have frequently centred on the legitimate use of analogy and its limitations (Hodder 1982: 12-16). One of the reasons for this situation is that the interests of ethnographers have not always been those of the archaeologist.

> Deficiencies in the ethnographic literature are encountered in a search for quantified demographic data, details of settlements' spatial organization, house layouts and architectural technology and chronology, information about the manufacture, distribution, and functions of portable objects and about subsistence economy, material correlates of variation in economic rank and relations among settlements (Kramer 1982: 8).

1.   The theory and practice can be seen in Binford (1967, 1977), whereas Aurenche (1981) assumes the comparability of contemporary Near Eastern traditional housing and ancient mud brick structures. More recent work by Aurenche and Desfarges in Syria and Jordan is expressly ethnoarchaeological (Aurenche and Desfarges 1983: 147-85). For a combination of approaches, utilizing both archaeological inference and ethnographic analogies, see Dever 1985.

In response to these deficiencies, archaeologists themselves, working in the Middle East and elsewhere, have been led to engage in the systematic observation of contemporary behaviour and its material correlates. Such observation enables them to refine their judgments concerning ancient behaviour especially when a strong similarity in life styles, environments and technologies between the cultures involved can be demonstrated (Kramer 1982: 1-2). Archaeologists engaged in both ethnographic observation and field work are able, by analogy, to formulate hypotheses concerning ancient behaviour and to test them against the results of their current excavations. Such ethnoarchaeological analysis can also provide a starting point for the re-evaluation of material previously excavated and published.[1]

In both of these cases, however, ethnographic observation tests the interrelationship between cultural assemblages and patterned behaviour (Watson 1979: 3). At the present time, scholarly discussion of method and theory in archaeology has not yet resulted in a consensus of opinion regarding the value and use of ethnographic analogy.[2] Watson recommends the use of ethnographic information from a society in a particular geographic area where there is great cultural continuity with ancient societies known archaeologically. This direct historical approach enables the archaeologist to construct models representing behaviour patterns that would result in a given material culture complex. The models can then be compared to relevant archaeological remains to determine the degree of fit (Watson 1979: 7).

The fact that there are instances when the models and the archaeological data do not fit is also a source of information. What is affirmed in such cases is that there are contemporary complexes of ideology

---

1.   See Watson 1979: 119-215 and Kramer 1982: 99-116, and detailed analysis below. Another example is the use of ethnographic studies from the late nineteenth century AD compared with the archaeological analysis of remains of a community that continued to exist until recent times, namely, the Pueblo people of Arizona (Ciolek-Torrello 1984: 127-28).

2.   Watson discusses the viewpoints of various schools of thought concerning ethnographic analogy (1979: 3-7). Glock makes use of ethnographic analogy but notes that its uniformitarian assumption does not prove anything. Rather it demonstrates a degree of probability (1983: 172-73). On the other side of the issue, Gould (1980: x) asserts that analogy, understood as an 'approach to the use of ethnographic observations as a way of explaining archaeological findings' is an idea whose time is gone!

and behaviour, along with their material correlates, for which there are no comparable complexes in the past. The reverse is also true, that there are complexes of ancient ideology and behaviour for which there are no modern parallels. In an attempt to broaden the range of ethnographic resources, some archaeologists use a cross-cultural approach drawing on cultures widely separated in space, time and cultural continuity from the ancient society recovered through excavation. In this case, the distinct culture is a resource in the formulation of hypotheses to be tested against the archaeological remains.[1]

Activity Areas

In this study of domestic architecture and ancient behaviour, the identification and location of activity areas plays a central role. However, certain assumptions regarding the identification of activity areas, employed by ethnologists, must be re-examined by archaeologists in order to better understand ancient remains. Susan Kent has identified the most common ethnological assumptions regarding activity areas: (1) activity areas can be discerned from content and the spatial patterning of artefact and faunal remains assemblages; (2) most activity areas are sex specific; and (3) most areas are monofunctional (Kent 1984: 2). The potential and limitations of each of these assumptions must now be explored before they can be adopted for the purposes of this study.

The operating presupposition of all archaeologists is that the material remains uncovered in an excavation are correlated to the behaviour of the ancient inhabitants. In a recent study of patterned sherd scatter at Tell el-Maskhuta, J.S. Holladay, Jr has shown that such scatter can be quite extensive. At the same time, the heaviest concentration seems to indicate the location where the vessel, or a series of similar vessels, was broken. Such a locus, in the greater number of cases, would be the area where this sort of vessel was regularly used (Holladay 1984). That this locus is significant for a functional analysis of the find spot is fairly certain. Although the vessel may have been broken while being transported from one area of use to another, this

---

1.   Dever's use of cross-cultural examples of circular, as opposed to rectilinear, house plans and the correlation of circular plans with certain aspects of life style and socioeconomic structure to explain the EB IV village at Be'er Resisim is a case in point (1985: 23*-24*).

would not be common enough an event to be statistically meaningful. More often, contamination is encountered when fragments of a vessel are found as part of an earthen fill brought in to level an area before rebuilding. In this case, the function of the find spot may be completely unconnected with the vessel itself.

In certain cases, the distribution pattern of artefacts that have been abandoned varies considerably from the same items in use. Kent points out that this discrepancy has rarely been noted in ethnographic studies (Kent 1984: 3). This is an important caveat when employing ethnological observation in distribution studies and challenges the archaeologist to distinguish between primary and secondary deposition, that is, artefacts and debris that were abandoned as part of a patterned assemblage in the area where they were used, and the remains that accumulated as the result of secondary usage or after abandonment (Kent 1984: 2).

The second assumption which Kent sees as characteristic of current ethnographic studies, that is, that most activity areas are sex specific, may be suitable for certain cultures but remains to be demonstrated for ancient Near Eastern societies before the rise of Islam. Ethnologists assert that the distinction between men's tasks and women's work functions in tribal societies the world over.[1] At the cultural stage of professional handicraft, however, men undertake functions previously reserved to women (Birket-Smith 1965: 93). This view suggests a hypothesis of social and economic organization in complex societies, as opposed to tribal societies, for archaeologists to test in regard to Bronze Age Palestinian culture.

The assumption that most areas were monofunctional is generally accepted. That one type of activity dominated an area does not exclude the possibility that other functions also occurred in the same room, and, indeed, this probably was usually the case. On the other hand, there are examples of an entire room dedicated to one function.[2] In addition, the same function may be located in more than one place. Kent observed that certain activities were moved depending on changes in climate and season. However, in some cases, such relocation left no physical evidence (Kent 1984: 65-66).

1. Kent's study of semi-traditional Navaho households showed 'few to none' sex specific activity areas (1984: Table 7).
2. For a discussion of the spatial distribution of activity areas based on the nature of the activity itself, see Yellen 1977: 95-96.

In attempts to correlate ethnographic studies with archaeological remains, Kent found considerable variation between ideal behaviour and actual practice. In the houses she studied there were areas set aside for specific functions, such as eating and sleeping. Nevertheless, these functions were frequently carried out in areas which had a different primary purpose (Kent 1984: 65).

It is clear, however, from current ethnographic studies of village life that the location of an activity is not completely random. Each activity requires a series of conditions and requires the use of associated objects that form a pattern. It is the recognition of these patterns or portions thereof, in the archaeological record, that makes possible the analysis of the spatial distribution of the artefacts and by-products of the activities themselves. Each pattern, whose signature is only partially erased by its deposition history, enables the archaeologist to distinguish and identify activity areas within the domestic space.

The present study does not include, to any significant extent, original ethnographic observation. Instead, it depends on the recent work of Kramer and Watson on village life in western Iran (Kramer 1982; Watson 1979) and on Gustaf Dalman's detailed study of Palestinian life which has not yet been surpassed (Dalman 1928–1937, 1964). These resources will be the basis for the formulation of operational paradigms for functional tool kits representative of various domestic activities.

The organization of activities within the domestic space is culturally conditioned and reflects the cognitive framework of the inhabitants. While it is not possible for archaeology to recover completely this mental framework, some resources are available from the past which illustrate aspects of ancient life. One such resource for the second millennium BC is the iconography of the ancient Near East, especially Egyptian tomb paintings and house models. These paintings are rich in the depiction of scenes from daily life showing all classes of Egyptian society. Many of these paintings, classified in Vandier's *Manuel d'archéologie égyptienne*, are of interest to this study, especially those from Middle and New Kingdom tombs. While these paintings show, for the most part, Egyptian customs, there is evidence that certain behaviour patterns were shared throughout the Levant. More particularly, Egyptian traditions were influential in the material culture of Egypt's many trading partners, especially the coastal cities of the Levant, as well as the regions under Egypt's direct military or political control. Because that control was strongest in Syria-Palestine during the second millennium BC (Weinstein 1975, 1981), this rich iconographic resource can be used with some confidence to illustrate a variety of ancient Near Eastern life ways. As with ethnographic observation, the tomb paintings show a variety of material culture items in use and articulate the groupings of these items in relation to specific activities.

The small house models from Egypt add a significant component to our mental images of mudbrick houses. Since few excavated houses have been preserved above ground floor level (cf. the excavations at Thera/Akrotiri), house models that are two and three stories high illustrate what might be expected as typical housing within a walled town. At the same time, such models point to a possible source of contamination or mixing of artefact assemblages in the archaeological record, namely the collapse of upper stories.

The third resource for this study of Palestinian domestic architecture is the archaeological record itself. Unfortunately, this study cannot begin with complete, unprocessed archaeological data because it is concerned with the remains from previously excavated sites, whose finds have already been processed and selected before publication. The samples of finds that have been included in the report, along with the descriptions of the architecture, are not only incomplete but also arbitrarily chosen without any indication of the total amount of material recovered during excavation.

This lack of quantification in the selection process makes it difficult, and at times impossible, to distinguish between primary, secondary and tertiary deposits. There is no way of determining, with complete accuracy, the relationship of the reported finds to the archaeological record itself. This is true not only of the published plates illustrating the ceramic wares and artefacts, but also of certain styles of architectural drawings and verbal descriptions that refer to the construction techniques and architectural features. In spite of these limitations, the hypothesis to be tested is that the data assembled from these three sources will provide new insights into the relationship between domestic activities and architectural traditions.

Goals and Tasks

The goals of this study are threefold: (1) to test the extent to which ethnoarchaeology and ancient iconography can assist in developing models describing how people lived, the variety of domestic activities in which they engaged, and the use of space in domestic structures; (2) to develop a set of characteristic model-specific paradigms which consist of characteristic groupings of portable objects, features and debris products by which particular activities can be inferred; and (3) to attempt to determine the location and variety of specific domestic activities within (and near) second millennium Palestinian houses by assembling into locus groups the associated finds, features and debris recovered from these houses, and comparing these assemblages with the models just proposed.

In view of the limitations on my access to the relevant data occasioned by earlier excavation and recording techniques and prevailing publication standards, this study will focus on three tasks: (1) to select the most representative excavations of Middle and Late Bronze Age Palestinian houses and to undertake an analysis of the material culture assemblage reported for each locus in order to establish room function and housing units; (2) to evaluate, where possible, room size, overall architectural plan including the arrangement of functionally specific rooms, and construction techniques that may further assist in identifying room function and activity areas; and (3) to compare the range of activities reflected at particular sites where the precise location of activities is not possible.

Chapter 2

MODEL BUILDING

Ethnographic Observation

Patty Jo Watson's study of the life ways of the inhabitants of
Hasanabad, a village in western Iran, has become a classic in ethnoarchaeology. Her observations on the construction techniques of
domestic architecture,[1] the tool kits of daily life and the social
organization of the community provide a starting point for understanding traditional behaviour patterns that may be reflected in the
archaeological record of ancient Near Eastern sites. Indeed, from her
own experience, Watson refers to finds from recent excavations of
Neolithic sites to show the continuity of subsistence patterns, craft
techniques and exploitation of natural resources (1979: 36, 300).

Watson's study is of particular value because the community at
Hasanabad was not heavily influenced by modern technology and con-
sumer goods purchased from outside the village. This makes it possible to catalogue the traditional classes of items and installations necessary for the basic activities of food production, preparation, consumption and storage.

By contrast, the analysis by Kramer of village life at Aliabad is that
of a more complex society. While there may be less direct continuity
between this community and the prehistoric villages of the Zagros
region, there are some important points of contact with the complex
societies of second millennium Palestine. At Aliabad, this is seen most
clearly in the range of personal possessions which were produced

1. Knowledge of the processes of mudbrick collapse and decomposition
(Margueron 1985: 1-20; see also Schiffer 1987) is useful for excavators who need to
be aware of the formation of debris layers within an ancient structure. Needless to
say, if the process of decomposition and the construction techniques employed by the
ancient builders are not described in the excavation report, the analysis must proceed
more along the lines of inference or supposition than of evidence.

outside the village in urban areas and were purchased. The result is a society that is basically pastoral and agricultural but has been influenced by the larger industrial complex of which it is a small part. By combining the results of Watson's study with the later work of Kramer (1982) it is possible to compile a series of possible activity sets which include the associated artefacts and installations of various domestic activities.[1] These sets are seen in Table 2.1.

Table 2.1. *Ethnographic Activity Sets*

Activity	*Artefacts*	*Installations*
Food Preparation		
Hasanabad	deep pots	hearth
	shallow pans	bin
	iron bread plate	niches
	tripod	pegs
	tongs/poker	storage pit
	metal bowl/s	bench
	pot lids	
	wooden spoon	
	tea kettle and tray	
	wooden sugar bowl	
	sugar hatchet	
	basket rice drainer	
	wooden pounder	
	bread board	
	stone pestle	
	boulder mortar	
	skin water bag	
	rotary quern	
Aliabad	lamps	oven
	dung fuel	bee hive in wall
	goat skin churn	
	barley sacks	
	flour, lentils, beans	
	chickpeas, tea, sugar	

1. Watson's catalogue of items in daily use is more complete than Kramer's. What Kramer adds are items acquired from the more developed centres that reflect wealth or status. While each researcher has a particular hypothesis to be tested and does not necessarily record the type of information that would be useful for a different project, the combined work of Kramer and Watson provides an adequate resource for the present study (see the evaluation of Rothman 1983, especially p. 76).

Table 2.1—*Continued*

Activity	Artefacts	Installations
Food Consumption	tea pot	
	cups and saucers	
	(items used in food preparation)[1]	
Food Storage	large jar	clay bin
		straw-lined pit
Storage	fodder, dung	pit
	clothes, utensils	
	bedding	
Weaving and Sewing	spindles and whorls	looms
	needles, thread	sewing machine (Aliabad)
	awl	
	weft pounder	
	warp scraper	
	yarn, goat hair	
Personal Adornment	cosmetics, comb	
	beads/shell, rings	
	necklaces, anklets,	
	pendants	
Games and Music	astragali (knuckle bones)	
	pebbles for 'jacks'	
	dolls, figurines	
	reed pipe, drum[2]	
Animal Husbandry	goads, scrapers	mangers
	shearing tool	dung storeroom
	bones	
	milking bowl, churn	
	harness, yoke	
	salt bag, sling stones	
Food Production and	fish nets	stable
Acquisition	fish hooks	manger
	utility room	straw storage
	hooks to make nets	poultry coop
	plough	
	sickle	
	threshing sledge	
	winnowing sieve	

1. Typically, food consumption occurred in the living room rather than in the kitchen. However, the specific items utilized for serving and eating were not enumerated (Kramer 1982: 102).

2. Watson did not observe these items in the possession of villagers living in Hasanabad. The musicians were itinerants (1979: 31).

Table 2.1—*Continued*

Activity	Artefacts	Installations
	winnowing fork	
	traps	
	gun	
Multipurpose items	baskets	
	goat hair nets	
	reed screen[1]	
Aliabad	photographs, souvenirs	
Possessions	costly utensils	
	mirrors	
	clocks	
	carpets	
	trunks	
Status Items	bicycle	
(from Kramer 1982:	motor vehicle	
Table 3.7)	radio	
	record player	
	tape recorder	
	sewing machine	
	scythe	
	metal sledge blades	
Idalion	slow wheel—upper	seat
Pottery Production	slow wheel—lower	support for wheel
	fast wheels	bin
	forming tools	kiln
	paddle	fuel
	clay, water	

Room Function

An integral part of the activity sets detailed above is the location of the activities themselves in relation to each other and within the total domestic space. Recognition of activity clusters, their location, and their association with certain family members adds to our knowledge of the material culture correlates of patterned behaviour.

In the houses observed by Watson at Hasanabad, the main room was the living room. Typically, this room included a central hearth, a storage area, food preparation and consumption equipment, bedding,

1. For the most part, these items were noticed by Watson at Hasanabad (1979: 79-202) and by Kramer at Aliabad (formerly called Shahabad) (1982: 99-116).

and occasionally a loom (1979: Figs. 5.12, 21). Several Hasanabad families had more than one living room, a 'best' room for guests and a family room (Watson 1979: 126). The flour chest was a prominent part of the living room equipment. In only 1 out of 16 occurrences was the flour chest in the *aywan* rather than in the living room (Watson 1979: Table 5.1). Grain was also stored in pits in the floor. Eight examples of such pits were observed in living rooms and 3 in courtyards (Watson 1979: Tables 5.1, 3). Watson did not observe any occurrences of a separate kitchen although several examples of a summer hearth, used for cooking in the courtyard, were identified (1979: Table 5.3).

Additional possible rooms in a given house might include an *aywan* or entry hall, a utility room, a storeroom and a stable. Several underground stables were also in use (Watson 1979: Table 5.3). The *aywan* could serve as an entrance to the stable as well as to the living room (Watson 1979: Figs. 5.9, 10), although, in most instances, the stable opened directly into the courtyard (Watson 1979: Figs. 5.19, 20). In fact, above ground stables have their own entrance from the courtyard or *aywan* in 9 out of 12 instances. In only one instance was the primary entrance through the living room (Watson 1979: Figs. 5.6-5.29). Direct access to the outside seems to be an important feature of the location of stables.

Utility rooms and storerooms were used to store straw, fuel (dung), tools and equipment, and miscellaneous household goods (Watson 1979: 160). In some instances, stabling and storage activities were reported for the same room (Watson 1979: Fig. 5.20).

By contrast, the first room of a village house to be built at Aliabad was the kitchen. Storage and food preparation commonly took place there. Food consumption would also take place in the kitchen if there were no living room, although such small houses were rarely observed by Kramer and Watson (Kramer 1982: 99). A cooking oven, flour bin (a packed mud chest set on short legs) and loom were standard kitchen features, at least at Aliabad (Kramer 1982: 100). The floor was smoothed and plastered but uncarpeted—unless the room was also used as a living room (Kramer 1982: 102). An additional oven, for summer cooking, was located in the courtyard, as were storage pits for surplus grain (Watson 1979: 122-28, 157).

Kramer observed that textile production and food preparation were tasks commonly performed by women in the kitchen. This twofold activity cluster should be expected in ancient houses as well. Indeed, at Hasanabad, the kitchen served as the women's room whereas the living room was the men's room (Kramer 1982: 102).

The main room of the housing complex, the living room, was used for eating, entertaining and sleeping (as at Hasanabad). This room was the most public room in the house and was decorated with the family's most important possessions and carpeted with rugs. The bedding, rolled up during the day, served as seating. In the centre of the room was a hearth covered by a wooden frame to deflect the heat. During the summer, the hearth was filled in and covered by a carpet. It was not uncommon, at Aliabad, to have a summer living room on the second story where cool breezes could be enjoyed (Kramer 1982: 103).

In addition to these two basic rooms, each house had a storeroom, one or more stable rooms and a courtyard. The storerooms were used to contain fuel, fodder and a variety of household equipment. When there were several storerooms, each served a specific function. Occasionally, a grain storage pit was sunk in the floor, filled with barley and plastered over (Kramer 1982: 105).

At Aliabad, the stable rooms were either on the ground floor level, separate from the family rooms, or underneath the courtyard. The only feature in the stable was a feeding trough. Kramer noted that little attention was paid to the stable floor, in contrast to the kitchen and living room floor, and concluded that floor treatment could be a clue to the function of a particular room (1982: 106-107).

The main function of the courtyard for its occupants, both human and animal, was traffic circulation within the compound. In addition, this enclosed area served a variety of secondary functions, such as temporary kitchen, storeroom and animal pen. Certain built-in features were associated with these activities, for example, an oven, trough, grain storage pit, chicken coop, well or sleeping platform (Kramer 1982: 108-109).

The villages observed by Watson and Kramer were poor communities with little industry, craft production or trade. The economy of these villages was based on animal husbandry and agriculture. While many of the artefacts mentioned in Table 2.1, such as tools and weapons, were not used in the home, they may be found in the domestic compound when not in use elsewhere. The utility room or storage area may, therefore, contain a variety of items representing different functions which are incidental to the primary function of that particular room.

The activities and room functions described here reflect not only a certain environment and subsistence level but also the influence of a religious tradition. The customs of Islam impose restrictions on the production and consumption of certain foods, especially wine, beer and shell fish. Because such foods were not prohibited in second millennium societies of the Levant, and, indeed, wine was a major commodity, ethnographic studies which include the activities associated with these foods must be sought.

The storage of oil in a room of the house, along with wine and possibly beer, is usually located in a dark, interior room or cellar (Dalman 1935: IV, 251-52). The items commonly associated with this activity are storejars or jar stands. An earlier ethnographic account of the location and function of domestic storerooms is presented by Schliemann in his description of a nineteenth-century house in a village of the Troad visited by Professor Rudolf Virchow, his associate. The stone walls of the ground floor had no doorway.[1] Its rooms, used for storage, were entered from the first floor living rooms above (1881: 53-54). Unfortunately, Schliemann did not mention what items were stored in these rooms, although he did compare them to the storerooms of Troy III which were filled with pithoi. Little evidence of items used in the production of these liquids was found in the average house. Preparation of olives and grapes for crushing and the production of olive oil and wine usually took place outside the home in a functionally specific location (Cf. Dalman 1935: IV, 355-56), namely at the olive crusher or grape press (Dalman 1935: IV, 212, 354), either outdoors or in a special building. While it will be necessary to consider the implications of storing such staples in ancient houses, no additional activity sets need be postulated for the preparation and production of these items for Middle and Late Bronze Age domestic areas.

Although the inhabitants of Hasanabad were influenced by Islam in many ways, they were not observant Muslims. They did not engage in regular prayers or fasting and there was no mosque or teacher in the village. This means that there were no material remains of cultic

---

1. In some village houses, the ground floor did have a doorway. This entrance led into one room which served as a stable (Schliemann 1881: 54). All other ground floor rooms were entered from above. Comparable houses are depicted in the Town Mosaic, a collection of faience house plaques from Knossos, showing the long history of this style (Burn 1980: 33).

activity. There were, however, some superstitious beliefs reflected in the use of certain items of personal adornment, such as wearing cowrie shells and blue beads to ward off the evil eye (Watson 1979: 26). At Aliabad, where the literacy level was higher, some families owned copies of the Quran (Kramer 1982: 103-104). Here again, it would be useful to have an ethnographic resource which includes religious customs and the material remains of such practices for comparison with ancient cultures where religious life was an important component of daily life, both in the home and at the holy place.

The local climatic conditions and native crops, as well as modernization, influence the type of cooking oil and fuel used by Iranian villagers today. While dung is generally used for baking, kerosene can also be purchased and is frequently used for lighting (Kramer 1982: 47; cf. Dalman 1935: IV, 252, olive oil continued to be used for lighting at Kerak). For the ancient inhabitants of the Levant, the production of olive oil, used for lighting, cooking and various other purposes, was a major industry. This product continues to be an important part of the economy of many peoples living in the Mediterranean basin where traditional practices can still be observed.

One significant change in the olive oil industry has come about through the use of metal containers, instead of ceramic jars, for packing and shipping. Indeed, ethnographic observation of traditional potters working in the Near East is increasingly difficult, due to the decline in demand for their products.[1] Earlier studies, primarily of Cypriot potters, continue to be an important resource for understanding the production and distribution techniques of this industry which was an essential ingredient in daily life and regional trade.

While oil processing does not usually take place inside a house, the production of pottery can take place in a courtyard or even in an interior room of a dwelling. Therefore, this activity can be considered one of the possible, domestic behaviour patterns able to be identified in the archaeological record.

As part of the expedition to Idalion, Robert H. Johnston carried out ethnographic observation of traditional potters working in Cyprus.[2]

---

1.   Personal communication, Gloria A. London, July 13, 1987. Dr London, a ceramic specialist serving with the Madaba Plains Project, 1987 season, visited potters in Jordan hoping to observe traditional methods in use. See London and Sinclair 1991: 420-26.

2.   Johnston's study of Cypriot pottery technology served as the basis for his

Johnston recognizes that his work is only one in a series of ethno-graphic studies into the continuing tradition of pottery technology.[1] Of special interest is the equipment utilized by both men and women in pottery production. Johnston observed the method of construction of large pithoi built by hand on a tree bark base (bat) or round stone. For smaller vessels, a two-piece potter's wheel, the slow tournette, was used. These wheels are round or square and many are currently made of wood (Johnston 1974b: 133). Observations of the use of the fast wheel by Turkish potters may also be relevant to our study of the second millennium in view of the consensus that a fast wheel was already in use in Palestine during the Middle Bronze Age (Albright 1933: 68). Johnston documented a variety of tools used to smooth the vessels during the forming process which included pieces of wood, paddles, smoothing cloths and rubbing stones. Not all of these items will survive to become part of the archaeological record of the future. So too, it is evident that some ancient tools were subject to decomposition and are irretrievable.

Several items in this activity set would vary in shape and size from one culture to another. However, of those preserved in the archaeo-logical record, the wheel thrust bearings are the most easily identifi-able. The comparisons made by Watson and Kramer with ancient sites are usually to Neolithic life ways uncovered in the same Zagros mountain area (Watson 1979: 91, Kramer 1982: 230-50). Johnston, on the other hand, compared the work of contemporary potters on Cyprus with biblical potters in Palestine, assuming a long tradition of comparable techniques (1974a: 88). It is at this point that other resources can be used to strengthen the link between the ethnographic studies and the archaeological remains of second millennium domestic activity in Palestine.

1974 article on 'The Biblical Potter' (1974: 86-106).

1.   Other examples can be found in Matson 1965, Yon 1981, and the most recent study by G.A. London (1990). Johnston himself has undertaken experiments in radio-xerography of ceramic vessels to determine the best methods for illustrating manufacturing techniques and clay contents. The use of the mammogram made pos-sible, without sawing, a view of the interior. The inclusions are also clearly visible using this method. A sample of the results is in my possession. In spite of all these studies, Wood notes that there have been few ethnographic studies on the sociology of pottery production (Wood 1985: 209, n. 3), how pottery was made, sold, traded, and so forth. See now Wood 1990.

Iconographic Evidence

Several types of iconographic materials from Egypt, extensively documented by Erman (1894) and Vandier (1952–1964), dating to the third and second millennia BC, are useful in relating data from ethnographic studies to ancient life ways. The abundant materials from the Middle and New Kingdom periods that are contemporary with the artefact assemblages under study here include drawings, especially tomb paintings, and clay or limestone models and figurines. Such illustrations and models show men and women involved in a great variety of activities, the location of those activities in the domestic space, and the associated tools and installations. While there remains some difference of opinion regarding the use of certain vessels and objects, many functional classes of items can be clearly identified.

As we have seen above, the largest number of items in any home, reported by ethnoarchaeologists, were those associated with food preparation and consumption (Table 2.1). This subject was also a common motif in Egyptian tomb paintings which illustrate numerous banquet scenes as well as funerary offerings. Both of these activities were combined in a painting from the Tomb of Djeserkeresonb (Davies 1963: Pl. I) where food preparation is shown on the lower register with an offering scene above. Such a painting shows a wide variety of food items as well as ceramic and stone vessels, knife blades, and jar stands.

Limestone models from the time of the Old Kingdom depict ancient Egyptians performing many specific tasks. One statuette shows a woman kneeling in front of a quern grinding grain with a loaf-shaped stone (Breasted 1948: Pl. 16b). Other figurines show a man standing forming bread loaves (Breasted 1948: Pl. 26b) and another squatting in front of an oven where bread is being baked (Breasted 1948: Pl. 26c). An associated activity is illustrated by a statuette that represents a brewer standing in front of a jar stand that supports a large bowl in which he is kneading mash (Breasted 1948: Pl. 30a). From the time of the Middle Kingdom, a model of both a bakery and brewery depicts the basic activities of grinding, kneading, baking and fermenting but does not add significantly to our knowledge of the equipment used (Winlock 1955: Pls. 22-23). A wall painting from the tomb of Rameses III depicts the entire baking process; bakers knead dough with their feet, the dough is then formed into a variety of shapes and baked on a bread oven (Erman 1894: 191). These statuettes and the tomb scene of bread baking illustrate numerous items of kitchen equipment including querns and grinding stones, bread ovens, jars and bowls.

Closely associated with food preparation and consumption is storage. Evidence for storage assemblages from the ancient world is seen clearly in Egyptian tomb paintings that illustrate the interior of large houses. The best example is, indeed, that of a palace depicted in the Tomb of Meryre' at Amarna (Davies 1903: Pl. 18). In one view, the palace is shown from the side with the contents of the interior rooms clearly visible. Several rooms are filled with storejars while others include both jars and bread loaves.

The diversity of activities performed in the private house is shown in the illustration of the house of Djehuty-nefer in Theban tomb 104 (Davies 1929: Figs. 1A, 1B). The side view of the house (Fig. 1) shows textile production in the lowest register. Here, fibres are being spun using spinning bowls and weights. In the next room, weavers work on vertical looms of various sizes; two weavers on the large loom and one on the smaller. In a third room on the same level, bakers are shown grinding flour and forming bread loaves. Upstairs, the owner eats a meal in a large room while servants carry jars and food stuffs from one floor to another.

The rooms in this house include items of furniture—tables, chairs and stools—as well as architectural features, such as pillar bases and pillars supporting the ceiling, windows and granaries. While such a house is in sharp contrast to the village houses of western Iran, it may provide some insights into the range of activities that were carried out by the occupants of houses in the walled towns of ancient Canaan.

Additional examples of textile production are illustrated by the Middle Kingdom model of a weavers' shop from the tomb of Meket-re (Winlock 1955: Pls. 25-27). Here the many stages of textile production are shown, preparing the yarn, spinning, using spinning bowls, spindles and whorls, and weaving on horizontal looms.

A variety of activities shown in the tomb paintings focus on personal adornment, recreation, commerce and religious practice. Extensive use of cosmetics by both men and women is illustrated, in some detail, in New Kingdom art. For example, in the tomb of Ipuy (Theban tomb 217), a scene shows a man applying kohl to the eyes of a workman (Davies 1927: Pl. 38). Cosmetic containers and a kohl

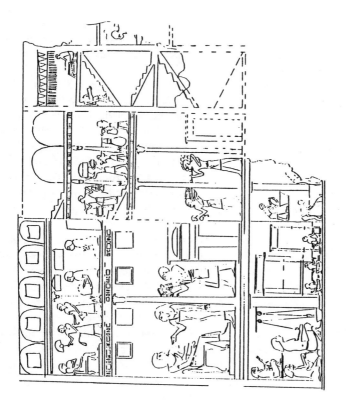

Figure 1. *The town house of Djehuty-Nefer, after Davies 1929: Figs. 1a, 1b*

stick are also shown. In another painting (Turin 55001), a woman holds a mirror and cosmetic container while she applies colour to her lips (Museum of Fine Arts 1982: Fig. 53). Such drawings show quite a number of personal possessions that would be customarily kept in the home.

Besides cosmetics, Egyptians adorned themselves with floral necklaces and headbands, perfume cones and jewellery. While examples of floral necklaces have been found preserved in tombs, such as the tomb of Tutankhamun (Hayes 1959: Fig. 188), the items most likely to be preserved in the archaeological record are those that were less perishable; for example, jewellery made of metal and precious stones. The depiction of musicians and dancers in a fragment of painted relief illustrates a variety of earrings, bracelets and beaded girdles (Vandier 1964: Fig. 197). At the same time, this scene also shows several types of musical instruments which could be included in the category of personal possessions.

While the scene of a banquet with entertainment seems to represent the most popular recreation of the wealthy, drawings of individuals from various classes show them playing a board game. The most unusual example of this scene appears on a satirical papyrus (EA 10016 sheet 1) (Peck and Ross 1978: Figs. 75-76) which shows a lion and an antelope playing senet.

Activities that involve business transactions are shown in scenes that illustrate the use of weights and balances and the conferring of seals of authority. A market scene from Theban tomb 162 of Kenamun shows a pair of hand-held scales (Davies 1963: Pl. XV), while a different scene from Theban tomb 100 depicts a weight in the form of a bull's head set in a balance (Davies 1943: Pl. LV). Many business transactions involve official documents or sealings on containers of goods. These items are frequently stamped with a private or official seal in the shape of a scarab or a geometric shape (cylinder or stamp seals). A scene in the tomb of Huy shows the conferral of such a seal in a ring (Davies and Gardiner 1926: Pl. VIII).

Another activity that could be carried out in a private home or courtyard is pottery production. Several Egyptian models show potters at work forming bowls on the tournette. One statuette is of a single potter squatting in front of a tournette which he turns with his left hand. On the wheel he forms a bowl. Leaning against the base of the model are several completed vessels (Johnston 1974a: 85). A model from the Tomb of Karenen at Saqqara includes two potters. One works with the slow tournette and a second potter prepares the clay in the potters' shop. A conical feature beside the second potter may represent a kiln although it does not seem to be to scale (Quibell 1908: Pl. XIX). A tomb painting from the New Kingdom (Theban tomb 93) also illustrates the process of pottery production, but in somewhat greater detail. Stages in the process include mixing the clay, forming the pot on the wheel, and preparing the kiln (Davies 1930: Pl. LIXA).

Egyptian tomb paintings and models illustrate many other tasks that servants performed in the palace or in special industrial quarters, such as brewing, animal slaughter, wood working and jewellery manufacture. These tasks appear to be unsuitable to a discussion of activity areas in domestic structures. For this reason, the only crafts illustrated from ancient iconography are those which ethnographic observation has shown were performed in the house or in the family courtyard. As was noted by Kramer and Watson, certain items occurred in the home that were not used there (see Table 2.1 above—Food production and acquisition). It is always possible that comparable items (tools and weapons) will appear in the archaeological record, but it must be assumed, in any functional and spatial analysis, that the proportion of such finds to other activity sets will show them to be random, or, at least, in storage. Therefore, the wide variety of agricultural and industrial tools and military weapons represented in ancient iconographic sources will not be included here.

Functional Paradigms

On the basis of ethnographic observations of village life and ancient iconographic representations, I have constructed a series of ideal functional paradigms[1] or activity sets (Tables 2.2–2.8) for comparison with the recorded finds from second millennium Palestinian houses. The series includes paradigms for food preparation and/or consumption activities, storage, textile production, weaving, personal adornment and possessions, business transactions and wealth, and pottery production. The two most basic activities represented in every house are food

1. Ideal types are seen by Kent Flannery as useful models for archaeological analogy. See his empirically derived ideal types of early sedentary villages developed for his study of Near Eastern and Mesoamerican villages (1972: 29).

preparation and storage. While these activities may be carried out in one and the same room, they may also be spread over several rooms. In view of this possibility, two separate paradigms have been designed, one representing the activity set of a food preparation and/or consumption area and the other representing the activity set for a storage area. In fact, the items included in these activity sets often overlap. Two paradigms can be considered of secondary value because they may be absent from any given house, namely, those representing the domestic industries of textile manufacture and pottery production. The remaining paradigms indicate the wealth and status of the inhabitants while, at the same time, pointing to the areas used as living quarters. These areas were not necessarily spatially segregated from other activity areas although, in some cases, they were. Thus, no separate activity set has been designed to indicate the location of the living room.

Table 2.2. *Paradigm for Food Preparation and/or Consumption*

Item	Code	Feature
	AA05	Bench
	AA06	Shelf
	AA07	Oven
	AA08	Hearth
	AA09	Bin
	AA10	Silo
Charred grain	D001	
Seeds/nuts	D002	
Animal bones	D003	
Ashes/charcoal	D004	
Food Preparation	H001-005	
Grinders	G001-007	
Debris	D001-004	
Baking Tray	Q001-003	
Cooking Pot	E001-079	
Krater	D001-083	
Bowl	A001-247	
Jar	G001-107	
Pithos	F001-011	
Jug	J001-124	
Juglet	K001-098	
Jar Stand	T001-003	
Other		

Table 2.3. *Paradigm for Storage Area*

Item	Code	Feature
	AA06	Shelf
	AA09	Bin
	AA11	Pit
Strainer	H001	
Funnel	H002	
Scoop	H003	
Jar stopper	H004	
Lid	H005	
Grinder	G001/3	
Mortar	G002/4/5/7	
Bowl	A001-247	
Jar	G001-107	
Pithos	F001-011	
Amphora	H001-018	
Jug	J001-124	
Juglet	K001-098	
Jar Stand	T001-003	
Stirrup Jug	V001-006	
Other		

Table 2.4. *Paradigm for Pottery Production*

Item	Code	Feature
	AA06	Shelf
	AA07	Oven
	AA09	Bin
	AA18	Pit for wheel
	AA22	Kiln
Clay/temper	D005	
Wheel thrust bearing	P001	
Burnishing tool	P002	
Kiln furniture	P003	
Clay rolls	P004	
Kiln wasters	P005	
Funnel	P006	
Forming tools	P007	
Flat stone	P008	
Potting bowl	P009	
Other		

Table 2.5. *Paradigm for Textile Manufacture and Weaving*

Item	Code	Feature
	AA21	Loom
Fabric remains	B001	
Loom weight	B002	
Spindle	B003	
Whorl	B004	
Pick/shuttle	B005	
Needle	B006	
Spinning bowl	B007	
Awl	T002	

Table 2.6. *Paradigm for Personal Adornment*

Item	Code	Feature
Cosmetic boxes	C001-002	
Kohl pot	C003	
Kohl stick	C004	
Kohl tube	C005	
Palette	C006	
Cosmetic spoon	C007	
Comb	C008	
Mirror	C009	
Pestle	C011	
Jewellery	J001-015	
Other		

Table 2.7. *Paradigm for Economic Affairs and Recreation*

Item	Code	Feature
Written documents	E003-004	
Seals	E001-002, E005-008	
Weights	V001-002, V006	
Exclusive items	R001-015	
Weapons	W001-011	
Miscellaneous	Z001-008	
Other		

Table 2.8. *Paradigm for Animal Care Facilities*

Item	Code	Feature
	AA23	Manger
Debris	D009-010	
Harness	W013	

Organization of Excavated Finds

In order to recognize individual activity areas in ancient houses, it is necessary to recover and identify the artefacts used in a particular area and determine their distribution. The classification of excavated artefacts, ceramic vessels and architectural features and their organization in locus groups provides the data for identifying various functional tool kits and locating discrete activity areas, as well as activities that cluster together in the same room.[1] While some artefacts may themselves have multiple uses, the distribution of associated finds can indicate, ideally, the precise tasks performed in a given area. The incomplete recovery and publishing of finds are limitations that are compensated for, only in part, by analogy to the functional paradigms.

Evidence for the presence of individual objects in a particular locus is taken primarily from the plates included in reports of the sites to be studied. In some instances, an excavator will refer in the text to the presence of broken objects or vessels of a certain type without illustrating them. In organizing assemblages for each locus that are as complete as possible, this information is included in the appropriate artefact category.[2]

In the present study, three major divisions of archaeological finds have been utilized: artefacts, ceramic vessels and architectural features. Within each division, various categories have been developed which are functional rather than stylistic (see Tables 2.9–11, below). Individual items within each category are further distinguished on the basis of form or style,[3] but, in some cases, this distinction

1. Yellen severely criticizes Whallon for his correlation of associated tools to a single task rather than with multiple related tasks (1977: 97).
2. The code consists of the letter of the particular artefact or ceramic category and the number 000.
3. In order to reassemble the contents of each locus, all artefacts, ceramic ware forms, and architectural features from published reports of second millennium houses have been entered into dBASE III files. Each category is identified by a letter.

reflects chronological rather than functional developments.

Artefact Corpus

Small objects serve as important indicators of past human behaviour because they provide, in many cases, unambiguous functional identification. At the same time, it is important to remember that objects found in the excavated debris may well reflect both the latest use of a room and casual discard that occurred during or following abandonment or destruction. Among the objects that can be considered functionally certain are such items as seals, tablets or ostraca that reflect the social, economic or political life of Palestine and its neighbours during the second millennium. Other well known artefacts that provide evidence of local crafts and industries include potters' wheel thrust bearings, perforated stone weights and a variety of tools: adzes, axes, chisels, knives, and the like, as well as those objects necessary for food preparation activities, including mortars, pestles, querns, grinding stones and baking trays.

On the other hand, debris resulting from food preparation, while an important indicator of area function and daily diet, has frequently been overlooked in excavation. In ancient Canaan the most important foodstuffs were wheat, barley, olives, grapes, pulses, figs, dates and nuts (Amiran 1978: 64-77), along with animal products, such as meat, yoghurt and cheese. One item in this inventory of debris, namely animal bones,[1] could be reused for decoration and as tools in a variety of domestic industries, especially in textile manufacture. Loom weights, spindle whorls, needles, awls and buttons, often made of bone, indicate quite specifically the production of clothing and fabrics.

Unfortunately, not all objects of Palestinian material culture are so well understood and, indeed, in some cases, small objects have been badly misinterpreted, for example jar stoppers, gaming pieces and unique objects without known parallels. The importance of precise and certain identification of artefacts is emphasized by Gibbon in his

---

Subdivisions within each category are individually numbered and the resulting code is entered in a database file. These data have been indexed and sorted in a variety of ways to show the pattern of finds and their association with various structures.

1.   Rosen presents information that can be gleaned by microarchaeological analysis of floors and soil layers in multifunctional areas (1986: 5-6). Fragments of bone are frequently found where slaughtering or food consumption took place. However, without microscopic examination of the dry debris layer, much of this information is lost.

assertion that assigning appropriate symbols to nominal data is essential to the accurate counting of items (1984: 54). Mislabelling seems to be most frequently the case with those artefacts that are identified with cultic activity (Deetz 1967: 79) and are not usually understood to be domestic equipment. On the Palestinian scene these include figurines, plaques, stelae, metal objects and weapons.[1] In this study, all artefacts from domestic loci will be studied for the evidence they provide for domestic activity areas even though some objects may point to events in the lives of the inhabitants or to their professional occupations performed outside the home, for example arrowheads may relate to the 'last attack' or indicate the home of a military man.

One category of artefact easily lost in an occupied area is jewellery, especially beads and amulets. Because their loss may be more random than that of other artefacts, due to their small size and light weight, they do not serve as clear indicators of the function of their find spots, unless they are found in an associated group. These items probably tell us more about the beliefs and wealth of the inhabitants than about the function of the rooms in their homes. Nevertheless, as we shall see, these artefacts can be an important indicator of the location of the main living room. Other personal possessions, especially imported artefacts from Egypt, Cyprus and Syria which reflect the wealth of individual households, may also point to the public areas of the house while, at the same time, indicating the international relations and trade networks operative in the Levant.

For the purposes of this study, classification of all objects in the excavation reports of the sites chosen for analysis have been organized in specific categories (Table 2.9). The categories themselves are organized in specific functional classes derived from the catalogue of the Museum of Fine Arts, Boston, *Egypt's Golden Age: The Art of Living in the New Kingdom 1558–1085 BC*.

1.   The frequent association of temples and workshops for the production of metal objects is best seen on Cyprus where this association has been documented for various periods and at various sites; at Kition (Karageorghis 1976: 113), and at Maa (Karageorghis, oral communication, Brock University, 21 March 1986). See also the excavations at Athienou (Dothan and Ben-Tor 1983).

Table 2.9. *The Basic Artefact Categories apart from Pottery*

A	Architectural elements
B	Clothing
C	Cosmetics
D	Debris materials
E	Epigraphic materials
F	Figurine/Plaque
G	Grinder
H	Food Preparation equipment
I	Musical Instruments
J	Jewelry
M	Traces of Metallurgy
P	Pottery production equipment
R	Exclusive Items
T	Tools
V	Weights
W	Weapons
Y	Monumental Sculpture
Z	Miscellaneous

Ceramic Corpus

The identification of activity areas and room function in Palestinian houses should be based not only on the functional character of individual artefacts that can be clearly distinguished, but on the total assemblage of objects and ceramic vessels in their architectural context. In most excavations, pottery sherds far outnumber objects. But the functional character of individual vessels is not always as apparent. For example, small juglets, whole or broken, may serve a variety of purposes—container, scoop or small pitcher—and may be identified with various functions: storage, cosmetics, food preparation and consumption.

Concern for the integrity of the excavated assemblage has not in the past been the primary concern of archaeologists. The history of ceramic analysis has focused, for the most part, on pottery typology, clay type, manufacturing techniques and relative date. Differences in form of vessels of the same type have been understood to be chronological or ethnic indicators. For some of the same reasons, imported wares have been valued for their historical and economic implications.[1] In her study of the burial customs of the beginning of the

---

1. This is true even of Wood's recent study with its concern for the social

second millennium in Palestine, Kenyon attempted to distinguish various cultural groups on the basis of varying ware forms (1970: 135-53). Neglected in such studies has been the careful specification of the function of various ware forms on the basis of their inclusion in a particular assemblage. Any attempt to identify functionally meaningful tool kits and determine the activities performed in a specific room will have to consider carefully the pattern of associated finds. The majority of vessel forms found in Palestinian houses can be related to the domestic paradigms designed for this study. Bowls, kraters, cooking pots, juglets, jugs, flasks, stirrup jars, store jars and goblets are all ware forms that reflect the preparation and consumption of food. Other ceramic forms, occasionally found in domestic settings, such as cup and saucer vessels, zoomorphic vessels, lamps, jar stands and pyxides, are not as clearly related to a particular activity.[1]

My categories for the classification of all published pottery have been designed in order to facilitate comparison with the tool kit paradigms. These general categories are divided into specific ware form styles on the basis of criteria derived from Ruth Amiran (1969: Pls. 25-59).[2] These plates include the pottery of the MB IIA period to LB IIB. The sequence of types in Amiran has also been adopted because it is similar to that employed in the published report of the excavations at Hazor, a major site for this study, and of other more recent excavations.

setting of pottery production and exchange. In the detailed analysis of each site, the focus is on the stylistic features that establish the relative chronology of the excavated strata (1985: 553-54).

1. For an analysis of the artifact assemblage employed in the Iron Age domestic cult which includes some of these forms, see Holladay 1986: 249-99.

2. A code book for each ceramic ware form has been designed in order to facilitate entry into dBASE III files. The individual items are organized into categories, represented by a letter, A-Z. Each type within the category has its own number, e.g. B15, a chalice.

Table 2.10. *The Categories for Ceramic Ware Forms*

A   Bowl
B   Chalice
C   Goblet/Mug
D   Krater
E   Cooking Pot
F   Pithos
G   Jar
H   Amphoriskos
J   Jug
K   Juglet
L   Pilgrim flask
M   Bilbil
N   Pyxis/Alabastron
O   Lamp
P   Cup and Saucer
Q   Baking Tray
R   Vase/Bottle
S   Kernos
T   Jar stand
U   Incense vessel
V   Stirrup jar
Y   Miscellaneous
Z   Zoomorphic vessel/rhyton

Additional forms, that do not appear in Amiran, have been appended to the core collection where needed. These forms reflect the divergence in vessel style from north to south in the country as well as the degree of access to trade goods, especially imported wares (Anderson 1984: 72). Several ware forms have been renamed[1] and certain forms, included in Amiran for comparative purposes, have

1.   These categories were based on shape, size, or parallel ware forms in Amiran or her sources. These changes involve Bowls 27:16-17 to Vase R1, R2; Bowl 27:20 to Chalice B1; Goblets 28:7, 8, 9 to Chalices B11, B12, B13; Krater 29:9 to Goblet with spout C10; Jugs 34:9, 12 to Juglets K7, K10; Jug 35:9 to Juglet K16; Jugs 37:8, 10 to Juglets K34, K35; Bowl 39:4 to Krater D23; Goblets 40:1, 2, 4, 5, 9, 10, 11 to Chalices B14, B15, B17, B18, B21, B22, B23; Chalice 40:8 to Bowl A108; Jugs 46:13, 19, 21 to Juglets K41, K45, K46; Goblets 50:6, 10 to Chalices (?) B22; Chalice 50:8 to Krater D29; Jug 54:2 to Bilbil M2; Jugs 55:8, 9 to Juglets K55, K56; Jugs 56:6, 14, 15 to Juglets K61, K62, K63; Bowls 57:12, 13 to Kraters D32, D33; Jug 58:8 to Goblet/mug C11; Cup Photo 193 to Bowl with handle A68. (All plate references are to Amiran 1969).

been omitted because they are not found at Palestinian sites.[1] When this large number of types becomes cumbersome in forming meaningful comparisons to the functional paradigms, clusters of closely related types are formed into subcategories.[2] This is useful because it is precisely the function of the vessels that is the concern of this study. In view of this consideration, the size or capacity of various ware forms is usually of greater significance than the particular ceramic style in determining their appropriate functional subcategory.[3]

In several cases, published reports indicate the presence of 'a room full of smashed pithoi' without drawing any of the forms in the plates (e.g. Yadin *et al.* 1960: 99). Because the main focus of this ceramic analysis is functional rather than stylistic, such information can be utilized in the formation of the artefact assemblage pattern for a particular activity area or room.[4]

Architectural Context

The assemblages of objects and ceramic vessels alone do not tell the complete story of domestic activity areas. These tool kits are only complete when they are located in the domestic space and associated with the architectural features that supported these assemblages. On the other hand, the features themselves may be ambiguous. Does a

---

1. These include Pl. 35:1-6 and 43:6-7, 11-13. Other ware forms that were duplicates of those already identified were also omitted. These involve B4, 28:10 = 27:23; C1, 35:10 = 28:1; G3, 35:12 = 31:3; A74, 39:11 = 39:10; B22, 50:10 = 40:10; A62, 50:11 = 38:24; A64, 50:12 = 38:26; K38, 52:2 = 46:6; A38, 53:1 = 37:14; K56, 56:5 = 55:9.

2. Subcategories have been developed by Bryant G. Wood in his study of the Late Bronze Age pottery of Palestine which are quite specific in regard to ware form (1985: Pls. 4-69). The appropriate subcategories for our purposes need not be so specific as Wood presents, for example, 'conical bowls with inward-folded-rim' versus 'conical bowls with plain rim' (Wood 1985: Pls. 15, 17). Although most of these distinctions are stylistic, they may reflect functional diversity.

3. In his study of LB pottery, Wood developed a reference corpus against which he compared all other published ware form types. Wood employed Cowgill's system of 'similarity coefficient' for determining ceramic ware form morphology. In this system, excellent parallels receive the coefficient of five, good parallels the coefficient of three, and fair parallels the coefficient of one. With this method, Wood establishes a series of contemporary phases between sites (Wood 1985: 228-29, 254-63). The careful analysis prepared by Wood for LB IIB is accepted in this thesis as a basis for the chronological ordering of Late Bronze occupation levels.

4. See discussion of the artefact code, p. 53 n. 2 above.

platform function as a bench, a bed, a shelf or all three? Are pits used for storage or garbage disposal? These questions cannot be answered unequivocally but the chances of understanding these features increases when they are associated with the artefacts uncovered in the same locus. This completed pattern of finds, located in the domestic space, can be compared to the functional paradigms to ascertain their degree of similarity and the probable identification of activity areas and room function.

Ideally, the construction techniques employed in the domestic structures themselves and the associated architectural features should be explored in order to identify the function of individual rooms. For example, thick walls that can support a second storey, and drain pipes that funnel water away from the building's interior are important clues to room arrangement. Other features, such as doors, doorsills and jambs, windows, and interior decoration would greatly expand our understanding of the functioning of the total structure, as well as the wealth and status of the inhabitants, but most house remains preserve only the foundations. Although we must imagine many of these features in a second millennium house, we are reduced to one basic assumption that seems very probable, namely that the walls in the majority of instances were constructed of mudbrick with a plaster coating. Evidence to the contrary would be a significant indication of status or wealth. A detailed analysis of construction techniques, however, is a complete study in itself (e.g. Aurenche and Braemer cited above) and beyond the scope of this work.

Nevertheless, in this study the identification of certain structures as 'houses' depended in part on the distinctions that could be made between domestic and public buildings in the published record. The overall size, the building materials used, the number and shape of rooms are all evidence for the type of structure intended by the original builders.[1] At the same time, ancient buildings were occasionally

---

1. The excavation of the Palace of Zimri-Lim at Mari is a very different problem than the typical excavation of domestic remains in Palestine. At Mari, the palace contained 140 rooms, standing walls (at times 1.5-2.0 m high), complete doorways, numerous built-in features, paved floors, as well as numerous artefacts. Room layout and decoration, along with the artefact remains, were significant indicators of room function. The architectural remains indicated the extent and integrity of the palace complex. On the contrary, most Palestinian domestic structures are known only from their wall foundations and artefacts. In many cases, evidence for doorways was missing or not recognized during excavation.

remodelled, redesigned, and used for secondary purposes not related to their intended function. This may apply to public buildings that were abandoned and later used for domestic purposes as well as to houses that were converted into workshops.

A construction technique which has been preserved and noted in a significant number of cases is the treatment of the floors, that is, whether they were made of beaten earth, were stone paved or plastered. A plastered floor, in particular, may indicate something of the function of a room and indeed of the building as well.

So, too, certain features such as benches, bins, silos, shelves, ovens, hearths, drains and stairs can point to room function, wealth or status, house size and cultural affinity. The size of each room and its relative location may also be indicative of its function in relation to the total house plan. In many cases, however, excavation reports do not describe these features, although ovens are usually drawn on the plans.

Table 2.11. *The Architectural Features*

1	Room/Locus
2	Floors
3	Pillar base
4	Steps
5	Bench
6	Shelf
7	Oven
8	Hearth
9	Bin
10	Silo
11	Pit
12	Cistern
13	Drain
14	Toilet
15	Bath
16	Roof
17	Unidentified
18	Base for potter's wheel
19	Threshold
20	Partition wall
21	Loom
22	Kiln

All identifications, at the time of excavation, are a matter of judgment concerning the function of a particular feature along with an assessment of the associated finds. For example, the distinction between a shelf and a bench may be only a matter of width or height because low benches were used as shelves to keep store jars above floor level. Benches themselves seem to be approximately 50 cm wide whereas shelves vary in width, shape and height above the floor. In spite of this distinction, shelves that run alongside a wall are not always recognized as such.

Other distinctions which may be ambiguous are those among ovens, hearths and braziers. Modern definitions are not very helpful in this case due to the great advances in the design of cooking ovens and of furnaces present in modern culture. However, certain aspects of both of these features enable archaeologists to recognize baking ovens, ovens for baking bricks or burning lime, and kilns for firing ceramic vessels.[1] While not all of these heat-producing installations occur in the archaeological record of second millennium Palestine, especially in domestic contexts, they do indicate the possible range of such features. What is not included here is a simple cooking area located directly on the floor of a room or courtyard.

The basic function of the oven is the same regardless of its individual specification, namely to heat and transform an item in an enclosed structure. The fuel is placed outside, or occasionally inside, the oven and, once it is hot, the item to be cooked can be placed on the inside wall of the oven.[2] This method is one way of baking bread. In a study of domestic architecture, only the cooking oven—or bread oven—is intended by category 7.[3] Large ovens used for industrial purposes have not been included in this study.

A hearth is also a structure where combustible material is burnt. Hearths may be either embedded in the floor, at floor level, or raised above the floor on a platform. In some cases, the hearth is separated from other features by a partition wall. The primary distinction between a hearth and an oven is the manner of heat utilization. The

1. The French term *four* covers all types of ovens. Distinctions are indicated by additional adjectival phrases, such as, *à poterie, à briques* (Aurenche 1977: 89).

2. This type of oven was common at Tell el-Maskhuta in Egypt during the Middle Bronze Age although most were found in a very ruined condition (Personal communication, John S. Holladay, Jr, 15 December 1988).

3. See examples of cylindrical bread ovens from Syria (Aurenche 1977: Figs. 240, 241). Large communal bread ovens are also illustrated (Aurenche 1977: Figs. 242, 243). See the description of ovens at Khirbet el-Meshash from the Iron Age (Fritz and Kempinski 1983: 106-12).

food to be cooked is placed in a cooking vessel inside the hearth (Aurenche 1977: 90). With the use of a baking tray or *saj*, bread can be baked in a hearth or directly on an open fire (Watson 1979: 205).[1] Although the terms used for storage bin, storage pit and silo are all translated as 'silo' in French and Italian, there seem to be some distinctions that can be made in English and in German (Aurenche 1977). For the purposes of this study, a silo is a cylindrical feature, standing independent of other features, that is either built above ground or sunk into the ground. The primary function is that of a granary or storage pit. A pit (category 11) is understood to be any natural or excavated hole in the ground of any shape, used in a wide variety of functions, such as storage, refuse dump, burial pit,[2] potter's installation, or simply existing due to prior soil removal.

The term 'bin' is reserved for those features that are constructed on or above floor level and are built up against another feature, such as a wall or the corner of two walls. The bin is usually understood to be a container. However, the term is used in the feature database file to identify all structures meeting the basic definition. The determination of specific function (storage bin, manger, potter's installation) is withheld until an assessment of the feature along with its associated artefacts and its location can be made.

Although it is not always easy to distinguish an in-the-ground silo from a cistern, their functional differences are easily defined. While the silo serves as a food and grain storage facility, the cistern serves as a water reservoir. In some cases, the cistern is related to a drainage system that carries water into the storage facility. (In other instances, drains serve to carry water away from unroofed areas to the exterior of a structure.) In this case also, a final judgment on the function of a particular feature may rest on the evidence of associated finds and comparison of the resulting tool kit with a particular functional paradigm.

---

1.   Most ovens excavated in Palestine are formed of pot-sherds or of a portion of a large vessel and are plastered with mud (Wright 1962: 109). At the same time, hearths or portable braziers used for heat are not common in Palestine. Rectangular hearths found on Crete are discussed by P.M. Muhly 1984: 107-22.

2.   See Iron Age levels at Ashdod in Area D (Dothan and Freedman 1967).

Functional Tool Kits

Designing paradigms that functionally distinguish the items included in the tool kit assemblages is crucial for the proper use of analogy (Shipman 1986: 94, 102). As the knowledge of traditional and ancient life ways increases, our ability to develop suitable analogies also increases. Indeed, hypotheses concerning room function cannot actually be proved or falsified. All that can be achieved is a demonstration that the ideal types or paradigms are theoretically good analogies in their relationship to the data (Hodder 1982: 9). Hodder lists three elements needed to support a hypothesis: (1) relevance, (2) generality, (3) goodness-of-fit, which involves the similarities between the analogy and the data (1982: 22). The strength of such relational analogies is the demonstration of some links, natural or cultural, that exist between different aspects in the data. The associated patterns within the excavated assemblages, although incomplete, are interdependent and not randomly linked (Hodder 1982: 16). When the same pattern occurs in a particular paradigm, this type of analogy is at its best. For example, when a paradigm of weaving equipment can be compared with an archaeological assemblage which includes a needle, spindle whorls and a group of loom weights, the analogy functions easily.

The paradigms designed for this study are heavily based upon considerations from ethnographic research and the study of ancient iconography. These components strengthen the analogy because their relevance for comparison increases the likelihood that the analogy will disclose patterns of ancient behaviour by demonstrating parallels between past and present activities. In other words, 'material culture patterning can be predicted because of its functional relationships with other aspects of life' (Hodder 1982: 20).

In attempting to establish the functional identification of a particular set of material correlates presumably deriving from one or more sets of patterned activity within an archaeological context, it is necessary to select between different analogies or paradigms. As has been shown above, several features, artefacts and ceramic ware forms are multifunctional. If, however, a functional relationship between the items in a tool kit can be discerned, it becomes possible to make a comparison to an appropriate paradigm. Where such identifications of ancient behaviour can be made, the analogy can be strengthened by determining the pattern of association among activity areas themselves and their location in the architectural space. By such analysis, the links between particular aspects of ancient behaviour, as reflected in the distribution of the cultural evidence, can be recognized. Ideally, the setting or context of the activity areas should manifest something of ancient images of the home.[1] In certain instances, it will be possible to suggest the location of such areas as the living room, the kitchen, the utility or storeroom, the bath room and the bedroom or private quarters. However, in other cases, too few items have been published to constitute a useful assemblage. The patterned activities which took place in the physical setting, or locus, can only be understood in comparison to other areas identified by complete tool kits. In such cases, the basis of comparison will not be the paradigms exclusively, but room arrangement, location, or some other variables.

Method of Analysis

The tool kits assembled from the reports of Middle and Late Bronze Age sites in Palestine represent the published artefacts, but not the actual archaeological record, let alone the items in use in the domestic space. The preservation of artefactual remains in their use settings is affected by (1) the durability of the artefacts, (2) the customs of the inhabitants and (3) the history of the deposition of the debris. Houses destroyed suddenly and violently may preserve more finds *in situ* than deliberately abandoned structures. The details of this depositional history have not consistently been observed or reported so that no single method of analysis can be used for all sites. Each site must be evaluated independently.

In those cases where an artefact assemblage can be reconstructed, it must be kept in mind that precise numbers of artefacts found, especially pottery sherds, are rarely reported. So too the percentages of finds published is rarely indicated. As a result, the numbers of items in each tool kit are very small and, in many cases, attempts to compare the tool kits to the paradigms using statistics are impossible.

The paradigms, on the other hand, are constructs that represent, ideally, a complete functional assemblage. The task of determining the relative value or importance of each item to be included in a particular paradigm is not straightforward. First of all, certain objects or

1.   See Hodder's discussion of 'context' (1982: 24-27).

ceramic ware forms are more or less common depending on the period or phase of occupation; for example, miniature bowls, toggle pins, silos, and so forth. Secondly, certain items are not essential to any particular activity and therefore are not diagnostic for that activity, for example lamps. Thirdly, certain ware forms and artefacts are present in more than one paradigm because they are multifunctional. Where this is the case, the activity set is compared to whichever paradigm or paradigms are most likely to result in a 'good fit'.

Attempts to compare individual tool kits to the paradigms, using nonparametric similarity coefficients (see below), have demonstrated that the classes of items in the paradigms must be weighted and are, therefore, not absolute numbers. At the same time, all reported items for each site, clustered in appropriate locus groups and assigned to functional classes, have been enumerated to determine the percentage of occurrence in each locus group. The value of occurrence is then compared to the weighted, functional paradigms presented below.

Indeed the functional paradigms (Table 2.12) are most useful for comparison with locus groups of coherent activity areas at well stratified sites that were (1) carefully excavated and recorded and (2) yielded numerous finds which were (3) published in sufficient detail to enable comparison with the paradigms. The paradigms consist of a weighted list of functionally essential items, which have been assigned percentage values so that they can be compared numerically to the functional classes of finds from each locus group (see below, Tables 2.12, 2.13). Additional information, such as room size and location will be used, where possible, to strengthen the probability of activity identification.

Table 2.12. *Weighted Functional Classes—Working Paradigms*

Food Preparation and Consumption

Baking tray/oven	3%
Cooking pots	20%
Bowls	46%
Storejars	13%
Jugs/juglets	13%
Other	5%
	100%

Food Storage

Bowls	12%
Storejars	72%
Jugs/juglets	12%
Other	4%
	100%

Table 2.12—*Continued*

Pottery Production		Textile Manufacture	
Shelf	10%	Tools	10%
Bin	20%	Whorl	30%
Kiln	10%	Needle/spindle	10%
Wheel	30%	Spinning bowl	10%
Forming tools	20%	Other	40%
Other	10%		100%
	100%		

Weaving		Economic Affairs	
Tools	10%	Tablets	10%
Whorls	10%	Seals	50%
Needle/spindle	10%	Weights	10%
Weights	60%	Exclusive items	20%
Other	10%	Other	10%
	100%		100%

Personal Adornment		Animal Care and Management	
Beads	40%	Manger	60%
Jewellery	20%	Debris	10%
Cosmetic items	20%	Harness	20%
Other	20%	Other	10%
	100%		100%

The values chosen for each category in these weighted paradigms are based on several factors: the essential nature of the item/class for the activity involved, the likelihood of its preservation in the archaeological record, and the probability of its being recorded and published. These values represent my best judgment, based on selective testing of these values against the best preserved and reported assemblages for the most common activities, for example Hazor L. 6215 for food preparation and/or consumption, and Hazor L. 6217 for storage.[1]

1. Ruth Trigham points to several examples where low level identification was intuitively derived or assumed and was the weak point in very complex and sophisticated data analyses. (See especially her criticism of Binford's view that women were potters, 1978: 173-75). As we shall see below, the assemblages from Hazor used as a test case are not as close to the paradigms as are those from Tell Hadidi illustrated in Table 2.13. This may result from the fact that the assemblages at Hazor were more multi-functional than those from Hadidi. Two examples, Hazor L. 6215 and

Similarity Coefficients

A simple statistical test, suitable for groups of numerically few items, called Robinson's coefficient of agreement, has been chosen to measure the degree of similarity between 'defined categories for pairs of archaeological assemblages' (Doran and Hodson 1975: 139). This test of measurement defines the maximal distance or difference between any two units as 200%. 'By subtracting any calculated distance' or dissimilarity 'from 200 an equivalent measure of similarity or agreement is achieved' (Doran and Hodson 1975: 139).

In this study, the weighted value of each category in the paradigm is compared with the comparable items in the locus assemblage. The difference of presence is computed and this difference is subtracted from 200% to determine the degree of similarity. The formula for this procedure is

$$S_R = 200 - \sum_{k=1}^{a} | Pik - Pjk |$$

L. 6217, are compared to the paradigm:

Category	Paradigm	L. 6215	Difference	Similarity
Baking tray/oven	3%	0%	3	200
Cooking pots	20%	10%	10	–88
Bowls	46%	15%	31	112
Storejars	13%	25%	12	or
Jugs/juglets	13%	40%	27	56%
Other	5%	10%	5	
	100%	100%	–88	

In this example the number of storage related vessels is either unusually high, or our judgment concerning the relative percentage of items included in a typical food preparation assemblage needs to be modified.

Category	Paradigm	L. 6217	Difference	Similarity
Bowls	12%	9%	3	200
Storejars	72%	54%	18	–65
Jugs/juglets	12%	0%	12	135
Other	4%	36%	32	or
	100%	99%	65	67.5%

where the presence of each functional class k in the paradigm i and in the tool kit assemblage of a given locus j is expressed as a percentage P. The functional paradigms used most frequently were those for food preparation and/or consumption and for storage. Examples of the functional categories and their relative values within these paradigms are given below and compared to comparable items in selected assemblage groups (Table 2.13). The percentage value of each category represents the degree of expected occurrence and importance of each functional type in the specific paradigm (see above). In order to evaluate the closeness of fit of any individual activity set or tool kit for a given locus, the percentage of representation of each category of find included in the tool kit is computed. The values obtained are then compared to the paradigm using Robinson's coefficient of agreement.

Table 2.13. *Examples of the Degree of Similarity*

Food Preparation (Tell Hadidi Tablet House, Locus II):

Category	Paradigm	Finds	Difference	Similarity
Baking tray/Oven	3%	0.0%	3.0	200.0
Cooking pots	20%	18.7%	1.3	–37.0
Bowls	46%	43.6%	2.4	163.0
Storejars	13%	31.5%	18.5	or
Jugs/juglets	13%	6.2%	6.8	81.5%
Other	5%	0.0%	5.0	
	100%	100.0%	37.0	

Storage (Tell Hadidi Tablet House, Loci Ia and Ib):

Category	Paradigm	Finds	Difference	Similarity
Bowls	12%	0%	12	200
Storejars	72%	81%	9	–29
Jugs/juglets	12%	9%	3	171
Other	4%	9%	5	or
	100%	99%	29	85.5%

For each assemblage analysed by Robinson's coefficient of similarity, both the similarity coefficient and a percentage of closeness, normalized to base 100, have been assigned.

In a limited number of specialized cases where a hoard was found in a structure under analysis here, an artificial similarity coefficient of 199 or 99.5% has been assigned to the assemblage in question. These assemblages are anomolous in this study of domestic activity areas and this device was chosen to indicate clearly the unique nature of these finds.

Chapter 3

THE MIDDLE BRONZE AGE

The Physical Context

The geographical scope of this study extends from Tel Dan in the north to Tell el-Far'ah (S), and as far east as 'Amman in Transjordan. This region includes several geographic areas and extremes of topography, beginning with the Huleh Valley in the north (Fig. 2, Sites 2, 3), and extending south through the Jordan Valley (Fig. 2, Sites 10, 11, 14, 22), the Jezreel Valley (Fig. 2, Sites 7, 8, 9), Samaria and Carmel (Fig. 2, Sites 5, 12, 13, 18), Judah and the foothills (Fig. 2, Sites 20, 21, 23, 25, 26, 28, 32, 33, 34, 36, 40, 43), the Coastal Plain—north and south—(Fig. 2, Sites 1, 4, 6, 15, 16, 17, 24, 29, 31, 32, 35, 38, 39, 41, 42, 44), the Beersheba Plain (Fig. 2, Site 45, 46) and the Jordanian Highlands (Fig. 2, Sites 19, 27, 30, 37).

A total of 45 Middle and Late Bronze Age sites have been identified for the purposes of this study.[1] Twenty-four sites with Middle Bronze Age occupation remains appear on Table 3.1. Of these, nine sites yielded domestic architecture and associated ceramic vessels and artefacts that could be analysed to determine the nature and location of various domestic activities.

Among the many factors that influenced ancient house plans, an important feature was the local topography which, in Palestine, means the configuration of the tell itself. The interior space of walled towns was divided among public buildings, commercial and industrial areas, and domestic structures. Local topography, the fortification system and the underlying debris upon which the town was built, along with conditions created by existing buildings, established the contours of the tell and affected the size and plan of ordinary houses. Thus, it may

---

1. Sites without excavated or published domestic remains are Tel Dan, 'Afula, Tell Zeror, Aphek, Gibeon, Gezer, Beth-zur and Yabneh-yam.

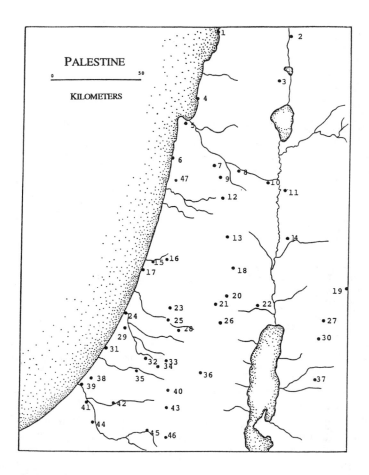

Figure 2. *Map of Palestinian sites, Middle and Late Bronze Age, after Tufnell 1948: 8*

Middle and Late Bronze Age Sites (key to Fig. 2)

1.	Tyre	24.	Tel Mor
2.	Dan	25.	Tell Batash
3.	Hazor	26.	Jerusalem
4.	Akko	27.	Heshbon
5.	Tell Abu Hawam	28.	Beth Shemesh
6.	Tel Dor	29.	Ashdod
7.	Megiddo	30.	Madaba
8.	Jezreel	31.	Ashkelon
9.	Tell Ta'anach	32.	Tell el-Ereini
10.	Beth Shan	33.	Mareshah
11.	Pella	34.	Lachish
12.	Dothan	35.	Tell el-Hesi
13.	Shechem	36.	Hebron
14.	Deir 'Alla	37.	Dibon
15.	Tel Jerishe	38.	Gaza
16.	Aphek	39.	Tell el-'Ajjul
17.	Joppa	40.	Tell Beit Mirsim
18.	Shiloh	41.	Tell esh-Sheri'a
19.	Rabbath-'Ammon	42.	Tel Haror
20.	Ai	43.	Tel Halif
21.	Bethel	44.	Tell el-Far'ah (S)
22.	Jericho	45.	Beer-sheba
23.	Gezer	46.	Khirbet el-Meshash
		47.	Tel Mevorakh

well be that, in certain periods, nearby towns or cities might well develop specialized architectural styles of little more than local spread. The partial excavation of second millennium strata, at most sites, allows for only limited observation of domestic structures and the relationship of such areas to the overall town plan. In most cases, the configurations of the tell which conditioned the architecture cannot be fully appreciated. Occasionally, however, it is possible to see clearly the internal topography of a large site such as the city of Hazor during the Late Bronze Age (see Chapter 4, below).[1]

Other factors which conditioned the construction and destruction of domestic buildings but which cannot be dealt with in the present study include the geological characteristics of each geographical region, the processes of tell formation (Rosen 1986) and the effects of destruction and erosion on the formation of debris layers (Margueron 1985). At present, each of these elements is an independent study (see Williams 1973; Ibach 1987; and Geraty *et al.* 1987, especially with regard to survey data). An additional element for understanding the occupation history of individual structures is the impact of a geographical region on available building materials and construction techniques employed in domestic architecture. A good example of such a study is the work of Aurenche in Syria (1981) and that of Schiffer (1987).

The Temporal Context

The houses included in this study are drawn from the reports of all sites within the study area with Middle and Late Bronze levels published during the past 60 years. The occupation phases of the Middle Bronze Age extend from Middle Bronze IIA to Middle Bronze IIC (Dever 1980a: 35; Gerstenblith 1983: 2-3). Occupational phases of interest for each site studied are shown on Table 3.1.

These sites fall into three categories: sufficient exposure of domestic architecture and adequate publication, partial exposure and publication, and inadequate exposure and/or publication. In the first category, complete, or almost complete, houses can be recognized and partial locus groups of ceramic vessels and artefacts can be reassembled so that functional/spatial analysis can be carried out. For a certain number

---

1. The internal topography at Ras Shamra/Ugarit, a major site outside the study area, can be seen to have had a serious impact on individual buildings; see, for example, the alabaster house (Saadé 1979: 123).

of sites, no functional analysis can be attempted because the published reports are incomplete or at a preliminary stage. Two such sites are discussed in the final section of this chapter. The third category includes sites for which there is evidence of Middle Bronze Age occupation, but not of domestic architecture and, as a result, are not included in this study.

Table 3.1. *Sites with Middle Bronze Age Strata*

Site	MB IIA		MB IIB		MB IIC	
Tel Dan						
Hazor	pre-XVII		XVII/4		XVI/3	
'Afula			V			
Megiddo	XIII		XII-XI		X	
Ta'anach					2 phases	
Tel Mevorakh			XV-XIV		XIII	
Tell Zeror	19-18					
Beth Shan			XB		XA	
Tell el-Far'ah(N)	Niveau 5					
Aphek						
Shechem	XX	XIX	XVIII	XVII	XVI	XV
Bethel	MB IIA		MB	IIB-C		
Gibeon			4			
Beth-shemesh	VI				V	
Gezer	XXI		XX	XIX	XVIII	
Beth-zur					III	
Yabneh-yam	Domestic		III		II	
Tell Batash					XI	
Tel Mor					12	
Tell Nagila						
Tell Beit Mirsim	G	F	E1	E2	D	
Tell el'Ajjul			City	III		
Tell el-Far'ah(S)					Z	
Khirbet el-Meshash					E	

Hazor (Map Reference 203/269)[1]

The site of Hazor is located in the southwestern corner of the Huleh Plain, 15.5 km north of the Sea of Galilee. This large city mound consists of two distinct areas, the tell or upper city (6 hectares or 15 acres), and the enclosed plateau or lower city (81 hectares or 200

1.　All references are to the Palestine Grid.

acres) (Yadin 1972: 14-17). Under the direction of Yigael Yadin, the James A. de Rothschild Expedition carried out five seasons of excavation: 1955, 1956, 1957, 1958 and 1968.

Bronze Age occupation, uncovered in Areas C and 210 of the Lower City, began in the Middle Bronze period (Yadin 1972: 48). The excavation of Area C during the first two seasons uncovered four strata of domestic architecture (Yadin 1960: 76). Although this area was not completely excavated, several discrete housing units were identified. These structures provide sufficient data, in some loci, for spatial/ functional analysis of activity areas in second millennium houses.

Stratum 3 Area C (Figs. 3, 4)

In Area C, only a limited area of Stratum 3 (MB IIC) was exposed (Squares 2-5/L-O—Yadin *et al.* 1960: Pl. 207). One complete structure and partial remains of a second were uncovered. Because the walls remained standing above floor level (c. 0.20–1.25 m) and the doorways were preserved with their sills, distinct building phases could be distinguished as well as the relationship of the rooms to one another. While these structures provide evidence for the architectural traditions that were operative at Hazor, it is unfortunate that the destruction debris could not be distinguished from the stones that were dumped into the rooms to raise the level of the area before the construction of Stratum 2 (Yadin *et al.* 1960: 92). Without this separation, the ceramic finds attributed to Stratum 3 may be contaminated and, in some cases, cannot be assumed to be *in situ*.[1] Because contamination would radically alter the reliability of any proposed tool kit assemblage and render the comparison with functional paradigms uncertain, this problem will be dealt with on a room by room basis.

The only complete structure in Area C is Building 6205 (Fig. 3), a series of five rooms built above the eastern corner of the supporting terrace wall (L. 6093-6164). The main entrance is on the west into Room 6191. A partition wall (with a pillar? 0.74 m high) separated the main area of traffic from an oven in the northeast corner. These features indicate food preparation activity near the doorway of the

1. The excavator saw the contamination of Stratum 3 pottery by that of Stratum 2 as a real possibility given the kind of fill material deposited by the ancient inhabitants as make-up for Stratum 2 structures (Yadin 1960: 92). However, in his synthesis of the excavations, Yadin describes the debris separating Stratum 2 from Stratum 3 as an ash layer, the result of a violent conflagration (1972: 31).

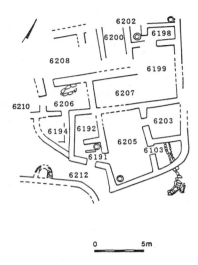

Figure 3. *Hazor Area C Stratum 3, after Yadin et al. 1960: Pl. CCVII*

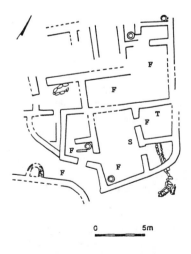

Figure 4. *Hazor Area C Stratum 3, spatial distribution*

house (Fig. 4). The ceramic assemblage found in association with the oven includes 1 cooking pot,[1] 3 narrow-neck jars, 1 jug and 1 juglet (Table 3.2) (tables follow the description). Because of the possibility of contamination, it is significant that these vessels, although smashed, could be reconstructed to a sizable extent.[2] The degree of similarity to the food preparation/consumption paradigm is 58.8%, based on a similarity coefficient of 117.7.

A square room, L. 6192, was located to the north of Room 6191. Because the east wall of Room 6192 was severely destroyed, its relationship to the central room (L. 6205), during the earliest phase of Stratum 3, cannot be established. However, in a later phase, the opening into Room 6191 was blocked,[3] suggesting a second doorway into Locus 6205.

The ceramic corpus published from this room (L. 6192) includes one krater, a cooking pot and a juglet. However, this apparently does not represent the total assemblage which is described by the excavator as a 'concentration' (Yadin *et al.* 1960: 79). Because of the destroyed condition of this room, contamination could be a significant factor although the published pottery sherds were uncovered on a fairly well preserved plastered floor. Such a small sample does not allow for functional analysis although all of the vessels indicate domestic activities related to food preparation. The fact that the floor was plastered may indicate that this room was used for grain storage, possibly in sacks. However, this suggestion is otherwise unsupported.[4]

---

1. Only one cooking pot is illustrated (Yadin *et al.* 1960: 110-12) but the text describes this room as containing 'chiefly cooking pots' (Yadin *et al.* 1960: 79). This description is at variance with the assertion of the excavator that 'everything, all the finds were published' (oral communication, Trudy Dothan, ASOR Annual Meeting, Atlanta, 1986). Evidently, the remaining pottery was not registered.

2. Only one vessel could be reconstructed, rim to base, Cooking pot C1227. The storejars and juglet were generally missing their rims; nevertheless, the form of the body was largely preserved. The most fragmentary vessel was represented by a large body sherd with handle, Jug C1461/2.

3. Yassine identified L. 6191 and 6192 as a separate house that shared its entryway with House 6205 (1974: 35). However, the blocked doorway between these rooms in their final phase indicates that, at one time, they were definitely related to the larger house, 6205. This view is supported by Yassine's own computation of total floor space for House 6191. At 15 m², it is the smallest house of his Type I–Simple, and is out of scale with the other houses of this type (1974: 37).

4. Watson rarely reports the condition of house floors, and in the instances where

The largest room in this house is Locus 6205. The excavator identified this locus as a central courtyard (Yadin *et al.* 1960: 78), even though it is narrow enough to be roofed—4 m at its widest. No evidence to distinguish this room from other roofed rooms was presented. One can only assume that the length of the room (7 m) and its location served as the basis for this judgment.

An oven, located in the southwest corner of L. 6205, along with the ceramic assemblage and objects reported for this locus, clearly reflects food preparation activities. Indeed the assemblage from this locus is the largest one reported for Stratum 3 (23 items). Along with a basalt bowl, probably used as a mortar, were 6 ceramic bowls, 3 cooking pots, 1 pithos, 5 narrow-neck storejars, 1 alabaster vessel and 4 juglets (Table 3.2). The similarity coefficient for this assemblage is 150.8 or 75.4% in comparison with the food preparation/consumption paradigm. At the same time, the presence of 6 storage vessels and several juglets in this assemblage clearly indicates that L. 6205 was a major location for food storage. In fact, no other storeroom was identified. Thus, this room seems to have been the location of several activity areas.

Two additional rooms are located along the east side of the central area, L. 6203 to the north and L. 6103 to the south. Beginning near the south wall of Room 6203 was a drainage channel which crossed Room 6103 and continued under the south wall of the house. Obviously, some activity involving a liquid took place in Room 6103, although the lack of description of the floor leads one to assume that it was not specially treated. At the same time, the dearth of reported finds, only one large jug (45 cm tall, rim missing) and a fragment of carved bone, makes it difficult to attempt any functional analysis.

The situation for room 6203 is very different. Here, the material correlates of several activities have been preserved. The ceramic vessels (Table 3.2) clearly represent food preparation activities—5 bowls, 1 chalice, 1 large cooking pot, 1 baking tray, 1 storejar (the rim of this 'jar' was missing but it was clearly a storage vessel, see Table 3.2) and 2 jugs. In addition, 2 spindle whorls are evidence of spinning, and 3 beads/buttons and 2 fragments of incised bone inlay reflect the economic status and life style of the inhabitants. At the same time that these finds witness to multiple activity areas, they also

she does, the floor of the living rooms is described as 'packed earth covered with a carpet' (1979: 282).

reflect activities common to women and strongly suggest a woman's workroom. When compared to the food preparation paradigm, this assemblage has a similarity coefficient of 120.1 or 60%.

Although the north wall of House 6205 is not well preserved along its entire length, it can be assumed that the rooms discussed above constituted a distinct unit. Analysis of the material culture correlates for each room indicates that the major activity was food preparation and consumption (for the distribution of activity areas, see Fig. 4). Every room, except for Locus 6103, contained the remains of a cooking pot although one or more may have been in storage. Two ovens, grinding stones, and a basalt mortar included in the tool kits of L. 6205 and 6091 support the functional identification of these activity areas.

There was little architectural evidence for a second storey in House 6205. While the walls were thick enough to support an upper floor (60–70 cm), no staircase was present. Neither was there any reported evidence for the type of roof or ceiling that must have covered, at least, the rooms on both sides of the central hall or court.

That L. 6205 was a courtyard remains uncertain. With a maximum width of 4 m it could be roofed without support, although by comparison with Tell Beit Mirsim, where a transition from the use of a central hall with pillar bases to an open central court occurred during the Middle Bronze Age (Albright 1938: 39), one might still expect pillar bases down the length of such a hall. At Hazor, there is insufficient evidence from Stratum 4 to Stratum 3 to see if the same transition can be documented. On the other hand, if L. 6205 were unroofed, it is surprising that the drain did not begin in this area. As things stand, it seems impossible to determine the exact nature of L. 6205 on the basis of the evidence presented.

To the northwest of House 6205, three phases of occupation were found in badly preserved condition. The state of these remains was due mainly to the fact that Stratum 2 floors were only 30 cm above the Middle Bronze Age floors (Yadin *et al.* 1960: 81) which, in this area, were generally 1 m higher than those of House 6205. Not one complete structure can be recovered but several rooms can be identified.

The most complete room was L. 6194, a triangular area that shared a common wall with Rooms 6192 and 6191. Along the east side of this wall was a shelf and, along the north wall, there was a bench. Both of these features appeared to be in use with the upper floor phase,

Stratum 3 (Yadin *et al.* 1960: 80). The published finds for this room, which include a chalice, a small cooking pot, a miniature vessel and a perforated stone (Table 3.2), do not correspond to any identifiable tool kit although the ceramic vessels may be related to cultic activities.[1]

Immediately north of Room 6194 was L. 6206, a room with an oval-shaped stone installation that contained ashes and charcoal, along with a nest of ceramic vessels. Of these vessels, only one bowl, a chalice, a Kamares ware krater sherd and an alabaster lid, were published (Table 3.2). The identification of the oval installation as a 'furnace' or hearth (Yadin *et al.* 1960: 80) does little to specify the activities carried out in this room. Clearly, neither of these adjoining rooms can be designated as unambiguous domestic activity areas.

To the west was an open area (L. 6210) that may have been related to Room 6206. Of special interest here was the large percentage of baking trays, 3 out of 7 items. The proximity of the baking trays to the 'furnace' in Room 6206 may indicate a continuity of function between these two areas on the assumption that the baking tray was used to make bread on an open fire. This may be the ancient version of the traditional bread-making practice observed by Watson where an iron convex disk (*saj*) is used over an open hearth (1979: 205). Unfortunately, no other association of baking trays and hearths can be documented at Hazor that would strengthen the correlation of these remains with baking activities; cf. L. 2007 and 2008 below.

Locus 6207, a room with two floor levels, was located north of L. 6205. Assigned to Stratum 3 were 11 ceramic ware forms (Table 3.2) that have a similarity coefficient of 153 or 76.5% in comparison with the food preparation and consumption paradigm. Also found in this room was a cup-and-saucer vessel which does not usually fit into any assemblage associated with secular domestic activities. However, it is possible that such a vessel, along with the chalice, was related to cultic activity performed in the home.[2]

The rooms in the northern section of the excavation area represent three phases of rebuilding during Strata 4 and 3. The finds from these

1. For an example of cultic artefacts and vessels from Hazor, see the discussion of the Late Bronze Age shrine in Stratum 1B below.

2. See the discussion of John S. Holladay, Jr in which he enumerates the items found in Iron Age domestic contexts that were patently cultic (1987: 276) and includes among them the cup-and-saucer vessel.

rooms, however, were all assigned to Stratum 3. The largest Room was L. 6199, in which all three floor levels were recovered. The assemblage of pottery and objects (Table 3.2) supports the identification of a food preparation and consumption tool kit with a similarity coefficient of 128 or 64%. A lamp and strainer were also included. In fact, 60% of the assemblage consisted of bowls and may indicate an emphasis on food consumption, suggesting that this room may have served as a living room.

Room 6199 opened into Room 6198 which also had three floor levels preserved. Only one bowl was reported from this locus. In the final occupation phase, an oven was located here. Another oven, related to the intermediate building phase, was located to the west of Room 6198. No finds were associated with these features, although in themselves, the ovens indicate domestic activities. The plan of these rooms seems to be similar to that of Building 6205 where two ovens were located, one in the entryway and the other in an inner room.

The walls of L. 6200, located to the west of the oven in the corner of L. 6202, were not completely preserved. The finds from this area consisted almost exclusively of bowl forms, 10 out of 14, including one krater. Two goblets were also present. No identifiable tool kit is represented by this assemblage although there seems to be an emphasis on food consumption and may represent a living room assemblage.

The ceramic ware forms and objects recovered from 'Sub-area 6200' cannot be distinguished according to building phase. As a result, the tool kits from these loci may be composite assemblages rather than the material correlates of activities carried out during discrete phases of occupation. Because of the fragmentary wall remains, it is not possible to assign particular activities to a coherent housing unit, although L. 6208, 6210, 6206 and 6194, and L. 6207, 6199, 6198 and 6200 may be considered as likely groupings. At the same time, the assemblages from the loci in this area seem to be more diversified than those in House 6205. While they point to a variety of domestic activities, some finds and features indicate activities beyond the scope of the basic paradigms designed for this study.

Domestic activities concentrated near House 6205 were evident in the ceramic remains from Street 6212. In fact, this assemblage forms a typical food preparation and consumption tool kit with a similarity coefficient of 160.8 or 80.4%. The full range of this functional tool kit is present: bowls, a chalice, kraters, cooking pots, storejars, a jug and baking trays (Table 3.2). The similarity is strengthened by the presence of Silo 6536[1] and a large loaf-shaped upper mill-stone. Actually, the eastern part of L. 6212 that ended at the entrance to House 6205 may have served as a courtyard for domestic activities. Along the same lines, the fact that many of the representative ceramic ware forms were only partially preserved, consisting mostly of rims and handles, may point equally well to a midden area.

Architectural remains seemed to continue to the southwest of House 6205 although excavation was not extended in this area because the building remains of the Late Bronze Age were left in place, making access to the underlying structures impossible. As a result, the only exposure of Middle Bronze Age architecture that revealed a complete housing unit was this section of Area C.

Table 3.2. *Hazor Stratum 3—Finds and Functional Classes*

Locus	Finds	Functional Class
6103	1 jug	food preparation/storage
	carved bone	special/status
	drain	drainage
6191	1 cooking pot	food preparation
	3 narrow-neck jars	liquid storage
	1 jug	food preparation/storage
	1 juglet	multipurpose
	oven	food preparation
	partition wall	divider

The similarity coefficient for L. 6191 is 117.7 or 58.8% when compared to the food preparation and consumption paradigm.

6192	1 krater	food preparation/consumption
	1 cooking pot	food preparation
	1 juglet	multipurpose
6194	1 miniature bowl	special/cultic
	1 chalice	food consumption
	1 cooking pot	food preparation
	perforated stone	unknown
	bench	multipurpose
	shelf	multipurpose
6198	bowl	food preparation/consumption

1. This silo (L. 6536) stands 18 cm above the street level and would, instead, be classified as a 'bin' in the features list for this study. Its location, outside the house proper, suggests that this feature was not used for storage because of the lack of security. It may instead have been a manger.

Table 3.2—*Continued*

Locus	Finds	Functional Class
6199	5 bowls	food preparation/consumption
	1 krater	food preparation/consumption
	1 narrow-neck jar	liquid storage
	1 lamp	lighting
	1 baking tray	food preparation
	funnel	food preparation

The similarity coefficient for L. 6199 is 128 or 64% when compared to the food preparation and consumption paradigm.

Locus	Finds	Functional Class
6200	9 bowls	food preparation/consumption
	2 goblets	food consumption
	1 krater	food preparation/consumption
	strainer	food preparation
6202	oven	food preparation
6203	5 bowls	food preparation/consumption
	1 chalice	food consumption
	1 cooking pot	food preparation
	1 jar[1]	storage
	2 jugs	food preparation/storage
	1 baking tray	food preparation
	2 spindle whorls	textile production
	1 bead	adornment
	2 buttons	adornment
	2 bone inlays	special/status

The similarity coefficient for L. 6203 is 120.1 or 60% when compared to the food preparation and consumption paradigm.

Locus	Finds	Functional Class
6205	6 bowls	food preparation/consumption
	3 cooking pots	food preparation
	1 pithos	dry storage
	5 narrow-neck jars	liquid storage
	4 juglets	multipurpose
	basalt mortar	food preparation
	alabaster vessel	special/status
	bone inlay	special/status
	oven	food preparation

The similarity coefficient for L. 6205 is 150.8 or 74.5% when compared to the food preparation and consumption paradigm.

1. All storejars are identified as either 'narrow-neck' or 'wide-neck' to suggest a particular type of storage, liquid or dry. In the case of a storejar with a missing rim, the vessel is identified merely as a 'jar'.

Table 3.2—*Continued*

Locus	Finds	Functional Class
6206	1 bowl	food preparation/consumption
	1 chalice	food consumption
	1 Kamares krater	food preparation/consumption
	jar stand	food preparation/storage
	alabaster vessel	special/status
	hearth	heat/cooking
6207	3 bowls	food preparation/consumption
	1 chalice	food consumption
	1 krater	food preparation/consumption
	1 cooking pot	food preparation
	1 jar	storage
	1 narrow-neck jar	liquid storage
	1 jug	food preparation/storage
	cup and saucer vessel	special/cultic
	jar stand	food preparation/storage

The similarity coefficient for L. 6207 is 153 or 76.5% when compared to the food preparation and consumption paradigm.

6210	3 kraters	food preparation/consumption
	1 narrow-neck jar	liquid storage
	3 baking trays	food preparation
6212	3 bowls	food preparation/consumption
	1 chalice	food consumption
	2 kraters	food preparation/consumption
	4 cooking pots	food preparation
	1 jar	storage
	2 wide-neck jars	dry storage
	1 jug	food preparation/storage
	2 baking trays	food preparation
	basalt grinder	food preparation
	bin	storage

The similarity coefficient for L. 6212 is 160.8 or 80.4% when compared to the food preparation and consumption paradigm.

Area 210

One 5 × 5 m square in the middle of the Lower City of Hazor revealed the complete sequence of Middle and Late Bronze Age occupation, Strata 4–1A. Because of its limited size, Area 210 included only one complete room and sections of three others. For the Middle Bronze Age, both Stratum 4 and Stratum 3 levels were present and clearly distinguishable even though the earlier wall lines were reused (Yadin 1972: 48).

Stratum 4 (Fig. 5)

Little can be said concerning the domestic activities of Stratum 4 because of the limited exposure and small number of domestic finds. Under the floor of Room 2011 were three infant burials, one in a jar and two in jugs. Juglets were found in association with these burials, either in the storejar or nearby (Yadin 1972: 48). While these vessels probably were in use as part of a domestic assemblage at an earlier time, it is certain that they had been reused for burial purposes. As a result, they cannot be included among the finds representing the latest activities in Room 2011. The remaining assemblage (Table 3.3), 1 bowl, a baking tray, 2 pestles and a weight, is insufficient to constitute a recognizable tool kit but is certainly suggestive of food preparation activities.

Of the other three rooms, only L. 2012 yielded published finds; 1 bowl, 1 chalice, 1 cooking pot and 1 bone spinning whorl. This assemblage is too small for analysis but does point to expected domestic activities of food preparation and textile production. Room 2010 had a cobbled floor but no pottery or objects were recorded for this locus.[1] The smallest room (1.2 × 2.4 m) was L. 2009. This room had a beaten earth floor and well preserved walls. In view of the fact that no doorway was reported, it is possible that this room was entered from above. Unfortunately no pottery or objects were published (see Fig. 5).

Stratum 3 (Fig. 6)

Four rooms appeared 40 cm above the floor levels of Stratum 4. The corpus of reported finds from these rooms is small; however, several items, interesting for the purpose of this study, do appear. Baking trays were found in two rooms, L. 2007 and 2008. In Room 2008, one corner consisted of a raised platform and a 'nest of vessels' (Table 3.3), namely, cooking pots and baking trays (Yadin 1972: 49). Only one example of each form was published but the association of these finds with an ash layer supports the excavator's identification of a cooking corner. Also found in this room was a bronze toggle pin and a bone stopper(?).

---

1. Cobbled rooms were found in every Late Bronze Age house in Area C, Stratum 1B. These rooms were consistently empty of artefact remains. This same phenomenon also occurred in Area F, House 8039 (see below).

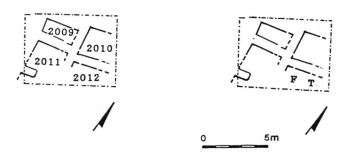

Figure 5. *Hazor Area 210 Stratum 4, after Yadin 1972: Fig. 10*

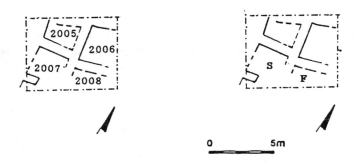

Figure 6. *Hazor Area 210 Stratum 3, after Yadin 1972: Fig. 10*

The finds in Room 2007 included 1 chalice, 2 narrow-neck jar rims, 1 baking tray and a small basalt pestle (Table 3.3). Too few to be useful for analysis as a functional tool kit, these finds are, nevertheless, consistent with basic food storage and preparation equipment. A spindle whorl from Room 2005 was the only evidence of textile production in the Stratum 3 house. Also included in L. 2005 was a lamp, suggestive of the probable location of this small room in the recesses of the house.

Area 210 clearly indicates continuous occupation from Middle Bronze II to the end of the Late Bronze period. Further exposure of this area to provide more complete house plans as well as evidence of town planning would be very useful. Because Area C and Area 210 were not in touch with other areas of Middle Bronze Age construction in the Lower City, it is not possible to say how these areas of domestic occupation related to the gate complex (Area K), the Double Temple (Area F), the Orthostat Temple (Area H), the cisterns, tombs and rock dwellings (Areas D and E), or with each other.

The domestic remains in Areas C and 210 did provide evidence of food preparation, cooking, eating and, possibly, storage. While 4 spindle whorls were recovered, there were not sufficient finds, in any one locus, to form a tool kit related to domestic arts and crafts, such as textile manufacture and pottery production. No evidence at all was reported for other activities, possibly performed in the domestic setting, such as flint knapping, dyeing and large scale food processing, especially crushing and pressing. It appears that Hazor still retains many secrets concerning the life style of its second millennium inhabitants.

Table 3.3. *Hazor Area 210—Finds and Functional Classes*

Locus	Finds	Functional Class
Stratum 3		
2005	1 juglet	multipurpose
	lamp	lighting
	spindle whorl	textile production
2007	1 chalice	food consumption
	2 narrow-neck jars	liquid storage
	1 baking tray	food preparation
	basalt pestle	food preparation
2008	1 cooking pot	food preparation
	1 baking tray	food preparation
	jug stopper	multipurpose
	bronze toggle pin	personal adornment

Table 3.3—*Continued*

Locus	Finds	Functional Class
Stratum 4		
2011	1 bowl	food preparation/consumption
	1 baking tray	food preparation
	basalt pestle	food preparation
	basalt pounder	food preparation/craft use
	limestone weight	special item
2012	1 bowl	food preparation/consumption
	1 chalice	food consumption
	1 cooking pot	food preparation
	bone spindle whorl	textile production

Table 3.4. *Hazor Area C Middle Bronze Age Loci*

Locus	Square	Description	Similarity Coefficient
6103	O2	Floor	
6191	M3	Room	117.7 or 58.8%
6192	M3	Room	
6194	M3	Room	
6198	O5	Room	
6199	O4	Room	128.0 or 64.0%
6200	N5	Room	
6202	N5	Oven	
6203	O3	Room	120.1 or 60.0%
6205	N3	Courtyard	150.8 or 75.4%
6206	M4	Room	
6207	N4	Room	153.0 or 76.5%
6208	M5	Undefined Area	
6210	L4	Undefined Area	
6212	M2	Street	160.8 or 80.4%

Two soundings, L. 6087 and 6247, have been omitted because the Stratum 3 finds in these loci cannot be related to the stratified remains. Loci 6257 and 6258 lie outside the structures under consideration.

Table 3.5. *Hazor Area 210 Middle Bronze Age Loci*

Locus	Square	Description
Stratum 4		
2009	A 1	Room
2010	A 1	Room
2011	A 1	Room
2012	A 1	Room

Table 3.4—*Continued*

Locus	Square	Description
Stratum 3		
2005	A 1	Room
2006	A 1	Room
2007	A 1	Room
2008	A 1	Room

Megiddo (Map Reference 167/221)

The ancient site of Megiddo was strategically located in the Jezreel Valley along the Via Maris.[1] Because of its historical importance, this mound has been more extensively excavated than any other in Palestine.[2] The excavations by the Oriental Institute of the University of Chicago continued for 14 seasons (1925–1939) before they were terminated by the outbreak of World War II. In these excavations, 20 strata of occupation were uncovered dating from the Chalcolithic Period to the Persian Era. Domestic architecture from the Middle Bronze Age was uncovered in two Areas, AA and BB.

The exposure of Bronze Age remains at Megiddo represents a major assemblage of objects and architecture for the period. Unfortunately, the stratigraphy, presented in the excavation report, is confused. Further complicated by the large number of tombs dug into the domestic areas, some of the architecture and artefacts have been assigned to the wrong strata. Many attempts have been made to interpret the stratigraphic record, the most important being those of Kenyon (1969), Dunayevsky and Kempinski (1973), and Gonen (1987).

Detailed study of artefact distribution is further complicated by the limited information recorded concerning incomplete pottery vessels recovered from each room, and by the fact that the majority of rooms drawn on the plans lack locus numbers. And among the numbered

---

1. Gonen details the references to Megiddo in Egyptian texts and concludes that the strategic importance of the site varied during its history. For example, Megiddo was of little importance in the 19th dynasty period when Egypt's northern border was no longer located in the Megiddo region (1987: 98).

2. During the years 1903–1905, G. Schumacher, C. Steuernagel and C. Watzinger excavated here on behalf of the Deutscher Palästina-Verein and the Deutsche Orient-Gesellschaft. The results of this work will not be considered here.

loci, those with recorded artefacts rarely contain more than two published items.[1] As a result, these small assemblages are not useful for comparison with functional paradigms. What is possible is the analysis of finds from each phase of each area. In this way some sense of the range of activities performed in the Middle Bronze houses can be discerned.

In Area BB, two discrete building complexes were separated by the sacred area, one to the southeast and the other to the northwest. Because of this spatial separation and the fact that the architectural style of the two complexes varied over time, the assemblages from these complexes have been studied separately.[2]

Stratum XIII Area BB SE (Fig. 7)
The earliest Middle Bronze Age phase in Area BB SE appears on Plan XIII A (Loud 1948). Two areas of houses are shown, separated by a north–south street. The houses to the west of the street may have been earlier than those to the east (Kenyon 1969: 44) because their wall alignment is not in harmony. While the architectural remains appear to form a housing complex, no complete houses can be reconstructed from the wall fragments.

The artefact remains from this complex include 10 items. Because of the limited number, no activity areas can be located with confidence. However, certain activities, represented by the assemblage, can be identified; 60% of the finds relate to food preparation or consumption and food storage, 2 bowls, 3 jugs and 1 storejar; 10% to personal adornment, 1 toggle pin; while the remaining 30% cannot be accurately categorized (Table 3.6). Indeed, the stone pommel, clay wheel and fragment of bronze shaped like a horn may represent a cultic or a non-domestic function. On the other hand, they may be in secondary use as domestic tools although it is difficult to assign precise functions.

The storage function of only one room can be suggested. L. 3119, a small, corner room with a paved floor, contained one large, wide-necked storejar. Unfortunately, there were no other finds from the immediate area to strengthen this suggestion.

1. A study of all 'clean' loci, those whose floors were indicated on the plans, did not improve the data retrieval process. Zero to two items remained the norm.
2. Kenyon's study of the stratigraphy suggests a series of phases which do not correspond, in some cases, with the published plan, that is, Phase M includes BB NW on Plan XIII with BB SE on Plan XII.

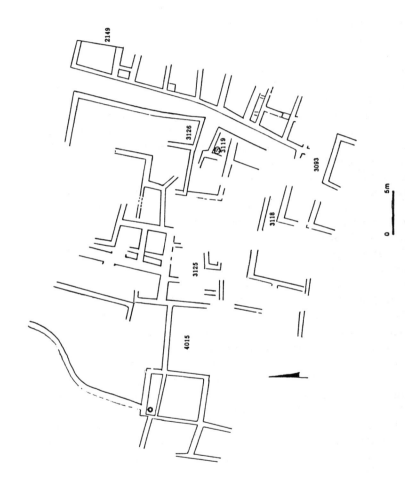

Figure 7. *Megiddo Area BB SE Stratum XIIIB, after Loud 1948: Fig. 397*

No finds were reported for the rooms along the east side of the north–south street. Because these structures were cut into by a later city wall, no complete plans can be reconstructed. It is assumed that these rooms were part of houses because of their size, the thickness of their walls, as illustrated, and the sharing of party walls, apparently a common feature of houses at Megiddo. The only architectural features indicated on Plan XIII A are a fragment of flooring and a corner bin.[1]

Stratum XIII Area BB NW (Fig. 8)
Two phases of occupation west of the temple area are represented on the published plans (XIII B and XIII A). In the assemblage from the houses of the earlier phase (B), the percentage of craft related artefacts is noticeably greater (44%) than for other Middle Bronze Age structures at Megiddo. This assemblage included 1 stone spindle whorl, 1 bronze chisel, a bronze dagger with a limestone pommel, a bronze blade, and a limestone mould (Table 3.7). Conversely, the percentage of finds related to food preparation, consumption and storage is less (25%); 2 bowls, 1 storejar and 1 krater. However, 2 flint sickle blades, originally related to food production, were part of the class of tools from this area. In this context, these blades and a bronze figurine (L. 5123), along with the limestone mould (L. 5093), may well be evidence of tool production and metallurgy in this area (see also L. 5034 below).

Several rooms of a complex to the north of the temple area (Square M13) should be considered separately because they cannot be related stratigraphically to the western houses (Kenyon 1969: 45). The assemblage of artefacts published from these northern rooms includes only one ceramic vessel, a juglet, whose precise function, in the circumstances, is uncertain (Table 3.7). Of the remaining artefacts, 60% are related to textile production, including 1 needle, 1 loom weight and 1 borer, and 10% (1 balance weight) to business.

A larger assemblage of artefacts was reported for the later phase (A) of houses in the northwest area (Table 3.8). The percentage of food preparation, consumption and storage related vessels (c. 50%) is more typical of domestic structures. It included 5 bowls, 1 goblet, 3 jars, 5 jugs and a basalt mortar. Several items related to the textile

---

1. The nominal identification of this feature as a bin is arbitrary because there is no indication of the level of the floor. It is the shape of the feature, rectangular rather than round, that suggests a bin rather than a silo.

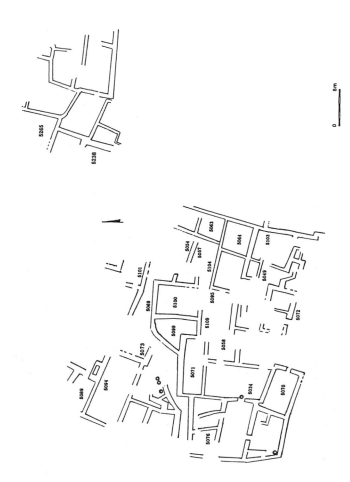

Figure 8. *Megiddo Area BB NW Stratum XIII, after Loud 1948: Fig. 397*

industry were also represented (14.8%), 3 loom weights, two of clay and the other of stone, and a bone awl. The stone weight may have been used in commerce along with the stone scarab (7.4% of the total assemblage), or in craft-related activities. Several items of special or cultic usage were also identified (14.8%), a serpentine adze head, a miniature jug, a clay wheel and an inscribed clay fragment. Two juglets and a limestone pommel, all without precise functional classification, were associated with a bin formed of large clay slabs in Room 5064 (Loud 1948: 87, Fig. 196). A unique find, uncovered in paved room 5034, consisted of a juglet that contained fragments of silver weighing 135 grams. These artefacts reflect common domestic activities as well as specialized or status items among the possessions of the inhabitants. Unfortunately, it is not possible to localize these activities in the Middle Bronze Age houses or to understand their relationship to one another.

The presence of lamps in an artefact assemblage could be a very useful indicator of roofed rooms or small rooms far from the main source of light. In the NW houses of Stratum XIII, 2 lamps were found near Locus 5073 (XIII B) and one to the east of Locus 5072 (XIII A). In both cases, however, these loci were undefined because 50–75% of the room walls were missing. In the case of Area BB SE, no lamps were recovered. Without additional information, this data cannot be used to determine the function of these rooms.

Table 3.6. *Megiddo Stratum XIIIA—Area BB SE—Finds and Functional Classes*

Locus	Finds	Functional Class
2149nr[1]	1 bowl	food preparation/consumption
	1 jug	food preparation/storage
	stone pommel	weapon
	toggle pin	adornment
3093nr	1 bowl	food preparation/consumption
3118E	clay wheel	special item/cultic
3118S	1 jug	food preparation/storage
3119	1 wide-neck jar	dry storage
3125N	bronze horn? frag.	unknown
3126N	1 jug	food preparation/storage

1. nr = near; this designation is made in the text by an equal sign preceding the locus number; e.g. =1733, Register of Finds (Loud 1948: 150).

Table 3.7. *Megiddo Stratum XIIIB—Area BB NW—Finds and Functional Classes*

Locus	Finds	Functional Class
5073nr	bronze chisel	tool
5073E	2 bowls	food preparation/consumption
	2 lamps	lighting
5073W	toggle pin	adornment
5087W	bronze dagger and limestone pommel	weapon
5093	stone whorl	textile production
	bronze blade	tool
	limestone mould	metallurgy
5114nr	1 narrow-neck jar	liquid storage
5123nr	flint sickle blade	agricultural tool
5123N	flint sickle blade	agricultural tool
5123S	bronze figurine	special/cultic
5260	1 krater	food preparation/consumption
5238nr	haematite weight	business
5265nr	1 juglet	multipurpose
	needle/awl	textile production
5265E	bronze borer	tool
5265W	clay loom weight	textile production

Table 3.8. *Megiddo Stratum XIIIA—Area BB NW—Finds and Functional Classes*

Locus	Finds	Functional Class
5034	1 juglet	storage—contained silver
	silver fragments	metallurgy/treasure
5049	1 jug	food preparation/storage
5049nr	1 narrow-neck jar	liquid storage
5054	1 jar/goblet	food preparation/consumption
	1 miniature jug	special/cultic
5057	toggle pin	adornment
5058	clay wheel	special item
5058S	stone weight	business/textile
5058W	clay incised object	unknown
5064	2 juglets	multipurpose
	limestone pommel	weapon
5070	clay weight	textile production
5072	1 bowl	food preparation/consumption
	1 jug	food preparation/storage
5072E	1 bowl	food preparation/consumption
	1 lamp	lighting
5076	1 bowl	food preparation/consumption

Table 3.8—*Continued*

Locus	Finds	Functional Class
5076N	stone scarab	business/adornment
5076NE	clay weight	textile production
5094N	serpentine adze head	status/cultic
5095nr	1 narrow-neck jar	liquid storage
5095E	bone awl	textile production
5100	basalt vessel	food preparation
5101	1 bowl	food preparation/consumption
5103nr	1 bowl	food preparation/consumption
5104nr	1 wide-neck jar	dry storage

House Plans. The area of houses northwest of the sacred area was divided by streets into discrete complexes. One street ran east–west, south of Room 5070, and intersected with a north–south street on the west side of the excavation area. A second east–west street meandered along the northern walls of Rooms 5076 and 5071 (Loud 1948: 84). The complex formed by these streets probably included several houses although the artefact assemblage does not provide sufficient evidence for distinguishing individual structures. A reconstruction designed by Yassine identified three houses among these rooms and a fourth outside this complex to the northwest (1974: Pl. VII.1). From the published report, it is impossible to attempt a further reconstruction than what has been suggested by Yassine. It is important to note, however, that a pillar base and part of a pillar to support the roof was uncovered in the northern part of Room 5034 making it likely that this room (4 × 6 m) was not an open courtyard.

The irregular shape of several rooms in these houses is caused by curving walls or corners that lack right angles. This irregularity is first seen on Plan XIII B and increases in the following phase. It does not seem to be the result of the topography of the underlying debris layers. Indeed, it may, as Yassine suggests, be the result of building techniques, especially the enlarging of houses over time (1974: 17).

Stratum XII Area BB SE (Fig. 9)
Several housing units on Plan XII BB, located southeast of the sacred area, were associated by Kenyon with the second phase of Stratum XIII houses in BB NW, (1969: 45-46, Fig. 19). Although these houses appear to be well preserved with many complete rooms articulated (p. 38), few finds were reported. A total of 16 items reflect common

domestic finds (Table 3.9); 56.25% of the assemblage reflected food preparation, consumption and storage. The ceramic corpus consisted of 2 bowls, 1 goblet, 1 cooking pot, 1 storejar, 2 jugs and a juglet.[1] Most of these items, except for 1 bowl, 1 storejar and 1 jug, cluster in the northeast room of the house (L. 2135W, 2142W, and 2147nr). No other significant cluster of food preparation vessels was found. One large storejar, together with a paste scarab, was found in a small room whose floor was not discerned during excavation, L. 3121. While the size of this room (2.0 × 2.5 m) and its location, in the southeast corner of the rooms immediately south of the sacred area, has similarities to the small room of Stratum XIII (L. 3119), there are no other artefacts to support the interpretation of storeroom. Both of these rooms, however, can be compared in size to the Stratum D storerooms (1 and 4) in the Patrician House at Tell Beit Mirsim (2.5 × 3.1 m and 2.9 × 3.1 m respectively), see Table 3.65.

Two bronze spearheads, whose precise function in this setting is unclear, represent 12.5% of the assemblage. There are not enough other tools or weapons to determine whether these points were the possessions of persons connected with military service or whether they were in some other context, for example, in re-use as household tools, in storage as scrap metal, or as votive offerings connected with the sacred area. The only item of personal adornment, apart from 3 scarabs, was a bronze toggle pin. However, the presence of a balance weight in the assemblage suggests that the scarabs may have been associated with business, rather than simply serving as jewellery. In this assemblage, the items related to business constitute 25% of the total assemblage, a significantly greater percentage than the previous stratum. These items, located in the rooms south of the sacred area, form the only other artefact cluster for this phase. The thickness of the walls in this area may be a clue that these rooms, while associated with the houses north and east, served a more specialized function.

---

1. The juglet could well be included in the food preparation/consumption and storage category because of its location in the same room as the cooking pot, a bowl, a goblet/jar and 2 jugs. In the tables, the juglet is classified as multifunctional, because it can serve as a dipper/scoop or perfume container, although, in this case, there were no other cosmetic or personal adornment items reported for this room, with the exception of 2 scarabs—themselves multifunctional.

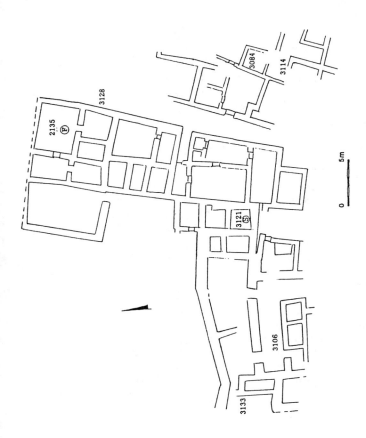

Figure 9. *Megiddo Area BB SE Stratum XII, after Loud 1948: Fig. 398*

Indeed, they may have been directly related to the sacred area.[1]

House Plans. Several discrete houses west of the north–south street can be identified with some certainty. In these structures, some of the thresholds were sufficiently well preserved to indicate the relationship between associated rooms. Three possible room clusters were preserved (Fig. 9). The northernmost included five rooms and measured 60 m^2 on the ground floor. Immediately south is another possible house with five rooms that measured 46.5 m^2. The third possible house, (east of L. 3121) included seven rooms, although two of these were very small and may have served as a stairway to the upper storey or roof. The total measurement was 66.3 m^2. To the east of the street, the remains were too fragmentary to attempt a positive reconstruction.[2]

Table 3.9. *Megiddo Stratum XII—Area BB SE—Finds and Functional Classes*

Locus	Finds	Functional Class
2135W	1 juglet	multipurpose
	steatite scarab	business/adornment
2142W	1 bowl	food preparation/consumption
	1 jar/goblet	food preparation/storage
	steatite scarab	business/adornment
2147nr	1 cooking pot	food preparation
2147E	2 jugs	food preparation/storage
3084S	1 bowl	food preparation/consumption
	1 jug	food preparation/consumption
3106	haematite weight	business
3106N	bronze spearhead	weapon
3121	wide-neck jar	dry storage
	paste scarab	business/adornment
3133N	bronze spearhead?	weapon/tool
	toggle pin	adornment

1. For the possible association of metallurgy and metal artefacts with cultic areas, see p. 55 n. 1.
2. Yassine (1974) has suggested one house in this area. However, because of the poor alignment of walls (due to the continuation or rebuilding of Stratum XIIIA remains?), no attempt is made here to locate a coherent house plan.

Table 3.10. *Megiddo Stratum XII—Area BB NW—Finds and Functional Classes*

Locus	Finds	Functional Class
5038E	1 jug	food preparation/storage
	bone comb	cosmetic
	toggle pin	adornment
5043	1 jar	storage
5048	1 jug	food preparation/storage
5077	loom weight	textile production
5077nr	spear/arrowhead	weapon
5081nr	1 jug	food preparation/consumption
5081S	haematite weight	business
5112nr	crystal pendant	adornment

Stratum XII Area BB NW (Fig. 10)

To the west of the sacred area are the poorly preserved remains of a series of rooms built on a somewhat different alignment than those of the underlying stratum. Only three complete rooms can be identified. No finds were reported for two of these rooms. The middle room, L. 5038E, yielded a comb, toggle pin and a juglet, all of which could function in the class of personal adornment and cosmetic use. One other item of adornment, a crystal pendant, found near Tomb 5112, completes this class of artefacts (Table 3.10). For this phase, items of adornment or cosmetic use constitute 40% of the entire assemblage.

Little in the way of food preparation and consumption or storage is represented in the assemblage. One Cypriot jug and a juglet, possible storage vessels, along with a wide-mouth jar or large goblet, all come from separate loci. As a result, no storeroom can be located with certainty.

From an undefined area to the north of the main housing complex, L. 5077, came a bronze spear/arrowhead and a loom weight. Because of their location, and the lack of associated artefacts, it is unclear whether these items were in primary or secondary use. In fact, due to the poor preservation of complete rooms, it is not possible to formulate a coherent house plan for this phase.

With the transition from Stratum XII to Stratum XI, the buildings to the west of the sacred area undergo a major architectural change. This is evident from Plan BB XI (Loud 1948: Pl. 399) which shows walls 1.2 m thick for the new structures as compared with typical house walls, c. 0.7 m thick, in the SE sector (Fig. 11). Comparison of

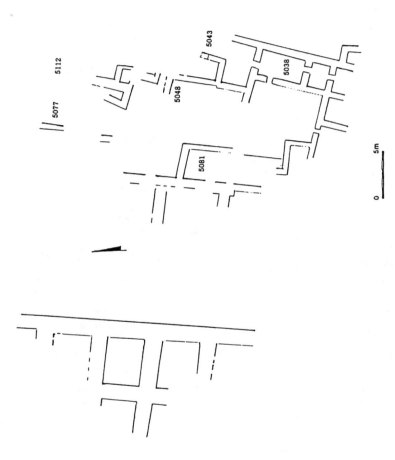

Figure 10. *Megiddo Area BB NW Stratum XII, after Loud 1948: Fig. 398*

the finds reported from both sectors clearly distinguishes the domestic structures.

Stratum XI Area BB SE (Fig. 11)

The structures in the southeast sector of Area BB represent a rebuilding of the earlier phase along both sides of the north–south street. In some cases, these houses share party walls and are, as a result, difficult to isolate. In this phase, functional analysis of the artefact assemblage is more rewarding because items tend to cluster in certain loci. Unfortunately, these clusters are scattered among the houses making any overall decisions concerning room arrangement impossible.

Forty objects were recorded for Stratum XI SE, one of the largest Middle Bronze Age assemblages from Megiddo. Of these finds (Table 3.11), 50% were ceramic vessels related to food preparation/ consumption and storage. Two important clusters of these vessels occurred, one in Room 3053 of the easternmost house, and another in a fragmentary room, L. 3096. The similarity coefficient of this latter locus with the food preparation paradigm is 147 or 73.5%. In view of the undefined nature of this locus, the degree of similarity is surprisingly good. The presence of a lamp in this room may indicate that it was roofed and far from the source of light. Indeed, the large room (4.5 × 7.0 m) immediately to the north contains a pillar base in the middle of the floor, suggesting that it, too, was roofed (Square O13).

The most unusual category of finds, 3 figurines and 1 zoomorphic vessel, represents 10% of the assemblage. The presence of such objects in houses bordering the sacred area may support Kenyon's view that the standing stones illustrated on Stratum Plan XII were still in existence (1969: 45). Three other categories of objects, each representing 10% of the total finds from the southeast sector, are (1) tools and weapons, (2) business, and (3) adornment and cosmetic use. Only one loom weight (2.5%) was published, providing minimal evidence for textile production during this phase.

House Plans. Several housing units, clearly distinguished by the north–south street, are separated by two east–west alleys, L. 3068 and an unnumbered alley opposite. While these alleys may have served as entrances to individual houses, they also separated the houses from one another. Within these houses some thresholds were preserved,

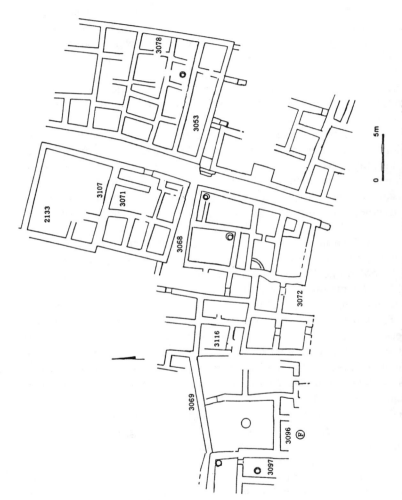

Figure 11. *Megiddo Area BB SE Stratum XI, after Loud 1948: Fig. 399*

although they are lacking in most walls. As a result, one can rarely be certain that two or more rooms are part of the same house. Two houses west of the street seem to be a rebuild of Stratum XII structures. The house to the north of the alley, including L. 3071, had 6 rooms in Stratum XI and a possible stairway. It is not clear what relationship this house had to the rooms on the north, L. 3107S and 2133. However, in size (56.4 m²), this area could well be a separate house. To the south of the alley, a redesigned version of the Stratum XII house can be distinguished. Due to the total lack of reported finds, it is unclear whether this house included the room cut into by Tomb 3070. Extending west of this house, south of the sacred area, was a series of rooms built above the wide Stratum 12 foundations. While it is clear from the finds that domestic activities were carried out in these rooms, it is difficult to reconstruct complete houses.

On the east side of the main street, the house units seem to have been larger. An entryway or small alley separated the houses to the north from the poorly preserved houses to the south. No artefacts were reported from these southern rooms. Although no thresholds were preserved in the house immediately north of the alley (L. 3053–3078), some doorways were preserved. In fact, this house may have had as many as 11 rooms (12 × 9 m, 108 m²). This house contained an assemblage of domestic vessels and artefacts, most of which clustered in L. 3053 (Table 3.10).

Further north, a second structure of the same length was only partially preserved (no locus numbers appear on the plan). The rooms appear to be comparable in size but no finds were recovered that would confirm its identification as a private house. However, the thickness of the wall foundations is the same as all the houses in the southeast sector during this phase.

Table 3.11. *Megiddo Stratum XI—Area BB SE—Finds and Functional Classes*

Locus	Finds	Functional Class
2133	1 narrow-neck jar	liquid storage
	1 juglet	multipurpose
	black stone scarab	business/adornment
	bronze blade	tool
	clay figurine	special/cultic
2133E	1 juglet	multipurpose
3053	1 bowl	food preparation/consumption
	1 krater	food preparation/consumption

Table 3.11—*Continued*

Locus	Finds	Functional Class
	1 wide-mouth jug	food consumption
	1 jug	food preparation/storage
	flint javelin head	weapon
	bronze figurine	special/cultic
3053N	1 jug	food preparation/consumption
3068	1 bowl	food preparation/consumption
	toggle pin	adornment
3068S	paste scarab	business/adornment
3068W	scarab	business/adornment
3069	paste scarab	business/adornment
	toggle pin	adornment
3071	1 juglet	multipurpose
	zoomorphic vessel	special/cultic
3072W	wide-neck jar	dry storage
3078	bronze adze	tool
3081nr	1 juglet	multipurpose
3096	6 bowls	food preparation/consumption
	1 chalice	food consumption
	2 jugs	food preparation/storage
	1 juglet	multipurpose
	1 lamp	lighting

The similarity coefficient for L. 3096 is 147 or 73.5% when compared to the food preparation and consumption paradigm.

Locus	Finds	Functional Class
3097	1 bowl	food preparation/consumption
	spear/arrowhead	weapon
	gold band	adornment
3107S	clay weight	textile production
3116	2 bronze figurines	special/cultic

Stratum XI Area BB NW (Fig. 12)

The impressive complex west of the sacred area was only partially preserved. Two distinct buildings were identified by the excavators: one with a V-shaped plan lay along the north and west sides of the sacred area, and a second, rectangular in plan, was further west (Loud 1948: 92). These buildings were not aligned with one another although they shared a similar style of construction (Loud 1948: Figs. 224, 226) and may have joined (Loud 1948: Fig. 399). Only two artefacts were reported for the western building, a bone spindle whorl and a haematite weight (Table 3.12). No functional interpretation can be attempted with such limited information.

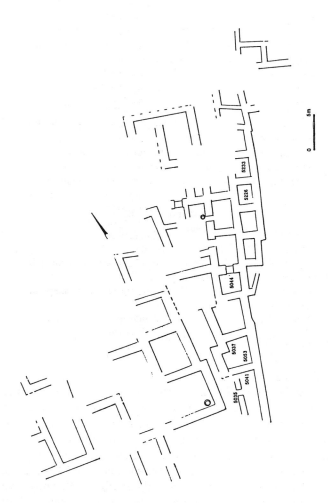

Figure 12. *Megiddo Area BB NW Stratum XI, after Loud 1948: Fig. 399*

The distinctive character of the V-shaped structure is evident in its artefact assemblage. Out of a total of 15 published finds, the percentage of rare or specialty items is greater than that of food preparation and consumption items, 41.5% versus 33.3% (Table 3.12). Several of the special items may be considered as cultic objects, for example, a bronze figurine and a miniature bowl. On the other hand, there were no items reported that could be specifically related to food storage with the possible exception of a juglet. Articles of personal adornment constituted 16.6% of the total finds, while weapons were 8.3%.

Building Plan. In the V-shaped building many complete rooms and paved floors were recovered. Along the east side was a row of small rooms situated behind a row of larger rooms. While the location and size of the smaller rooms might indicate storage, there were no finds to support this suggestion. Instead, these rooms contained jewellery and votive objects. The east wall of these small rooms is slightly thicker (1.2 m) than other interior walls (1.0 m) and probably served as a major exterior wall. The full extent of this structure cannot be determined although it probably extended to the west.

Few complete rooms can be reconstructed in the western building although it is clear from the plan that the average size of these rooms (5 × 5 m) is considerably larger than those in the southeast sector (3 × 2.5 m). The alignment of these rooms with those that appear in Squares M–N13 on the Stratum XII plan (Loud 1948: Fig. 398) led Kenyon to suggest that this western building was earlier than the V-shaped building further east (1969: 47). Unfortunately, the paucity of finds and the poorly preserved condition of the walls of the Stratum XI building makes further speculation on its function unproductive at this point (see Stratum X below).

Table 3.12. *Megiddo Stratum XI—Area BB NW—Finds and Functional Classes*

Locus	Finds	Functional Class
5031nr	bone whorl	textile production
	haematite weight	business
5035	1 bowl	food preparation/consumption
5037W	bronze object	unknown
5041nr	cooking pot	food preparation
5044	1 bowl	food preparation/consumption
5044E	clay object	unknown
5053nr	bronze figurine	special/cultic

Table 3.12—*Continued*

Locus	Finds	Functional Class
5226WRm	flint arrowhead	weapon
5231nr	gold ring	adornment
5231S	1 jug	food preparation/storage
5233	toggle pin	adornment
5233E	1 miniature bowl	special/cultic
	stone object	unknown

Stratum X Area BB SE (Figs. 13-14)

The houses in the southeast sector of Area BB were rebuilt on the foundations of Stratum XI structures.[1] The north–south street continued to separate the major housing units. The alley that ran off this street toward the east was extended to completely separate the houses (Loud 1948: 117), and connected with a second north–south street further east (Loud 1948: Fig. 400). The largest assemblage from Middle Bronze Age Megiddo was reported for this phase, 104 objects and ceramic vessels, along with a group of 26 loom weights (Table 3.13).

These clay loom weights constitute the most distinctive finds from an individual locus (3036E). There can be no doubt that weaving was being carried out in this area. A comparison with the weaving paradigm indicates a similarity coefficient of 136 or 68%. The only other finds in this room were a clay stopper and a bronze needle/toggle pin. Two other assemblages clearly reflect food preparation/consumption, L. 2032N and L. 2032S. The similarity coefficients for these assemblages are 139 or 68.5% and 141.5 or 70.7% respectively. The similarity is considerably strengthened if the other associated loci (2032 and 2032nr) are included, 166.3 or 83.2%. Unfortunately, all of these loci are undefined areas and appear to be outside of coherent housing units.

A similar food preparation/consumption assemblage was located in a series of rooms to the south, L. 3057, 3056Rm, and 3045E. Because of the small number of published bowls, the similarity of this assemblage with the standard paradigm is weak. Nevertheless, the concentration of 2 juglets, 1 jug, 1 chalice, 1 bowl and 2 lamps points predominantly to food consumption (Table 3.13; Fig. 14).

---

1. Gonen attributes Stratum X BB to early LB I (1987: 86). I accept Kenyon's view that this stratum was within the late MB IIC horizon (1969: 47).

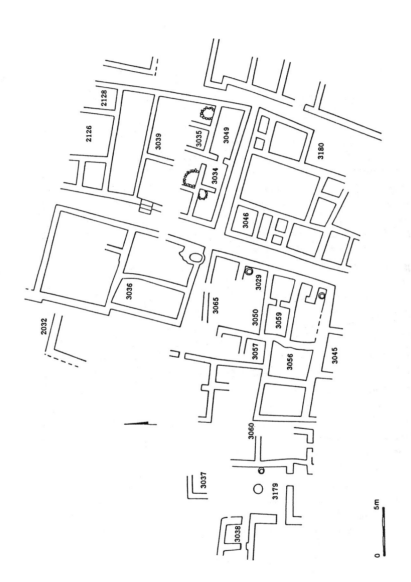

Figure 13. *Megiddo Area BB SE Stratum X, after Loud 1948: Fig. 400*

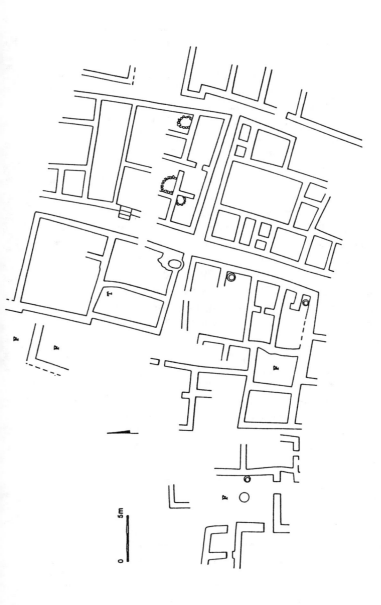

Figure 14. *Megiddo Area BB SE Stratum X, spatial distribution*

Another concentration of vessels associated with food consumption occurred in Room 3179, directly south of the sacred area. It is significant that all the bowl forms are domestic use forms; no miniature bowls were included. Altogether, 6 bowls and 2 chalices were recovered. While this assemblage does not correspond exactly to the standard paradigms, no other activity is represented in the assemblage.

Other activities are represented among the finds from the entire sector. Overall, food preparation, consumption and storage vessels constituted 46.3%, tools and weapons 4.6%, business 3.8%, adornment and cosmetics 7.7%, textile production 24.3%,[1] lighting 4.6%, and special items 7.7%. Several of the special items may have had a cultic function, such as the bronze serpent and the clay birds. The precise function of the clay disk cannot be determined although it may have been a gaming piece or a stopper.

The location of lamps in these houses is better understood than in previous strata. Two lamps were found in the area west of L. 2128, a room in the northeast house. In the house immediately south, 2 lamps were located in the rooms near L. 3034. Two lamps were also part of the assemblage of vessels in Room 3056 and another lamp occurred with 2 bowls in L. 3037. The presence of a lamp in this undefined area may indicate that this locus originally was a roofed room. This evidence is important because of the architectural changes evident in the plan of Stratum X.

House Plans. While the major Stratum XI house walls were reused in Stratum X, alterations in room arrangement are evident. Certain areas clearly were courtyards rather than roofed rooms (Loud 1948: 97). It is not possible to be certain, in every case, that a large room did actually serve as a court, because many walls have been cut into by later construction and intrusive burials.[2] Nevertheless, no pillar bases are reported for these enlarged areas. One can compare the size of the rooms in the northwest house (for example, Room E of L. 3036; 4 × 6.6 m) and the southeast house (Room E of L. 3046; 5 × 7.2 m)

---

1. All percentages have been computed on the basis that each item was counted as one. This principle was also applied to this group of loom weights in spite of the fact that several items in each functional category usually functioned together as a unit.

2. Great difficulty in determining coherent strata results from the paucity of elevations indicated on the plans of each stratum. It is not often clear what the impact of the underlying debris is on the level of wall foundations and beaten earth surfaces.

with Room 3179, which did have a roof support (4.4 × 6 m). A roof support would be expected if all of these areas were roofed. This transition from roofed main room to court was also observed by Albright at Tell Beit Mirsim in the transition from Stratum E to Stratum D (see below). Another feature of Stratum X is the increase in the number of bins or silos located within the houses. Without elevations, it is not possible to classify these features accurately. However, it may be that they served as storage facilities for food stuffs. This suggestion may have merit in view of the fact that few storejars were reported, although any accurate evaluation is difficult.

Table 3.13. *Megiddo Stratum X—Area BB SE—Finds and Functional Classes*

Locus	Finds	Functional Class
2032	1 bowl	food preparation/consumption
	1 chalice	food consumption/cultic
	bronze chisel	tool
2032nr	5 bowls	food preparation/consumption
	1 lamp	lighting
2032N	6 bowls	food preparation/consumption
	1 chalice	food consumption/cultic
	1 jar/pyxis	storage/cosmetic use
	jar stand	food preparation/storage
	2 clay birds	special/cultic?

The similarity coefficient for L. 2032N is 139 or 68.5% when compared to the food preparation and consumption paradigm.

2032E	bone spindle	textile production
2032S	9 bowls	food preparation/consumption
	3 chalices	food consumption/cultic
	1 jug	food preparation/storage
	jar stand	food preparation/storage
	2 faience pendants	adornment
	bead	adornment
	bronze snake?	special/cultic

The similarity coefficient for L. 2032S is 141.5 or 70.7% when compared to the food preparation and consumption paradigm.

2126S	1 bowl	food preparation/consumption
	crystal bead	adornment
	silver toggle pin	adornment
2126W	toggle pin	adornment
2126WRm	faience scarab	business/adornment
2128W	1 krater	food preparation/consumption
	2 lamps	lighting

Table 3.13—*Continued*

Locus	Finds	Functional Class
3029W	1 bowl	food preparation/consumption
3034nr	stamp seal	business/adornment
3034N	1 lamp	lighting
	2 bronze chisels	tools
3034W	1 lamp	lighting
3035E	bone object	unknown
3036E	26 clay weights	textile production
	needle/toggle pin	textile/adornment
	clay stopper	multipurpose

The similarity coefficient for L. 3036E is 136 or 68% when compared to the weaving paradigm.

Locus	Finds	Functional Class
3036S	toggle pin	adornment
3037	1 bowl	food preparation/consumption
	1 jug	food preparation/storage
	steatite scarab	business/adornment
3037E	red stone weight	business
3037S	loop-headed pin	textile production?
3037W	2 bowls	food preparation/consumption
	1 lamp	lighting
3038	1 bowl	food preparation/consumption
	1 jug	food preparation/storage
3038E	bone pommel	weapon
	toggle pin	adornment
3039nr	2 bowls	food preparation/consumption
	2 jugs	food preparation/storage
3040nr	clay 'disk'	storage
3045E	1 jug	food preparation/storage
3046S	1 bowl	food preparation/consumption
3049	1 jug	food preparation/storage
	needle/toggle pin	textile/adornment
	bone awl	multipurpose
3050nr	bronze chisel	tool
	toggle pin	adornment
3056Rm	2 jugs	food preparation/storage
	2 lamps	lighting
	bronze chisel	tool
	unguent spoon	cosmetic use
3057	1 bowl	food preparation/consumption
	1 chalice	food consumption/cultic
	green stone object	unknown
3059nr	bone inlay	special/status
3060W	toggle pin	adornment

Table 3.13—*Continued*

Locus	Finds	Functional Class
3065N	bronze borer	tool
3179	6 bowls	food preparation/consumption
	1 chalice	food consumption/cultic
3180	1 jug	food preparation/storage
	haematite weight	business
	clay weight	textile production

Stratum X Area BB NW (*Fig. 15*)

The structures of Stratum X were built along the same lines as the main walls of Stratum XI. However, it is clear, in this later phase, that the V-shaped building was joined to the rooms that lay to the west. Because of the poor state of preservation, individual structural units cannot be distinguished, except for Room 2005 and its associated loci north of the sacred area.

A variety of activities are represented by discrete assemblages, all too small for statistical analysis. Considered altogether, the finds reflect predominantly food preparation, consumption and storage, 53.2%, and textile production, 22.8% (Table 3.14). Tools/weapons, business and adornment are equally represented, 3.8%, while special/cultic objects, including 2 miniature vessels and a chalice with a human face, equal 11.4%. The only coherent assemblage was found in Room 5026 and nearby loci. The similarity coefficient for these finds when compared to the paradigm for food preparation and consumption is 143 or 71.5%, very close by the standards of this study.

Table 3.14. *Megiddo Stratum X—Area BB NW—Finds and Functional Classes*

Locus	Finds	Functional Class
2005	1 chalice	food preparation/cultic
	bone spearhead	weapon
2023nr	1 lamp	lighting
5008N	1 cooking pot	food preparation
	jar stand	storage
5021	cooking pot	food preparation
5026	loop-headed pin	textile production?
5026N	1 chalice	food consumption
	1 narrow-neck jar	liquid storage
5026S	1 miniature bowl	special/cultic
	1 bowl	food preparation/consumption
	loop-headed pin	textile production?

Table 3.14—*Continued*

Locus	Finds	Functional Class
5026NW	3 bowls	food preparation/consumption

The similarity coefficient for L. 5026, 5026N, 5026S, and 5026NW is 143 or 71.5% when compared to the food preparation and consumption paradigm.

5033	miniature jug	special/cultic
5033E	sherd with face	special/cultic
	needle	textile production
5143	5 bowls	food preparation/consumption
5225	bone whorl	textile production
5225nr	stamp seal	business
5225ERm	miniature bowl	special/cultic
	alabaster pommel	weapon
5240nr	needle	textile production
	loop-headed pin	textile production?
	silver earring?	adornment

Building Plan. Two building units are represented on Plan X (Loud 1948: Pl. 377) of Area BB (Fig. 15), a fragmentary building north of the sacred area, and the large complex to the northwest. Both of these structures share a common building style with large rectangular rooms and 1 m thick walls. Because the northern building (L. 2005) remained unexcavated to the east, too small an area was exposed to understand its complete plan.

Several complete rooms were preserved in the northwest building along with paved or beaten earth floors. Drains under the floors may point to the location of interior courtyards although the fragmentary walls makes it difficult to visualize the room arrangement and overall plan. An addition along the east side, Rooms 5026 and 5026S, differs from the main complex by reason of the thickness of its walls (0.5 m), although the size of the larger room (4.7 × 9.2 m) may be comparable to Room 5033. It was, in fact, in this addition that the most complete food preparation and consumption assemblage was located (Table 3.14).

Another feature that is distinctive of this phase in the northwest complex is the presence of stone-lined silos or bins. As we have already seen, similar features appeared for the first time during this phase in the southeast houses. Five bowls and a cooking pot were found in association with these features near L. 5143 and 5021. Unfortunately, these loci were located in poorly preserved rooms near

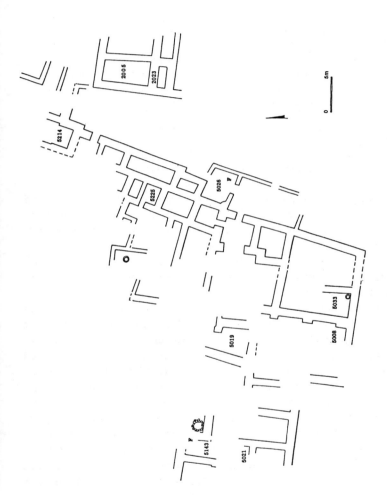

Figure 15. *Megiddo Area BB NW Stratum X, after Loud 1948: Fig. 400*

the western edge of the excavated area (Loud 1948: Plan 377). To the north of L. 5143, excavation only reached Stratum IV. As a result, the possibility of better understanding the plan of the northwest building is cut short.

There is, nevertheless, such a significant difference in construction style and room size between the northwest and southeast buildings in both Stratum XI and X that their primary function must be distinct. While the buildings in the southeast sector can be identified, quite surely, as domestic structures, so too, the complex in the northwest sector must be considered, at least initially, a public or monumental building. With this in mind, the sparse distribution of finds in this complex becomes more understandable. The additional rooms on the east side probably functioned as a kitchen area and the bins or silos in the western rooms as a storage area. The dearth of finds in the central area is not surprising if several of these rooms functioned as open courtyards. Such areas in public buildings served to channel traffic within the building and to separate functionally discrete quarters from one another. The importance of the northwest complex for this study is the contrast it makes to the domestic buildings in the southeast sector.

Stratum XIII Area AA (Fig. 16)
Several phases of Middle Bronze Age occupation were also uncovered in the northwest quadrant of the tell, Area AA. While the stratum numbers in this area cannot be correlated absolutely with those in Area BB, they will be used here for convenience.[1]

The earliest phase included an entryway, gate complex and city wall. Inside the gate, only a limited area, revealing major buildings, was excavated. From the broken wall lines, it is evident that the building west of the gate extended further south. From the rooms exposed, six items were reported. Of this small assemblage, 66.6% were related to food preparation and consumption (Table 3.15). On the plan, a corner bin, in an interior room, and two silos or pits are illustrated; Room 4087 and L. 4085 respectively. These features strengthen the functional identification of these activity areas. One loom weight and a carnelian bead were also included.

---

1. See Kenyon's correlation of the strata from Area AA with the phases she assigned to Area BB (1969: 59).

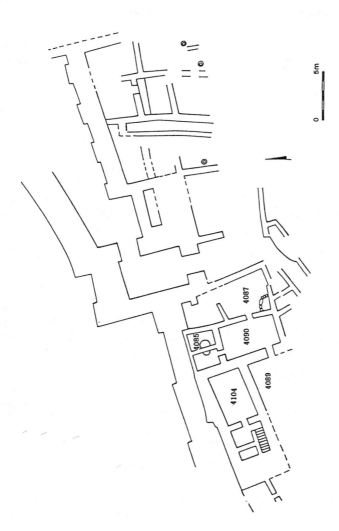

Figure 16. *Megiddo Area AA NW Stratum XIII, after Loud 1948: Fig. 378*

Room Arrangement. It cannot be determined with certainty that the rooms immediately west of the gate formed a distinct structure (Rooms 4087, 4090 and L. 4085), although the wall construction contrasts with the walls of Room 4104 further west which were twice as thick. It is probable that Room 4104 and its adjoining room and stairway belonged to a more impressive building. The thickness of the walls and the stairway leave no doubt that this was a multistoried building. Here, too, the area further south remained unexcavated.

Table 3.15. *Megiddo Stratum XIII—Area AA—Finds and Functional Classes*

Locus	Finds	Functional Class
4085	1 bowl	food preparation/consumption
4087	sherd jar stopper	storage
4089	clay weight	textile production
4089W	1 bowl	food preparation/consumption
	carnelian bead	adornment
4090	1 jug	food preparation/storage

Stratum XII Area AA (Fig. 17)
Three quite complete houses, built up against the city wall, were located above the gateway of Stratum XIII. While many complete rooms were uncovered, few finds were recorded—a total of 7 items. For the purpose of this study, no identification of activity areas can be attempted on the basis of artefact distribution (Table 3.16).

Individual items, however, are suggestive. For example, the large pithos from L. 4117E does confirm storage in the easternmost house, called House C by the excavators (Loud 1948: Fig. 23). Unfortunately, no other finds from this house can support this identification. So, too, the scarabs from House B, that constitute 42.6% of the total assemblage, indicate either personal adornment or business activities. However, no weights or other items associated with economic activities were found in the house. It cannot be ascertained whether these scarabs were in their original context in the room where they were found or had fallen from an upper storey.

House Plan. The plan of these houses was remarkably consistent even though House A, on the west, was somewhat irregular because it followed the street (Loud 1948: Fig. 23). These houses have been classified as central courtyard style with rooms on two or more sides of the court. Narrow rooms in both houses B and C may indicate

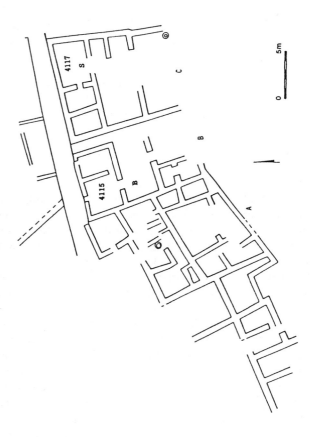

Figure 17. *Megiddo Area AA NW Stratum XII, after Loud 1948: Fig. 378*

stairways to an upper storey. This would mean that House B (7.2 ×
12 m) had a ground floor area of 86.4 m² and House C (8.8 × 12 m)
of 105.6 m², not to mention the rooms upstairs. The largest house
(A) measured 10 × 13.5 m or 135 m². Even on the ground floor alone,
these houses were quite spacious for congested urban dwellings
(Cf. Tell Beit Mirsim, Stratum G House = 93 m², Patrician House,
Stratum D = 116 m²).

Table 3.16. *Megiddo Stratum XII—Area AA—Finds and Functional Classes*

Locus	Finds	Functional Class
4115	toggle pin	adornment
4115S	1 bowl	food preparation/consumption
	3 scarabs	business/adornment
	bone inlays	special/status
4117E	1 pithos	dry storage

Stratum XI Area AA (Fig. 18)

Domestic structures continued to be built in the same area along the
city wall throughout the Middle Bronze Age. In Stratum XI, there was
extensive rebuilding of the earlier houses although some walls were
reused.[1] The most significant change was the construction of a new
north wall. Although discrete houses are more difficult to distinguish
than in Stratum XII, the number of reported finds for Stratum XI
rooms is greater (21 versus 7). On the other hand, no individual
assemblage is large enough for statistical analysis.

Overall, food preparation, consumption and storage is most heavily
represented in the assemblage, 61% (50% in the central house), while
business and textile production are represented equally, 9.4% (Table
3.17). One toggle pin, a lamp, an alabaster pommel and a limestone
ostracon drawing complete the reported finds.

House Plan. The walls of these houses were poorly preserved just at
those strategic points which would make it possible to reconstruct
complete housing units. As a result, only the plan of the western house
(L. 4056, 4077), which consisted of a series of rooms on three sides
of a large room or court (4.5 × 8.5 m), can be fully understood. The

---

1. Kenyon refined the phasing of these strata (AB-AE) in view of the redesign of
the gate area and city wall along the north side of the tell (1969: 55-57).

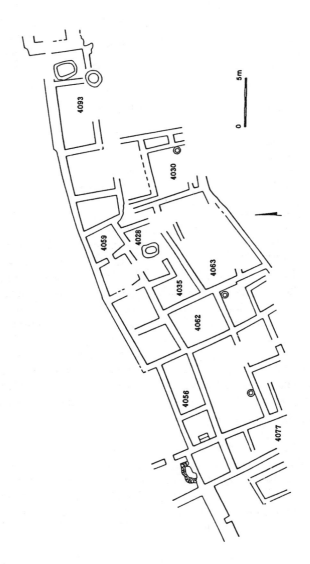

Figure 18. *Megiddo Area AA NW Stratum XI, after Loud 1948: Fig. 379*

plan of the central house (L. 4059–4062) is not as easy to discern, while the remains of the easternmost house (L. 4030–4093) were fragmentary.

Table 3.17. *Megiddo Stratum XI—Area AA—Finds and Functional Classes*

Locus	Finds	Functional Class
4028	1 narrow-neck jar	liquid storage
4028E	steatite scarab	business/adornment
4030N	toggle pin	adornment
4056nr	loom weight	textile production
4056E	1 lamp	lighting
4059	1 bowl in jar	food preparation/storage
	1 narrow-neck jar	liquid storage
	2 jugs	food preparation/storage
4059N	alabaster pommel	weapon
4059ERm	steatite scarab	business/adornment
	clay stopper	storage
	basalt pounder	food preparation
4062	1 bowl	food preparation/consumption
	1 wide-neck jar	dry storage
4063	loom weight	textile production
4077W	1 cooking pot	food preparation
	limestone pestle	food preparation
4093nr	1 jug	food preparation/storage
	drawing on stone	special/cultic
4093S	1 bowl	food preparation/consumption

Stratum X Area AA (Fig. 19)

The structures of Stratum X reused the walls of Stratum XI on the west but established a new building style on the east (L. 4031). This series of rooms continued into Stratum 9 where it was an integral part of the 'palace'. Because of its plan and the size of its rooms, this eastern unit was probably not a private house. Additional evidence is provided by its walls which were 1 m or more thick, somewhat thicker than the average for domestic structures (60–70 cm). Because the floors (Loud 1948: Fig. 480) appear to have belonged to Stratum XI (Kenyon 1969: 57), the finds from L. 4031 cannot be used to understand the function of this building.

In the housing units rebuilt on Stratum XI lines, 27 items were reported. The largest assemblage for a single locus is that for Room 4021, 7 items (Table 3.18). Unfortunately, no floor was identified in this room and the finds do not cluster in any one tool kit. Objects and

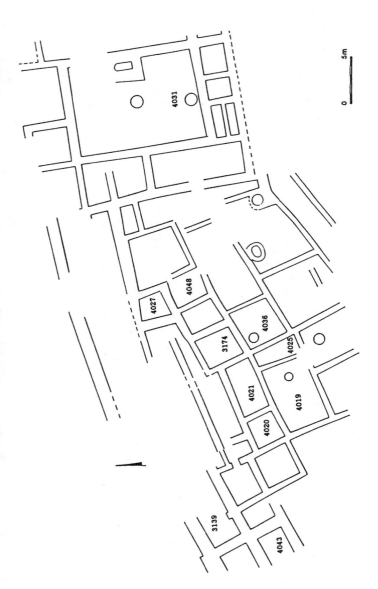

Figure 19. *Megiddo Area AA NW Stratum X, after Loud 1948: Fig. 380*

vessels associated with food preparation and consumption are represented along with business, and textile production. No other locus yielded more than three items. More than one third of the items from these rooms were used primarily for food preparation and consumption. Only one vessel exclusively indicated storage. Again, items involved in business and textile production were present in equal proportion, 18.5%. A silver pendant, along with several items whose functions are unknown, completed the reported finds (Table 3.18).

Table 3.18. *Megiddo Stratum X—Area AA—Finds and Functional Classes*

Locus	Finds	Functional Class
3139E	1 bowl	food preparation/consumption
	2 jugs	food preparation/storage
3174	1 jug	food preparation/storage
3174N	1 bowl	food preparation/consumption
	1 flask	storage
	clay loom weight	textile production
3174E	steatite scarab	business/adornment
3174W	amethyst scarab	business/adornment
4019	clay weight	textile production
	stone object	unknown/tool
4019SRm	2 jugs	food preparation/storage
4020	diorite object	special item
4020W	silver pendant	adornment/cultic
4021	1 bowl	food preparation/consumption
	1 jug	food preparation/storage
	diorite weight	business
	haematite weight	business
	bone whorl	textile production
	2 bone objects	textile production?
	ivory object	unknown
4025	clay loom weight	textile production
	clay 'disk'	unknown/food preparation
	stone pestle	food preparation
4027N	cylinder seal	business/adornment
4031	1 wide-mouth jar	dry storage
	1 jug	food preparation/storage
4043N	clay object	unknown
4048	2 jugs	food preparation/storage
4048W	limestone object	food preparation
	basalt object	unknown

House Plans (Fig. 19). Two possible houses can be distinguished on Plan AA Stratum X (Loud 1948: Fig. 380), although neither is complete. Each house might have had as many as 10 rooms on the ground floor even though the lack of doorways and wall elevations makes it impossible to be certain of room association and traffic patterns. For the most part, the rooms closest to the street in these buildings have been enlarged in comparison with those of Stratum XI. In the central house (L. 4036, 3174, 4048 and 4027) two bins or silos are shown. Other features are not described in the text leaving their specific function unclear. Beaten earth or paved floors were preserved in 8 rooms, 6 in the western house (L. 4019, 4020, 4020W, 4021, 4025, 4025S). It is not possible, on the basis of these floors or by room size to identify an inner courtyard. For example, Room 4019 measured 4.3 × 6.5 m, and the middle room of the central house measured 3.8 × 8.8 m. Both could easily have been roofed. On the other hand, the front room of the central house measured 5.8 × 7.5 m and could have served as an open courtyard. On this basis, no consistent plan, such as 'central courtyard', can be attributed to these houses.

Stratum IX Area AA (Fig. 20)

This stratum saw the continuation of the monumental building (L. 2314) begun in Stratum X. At this stage, it may have eliminated completely the domestic structures that had occupied this area during most of the Middle Bronze Age. In contrast to this view, Kenyon suggested that the western houses from Stratum X continued to be used during this phase (1969: 58).

This may indeed have been the case because no new structures are seen on Plan X AA and only one amulet, attributed to Room 4004, can be assigned to these rooms. As a result, no activities can be distinguished for the few locus entries in this phase.

Table 3.19: *Megiddo AA Middle Bronze Age Loci Stratum XIII*

Locus	Square	Description
4085	K7	Pit?
4087	L7	Room
4089	L7	Room?
4089W	L7	Undefined
4090	L7	Room
4104	L7	Room

Houses and their Furnishings

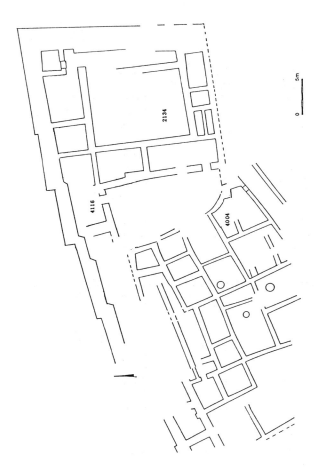

Figure 20. *Megiddo Area AA NW Stratum IX, after Loud 1948: Fig. 381*

Table 3.20. *Megiddo AA Middle Bronze Age Loci Stratum XII*

Locus	Square	Description
4115	K7-8	Room
4115S	K8	Room
4117	K8	Room

Table 3.21. *Megiddo AA Middle Bronze Age Loci Stratum XI*

Locus	Square	Description
4028	K7	Room
4028E	K7	Room
4030	K8	Paved Room
4030N	K8	Room?
4035	K-L7	Room
4056nr	K-L7	Room
4056E	K-L7	Room
4059	K7	Room
4059N	K7	Room?
4062	L7	Room
4063	L7	Room
4077W	L7	Room?
4093nr	K8	Room?
4093S	K8	Room

Table 3.22. *Megiddo AA Middle Bronze Age Loci Stratum X*

Locus	Square	Description
3139nr	K6	Room?
3139E	K6	Undefined
3174	K7	Room
3174E	K7	Room
3174N	K7	Room?
4019	L7	Room
4019SRm	L7	Room
4020	L7	Room
4020S	L7	Room
4021	K-L7	Room
4025	K7	Room
4027	K7	Room
4027N	K7	Room?
4031	K8	Room
4036	K-L7	Room

Table 3.22—Continued

Locus	Square	Description
4043N	L6	Room
4048	K7	Room
4048W	K7	Room

Table 3.23. *Megiddo BB-NW Middle Bronze Age Loci Stratum XIIIB*

Locus	Square	Description
5073nr	M12	Undefined
5073E	M12	Undefined
5073W	M12	Room
5085	N11	Pavement
5087	M12	Room
5087W	M12	Room
5093	N12	Room?
5093E	N12	Room?
5108	N12	Pavement
5114nr	M12	Undefined
5123nr	N11	Room
5123N	N11	Room
5123S	N11	Room?
5238nr	M13	Undefined
5260	M13	Undefined
5265nr	M13	Undefined
5265E	M13	Pavement
5265W	M13	Undefined

Table 3.24. *Megiddo BB-SE Middle Bronze Age Loci Stratum XIIIA*

Locus	Square	Description
2149nr	N-O15	Undefined
3093nr	O14	Room?
3118E	O14	Room?
3118S	O14	Room
3119	O14	Paved Room
3125N	O14	Room?
3126N	O14	Room
4015	O14	Paved Room

Table 3.25. *Megiddo BB-NW Middle Bronze Age Loci Stratum XIIIA*

Locus	Square	Description
5034	N12	Paved Room
5049	N12	Room?
5049nr	N12	Room?
5054	N12	Room?
5057	N12	Pavement
5058	N12	Room
5058S	N12	Room?
5058W	N12	Room?
5063	N12-13	Room
5064	N12	Room
5069	M12	Room?
5070	N12	Room
5071	N12	Room
5072	N12	Undefined
5072E	N12	Undefined
5076	N11	Paved Room
5076N	N11	Undefined
5089	M12	Room
5094N	M12	Room?
5095nr	N12	Room?
5095E	N12	Room
5100	N12	Room?
5101	M12	Undefined
5103nr	N12	Pavement?
5104nr	N12	Room?
5109	N12	Room

Table 3.26. *Megiddo BB-SE Middle Bronze Age Loci Stratum XII*

Locus	Square	Description
2135W	N14	Room
2142	N14	(same room as 2135)
2142W	N14	(same room as 2135)
2147nr	N14	(same room as 2135)
2147E	N14	(same room as 2135)
3084S	O15	Room
3106	O13	Room
3106N	O13	Room
3121	O14	Room
3128W	N14	Room
3133N	O13	Undefined

Table 3.27. *Megiddo BB-NW Middle Bronze Age Loci Stratum XII*

Locus	Square	Description
5038	N12	Room
5038E	N12	Undefined
5043	N12	Undefined
5048	N12	Room
5077	M12	Pavement
5081	N12	Paved Room
5081nr	N12	Room?
5081S	N12	Room?
5112nr	M12	Undefined

Table 3.28. *Megiddo BB-SE Middle Bronze Age Loci Stratum XI*

Locus	Square	Description	Similarity Coefficient
2133	N14	Room	
2133E	N14	(same room as 2133)	
3053	O14-15	Room	
3053N	O14	Room	
3068	O14	Ally	
3068S	O14	Room?	
3068W	O14	Undefined	
3069	O13	Undefined	
3071	N-O14	Room	
3072W	O14	Room	
3078	N-O15	Room	
3081nr	O15	Undefined	
3096	O13	Undefined	147.0 or 73.5%
3097	O13	Room	
3107S	N14	Room	
3116	O14	Room	

Table 3.29. *Megiddo BB-NW Middle Bronze Age Loci Stratum XI*

Locus	Square	Description
5031	N12	Undefined
5035	N12	Room
5037	N12	Room
5037W	N12	Room?
5041nr	N12	Room?
5044	N-M13	Room
5044E	N13	Room?

Table 3.29—*Continued*

Locus	Square	Description
5053nr	N12	(same room as 5035)
5226WRm	M13	Paved Room
5231nr	M13	Room?
5231S	M13	Room?
5233	M13	Room
5233E	M13	Undefined

Table 3.30. *Megiddo BB-SE Middle Bronze Age Loci Stratum X*

Locus	Square	Description	Similarity Coefficient
2032	N14	Undefined	
2032nr	N14	Undefined	
2032E	N14	Undefined	
2032N	N14	Undefined	139.0 or 68.5%
2032S	N14	Room?	141.5 or 70.7%
2126S	N15	Room	
2126W	N15	Room	
2126WRm	N14-15	Room	
2128	N15	Room	
2128W	N15	Room	
3029W	O14	Room	
3034nr	O14-15	Room	
3034N	O15	Room	
3034W	O14	Room	
3035E	O15	Room?	
3036	N-O14	Room	
3036E	N-O14	(same room as 3036)	136 or 68%
3036S	N-O14	(same room as 3036)	
3037	O13	Undefined	
3037E,	O13	Undefined	
3037S	O13	Room?	
3037W	O13	Undefined	
3038	O13	Room	
3038E	O13	Room	
3039nr	N15	Room	
3040nr	O15	Undefined	
3045E	O14	Undefined	
3046S	O14	Room	
3048W	O15	Room	
3049	O15	Room	
3050nr	O14	Room	

Table 3.30—*Continued*

Locus	Square	Description	Similarity Coefficient
3056	O14	Paved Room	
3057	O14	Room	
3059nr	O14	Room	
3060W	O14	Room	
3065N	O14	Room	
3179	O13	Room	
3180	O15	Room	

Table 3.31. *Megiddo BB-NW Middle Bronze Age Loci Stratum X*

Locus	Square	Description	Similarity Coefficient
2005	M13	Paved Room	
2023nr	M13	Paved Room?	
5008N	N12	Paved Room?	
5019	N12	Paved Room	
5021	N11	Pavement	
5026	N13	Paved Room	143 or 71.5%
5026N	N13	Room?	
5026S	N13	Paved Room	
5026NW	N13	Room?	
5033	N12	Room	
5143	M11	Undefined	
5214	M13	Paved Room	
5225	M13	Paved Room	
5225nr	M13	Room?	
5225ERm	M13	Room	
5240nr	M12	Undefined	

Tel Mevorakh (Map Reference 1441/2156)

Tel Mevorakh is located at the junction of the Sharon Plain and the Carmel coastal strip on the south bank of Nahal Tanninim. During four seasons (fall 1973, 1974, 1975, 1976), E. Stern excavated this small site of 1 dunam (1000 m^2) and identified fifteen strata. Although there was a gap in occupation during the twelfth and eleventh centuries BC, Stern uncovered a Middle Bronze Age fortress and a Late Bronze Age sanctuary as well as Iron Age and Roman period remains (1984: 1).

The Middle Bronze Age strata exposed at Tel Mevorakh are

restricted to an area of 150 m² in Squares D-E-F-G/10-11 with one small probe in E9. Excavations did not reveal complete building plans although several rooms with architectural features were uncovered. The most coherent Middle Bronze Age structure is a 'fort' in Stratum XIII (Stern 1984: 47). This structure and its finds are included in the analysis in order (a) to determine whether the finds can be distinguished from typical domestic assemblages and (b) as a partial test of the functional identification assigned by the excavator. Loci from other Middle Bronze Age strata are analysed to show the range of activities engaged in by the inhabitants of Tel Mevorakh.

Stratum XV (Fig. 21)
The earliest evidence for occupation at the site consists of 3 sections of 1 m thick walls that frame the west end of a large building (6.8 × ? m). The walls themselves were of clay bricks on stone foundations, overlying virgin soil. Stern assumes that this 'fortress' was the only building constructed in Stratum XV and he dates it on the basis of the ceramic finds to MB IIA (1984: 64).

Because the area in Probe Locus 349 is such a small sample of the total excavated floor space inside Building 349 (0.8 m² versus 7.2 m²), no interior architectural divisions or features were distinguished (Stern 1984: 51). The finds recovered from this structure were also restricted to L. 349 in the southwest corner. A ceramic assemblage of six items included 3 bowls or kraters, a cooking pot, storejar and jug.

Although this assemblage cannot be used to confirm the functional identification of Building 349, it is worth comparing it to those paradigms which have a large ceramic component. Indeed the assemblage from L. 349 falls into the category of food preparation and consumption and compares very well with the food preparation and consumption paradigm, having a similarity coefficient of 177.6 or 88.8%.

Two soil layers to the west of Building 349, Loci 351 and 355, were also identified as belonging to Str. XV.[1] Unfortunately, only one find was reported from each locus (Table 3.32), rendering them useless for our purposes.

---

1. Locus 351, uncovered in the southern probe in the central excavation area, was a soil layer attributable to either Stratum XV or XIV (Stern 1984: 51). Only one sherd, described as MB IIA, was published (Stern 1984: Pl. 16:5).

Figure 21. *Tel Mevorakh Stratum XV, after Stern 1984: Fig. 28*

Table 3.32. *Tel Mevorakh Stratum XV—Finds and Functional Classes*

Locus	Finds	Functional Class
349	2 bowls	food preparation/consumption
	1 krater	food preparation/consumption
	1 cooking pot	food preparation
	1 wide-neck jar	dry storage
	1 jug/narrow-neck jar	food preparation/storage

The similarity coefficient for L. 349 is 177.6 or 88.8% when compared to the food preparation and consumption paradigm.

351	1 bowl	food preparation/consumption
355	1 narrow-neck jar	liquid storage

Stratum XIV (Fig. 22)

At five locations on the tell, excavation uncovered remains of Stratum XIV which provided evidence of extensive occupation during the latest phase of MB IIA. In the central area of excavation, these remains extended under and beyond the earthen rampart of MB IIB Stratum XIII and were built up against the Stratum XV walls of Building 349 which probably continued in use during this phase (Stern 1984: 50). There are no complete Stratum XIV rooms excavated although two

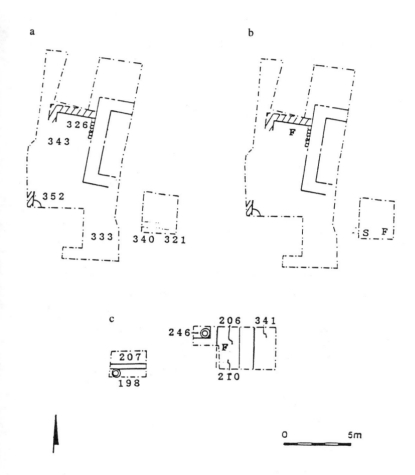

Figure 22. *Tel Mevorakh Stratum XIV, after Stern 1984: Figs. 28, 30*

walls do form a corner (W186 and W189; Stern 1984: Fig. 28).

Two soil layers (L. 326 and 343, Fig. 22a) were located within the perimeter formed by the Stratum XIV walls and by the west wall of Building 349. Locus 326 yielded only four published items (Table 3.33). While this is a very small corpus, these finds conform to the tool kit for a food preparation and consumption activity area with a similarity coefficient of 158 or 79%.

This evidence of food preparation is strengthened by the discovery of an oven, L. 352, that was built against a partially exposed wall (Fig. 22a) that Stern suggests was in line with the west wall of L. 326 to the north. Thus Oven 352 might have been in the same Stratum XIV structure (Stern 1984: 50). While this suggestion may have merit, it is not at all certain because excavation was severely limited at the point where such a connection could have been made. Nor could any connection be made with existing architecture for the small section of clay floor (L. 333) uncovered in a probe southeast of Oven 352. This floor was covered with a layer of ash and a few sherds (Stern 1984: 50-51). While the ashes could be suggestive, especially if their organic components were known,[1] no particular function can be assigned to this locus.

Stratum XIV remains uncovered in Probes D/5 and C/0-1 yielded domestic assemblages.[2] The best example is from Soil Layer 206 (Fig. 22c). While no objects appear in the assemblage, a ceramic corpus of 12 items does occur (Table 3.33). Although there is very limited exposure in these probes, this corpus is definitely that of a food preparation and consumption tool kit, consisting of 7 bowls and kraters, 3 cooking pots and 2 storejars, altogether having a similarity coefficient of 157 or 78.5%.

Separated from L. 206 by a major north–south wall, is a clay oven, L. 246, positioned in the corner of a nearby room. A similar oven, L. 198 in Probe D/5, was located alongside a partition wall. The fact that no finds were associated with the oven or with the stone-paved floor (L. 207) to the north of the partition wall makes it impossible to relate these features to any larger structure. These ovens indicate a heavy concentration of cooking areas, while, at the same time, leaving

1. Reports of carbonized grains, seeds and legumes are lacking. It appears that no flotation of ash layers was undertaken.

2. Locus 341 contained only one juglet body sherd; and Locus 210 yielded one published krater sherd.

unanswered the question of their precise relationship to the structures that occupied the tell.

While no Stratum XIV architectural remains were found in Probe E/9, several debris layers were present (L. 321, 340; Fig. 22a). The ceramic assemblage of L. 321 (Table 3.33) resembles that of L. 349 except that there were no cooking pot sherds preserved. The similarity coefficient is 144 or 72%, when compared with the food preparation and consumption paradigm. On the other hand, the assemblage published for L. 340 consisting of 10 storejars out of a corpus of 13 items suggests a storage tool kit (similarity coefficient = 168 or 84%). The three shallow bowls included in this corpus have a diameter range of 25–30 cm. That they were used as covers for the jars is possible but not certain.

Table 3.33. *Tel Mevorakh Stratum XIV—Finds and Functional Classes*

Locus	Finds	Functional Class
198	clay oven	food preparation
	stone floor	multipurpose
206	5 bowls	food preparation/consumption
	2 kraters	food preparation/consumption
	3 cooking pots	food preparation
	1 wide-neck jar	dry storage
	1 narrow-neck jar	liquid storage

The similarity coefficient for L. 206 is 157 or 78.5% when compared to the food preparation and consumption paradigm.

207	stone floor	multipurpose
210	1 krater	food preparation/consumption
246	clay oven	food preparation
321	3 bowls	food preparation/consumption
	1 wide-neck jar	dry storage
	1 jug	food preparation/consumption
	1 juglet	multipurpose

The similarity coefficient for L. 321 is 144 or 72% when compared to the food preparation and consumption paradigm.

326	2 bowls	food preparation/consumption
	1 cooking pot	food preparation
	1 narrow-neck jar	liquid storage

The similarity coefficient for L. 326 is 158 or 79% when compared to the food preparation and consumption paradigm.

336	1 narrow-neck jar	liquid storage
340	3 bowls	food preparation/consumption
	4 narrow-neck jars	liquid storage

Table 3.33—*Continued*

Locus	Finds	Functional Class
	6 wide-neck jars	dry storage

The similarity coefficient for L. 340 is 168 or 84% when compared to the storage paradigm.

Locus	Finds	Functional Class
341	stone floor	multipurpose
352	clay oven	food preparation

Stratum XIII (Fig. 23)

Stratum XIII is the earliest MB level with coherent architectural remains. Three rooms, two completely exposed, were identified as a 'fort' (Stern 1984: 47). Three doorways in the north–south wall (L. 143, 146, 179) indicate that the building continued east and its complete plan remains unknown.

Locus 335 was an interior room with only one entrance from Room 315, and was the only room which contained a lamp. Unfortunately, there is a discrepancy in the reporting of the finds from Room 335. On the one hand, the report says that the clay floor of this room 'was devoid of finds' (Stern 1984: 48) while, on the other hand, Figures 12, 13 and 14 depict 11 vessels and Plate 45.2 illustrates a bronze dagger. All of these finds are attributed to L. 335 and not to the burials under the floor which have their own locus numbers (L. 347, 348). In spite of these stratigraphic uncertainties, the assemblage of ceramic finds seems to represent a storage area tool kit. This is one of the larger assemblages published; it includes 2 bowls, 2 cooking pots, 4 storejars, 1 jug, 1 juglet, along with a lamp and the tip of a bronze dagger (Table 3.34). Although the presence of cooking pots in storage are not uncommon (see Tell Batash below), there is a similarity coefficient of only 122.8 or 61.4%.[1]

Room 315, to the east, served as a passageway between Room 318 on the south, Room 335, and the unexcavated rooms further east. In spite of this obvious traffic pattern, the floor was covered by an ash layer and the remains of 14 vessels (Table 3.34). Whether the ceramic finds are representative of the activities of Room 315 or come from the collapsed earthen rampart is not clear in this case either (Stern 1984: 47). Although there is possible contamination of this locus, the

---

1. The similarity between the assemblage for Room 335 and the storage paradigm is lessened with the addition of the lamp and the dagger fragment to 118.5 or 59.25%.

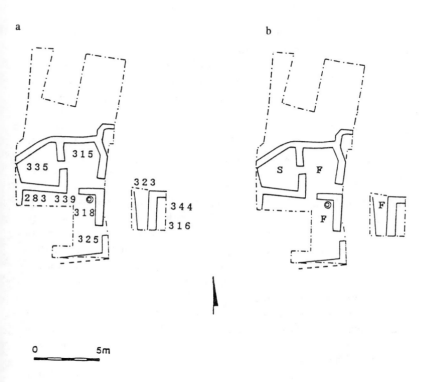

Figure 23. *Tel Mevorakh Stratum XIII, after Stern 1984: Fig. 27*

ceramic corpus resembles a food preparation and consumption tool kit with a heavy emphasis on bowl forms (10 out of 14 items, including 2 kraters). Also present are 1 cooking pot, 2 storejars, and 1 jug. The similarity coefficient in relation to the paradigm is 157.1 or 78.5%. This factor, in combination with the ash layer and the proximity of the oven in Room 318, is strongly suggestive that the activities performed in these rooms were well coordinated.

Room 318 itself, while only partially excavated, included an ash layer and animal bones, debris representative of food preparation. Both objects and ceramic vessels, along with Oven 357, support this functional interpretation (Fig. 23b). The most important objects are a loaf-shaped grinding stone and saddle quern. The ceramic assemblage consists of 9 bowls and kraters, 6 cooking pots and one storejar. However, the similarity coefficient, as compared with the food preparation paradigm, is 145 or 72.5%, due primarily to a large number of cooking pots. Two exemplars, however, were oversized, indicating that this was not quite a typical domestic assemblage. If the entire room had been cleared these unusual forms may have been better understood. As an example, the finds from loci uncovered in the western part of the room (one jug and three bowls from L. 283 and 339), include a bowl with a very heavy base, not common among bowl forms. At the same time, because of their association with stone paved Floor 283, these finds, which are too few to be statistically meaningful in themselves, may represent activities functionally distinct from the cooking area around Oven 357.[1]

At present the corpus from L. 318 does seem to support the view of the excavator that this room served as a kitchen area for the entire structure (Stern 1984: 49). This judgment is strengthened by the addition of another cooking pot reported for L. 325, which was contiguous with L. 318 on the south, and a jug and 2 bowls from L. 283 and 339 in the same room. While the large number of cooking pots testifies to a special emphasis on communal cooking, this fact, of itself, does not confirm the identification of the entire structure as a fort. Indeed, while the site was strongly fortified by an earthen embankment, the dearth of weapons seems to be an important factor that calls

---

1. Although the plan suggests that L. 283 and 339 may be part of the same room as L. 318 and 325, Stern suggests that there were here two separate rooms divided by a partition wall (1984: 49).

for a more precise functional understanding of this complex.[1]

In Probe E/9 (Fig. 23), there is one Stratum XIII locus (L. 323) whose finds demonstrate a more typical domestic pattern than Room 318, although no one activity can be assigned with certainty. Associated with this partially exposed stone-paved floor was an assemblage that included two bowls, two storejars, and a loom weight (Table 3.34). In contrast to Room 318, there is no evidence of weapons.

From the same probe, the excavator reports a section of clay floor, L. 316, that seals against the east side of Wall 185. The largest assemblage of finds (19 items) comes from this small space (c. 2.5 × 0.5 m). Again domestic activity is dominant: 10 bowls and kraters, 3 cooking pots, 4 storejars and 2 juglets. The assemblage has a very high similarity coefficient of 171.8 or 85.9% when compared with the paradigm for food preparation and consumption.

In summary the Stratum XIII structure at Tel Mevorakh clearly includes several spatially distinct activity zones which may be classified as food preparation areas as well as a storage room. Whether the building itself can be identified as a house is less certain, although the thickness of the exterior walls, in sharp contrast to the 1 m thick walls of Stratum XV Building 349, falls within the normal range for a domestic structure, 50–60 cm (see Table 3.62). Until further exposure of this building is undertaken, its overall function remains ambiguous.

Table 3.34. *Tel Mevorakh Stratum XIII—Finds and Functional Classes*

Locus	Finds	Functional Class
283	jug	food preparation/consumption
	stone floor	multipurpose
315	7 bowls	food preparation/consumption
	1 miniature bowl	special/cultic
	2 kraters	food preparation/consumption
	1 cooking pot	food preparation
	1 narrow-neck jar	liquid storage
	1 jar	storage
	1 jug	food preparation/consumption

The similarity coefficient for L. 315 is 157.1 or 78.5% when compared to the food preparation and consumption paradigm.

1. Examples of ceramic assemblages that witness to large scale food preparation and consumption are frequently associated with structures identified as cultic or funerary. For a discussion of such assemblages, see Holladay 1987, especially his discussion of Samaria Locus E 207, pp. 257-58.

Table 3.34—*Continued*

Locus	Finds	Functional Class
316	8 bowls	food preparation/consumption
	2 kraters	food preparation/consumption
	3 cooking pots	food preparation
	4 narrow-neck jars	liquid storage
	2 juglets	multipurpose

The similarity coefficient for L. 316 is 171.8 or 85.9% when compared to the food preparation and consumption paradigm.

318	8 bowls	food preparation/consumption
	1 krater	food preparation/consumption
	6 cooking pots	food preparation
	1 wide-neck jar	dry storage
	animal bones	food preparation/consumption
	ash layer	food preparation
	Nile shell	unknown
	basalt saddle quern	food preparation
	basalt grinder	food preparation
	bronze dagger	weapon

The similarity coefficient for L. 318 is 145 or 72.5% when compared to the food preparation and consumption paradigm.

323	2 bowls	food preparation/consumption
	1 narrow-neck jar	liquid storage
	1 wide-neck jar	dry storage
	1 jar/jug	food preparation/consumption
	1 loom weight	textile production
	stone floor	multipurpose
325	1 cooking pot	food preparation
335	2 bowls	food preparation/consumption
	2 cooking pots	food preparation
	2 narrow-neck jars	liquid storage
	2 wide-neck jars	dry storage
	1 jug	food preparation/consumption
	1 juglet	multipurpose
	1 lamp	lighting
	bronze dagger tip	weapon

The similarity coefficient for L. 335 is 122.8 or 61.4% when compared to the storage paradigm.

339	2 bowls	food preparation/consumption
	1 heavy-base bowl	unknown
344	2 bowls	food preparation/consumption
	1 juglet	multipurpose

Stratum XII (Fig. 24)

In Stratum XII,[1] seven loci were recognized, located in four rooms built against the south side of a northern retaining wall. While this wall is a reuse of the Stratum XIII east–west wall line, the plan of the adjoining rooms is new. The only locus whose assemblage of finds can be utilized to determine its functional identification is L. 317. The ceramic assemblage from this locus contains four ceramic items along with one bronze arrowhead (Table 3.35). Actually this configuration of finds does not compare closely with any domestic paradigm due to the paucity of published items. There is only a 142 (71%) similarity coefficient in comparison with a food preparation area even though a cooking pot, along with a bowl, a storejar and a jug, are part of the extant corpus. The presence of Bin 303[2] in the assemblage (Fig. 24b) does strengthen the case somewhat. Because food preparation areas are frequently the location of heavy traffic and of various other activities the random occurrence of an arrowhead does not actually weaken such an identification even though it must remain tentative.

No other locus had sufficient ceramic or artefact remains for analysis in determining activity areas. The smallest area, L. 219, contained only one pedestal bowl and a juglet, clearly random finds. The adjoining room, L. 220 and 304, did not have any recorded finds. Room 247 yielded only one toggle pin (Stern 1984: Pl. 18:4), L. 244, to the west, contained a needle, and L. 255 contained a dagger (Table 3.35). Unfortunately, these finds by themselves, while typically domestic, are not diagnostic. The size of the rooms, the wall construction and thickness, and the associated features provide a strong basis for understanding these loci as living areas.

Domestic activities may also have been carried on in the rooms to the east of the main north–south wall. The presence, in Probe E/9 (Fig. 24), of Soil Layer 312, along with Oven 358 and L. 22, indicate additional rooms and features. The paucity of reported finds (two bowls and a jug; Table 3.35) do not lend themselves to analysis. However, these finds, along with the oven, do conform to the

1. Stratum XII remains described here are designated Stratum XIIb by the excavator. Some remains of an upper phase, Stratum XIIa, were also identified but are quite fragmentary and susceptible to contamination (Stern 1984: 46).

2. L. 303 is partially built above floor level and is therefore identified as a 'bin' in my system. This identification does not imply a function distinct from that of a 'silo', as this feature is described in the text (Stern 1984: 47).

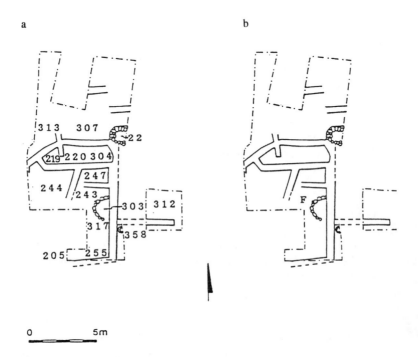

Figure 24.   *Tel Mevorakh Stratum XII, after Stern 1984: Fig. 26*

pattern already seen in the loci of this stratum. On the basis of the published report, it is not clear whether one or more buildings were present inside the ramparts during this final MB II phase. It is unfortunate that such a small area was exposed. Additional exposure might clarify the use history of this strategic site.

Table 3.35. *Tel Mevorakh Stratum XII—Finds and Functional Classes*

Locus	Finds	Functional Class
022	1 jug	food preparation/consumption
205	1 bowl	food preparation/consumption
	Mediterranean shell	unknown
219	1 bowl	food preparation/consumption
	1 juglet	multipurpose
244	bronze needle	textile production
247	bronze toggle pin	personal adornment
	stone floor	multipurpose
255	bronze dagger	weapon
	stone floor with lime coating	unknown
312	2 bowls	food preparation/consumption
317	1 bowl	food preparation/consumption
	1 cooking pot	food preparation
	1 jug	food preparation/consumption
	1 narrow-neck jar	liquid storage
	bronze arrowhead	weapon

The similarity coefficient for L. 317 is 142 or 71% when compared to the food preparation and consumption paradigm.

303	stone lined bin	storage
358	oven	food preparation

Table 3.36. *Tel Mevorakh Middle Bronze Age Loci Stratum XII*

Locus	Square	Description	Similarity Coefficient
022	F 10	Undefined	
205	D 10	Soil Layer	
219	F 11	West end of Room	
220	F 10	East end of Room	
243	E 10	Room	
244	E 11	Room	
247	E 10	Room	
255	D/E 10	Stone floor	
303	E 10	Bin	
304	F 10	East end of Room—220	
312	E 9	Undefined	

Table 3.36—*Continued*

Locus	Square	Description	Similarity Coefficient
317	E 10	Room	142.0 or 72.0%
336	F 10	Pit	
358	E 10	Oven	

Table 3.37. *Tel Mevorakh Middle Bronze Age Loci Stratum XIII*

Locus	Square	Description	Similarity Coefficient
022	F 10	Undefined	
283	E 11	Flagstone floor	
315	E/F 10	Room	157.1 or 78.5%
316	E 9	Room?	171.8 or 85.9%
318	E 10	North end of Room	145.0 or 72.5%
323	E 9	Flagstone floor	
325	D/E 10	South end of Room	
335	E/F 10-11	Room	122.8 or 61.4%
339	E 10-11	West end of Room	
344	E 9	Clay floor	
357	E 10	Oven	

Table 3.38. *Tel Mevorakh Middle Bronze Age Loci Stratum XIV*

Locus	Square	Description	Similarity Coefficient
198	D 5	Stone floor and Clay oven	
206	C 0	Soil layer	157 or 78.5%
207	D 5	Stone-paved floor	
210	C 0	Soil layer	
246	C 1	Clay oven	
321	E 9	Debris layer	144 or 72%
326	F 10	Soil layer	158 or 79%
333	D 10	Clay floor	
340	E 9	Debris layer	168 or 84%
341	C 0	Stone-paved floor	
352	E 11	Clay floor and clay oven	

Table 3.39. *Tel Mevorakh Middle Bronze Age Loci Strata XIV-XV*

Locus	Square	Description
326	F 10	Soil layer
343	F 10-11	Soil layer
351	D 10	Soil layer

Table 3.40. *Tel Mevorakh Middle Bronze Age Loci Stratum XV*

Locus	Square	Description	Similarity Coefficient
349	E-F 10	Soil layer	177.6 or 88.8%
351	D 10	Soil layer	
355	F 10	Soil layer	

Tell Beit Mirsim (Map Reference 141/096)

William F. Albright excavated the site of Tell Beit Mirsim during four spring seasons: 1926, 1928, 1930 and 1932 (Albright 1938: 6-7). These excavations were to establish the foundations for pottery chronology in Palestine for the next 50 years. In addition to its carefully studied ceramic corpus, the site yielded interesting objects and coherent architecture dating to the second and first millennia BC. The site itself is located in the Shephelah and covers an area of 3 hectares (Albright 1938: 1).

The earliest architectural remains were uncovered in the southeast quadrant and date to the Early Bronze III period. Five strata of domestic architecture from the second millennium include both Middle and Late Bronze Age structures. Changing styles of room arrangement and a diversity of activities, along with their artefact assemblages, can be traced in the Middle Bronze Age houses from Strata G, E and D (Albright 1938: 12-13, 20-21).

Stratum G (Fig. 25)

Only one complete house, located in Squares 32 and 33, could be successfully identified in Stratum G. Two distinct construction phases were separated by an ash layer that Albright assigned to a local conflagration (1938: 20). Unfortunately, few artefact remains from the earlier phase could be recovered because the original floor was removed and a new floor installed.[1] Only two ceramic ware forms were published, a bowl and a goblet, both from Room G 2. While this small sample is insufficient for statistical analysis, Albright's own understanding of the house plan is instructive.

House G included four rooms, a rectangular main hall on the east side, and three square rooms on the west, each averaging 14 m² in

---

1. Albright finds support for this view from the location of the pillar bases in relation to the floor level in Room G 1 (1938: 21-2).

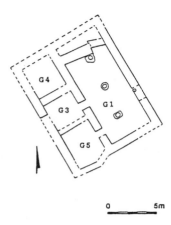

Figure 25. *Tell Beit Mirsim Stratum G, after Albright 1938: Pl. 56*

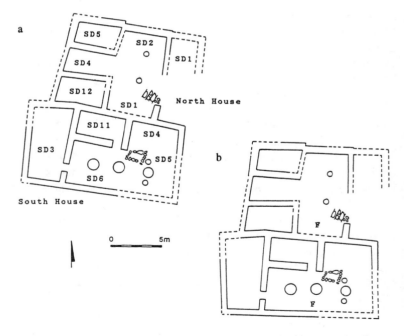

Figure 26. *Tell Beit Mirsim Stratum E North House and South House,*
          after Albright 1938: Pl. 50

area. Three pillar bases divided the main hall lengthwise and supported the roof. The presence of a door socket in the east wall indicates that this hall was broadroom style. Albright understood this structure as a two storey house with living quarters on the upper floor (1938: 22). His judgment is based on the fact that all of the house walls were 80 cm thick, somewhat thicker than the average range (50–70 cm).[1] Albright suggested that access to the upper storey was by means of a ladder at the north end of the main hall as no remains of a staircase were found (1938: 22). Further discussion of this house will only be possible at the conclusion of the analysis of Middle Bronze Age structures.

Because no complete rooms with artefacts in sufficient quantity for analysis have been identified in Stratum F, this phase of occupation at Tell Beit Mirsim will not be considered in this study. Better preserved were the structures of Strata E and D.

Stratum E (Fig. 26)
Separated from Stratum F by an ash layer, Strata E-D provide evidence of four phases of continuous occupation. While ash layers between Strata E and D were decisive in distinguishing these phases in some cases, a clear separation was not possible in all squares.

Two complete houses that share a common wall are attributed to Stratum E. The better preserved was South House (Fig. 26a). This house included a main hall, one perpendicular room across the back of the house, and a small room located in the corner of the main hall. In the hall there were three pillar bases along the main axis, and two others along the short axis (Albright 1938: 33-4). This room was certainly roofed.[2] Indeed, the thickness of the walls (c. 60 cm) would allow a second storey.[3]

The registered finds from this house were rich, with many special

1. See below the tables of wall thicknesses for structures at Hazor, Khirbet el-Meshash, Tell Beit Mirsim and Tell Mevorakh, Tables 3.57 and 3.58.
2. Yassine compares the houses of Stratum E to modern, rural Palestinian houses which have courtyards with posts that support arbors and grape vines. In addition, he assumes that no cooking was done in roofed rooms whereas Kramer reports ovens inside as well as outside the home (1982: 99). On the basis of his observations, Yassine rejects Albright's view that such rooms were roofed (Yassine 1974b: 106).
3. At Tell-i Nun, Jacobs records that 48 out of 59 houses were two-storey. These structures were built of bricks, $20 \times 20 \times 6$ cm and each wall consisted of $2\frac{1}{2}$ or 3 bricks (1979: 179). This would produce a wall 50–60 cm thick.

or status items (Table 3.41). Unfortunately, characteristic functional
tool kits are difficult to identify. Room SD11 yielded no finds, while
Room SD3 contained 1 Tell el-Yahudiyeh juglet found in a pit dug in
the floor. In the main hall, was a stone-lined bin between loci SD4 and
SD5. The purpose of this installation is not clear although it may have
been a hearth.[1] In the same room were 1 cooking pot, 1 krater, 1
store jar, 1 goblet and 1 juglet, which are related to food preparation or storage, along with 5 alabastra, a scarab, a bead and fragments
of bone inlay (Table 3.41). While it is clear that these status items
indicate the general life style and wealth of the inhabitants, they do
not point to specific activities carried out in this room. Nevertheless,
their diversity suggests that this hall, or the equivalent room above it,
was the main living room of the house (Fig. 26b).

To the north, the second house had a square plan (North House,
Fig. 26a). Stairs led down from the entryway (SD1) into the main
hall which was 53 cm below street level. This large main room (SD1–
SD2) contained two pillar bases, and was bounded on the west by two
smaller corner rooms (SD5 and SD12). The space between these
rooms (SD4) formed another narrow room. Although the major walls
of this house were reused in Stratum D, it cannot be determined with
certainty that there was a second storey in Stratum E. For the
purposes of this study, it is assumed that the Stratum E finds represent
the latest occupation and are not distinguished according to phase.[2]

Within the main hall (Room SD1–SD2), ceramic vessels and small
finds represent various domestic activities (Table 3.41). The assemblage for this room included items that most closely represent a functional tool kit for food preparation and consumption, namely, 1 bowl,
1 storejar, 1 juglet and a basalt mortar. Eight examples of a particular
vase form, found throughout the house (Albright 1933: 77), may also
have contributed to food preparation/consumption activities in the
main room. Because comparable vases of this particular form, a deep
closed 'bowl' with pedestal base (Albright 1933: Pl. 7: 11, 12, 13 and
14) are not found at other sites in functionally specific contexts, their

1. This feature is identified by Albright as a 'bin' (1938: 39). The elevations for
this feature on the published plan indicate that it was embedded in the floor and its
walls extended c. 20 cm above floor level.
2. Albright himself used two designations for the same room, 13-SD1 and 13-E1;
13-SD12 and 13-E12 (1938: 87-93). However, nowhere does he specifically indicate
that these designations correspond to phases within Stratum E.

precise function remains a matter for speculation. The remaining finds reflect the life style of the inhabitants. Personal adornment is represented by faience beads and a copper brooch; scarabs and a scaraboid may have been used as jewellery or for business; a bronze needle was used for textile production/repair; 2 alabaster dagger pommels and a limestone macehead could have been used as weapons or status items kept in the home or functioned, in secondary use, along with a chisel as tools; while bone inlays and an alabaster vessel, without a more specific context, reflect wealth or social status.

Corner room 12 contained 4 vases, 2 bowls and 2 faience flasks. These finds, in themselves, do not represent a functional tool kit but they do support the food preparation/consumption assemblage from the main hall. Similar finds were reported for the small room outside the house (12 SD1). These included 1 goblet, 1 jug, a scarab and 3 bone inlays. It is likely that these fragments of decorated inlay were part of the same object.

The houses of Stratum E reflect basic domestic activities and a rich and complex status of living on the part of their inhabitants. No functional tool kits, apart from food preparation/consumption, can be identified. This result, based on the evidence of the finds, indicates that the inhabitants were involved in typical domestic activities. At the same time, there was minimal evidence in these structures of craft activity, such as textile manufacture (1 needle, L. 13-E1; Table 3.41).

Several rooms located against the city wall to the south of the two houses described above may have been part of a house (not on the plan). Unfortunately, only 1 bowl and a Tell el-Yahudiyeh juglet were reported for these rooms. So, too, for the rooms uncovered further east in Squares 22 and 23 (See Albright 1938: Pl. 50), the finds were negligible.

Table 3.41. *Tell Beit Mirsim Stratum E—Area SE—Finds and Functional Classes*

Locus	Finds	Functional Class
South House		
03-SD3	1 juglet	multipurpose
13-SD4	3 alabaster vessels	special/status
	stone lined bin	storage?
13-SD5	1 lamp	lighting
	1 alabaster vessel	special/status
13-E6	1 goblet	multipurpose

Table 3.41—*Continued*

Locus	Finds	Functional Class
	1 juglet	multipurpose
	scarab	business/adornment
	faience bead	adornment
	alabaster vessel	special/status
	bone inlay	special/status
13-SD6	1 krater	food preparation/consumption
	1 narrow-neck jar	liquid storage
North House		
12-SD1	1 goblet	food consumption
	1 jug	food preparation/storage
	scarab	business/adornment
	3 bone inlays	special items
12-SD2	1 jar	storage
13-SD1	1 bowl	food preparation/consumption
	1 juglet	multipurpose
	special vessel	special item
	scaraboid	adornment/cultic
	3 faience beads	adornment
	2 alabaster pommels	weapons
13-E1	bronze needle	textile production
	3 scarabs	business/adornment
	basalt mortar	food preparation
	copper brooch	adornment
	alabaster vessel	special/status
	copper chisel	tool
	limestone macehead	weapon
	4 bone inlays	special/status
13-E12	2 bowls	food preparation/consumption
	4 vases	food preparation/storage
13-SD12	2 faience flasks	special/status

Stratum D (Figs. 27, 28)

The most impressive Middle Bronze Age domestic structures at Tell Beit Mirsim are found in Stratum D. Seven houses or complexes of rooms can be identified. The stratified finds from these rooms provide sufficient numbers, in some cases, for quantitative analysis to determine activity areas and room function.

The Stratum E houses in Squares 3, 12 and 13 were rebuilt in Stratum D. Unfortunately, the finds from these houses consisted of

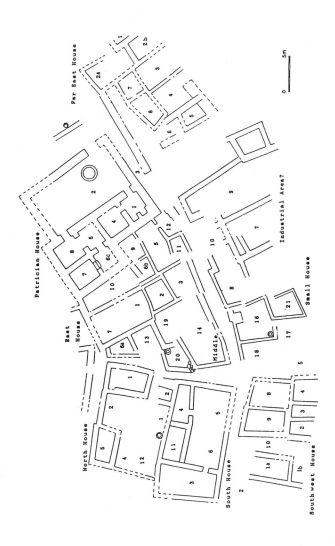

Figure 27. *Tell Beit Mirsim Stratum D, after Albright 1938: Pl. 51*

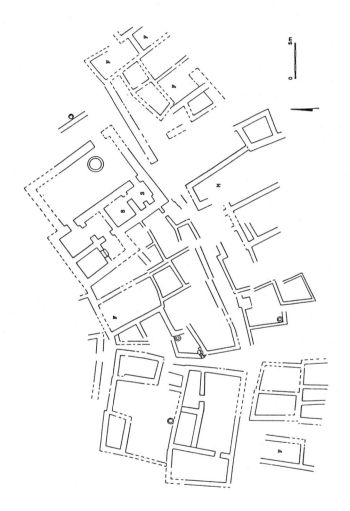

Figure 28. *Tell Beit Mirsim Stratum D spatial distribution*

sherds with few complete vessels. According to Albright's view, the archaeologist can assume that a vessel was in use in a particular location if it is found smashed *in situ*, or can be reconstructed from the sherds found in one room. In other cases, if the vessel can be reconstructed from sherds found in several rooms, it probably fell from an upper storey (Albright 1938: 38). As a result of this understanding of the archaeological record, Albright did not assign serial numbers to all the partial vessels and sherds which appear in the published plates of the Tell Beit Mirsim reports. This means that no provenience is available for 136 items from Stratum D (Albright 1932: Pls. 10-13, except Pl. 12: 12).

To the south of the lane that runs east–west through Area SE is a complex of rooms, which I have termed 'Southwest House.' The finds from only one room, 3-D1 (= Room 1a), are of sufficient number to determine functional use. That room contained 1 bowl, 2 cooking pots, 1 storejar, 1 jug and 2 juglets, along with a stone macehead (Table 3.42). The macehead, one of three found in Stratum D, could have been a weapon or symbol of authority or in secondary use as the support for a bow drill. However, no additional evidence is available to indicate what might have been manufactured here. The alabaster vessels, found in other houses nearby, are likely candidates, but could just as easily have been imports. The assemblage for Room 3-D1(a) forms a food preparation/consumption tool kit with a similarity coefficient of 125 or 62.5%. The small percentage of similarity to the paradigm probably reflects the limitations in Albright's recording system mentioned above. It may also be the case that small jugs and juglets tend to break into fewer pieces than bowls and are frequently recovered complete.[1] If this were the case in this instance, it would not be surprising that the percentage of these vessels is quite high in contrast to the bowl forms represented, unbalancing the assemblage.

From the plan (Fig. 27), it is not clear that the adjoining rooms formed part of the same structure. The reported finds from these rooms (10, 9, 8 and 2, 3, 4, 5) are too few to identify activity areas and may have been lost or discarded at random. The presence of 3 bowls and 1 vase are consonant with domestic activities and the loom

---

1. The only complete vessel from Field D at Tell el-'Umeiri recovered during the 1987 season was an EB III juglet, see Daviau 1991. Two additional complete juglets from Tell Jawa were recovered in the 1989 season (Daviau, in preparation) even though one juglet was buried under several smashed pithoi.

weight and pieces of bone inlay (Table 3.42), in themselves, do nothing to weaken this understanding of Southwest House.

Directly east of the Stratum E-D twin houses (North House and South House) is a complex of rooms divided by Albright into 2 structures (1938: 41) and referred to by me as East House (Rooms 6a, 7, 13, 1, 10, 6b and 9) and Middle House (D14, 19, 20, 2, 3 and 11).[1] Middle House (omitting Room 11, Fig. 27) shares some similarity in plan to North House and was comparable in size to South House (c. 90 m²). Unfortunately, the finds published are insufficient for functional analysis (Table 3.42). It should be noticed, however, that a lamp was reported for Room 23-D3, a locus which Albright described as an open court (1938: 41). Actually, this room was small enough to be roofed easily (3.3 × 3.6 m) and was an interior room comparable to Room 7 of the Patrician House. This Room also contained a lamp; nevertheless, Albright affirmed that it was roofed (1938: 38). The remaining finds from Locus 23-D3 do not constitute complete functional tool kits although in themselves they are very interesting. In Room D20 there was an oven and a juglet. While this was probably a food preparation area, an assemblage of one reported find must be considered random.

To the north in East House, the finds in the main room (D7) included 2 lamps, leaving open the question of whether this room could have been roofed. The remaining items reported from this locus should be associated with those from Locus D1 (Table 3.42). The total assemblage of ceramic vessels and objects from these two loci cannot be compared successfully to any of the paradigms because they are too diverse. The alabaster vessels, copper adze and copper macehead, included in this assemblage, seem to point to status or wealth rather than use as tools or weapons. No other room in this house could be analysed on the basis of reported finds.

The relationship of Rooms D9, 10, 5, 6 and 11 to either East House or Middle House remains uncertain. Albright understood these rooms to have been a small courtyard area associated with the Patrician House in its second phase when Room D6 (= 6c, Fig. 27) was opened

1. In the assignment of rooms I differ from Albright by including Rooms 23-D5, 6, 11 in Middle House, and Rooms 22-D9, 10 in East House. In terms of size, a complete house could include 22-D14, 19, 20 and 23-D2, 3 with the result that Rooms 23-5, 6, 11 and 22-D9, 10 would form a discrete house (Albright 1938: Pl. 51).

out into D9 and 10. The only reported finds from D9 consisted of 2 bowls and 1 bone awl. How these rooms functioned during the earlier phase of the Patrician House, when the walls of Room D6(c) were still standing, is unclear. In association with East House Rooms D5 and 11, certain rooms (D6[b], 9 and 10) may have formed a separate house opening onto the lane from Room D12. Two basalt grinders and a vase, along with a toggle pin, an adze and bone inlay, were found in East House Room D5 (Table 3.42). While the grinders point to food preparation, there are no other items from that tool kit to support this identification. Thus, it is possible that the grinders were used to pulverize materials other than food stuffs.

The largest house of Stratum D was the Patrician House, so named by Albright because of its fine construction and rich contents. Although Albright could distinguish several construction phases, the finds represent only the latest phase, because the earlier floors were removed or scraped down (1938: 35). Rooms 22-D1 and D4 both served as storerooms. The finds reported for Room D1 had a similarity coefficient of 164 or 82% while those from Room D4 equalled 152 or 76% with respect to the storage paradigm. Included in the assemblage from Room D1 was the stela of the 'serpent goddess'[1] along with a copper blade and a stone macehead which Albright attributed to second story debris (1938: 37). Indeed, the walls of this house were thick enough to support a second storey, at least over the side rooms southwest of the main court.

All the finds from Rooms D5 and 8 were assigned to the upper story because they could not be completely restored (Albright 1938: 38). While no complete tool kit can be reassembled, items representing typical domestic activities can be discerned. While one or more of these activities may have taken place in Room D8, contamination from upstairs rooms is possible. Vessels indicating food preparation and consumption include a cooking pot, a krater and a chalice; 10 spindle

---

1. Numerous examples of plaques, reliefs and statues of figures dressed in robes with thick hems now provide parallels for this stela showing that the 'serpent' was most probably the hem of a garment, that is, the bronze plaque of a man (Yadin *et al.* 1961: Pl. 339:1), a goddess statuette from Ras Shamra (Schaeffer 1939: Pls. 28-30), the statue of Idri-mi (Smith and Woolley 1949: frontispiece), and a seated god statuette from Megiddo (Loud 1948: Pl. 235: no. 23). A recent study by Schroer (1985: 49-115) discusses this motif in the Middle Bronze period, although it is clear from the examples presented above that the style continued to appear in artistic representations during the Late Bronze and early Iron Ages.

whorls are evidence of textile production, gaming pieces indicate recreation, beads and amulets were items of personal adornment, and a scarab may indicate business. One weapon, a copper arrowhead, was also reported (Table 3.42).

A second copper arrowhead was among the assemblage of the main room or court, D2. The size of this area makes it unlikely that it was roofed (6.2 × 11.7 m). Unfortunately, the finds do not indicate any specific activities that had been carried out in the courtyard. Instead, they continue the pattern of common luxury items represented in the assemblages of all the houses of this stratum and suggest a living room area. The shallow basin in the courtyard had a diameter of nearly 2 m and was lined with plaster. No comparable feature appeared in any other house and its function remains unknown.

In the final phase of the Patrician House, Room D6 was open to Rooms D9 and 10 (Fig. 27) while the floor in D7 was raised and plastered. Few finds were recorded from these rooms and their function remains unclear. Albright himself related Room D7 to food preparation, a view based primarily on the fact that there were cup marks in the plastered benches along the walls (1938: 35). Since no functional analysis of the finds is possible, no further clarification of the relationship of this room to the house as a whole can be attempted.

A series of rooms southeast of the Patrician House may have been two separate houses. In this study, they are known as the Far East House (Fig. 27). Items representing food preparation/consumption were found in several rooms. The most valuable assemblages are those for Room D2(b) with 138 or 69% and Room D4 with 113 or 56.5%. This plurality of food preparation/consumption areas may be an indication of more than one house. Because the plans appear to be incomplete, no definitive assessment of these houses is possible.

The houses in the Southeast quadrant of Tell Beit Mirsim are some of the best examples of Middle Bronze Age domestic architecture. The publication of numerous finds makes possible the functional analysis of various rooms and this, in turn, indicates a variety of domestic activities. In association with these houses is an area that may have served an industrial purpose. Because copper working was not expected in domestic structures, no paradigm for this industry was designed in this study. Comparison of the finds from Room 9, a crucible and a limestone mould, with those from other industrial areas would be necessary before any suggestion of copper working in

Area SE could be made. This is beyond the scope of the present study.

Table 3.42. *Tell Beit Mirsim Stratum D—Area SE—Finds and Functional Classes*

Locus	Finds	Functional Class
Southwest House		
3-D1(a)	1 bowl	food preparation/consumption
	2 cooking pots	food preparation
	1 wide-neck jar	dry storage
	1 jug	food preparation/storage
	2 juglets	multipurpose
	diorite macehead	weapon

The similarity coefficient for L. 3-D1(a) is 125 or 62.5% when compared to the food preparation and consumption paradigm.

Locus	Finds	Functional Class
3-D2	1 vase	food preparation/storage
	loom weight	textile production
14-D1	2 bone inlays	special/status
14-D3	2 bowls	food preparation/consumption
14-D5	bone inlay	special/status
13-D8,	1 bowl	food preparation/consumption
SD8	scarab	business/adornment
Middle House		
13-D14	Astarte plaque	cultic
13-D20	juglet	multipurpose
23-D3	lamp	lighting
	stamp seal	business/adornment
	scarab	business/adornment
	alabaster bowl	special/status
	javelin point	weapon
East House		
12-D7	2 juglets	multipurpose
	2 lamps	lighting
22-D9	2 bowls	food preparation/consumption
	bone awl	multipurpose
23-D5,	1 vase[1]	food preparation/storage
SD5	2 basalt grinders	food preparation
	toggle pin	jewellery

1. Vase R2 (Albright 1933, 7:11, Reg. no. 2272), popular in Stratum E, is given the provenience 23 E-5 which does not appear on the plan (TBM 2, Pl. 50). In view of the fact that Locus 23 D-5 is a well defined room, this vessel has been included in its assemblage. In fact the assemblage is too diverse to designate a functional tool kit and therefore the inclusion of this vase does not significantly alter the assemblage.

Table 3.42—*Continued*

Locus	Finds	Functional Class
	copper adze	tool
	bone inlay	special/status
23-D6	1 bowl	food preparation/consumption
23-D1	1 bowl	food preparation/consumption
	1 wide-neck jar	dry storage
	1 bronze bowl	special/status
	2 alabaster vessels	special/status
	copper adze	tool
	copper macehead	weapon

Far East House

32-D2(a)	2 cooking pots	food preparation/consumption
	1 narrow-neck jar	liquid storage
	1 jug	food preparation/storage
	3 scarabs	business/adornment
	copper ingot	metallurgy
	faience vessel	special item
33-D1	3 bowls	food preparation/consumption
	zoomorphic vessel	special item
33-D2(b)	5 bowls	food preparation/consumption
	1 cooking pot	food preparation
	4 juglets	multipurpose

The similarity coefficient for L. 33-D2(b) is 138 or 69% when compared to the food preparation and consumption paradigm.

33-D4	2 bowls	food preparation/consumption
	1 cooking pot	food preparation
	1 lamp	lighting
	copper dagger	weapon

The similarity coefficient for L. 33-D4 is 113 or 56.5% when compared to the food preparation and consumption paradigm.

Patrician House

22-D1	8 jars	storage
	3 narrow-neck jars	liquid storage
	3 wide-neck jars	dry storage
	stela	special/status
	copper blade	tool
	diorite macehead	weapon
	partition walls	

The similarity coefficient for L. 22-D1 is 164 or 82% when compared to the storage paradigm.

22-D2	scarab	business/adornment
	alabaster vessel	special/status

Table 3.42—*Continued*

Locus	Finds	Functional Class
	game board	recreation
	arrowhead	weapon
	5 bone inlays	special/status
22-D4	8-10 jars	storage
	brooch	adornment
	box and bone inlays	special/status

The similarity coefficient for L. 22-D4 is 152 or 76% when compared to the storage paradigm.

Locus	Finds	Functional Class
22-D5	2 awls	multipurpose
	haematite weight	business
22-D6	toggle pin	adornment
	haematite weight	business
22-D7	lamp	lighting
	gold bead[1]	adornment
22-D8	1 chalice	food consumption
	1 krater	food preparation/consumption
	1 cooking pot	food preparation
	4 (+ 6) spindle whorls	textile production
	scarab	business/adornment
	amulet	adornment
	2 beads	adornment
	alabaster vessel	special item
	gaming pieces	recreation
	arrowhead	weapon

Table 3.43. *Tell Beit Mirsim Area SE Stratum G Loci*

Locus	Square	Description
G1	33	Hall
G3	33	Room
G4	33	Room
G5	33	Room

1. This bead, Reg. no. 2185, is assigned to phase D1.

Houses and their Furnishings

Table 3.44. *Tell Beit Mirsim Area SE Stratum E Loci*

Locus	Square	Description
South House		
SD3	03	Room
SD4	13	Hall
SD5	13	Hall
SD6	13	Hall
SD11	13	Room
North House		
SD12	13	Room
SD1	13	Hall
SD2	12	Hall
SD1	12	Room
SD4	12	Room
SD5	12	Room

Table 3.45. *Tell Beit Mirsim Area SE Stratum D Loci*

Locus	Square	Description	Similarity Coefficient
South House			
3	03	Room	
6	13	Hall	
5	13	Room	
4	13	Room	
11	13	Room	
North House			
1	13	Hall	
2	13	Room	
12	13	Hall	
1	12	Room	
2	12	Room	
5	12	Room	
4	12	Hall	
East House			
6	12	Room	
7	12	Hall, part of L. 1	
1	23	Hall	
13	13	Room	
14	13	Room	
19	13	Hall	
20	13	Room	

Table 3.45—*Continued*

Locus	Square	Description	Similarity Coefficient
2	23	Room	
3	23	Room	
5	23	Room	
6	23	Room	
11	23	Room	
10	23	Room	
Patrician House			
2	22	Hall	
1	22	Room	164 or 82%
4	22	Room	152 or 76%
5	22	Room	
6	22	Room	
7	22	Room	
8	22	Room	
Second Phase			
6	23	Room	
9	22	Room	
10	22	Room	
Far East House			
2a	32	Room	
3	32	Street	
1	33	Room	
2b	33	Room	138 or 69.0%
3	33	Room	
4	33	Room	113 or 56.5%
5	33	Room	
6	33	Room	
7	33	Room	
8	33	Room	
Small House			
16	13	Hall	
17	13	Room	
18	13	Room	
21	13	Room	
Southwest House			
8	13	Room	
9	13	Room	
10	13	Room	
2	14	Room	

Table 3.45—*Continued*

Locus	Square	Description	Similarity Coefficient
3	14	Room	
4	14	Room	
1a	3	Room	125 or 62.5%
1b	4	Undefined	
2	3	Street	
Industrial Area?			
12	23	Room	
10	23	Open Area	
9	23	Hall	
8	23	Open Area	
7	23	Open Area	
4	23	Room	
S8C	23	Room	
S9C	23	Room	
S1C	24	Room	
S2C	24	Room	

Khirbet el-Meshash (Map Reference 146/069)

The site of Khirbet el-Meshash is an Iron Age settlement with several phases of Iron Age houses (Fritz and Kempinski 1983: 186). At a distance of 400 m from the site, a Middle Bronze Age fortified settlement was identified by Aharoni in 1964. Although much of this site has eroded away, the eastern and southern flanks of the fortifications have been preserved. Excavations through these fortifications and into the Middle Bronze settlement (Area E) were carried out in 1972 and 1974 by the staff of the Khirbet el-Meshash team directed by A. Kempinski (Fritz and Kempinski 1983: 186-87).

Area E2 (Fig. 29)

The most coherent architectural unit comes from Area E2 where three rooms were identified (Rooms 807, 808 and 815). Because of the poor state of preservation, only the foundation walls of these rooms remained intact. In view of the possibility of contamination, the finds must be analysed in relation to the features identified for each locus to determine the probability that a distinct tool kit can be identified. When such features have not been preserved, this task is

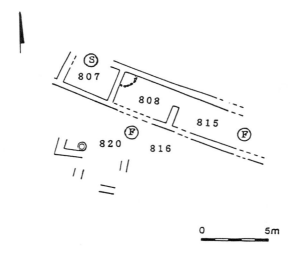

Figure 29. *Khirbet el-Meshash Area E2, after Fritz and Kempinski 1983: Plan 30*

restricted further by the publication of pottery forms only, with no mention of objects.

The best preserved locus is the central room (808) where a stone doorjamb remained in place in the entrance to Room 815. The floor associated with Room 808 walls was eroded away except in the interstices of the wall stones (Fritz and Kempinski 1983: 188-89). The ceramic remains from this locus present only a partial picture of the tool kit(s) utilized in this room and, as a result, must be evaluated cautiously (Table 3.46). For example, the only feature recovered in Room 808, for the later phase, is an undifferentiated quarter circle of stones in the northwest corner. While the function of this circular feature is not identified by the excavators, its location points to the likelihood that it was a bin.

The rooms on either side of L. 808 do not seem to be as well preserved. No floor was found in Room 807, to the west, and in Room 815, two patches of flagstone pavement, found at the level of the wall foundations, may have belonged to structures of an earlier period (Fritz and Kempinski 1983: 189).

The remains of this earlier phase were only partially exposed. For locus 815, a small number of ceramic ware forms (3 items) were published. The size of this assemblage is too small to be used statistically for comparison with the paradigms being tested in this study. Nevertheless, these vessels (1 bowl, a cooking pot and a storejar) represent domestic forms common in food preparation or consumption areas.

In addition to the pavement in Room 815, there was a paved stone floor under the walls of Room 808, from which most of the pottery reported for this room was recovered.[1] A flat stone located near the 'centre' of the room was identified as a possible pillar base, although the associated walls of the earlier stratum were not found. Room 808 included 6 ceramic items, 3 cooking pots, 2 jugs and a juglet, along with a possible bin. Because no bowls were recorded, this assemblage is insufficient for analysis even though the finds suggest that this room was probably a food preparation area, in spite of the poor preservation of this locus.

While Room 807 is represented by a small assemblage of five items, the percentage of storejars (60%) is significant. The large cooking pot fragment, along with a second cooking pot rim sherd, is not an uncommon item in storerooms associated with food preparation areas. Therefore it seems likely that this room functioned as a storage area although the finds are too few to be certain.

South of this row of rooms, additional architectural elements from structures of the earlier phase were identified: sections of walls, a large-stone pavement and a clay oven (L. 820). This locus does not represent a complete architectural unit as the walls were only partially preserved. The vessels published from this stone-paved floor include 4 bowls and a jar rim. Although such an assemblage is the minimum required for a statistical sample, it compares poorly to a food preparation and consumption area because the sample is unbalanced due to the lack of cooking pots.

The remaining locus, L. 816, is the area between Pavement 820 and Room 808 and may have been a part of L. 820. While it is not clear to which phase this locus belonged, its finds might shed light on the activities carried out in this space as well as on the function of the

---

1. Because there was no distinct locus number distinguishing the pottery in the interstices of the walls, marking the floor level of Room 808, from the pottery found on the floor that ran under the walls, it cannot be assumed that this corpus is free of contamination.

architectural units themselves. Unfortunately, the only recorded find was a cooking pot. Nevertheless, this vessel is in no way foreign to the assemblages compiled for the loci of this phase in Area E2.

All the ceramic ware forms published for Area E2 are typical of those occurring in tool kits for food preparation and storage activities although, as locus groups, these samples are too fragmentary to form representative assemblages. At the same time, the problem of the phasing for this area remains,[1] but the domestic function of the architectural units seems certain even though no plan of a complete house could be reconstructed.

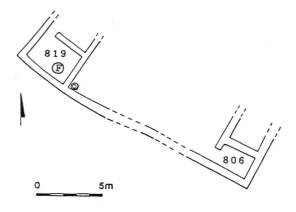

Figure 30. *Khirbet el-Meshash Area E1, after Fritz and Kempinski 1983: Plan 29*

Area E1 (Fig. 30)

In area E1, there was additional evidence of occupation along the inner side of the rampart retaining wall. This wall, preserved to a length of 20 m and a height of 1 m, served as the back wall of several rooms (L. 806, 819 and a central courtyard).[2] The smallest room (2.5 × 1.5 m) at the east end of the retaining wall was in a poor state of

1. The phasing is especially uncertain between Room 808 and L. 820 and 816.
2. Rooms 806 and 819 are separated by Trench 1 which cuts through the retaining wall and the 'central courtyard'. It is not certain, therefore, that the two rooms under discussion were indeed part of the same structure.

preservation (L. 806). The floor was barely discernible although a stone doorjamb and threshold marked the floor level. Only one bowl (Table 3.47) was reported (Fritz and Kempinski 1983: 191). A second room, to the north, was partially exposed but no finds or discussion are published. The second complete room (L. 819), located to the west of Trench 1, had a concentration of sherds marking its floor but no preserved architectural features. An additional room to the north of Room 819 was recognized but was too badly destroyed to yield any information (Fritz and Kempinski 1983: 191).

While the published finds for L. 806 of only one vessel make any statement regarding the function of that room impossible, a more adequate sample of 6 vessels is recorded for Room 819 (Table 3.47). This assemblage of 4 bowls and 2 storejars demonstrates only a weak similarity to a food preparation area due to the lack of other associated objects and features (a similarity coefficient of 118 or 59%). The ratio of bowls and storejars to the total sample of ceramic wares is 17 out of 27, strongly suggestive of domestic activities.

The excavators posit a courtyard that extends between Rooms 806 and 819 although the evidence for this connection was destroyed by the cut of Trench 1. In the 'courtyard' were the remains of an oven and a cooking pot (Fritz and Kempinski 1983: 191). No other features were identified.

These remains are very fragmentary and do not allow for a study of the complete building plan of the structure or structures involved. Nevertheless we are able to recognize these rooms as possible domestic areas on the basis of the preserved finds, the wall thickness, and room size (Table 3.60).

Table 3.46. *Khirbet el-Meshash Area E 2—Finds and Functional Classes*

Locus	Finds	Functional Class
807	2 cooking pots	food preparation
	2 narrow-neck jars	liquid storage/food preparation
	1 wide-neck jar	dry storage/food preparation
808	3 cooking pots	food preparation
	2 jugs	food preparation/consumption
	1 juglet	multipurpose
815	1 bowl	food preparation/consumption
	1 cooking pot	food preparation
	1 narrow-neck jar	liquid storage

Table 3.46—*Continued*

Locus	Finds	Functional Class
816	1 cooking pot	food preparation
820	4 bowls	food preparation/consumption
	1 narrow-neck jar	liquid storage

Table 3.47. *Khirbet el-Meshash Area E1—Finds and Functional Classes*

Locus	Finds	Functional Class
806	1 bowl	food preparation/consumption
819	4 bowls	food preparation/consumption
	1 wide-neck jar	dry storage
	1 narrow-neck jar	liquid storage

The similarity coefficient for L. 819 is 118 or 59% when compared to the food preparation and consumption paradigm.

Table 3.48. *Khirbet el-Meshash Middle Bronze Age Loci*

Locus	Square	Description	Similarity Coefficient
800	L 2-6	Trench 2/Rampart	
801	L 7	Surface	
802	L 8	Surface	
803	L 9	Surface	
804	A 8/9	Debris	
806	A/B 8/9	Room	
807	M 8/9	Debris	
808	M/N 8	Room	
809	M 9	Debris	
811	Q-U 3-11	Trench 1/Rampart	
814	L 9	Surface	
815	N/O 7/8	Room	
816	N 7	Debris	
817	O 7	Debris	
818	M 4	Probe	
819	S-U 9-10	Room	118 or 59%
820	M 7	Debris	
821	M 5	Probe	
822	U-E 10-12	Trench 3/Rampart	
823	M 6	Probe	
824	N 4	Probe	

Tell el-'Ajjul (Map Reference 093/097)

Tell el-'Ajjul is located on the north bank of Wadi Ghazzeh, 6 km southwest of Gaza. The enclosure ditch of this large site encompasses 28 acres or 11.3 hectares of ruined city. During four seasons, 1930–1934, Flinders Petrie conducted excavations under the auspices of the British School of Egyptian Archaeology. The excavations were concluded during a brief season in 1938 directed by E.H. Mackay and M. Murray (Avi Yonah 1975: I, 52).

The earliest domestic occupation on the mound dates to the Middle Bronze Age and was called by Petrie, Level III. Probably from the same period is Palace I, although no stratigraphic connections can be established. Indeed, the excavation method and recording procedures employed by Petrie make all phasing very tentative. Attempts to determine the duration of various architectural phases lack consensus. The most recent attempt by Weinstein rejects the views of Tufnell (Avi Yonah 1975: I, 60), Stewart (1974: 12-13) and Kempinski (1974: 147-50) that Level III ended during MB IIC and that Level II represented the transition from Middle Bronze to Late Bronze. His own view, based on the ceramic evidence, suggests that City III was in existence during the end of MB IIC and the beginning of LB I, was subsequently destroyed, and City II marks a reoccupation during LB I (1981: 4). Weinstein was careful to point out that the end of City II cannot be dated precisely.

Level III

The Middle Bronze Age occupation uncovered in the southwest corner of the mound was concentrated in Areas B and D.[1] These units were below the burnt layer which separated them from Area A structures built above the destruction debris. What is not clear is whether Areas B/D represent one or more phases in this period. Indeed, Petrie presented a confused picture by equating rooms with A or B prefix to City II and those with C or D prefix to City III (Petrie 1931: 9) while

---

1. These units were located near the benchmark labelled B. However, at this stage of the excavations, Petrie had not decided on a consistent system of designation with the result that some rooms were assigned one letter and others two. In this study, Area B includes all the rooms with B as the first of two letters and Area D includes all those with D as the first letter. Rooms B and D, on the other hand, belong to Area A, the upper level in this sector of the city—see Late Bronze Age Tell el-'Ajjul.

on the plan (Petrie 1931: Pl. LIV) there are no rooms with C prefix and both the rooms with B and D prefix have outlined walls, indicating structures beneath the burnt layer (Petrie 1931: 5). The elevations for the ash layer in this area, 726–744 inches, do not help to clarify the stratigraphic mixup. For the purpose of this study, both Areas B and D will be considered as MB IIC phases.[1]

To add to the confusion, provenience designations were not assigned to every registered object or vessel, or, where they were assigned, were not consistent. Both BM and BM' appear (Petrie 1933: III, 23, 25), although only one Room BM is shown on the plan. Attempts to analyse artefact distribution are, therefore, seriously frustrated even though a total corpus of 867 items could be identified from domestic structures of the Middle and Late Bronze Ages (see below, Tables 3.49–3.55).

Area B (Fig. 31)

Two complexes of rooms were assigned to Area B, one on either side of Street DO. In the northern unit, no finds were recorded for Rooms BK, BO or BP. The three remaining rooms (BL, BM, BN), for which finds were reported, do not form a complete architectural unit. The major activities that took place in these rooms seem to have been food preparation and consumption, and business (Table 3.49).

The single room with the largest assemblage, BJ, does not seem to have clearly defined architectural features. It is located to the west of Room BK, in the area of Rooms DD and DE. Strangely enough, no finds were reported for these loci. Several activities are represented by the assemblage of vessels and objects from Room BJ; three deep bowls indicate food preparation/consumption; scarabs point to business or adornment, while ground stone vessels, a zoomorphic vessel or figurine and a clay wheel reflect wealth and/or specialized articles of unknown function (Table 3.49). While these items are quite suggestive in themselves, no complete tool kits of any one activity are represented. Because it is not clear what relationship this room had to other Area B rooms on the north side of the street, its assemblage cannot be associated with any other activities.

To the south of Street DO, another complex of Area B rooms was

---

1. The pottery assemblage is too small to be useful in determining the exact phasing. Because of the continuity of occupation in the Late Bronze I period, no break can be seen in pottery styles for Area B.

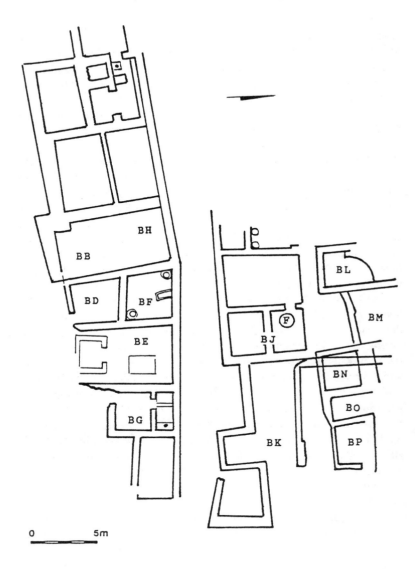

Figure 31. *Tell el-'Ajjul City III Area B, after Petrie 1931: Pl. LIV*

located. No finds were reported for Rooms BD or BG. In fact, the level of the artefacts from Room BF (678) is c. 1.5 m below the levels on the plan (Petrie 1933: Pl. LIV). The assemblage may very well be contaminated or reflect an earlier phase. For this assemblage, which consisted of incomplete vessels, 1 scarab and a clay wheel, a clear functional assignment cannot be made. Finds from the remaining rooms are too few to be relevant for determining activities, let alone for determining activity areas within structures (Table 3.49).

Petrie illustrated several domestic features on his plan (1931: Pl. LIV), namely ovens and toilets, along with two kilns. Because the toilets were attributed to phase D and the kilns were understood to precede all domestic structures in this area, only the ovens will be discussed here. These features are not labelled on the plan (in contrast, see the oven in L. EAQ below), but the unnumbered circles can scarcely represent anything other than an oven as all other numbered circles or ovals represent intrusive burials. Two ovens can be attributed to Room BF (Fig. 31) along with a trough[1] against the north wall. Petrie thought that the trough was built when the room went out of use because it was constructed at a higher level (1931: 6). The levels of the ovens, 720 and 740, seem to relate well to the levels of the nearby walls, 715–752 inches, indicating that they were in use during the main occupation phase of the room itself. The presence of the ovens correlates well with the artefact assemblage of this room which contained a cooking pot, 2 bowls and a juglet. Together, these finds result in a similarity coefficient of 138.2 or 69.1% when compared to the food preparation paradigm. Because of the small number of bowls included in most other assemblages, no comparison can be made to the standard paradigms. Nevertheless, the contents of Room BF strongly supports the identification of a food preparation and consumption area.

---

1. Petrie identified the room with the trough as Room DR although on the plan 'DR' is shown as a locus in Room BH-BB. He also attributed the two square pits dug into the bedrock as being in Room DR while they are shown on the plan in Room BE (Petrie 1931: Pl. LIV).

Table 3.49. *Tell el-'Ajjul City III—Area B—Finds and Functional Classes*

Locus	Finds	Functional Class
BB	bulla	business
BC	clay wheel	cultic?
BE	1 juglet	multipurpose
	scarab	business/adornment
BF	2 bowls	food preparation/consumption
	1 cooking pot	food preparation
	1 juglet	multipurpose
	scarab	business/adornment
	clay wheel	cultic?

The similarity coefficient for L. BF is 138.2 or 69.1% when compared to the food preparation and consumption paradigm.

Locus	Finds	Functional Class
BJ	1 bowl	food preparation/consumption
	2 kraters	food preparation/consumption
	1 jug	food preparation
	2 scarabs	business/adornment
	zoomorphic vessel?	special/status
	2 stone vases	special/status
	clay wheel	cultic?
BL	3 bowls	food preparation/consumption
	2 scarabs	business/adornment
BM	1 cooking pot	food preparation
	1 lamp	lighting
	4 scarabs	business/adornment
	macehead	weapon
	bone inlay	special/status
BN	1 miniature goblet	cultic

Area D (Fig. 32)

Within the same area as the Area B domestic complexes, several Area D houses can be distinguished. To the north of east–west street DO, one housing unit can be identified with Rooms DA-DE. Both Rooms DA and DB are incomplete on the west and few finds were preserved (Table 3.50). Two ovens, located in Room DB, correlate well with the assemblage of DC, which contains typical food preparation and consumption items—a bowl, cooking pot and jugs. The total assemblage has a similarity coefficient of 112.6 or 56.3% in comparison with the paradigm. In addition, Room DC may have been the largest room in the house, although the relationship of Room DF to this house is unclear. What is likely is that Room DS, to the north, was a part of House DA-DE. The assemblage from this room is a mixture of

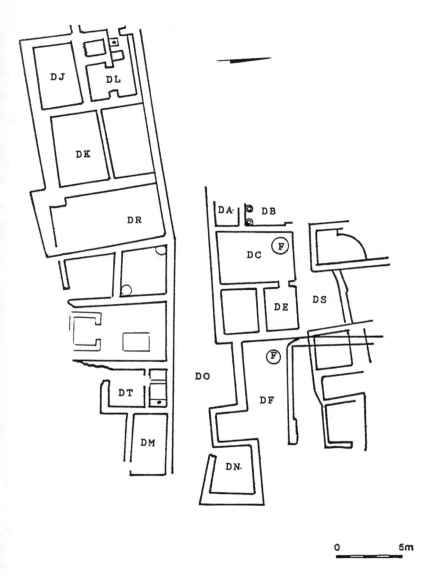

Figure 32. *Tell el-'Ajjul City III Area D, after Petrie 1931: Pl. LIV*

personal possessions, some of which may have served as tools. However, no specific activity sets can be distinguished.

Rooms DF and DN, to the east, also contained artefacts connected with food preparation. Indeed, the best assemblage for a food preparation/consumption tool kit is that for Room DH (Table 3.50), which was not recorded on the plan. Because of the subtle phasing in this area, no complete plan of House DF-DN can be attempted. It was intruded upon by Rooms BN-BP, built on a different alignment (Fig. 32).

To the south of Street DO, Petrie distinguished several phases of construction although he could not reconstruct complete Area D houses. No finds were recorded for Room DM (east of complex BB-BE) while only 1 chalice and a krater were assigned to Room DT. However, Room DT proved very interesting because it led into a toilet. The toilet, located in a small room (1.1 × 2.8 m), consisted of a white plastered bench positioned over a large jar. A second toilet of similar construction was located between Rooms DP and DL, west of Complex BB-BE. Unfortunately, the finds from the neighbouring rooms were too few to indicate room function (Table 3.50).

The most complete assemblage, reported for Room DJ, reflects food preparation or consumption activities. Along with 3 bowls, a jug and juglet was the ever present scarab and a bronze dagger (Table 3.50). A total of six daggers were found in Middle Bronze Age levels, not counting other types of bronze blades and javelin points. Whether these weapons were in secondary use as cutting implements or still retained their original purpose is unclear.

Several combined construction phases (Petrie 1931: Pl. LIV) make it impossible to determine whether one or more complete houses were exposed. The southern wall of Room DK measured 1.2 m thick, not typical of house walls in Area D which averaged 0.7 m (Fig. 32). This may indicate that Rooms DJ-DR were part of a discrete housing unit bordering the southwest defences, overlooking the wadi. While food preparation activities can be postulated as having taken place in these structures, few other typical domestic tool kits were preserved. This is in contrast to the remains from other Middle Bronze Age areas, such as Area G (see below).

Below the walls of Rooms DF and DR were two kilns (Petrie 1931: Pl. LIV). These structures clearly indicate the industrial nature of this area before the houses were built. The relationship of these kilns to the one near Pit AT, further north, cannot be determined (not on the plan). Within the B and D houses themselves, several large rectangular pits were excavated in the bedrock. Whether these were in use with the kilns or the houses is not clear. While they may have served as storage areas, there is no evidence to support this suggestion.

Table 3.50. *Tell el-'Ajjul City III—Area D—Finds and Functional Classes*

Locus	Finds	Functional Class
DB	bowl sherd	food preparation/consumption
	2 ovens	food preparation
DC	1 bowl	food preparation/consumption
	1 cooking pot	food preparation
	1 jug	food preparation
	1 juglet	multipurpose
	gaming piece?	recreation?
	bronze dagger	weapon

The similarity coefficient is 112.6 or 56.3% when compared to the food preparation and consumption paradigm.

DF	2 bowls	food preparation/consumption
	3 cooking pots	food preparation
	clay wheel	special
DG	3 bowls	food preparation/consumption
DH	3 bowls	food preparation/consumption
	5 cooking pots	food preparation
	2 kraters	food preparation/consumption
	1 jug	food preparation

The similarity coefficient for L. DH is 149 or 74.5% when compared to the food preparation and consumption paradigm.

DJ	3 bowls	food preparation/consumption
	1 jug	food preparation
	1 juglet	multipurpose
	scarab	business/adornment
	bronze dagger	weapon
DK	1 jug	food preparation
	scarab	business/adornment
	bronze dagger	weapon
DL	1 jug	food preparation
DN	scarab	business/adornment
	strainer	food preparation
DO	1 bowl	food preparation/consumption
	1 cooking pot	food preparation
	1 jug	food preparation
DP	finger ring	adornment

Table 3.50—*Continued*

Locus	Finds	Functional Class
	figurine	cultic
DR	1 bowl	food preparation/consumption
	1 chalice	food consumption/special
DS	1 bowl	food preparation/consumption
	3 scarabs	business/adornment
	2 toggle pins	adornment
	bronze blade	tool
	macehead	weapon
DT	1 chalice	food consumption
	1 juglet	multipurpose

Level III, Area E (Fig. 33)

Extending northeast, additional remains can be related to this early level; these include the stone foundations in Areas T and E and the lower phase of Area E (Table 3.56).[1] While many complete rooms were preserved, few coherent house units can be identified with certainty. Although the limits of individual houses are uncertain, housing clusters, separated by cross streets that connected two parallel ring roads (Yassine 1974: 129-33), are easily distinguished. A similar style of construction was continued in the better preserved Late Bronze Age levels.

Analysis of these dwellings is skewed by the reporting system used during the fourth excavation season. In some cases, the same designation was applied to more than one room, as in the case of L. EU, EW, EX, EY and EZ (Petrie 1934: Pl. LXII). A second weakness is the publication of a large corpus of ceramic vessels without provenience designation. The result is that many loci are assigned only one or two artefacts, too small a number to be useful in statistical analysis. In fact, the presence of one small item, such as a scarab, may reflect the debris that washed into an unused room rather than the original

1. Two phases of rooms (not counting the stone foundation level) are distinguished on the plan of Area E (Petrie 1934: Pl. LII). Unfortunately, insufficient finds were recorded to determine the exact dating of these phases. Petrie tried to connect the Area E houses, earlier phase, with those from Area A with black walls on the plan (Petrie 1931: Pl. LIV). However, these houses were originally phased by him as the upper level (above the ash layer) of Area A (Petrie 1931: 5). The levels of Room AQ (Petrie 1931: Pl. LIV) may indicate that these rooms are on a higher level than the early Area E rooms, 770-831 versus 709-750 inches.

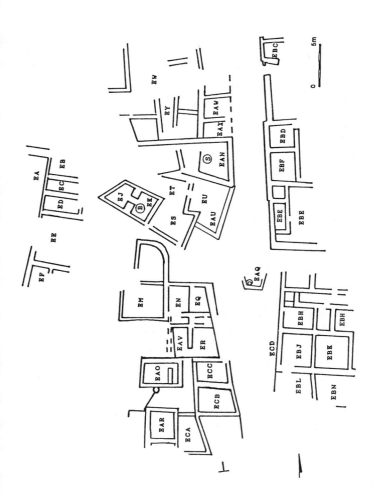

Figure 33. *Tell el-'Ajjul City III Area E, after Petrie 1934: Pl. LXII*

function of the room itself. This is the case for the complex of rooms along the west side of the excavation area, Rooms EA-EF, where only Room EE had an assemblage of valuable items that might have been in use in that room (Table 3.51). However, even this can be questioned in view of the extremes of elevation among the finds, the greatest being 2.6 m (680 versus 786 inches).

Room EK, to the east, had the largest number of reported finds (13). But the nature of these items does not reflect the primary domestic activities of food preparation, consumption and storage (Table 3.51). Instead, these artefacts reflect the type of activities that were likely to have been carried out in second storey rooms, such as business, personal adornment and the possession of status items. No finds were reported for the rooms on either side of EK, making it impossible to better understand the domestic unit formed by these rooms (EJ and ES, Fig. 33).

Along the main street, Room EAN contained the remains of two storejars. Such an assemblage is rare at Tell el-'Ajjul because Petrie published so few storejars in contrast to the reports from other Middle Bronze Age sites. This may have been due, in part, to the fact that most jars were severely smashed and rarely found intact. The style of Petrie's excavations did not allow him to record rooms filled with smashed jars, eliminating an important source of information for analysis of domestic architecture.

Two possible house units, located to the south of EJ-ES, included Rooms EAO-ECC and EAV-EL (Fig. 33). Unfortunately, the same kinds of artefacts were reported for these houses, scarabs and status items (Table 3.51). No finds characteristic of typical domestic activities, with the exception of the omnipresent scarab, were mentioned. Outside of Room EAR was a plastered bathroom with a drain that led into a sump. From the plan (Petrie 1934: Pl. LXII), it is unclear whether the bath was an integral part of House EAO-ECC. It appears to have been similar to those located in Areas B and D (see above).

To the east of the main, north–south street were two additional housing complexes, Rooms EBC-EBE (three rooms with the same designation), and Rooms EBH-EBN (Fig. 33 and Petrie 1934: Pls. LXII-LXIII). No artefacts were recorded for these loci, making it impossible to identify and locate domestic activities. In the middle of the street, an oven is shown surrounded on three sides by walls, L. EAQ. This feature does not appear to have been associated with any particular housing unit distinguished by the excavator. Its location suggests that this single oven may have been used by the inhabitants of several nearby houses. Indeed, no other ovens were shown on the plan of these eastern houses.

Table 3.51. *Tell el-'Ajjul City III—Area E—Finds and Functional Classes*

Locus	Finds	Functional Class
EA	arrowhead	weapon
EAN	2 narrow-neck jars	liquid storage
EAW	scarab	business/adornment
EB	scarab	business/adornment
ECA	scarab	business/adornment
ECC	1 scarab	business/adornment
	gaming piece	recreation
	faience vessel	special/status
EE	earrings	adornment
	1 toggle pin	adornment
	2 alabaster vessels	special/status
EF	scarab	business/adornment
EK	1 whorl	textile production
	kohl tube	cosmetic
	5 scarabs	business/adornment
	stone double vessel	special/cultic
	dagger	weapon
	4 bone inlay pieces	status
ER	2 scarabs	business/adornment
EU	toggle pin	adornment
EW	1 needle	textile production
	2 scarabs	business/adornment
	Egyptian figurine	cultic
	bone inlay piece	status

Area G (Figs. 34, 35)

Two phases of occupation in Area G were clearly separated by a layer of destruction debris. The earlier phase, late Middle Bronze Age IIC (Weinstein 1981: 4), was better represented, both architecturally and in terms of artefact remains (Table 3.52). Evidence for a variety of activities can be seen in the assemblages reported for this area.

Two major streets divided the housing complexes, GAL-GAN and GFD. One street, GAL-GAN, ran northeast by southwest in the

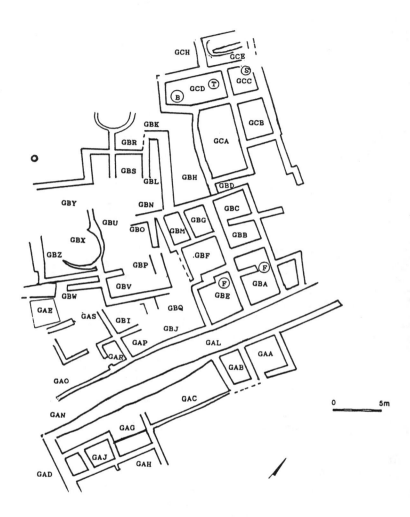

Figure 34. *Tell el-'Ajjul City III Area G, after Mackay 1952: XXXV*

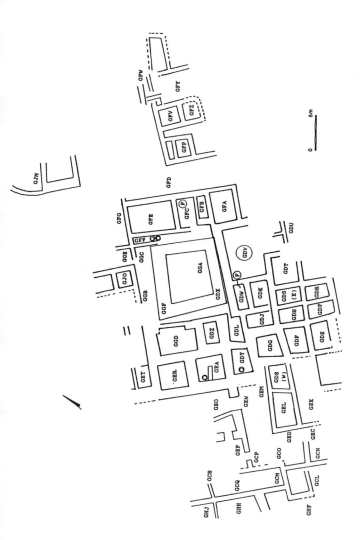

Figure 35. *Tell el-'Ajjul City III Area G, after Mackay 1952: XXXV*

southern part of the excavated area.[1] A series of rooms excavated
along the east side of this street do not constitute a complete house
(Fig. 34). This is clear not only from the arrangement of rooms but
also from the doorway in Room GAA which opened to the east.
Because only one juglet was reported from this room, no evidence of
its function was preserved.

The largest assemblage of ceramic vessels and artefacts from these
rooms, 13 items, was found in Room GAC. While no single tool kit
was completely represented, several activities appear to have been
carried on here. Included were ceramic vessels for food preparation
and storage, needles for textile production, personal possessions and
jewellery, tools and weapons (Table 3.52). While it is always possible
that many of these items were in secondary usage, their primary
functional characteristics are the first line of evidence for the activities
that occurred in these rooms.

To the north and south of Room GAC were two small rooms with
plastered floors, Room GAB and GAG. These rooms were empty of
finds except for a spindle whorl in Room GAG. The mud floor in
Room GAB was plastered with gypsum while that in Room GAG was
white stucco. The walls of Room GAG were also whitewashed
(Mackay *et al.* 1952: 24). What the significance of these features was
remains unknown. In fact, they may not have been contemporary
because the floor of Room GAB was 0.7 m above the bedrock and was
considered by the excavators to have been a second use phase (Mackay
et al. 1952: 24). Unfortunately, the lack of finds leaves the mystery of
these rooms intact.

Only one other room in this complex yielded finds, Room GAJ.
Again a variety of activities are represented in the assemblage: food
preparation or storage, personal possessions and tools. Because of
its small size, 2.2 × 2.0 m, and interior location, this room was
probably a storeroom. Unfortunately, its relationship to Room GAG
was not preserved. In fact, few doorways were uncovered among
these rooms although the walls remained standing 0.3–0.9 m high.

---

1. While Area G itself was never precisely located in the published report, Tufnell
indicated the excavation area on her plan of the city (Ani-Yonah 1975: I, 53). While
the excavators did indicate that the southeasternmost rooms 'rested on the steep slope
of the artificial rampart which encircles the tell' (Mackay, Petrie and Murray 1952:
24), this association of features does not appear on Tufnell's plan.

This combination of circumstances suggests that these rooms may have been entered from above.

Extending west of Street GAL-GAN was a large complex of rooms that belonged to one or more houses. Many rooms were badly ruined due to intrusive burials and pits while others show evidence of rebuilding. Rooms GAE-GAR (Fig. 34) yielded few finds and were poorly preserved except for Room GAR. This small room had a plastered floor and walls, all covered with white stucco. The room sloped toward a drain that ran under the wall. Under the floor was a pit 2.25 m deep cut into the bedrock. This well drained room may have served as a bath (Mackay *et al.* 1952: 24). Only one alabaster vessel was found *in situ*.

Doorways were preserved between Rooms GAR and GAO and GAO and GAS. Unfortunately, the finds reported for these rooms are too few for meaningful analysis (Table 3.52). In Room GAO, a large irregular pit may have served an industrial purpose. The sides of the pit were lined with mud and showed signs of burning (Mackay *et al.* 1952: 24). Whether this was secondary usage of this room or its primary function is unclear. In fact, the level of the pit (769 inches) calls into question the function of the adjoining 'bathroom' (GAR; 840 inches) because the doorway opened directly onto the pit.

To the north, a more coherent complex can be identified, GBA-GBC and GBE-GBM (Fig. 34). Whether these nine rooms were all part of the same house cannot be ascertained. The main east–west wall that divided the rooms was 0.8 m. thick whereas the cross walls were c. 0.5 m thick. Few doorways were preserved; as a result, the traffic pattern between the rooms cannot be reconstructed. Only two rooms yielded finds that indicate a range of activities, GBA and GBE (Table 3.53). In Room GBA, 2 bowls, a jug and a strainer point to food preparation or consumption. Also included in the assemblage were items of personal adornment, tools, weapons and a pyxis. On the basis of the room arrangement, the excavators suggested that Room GBA, separated from a small adjoining room by a partition wall, functioned as a shop on the main street (Mackay *et al.* 1952: 24). This interpretation does not explain the relationship of the finds to that function nor the fact that no opening onto the street was found although the foundation and wall together were preserved to a height of 1.07 m.

Next door, in Room GBE, the assemblage included a large goblet and three jugs that may have been used in food preparation, as well as

5 scarabs and a toggle pin. The finds from the remaining rooms were in the same functional classes as the assemblages detailed above (Table 3.53). Unfortunately, there were too few recorded for each individual room to be assured that they were not just random items contained in the destruction debris. This is especially true of the scarabs and beads.

Another coherent unit, located further west, consisted of Rooms GBD-GCD (Fig. 34). A 1 m thick wall along the south side of L. GCH separated this complex from the rooms to the south (GBK-GBV). The relationship of L. GBH to the northern house is unclear; it may have served as a street although its width (4.2 m) seems extreme, even though it is comparable to Street GFD to the north. The main room (GCA) contained an oven in a corner[1] along with a functionally mixed assemblage of objects related to personal adornment and crafts (Table 3.54). It is surprising that no items related to food preparation and consumption were recorded for this room. However, in view of the excavation and recording methods employed, smashed bowls and jars would have been customarily ignored.

The other rooms in this house yielded more interesting assemblages. For example, in Room GCC, 60% of the finds were status items and 40% were storage-related vessels (Table 3.54). In Room GCD, 37.5% of its finds were related to textile production, 37.5% to business activities, and the remainder to personal adornment and weaponry. While these finds do not indicate clearly the activity areas within individual rooms where they were used, they nevertheless show the range of activities typical of domestic structures. The inclusion of 13 weapons, such as daggers, arrowheads, javelin points and dagger pommels, from as many loci, may indicate the occupation of the inhabitants, at least in their primary usage. The location of a weapon in a particular room possibly reflects secondary usage as no hoard of stored weapons seems to have been found (Cf. Tel Batash below).

Under the floors and walls of these houses were numerous pits cut into the bedrock. Some pits were as much as 2 m deep and were

---

1. Mary Eliza Rogers described a house that she visited in Tanturah that had one main room with an oven in the corner farthest from the door (1862: 73). This oven had been heavily used as the ceiling was blackened with soot. The location described by Rogers did not seem to be unusual in her experience although most archaeologists assume that this would have been an unlikely place for an oven, see Yassine 1974: 106, and Chapter 6 below.

either round or rectangular. The original function of these pits (suggested by the excavators) as storage pits cannot be confirmed. They may have been refuse pits or used in some industrial capacity. However, it is clear that they had no relationship to the later pits, such as GAD and GBX, that impinged upon the architecture of the houses themselves, or Pit GGA around which several housing complexes were built (Fig. 35; Area G continued). This massive structure, c. 5.5 m deep and 9.6 × 9.2 m in area, was obviously built before the surrounding buildings, although how much before is unclear. Was it in use with complexes GD, GE and GF? If so, how did it function? The excavation provided little data on which to base an interpretation of this important structure. It appears to have been unplastered which would have made it useless as a reservoir because of the porosity of the stone (Mackay *et al.* 1952: 25). Walls built over the pit during the later phase indicate that, at some time, it was filled up with debris. However, there is no indication that this was its primary function.

The room complexes surrounding Pit GGA exhibited several serious differences in architectural style from those further east (discussed above). A 1 m thick north–south wall separated Rooms GDE-GDT from those further west. The rooms to the east (GDE-GDT) were more consistent in size and were quite small (2 × 3 m). The finds from these rooms indicated no food storage activity and only 15.4% indicated food preparation or consumption, while 30.8% were related to business, 23% to weapons, 15.4% to textile production and 15.4% to status or special functions.[1]

Rooms of similar size and wall thickness (GDG-GDY) were located at the southeastern corner of Pit GGA. One of these rooms (GDG) had been rebuilt along the lines of the rooms further west (GEA-GDZ), which had even thicker walls (1.4 m). Room GDY contained an oven but no vessels or objects related to food preparation (Table 3.54). Only Room GDW contained jugs that could be part of a food preparation/consumption or storage tool kit. Of the total assemblage from all rooms southeast of Pit GGA these jugs equalled 21%, while an equal number of objects (21%) were related to adornment. Only 7% were business related, 14% were weapons, and 21% were special

1. Room GDS in this complex has the same designation as another room immediately west of Room GDG. Such confusion skews the artefact assemblage. On the basis of the elevations recorded for each artefact, it is possible that 1 needle and 1 scarab should be assigned to Room GDS (South) rather than to GDS (North).

or status items. This last category included a silver bowl and two rhyta. The suggestion that Rooms GDJ and GDK served as storerooms because they were connected by an opening smaller than the normal size doorway may have some merit (Mackay *et al.* 1952: 26) although the finds (a plumb bob, 2 rhyta, a toggle pin and a javelin head) do not support this view (Table 3.54).[1]

Along the southwest side of Pit GGA were a series of rooms with walls 1.5–1.8 m thick. This unusual construction is paralleled only in the rebuild of Room GDG. Two rooms (GEA and GER) are quite square (c. 3.4 × 3.6 m), while the remaining rooms (GGD and GDZ) are rectangular and vary in size (2.8 × 1.8 m versus 3.4 × 5.1 m). Room GEA contained an oven but no food preparation or consumption related vessels although a cooking pot was found in Room GDZ (Table 3.54). The finds from Room GER were not related to any particular domestic activity. Rather, they were a group of status items that included a ceramic bowl with a rosette design inside, the lid of a kohl pot, a piece of ivory inlay, a bronze blade and a scarab. The paucity of finds from these well-built rooms may be additional evidence that this structure was somehow different from the other houses in Area G. Whatever other valuables were originally used here were removed or stolen when the building went out of use. Ordinary items may have existed in large numbers in these rooms but very few were preserved or reported.[2]

On the far side of the great pit, an alley (GFF) with 2 ovens fronted on a row of rooms, GFA-GFE (Fig. 35). No complete functional tool kits were preserved, but the individual assemblages did contain some items related to food preparation, and in accord with the presence of the ovens. For example, in Rooms GFC and GFE there were 1 bowl, 1 krater, a pestle and a juglet (Table 3.55). The presence of 7 scarabs and 2 weights point to business activities while the pyxis and toggle pins indicate personal adornment and cosmetics. Although only the most ordinary finds were recorded for Room GFC, it may have been the focal point of this house. Its floor was plastered with 13 cms of mud plaster which covered a bowl of sheep/goat bones positioned in

1. Although the thickness of the walls in this part of Area G strongly suggest basement rooms there is no published artefactual evidence that would support this interpretation.

2. Petrie's recording and publishing methods must be kept in mind here as is evident by the large number of status items reported in contrast to ceramic vessels.

the west corner of the room. In view of this special treatment and on the basis of its size (3.8 × 6.0 m), Room GFE probably functioned as the main living room in this complex.

Only one doorway from Room GFC to the space along the north side of the pit was recorded. Because Rooms GFB-GFE occupied the total space between Pit GGA and Street GFD, and because the rooms to the east and west were not excavated, there is no way of determining whether a complete house plan is represented here. However, the width of the walls of Rooms GFB-GFE is typical of houses elsewhere in Area G and in sharp contrast to the thick-walled rooms opposite. In fact, a 1 m thick wall separated Room GFA from courtyard GDV which seems to have functioned in relation to Rooms GDU-GDW. This supports an understanding of Room GFA as part of a separate house, whether or not it was associated with Room GFB to the west (Fig. 35).

To the north of Street GFD, several units of rooms were excavated. Unfortunately, no complete house plans can be identified nor are the finds from these rooms (GFP-GFZ and GFK-GJM) sufficient to understand how the rooms functioned (Table 3.55). From House GFP-GFZ, only 2 jugs, 2 toggle pins, 1 scarab and a stone axe were recorded. These finds do support the view that this was a domestic structure but little more.

Table 3.52. *Tell el-'Ajjul City III—Area G—Finds and Functional Classes*

Locus	Finds	Functional Class
GAA	1 juglet	multipurpose
GAC	1 narrow-neck jar	liquid storage
	1 jug	food preparation/storage
	2 needles	textile production
	3 scarabs	business/adornment
	2 toggle pins	adornment
	gaming piece	special
	scraper	tool
	2 javelins	weapon
GAD	1 jug	food preparation
	1 scarab	business/adornment
	awl	textile production
GAE	1 scarab	business/adornment
GAG	spindle whorl	textile production
GAH	3 scarabs	business/adornment
GAJ	1 bowl	food preparation/consumption

Table 3.52—*Continued*

Locus	Finds	Functional Class
	1 narrow-neck jar	liquid storage
	1 scarab	business/adornment
	1 toggle pin	adornment
	lead fragment	special
	flint drill point	tool
GAO	1 scarab	business/adornment
	bronze dagger	weapon
GAP	faience vessel	special/status
GAR	alabaster juglet	special/status
GAS	bronze hook	textile production
	toggle pin	adornment
	2 faience vessels	special/status

Table 3.53. *Tell el-'Ajjul City III—Area G—Finds and Functional Classes*

Locus	Finds	Functional Class
GBA	2 bowls	food preparation/consumption
	1 jug	food preparation/storage
	1 pyxis	special/cosmetic
	strainer	food preparation
	2 scarab rings	business/adornment
	1 toggle pin	adornment
	awl	textile production
	bronze dagger	weapon
GBB	1 scarab	business/adornment
	shell ring	adornment
	haematite weight	business
GBC	1 juglet	multipurpose
	flint blade	tool
GBE	1 goblet	food preparation/consumption
	3 jugs	food preparation/storage
	5 scarabs	business/adornment
	1 toggle pin	adornment
GBG	1 jar	storage
	bone saw	tool
GBH	3 scarabs	business/adornment
	2 toggle pins	adornment
	3 haematite weights	business
GBK	bronze needle	textile production
GBL	1 bowl	food preparation/consumption
GBM	2 scarabs	business/adornment

Table 3.53—*Continued*

Locus	Finds	Functional Class
	1 bead	adornment
GBO	1 whorl	textile production
	1 scarab	business/adornment
GBQ	1 scarab	business/adornment
GBR	1 jug	food preparation
	3 scarabs	business/adornment
	1 toggle pin	adornment
GBS	lid?	unknown
	3 jugs	food preparation
	1 juglet	multipurpose
	1 pyxis	special/cosmetic
	1 scarab	business/adornment
	1 toggle pin	adornment
	5 haematite weights	business
GBU	1 scarab	business/adornment
GBV	alabaster bowl lid	special/cosmetic
	1 scarab	business/adornment
	bronze awl	textile production
GBW	limestone pommel	weapon/tool
	sandstone disk	special
GBY	1 scarab	business/adornment
	1 bead	adornment
GBZ	1 bowl	food preparation/consumption
	jar sherd	storage

Table 3.54. *Tell el-'Ajjul City III—Area G—Finds and Functional Classes*

Locus	Finds	Functional Class
GCA	1 scarab	business/adornment
	1 toggle pin	adornment
	1 awl	textile production
	bronze chisel	tool
GCB	1 jug	food preparation/storage
	1 scarab	business/adornment
GCC	1 narrow-neck jar	liquid storage
	1 juglet	multipurpose
	alabaster bowl lid	special/cosmetic
	1 scarab ring	business/adornment
	faience vessel	special/status
GCD	1 whorl	textile production
	2 bronze needles	textile production

Table 3.54—*Continued*

Locus	Finds	Functional Class
	2 scarabs	business/adornment
	shell pendant	adornment
	haematite weight	business
	flint arrowhead	weapon
GCE	haematite weight	business
GCH	stone knob	multipurpose
	bronze needle	textile production
GCL	knob	unknown
	whorl/button	textile
	1 bead	adornment
	1 toggle pin	adornment
	bronze awl	textile production
	drill cap	tool
	bronze dagger	weapon
GCM	9 weights	business
GCN	1 bronze needle	textile production
	earrings	adornment
	haematite weight	business
	flint arrowhead	weapon
GCO	whorl	textile production
	1 scarab	business/adornment
	alabaster vessel	special/cosmetic
GCP	horse bit	riding
GCR	macehead	weapon
GDE	1 scarab	business/adornment
	alabaster vessel	special/cosmetic
	macehead	weapon
GDF	knob	unknown
	dagger pommel	weapon
GDG	bronze needle	textile production
	ivory awl	textile production
GDH	1 scarab	business/adornment
GDJ	plumb	tool
GDK	2 rhyta	special
	ivory toggle pin	adornment
	bronze javelin	weapon
GDL	bronze javelin	weapon
GDP	2 bowls	food preparation/consumption
GDR	bronze arrowhead	weapon
GDS	1 whorl	textile production
	1 bronze needle	textile production
	2 scarabs	business/adornment

Table 3.54—*Continued*

Locus	Finds	Functional Class
GDW	3 jugs	food preparation
	1 melon bead	adornment
	silver bowl	special/status
GDX	1 whorl	textile production
	1 bead	adornment
GDY	1 bead	adornment
GDZ	1 cooking pot	food preparation
	alabaster bowl lid	special/cosmetic
GED	bronze awl	textile production
GEF	1 toggle pin	adornment
GEN	1 jug	food preparation
	spouted bowl	food preparation/consumption
	alabaster vessel	special/status
GEO	1 scarab	business/adornment
GER	rosette bowl	special/status
	kohl pot lid	cosmetic
	1 scarab	business/adornment
	bronze blade?	tool
	ivory inlay	special/status
GET	pestle	pounder of red paint
	awl	textile production

Table 3.55. *Tell el-'Ajjul City III—Area G—Finds and Functional Classes*

Locus	Finds	Functional Class
GFC	1 bowl	food preparation/consumption
	1 krater	food preparation
	2 scarabs	business/adornment
	dolerite pestle	food preparation
GFE	1 juglet	multipurpose
	1 pyxis	special
	3 scarabs	business/adornment
	2 toggle pins	adornment
	awl	textile production
	plumb	tool
	haematite weight	business
GFF	ovens	food preparation
	2 scarabs	business/adornment
	haematite weight	business
GFP	dolerite axe	tool
GFV	2 jugs	food preparation/storage

Table 3.55—*Continued*

Locus	Finds	Functional Class
	1 scarab	business/adornment
	2 toggle pins	adornment
GGD	1 scarab	business/adornment
	ceramic jar lid	storage
GGE	1 bowl	food preparation/consumption
	bronze tweezers	tool
	blade	tool
GHH	1 narrow-neck jar	liquid storage
	2 pyxides	special/status
GHJ	1 bronze needle	textile production
	2 scarabs	business/adornment
	basalt mortar	grinder for red paint
	bronze javelin	weapon

The Function of Scarabs

The large number of scarab stamp seals recovered from the excavations at Tell el-'Ajjul provides an opportunity to explore the various functions this object could have served in the life of this site. More than 1050 scarabs were published from all the areas, including the palace and the cemeteries. In addition, there were 7 bullae and 18 cylinder seals which must be considered as part of the total picture.

An understanding of how scarabs functioned in Egypt serves as the starting point for interpreting their role in Palestine. Of most immediate relevance is the practice of the Middle Kingdom where both private name and design scarabs were used to stamp documents and personal possessions including papyri, ceramic vessels, boxes and so forth. During the late 12th and 13th dynasties, seals with names and/or titles were recovered in abundance from the administrative centres at Kahun and Lisht as well as from the forts along the Nubian border (Johnson 1977: 141).

Some of the titles on Egyptian scarabs seem to be administrative while others point to the use of the scarabs as amulets. It is clear that the scarabs found in tombs with epithets appropriate for a dead person were not used as seals while the owner was alive. Also, royal name scarabs which honoured a Pharaoh long dead were probably used as good luck charms or jewellery. The more numerous design scarabs, on the other hand, were probably used by ordinary people both as

seals and amulets, especially in view of the identification of the god
Khepri with the scarab beetle (Johnson 1979: 142).

At Tell el-'Ajjul, the number of scarabs seems to reflect the
Egyptian practice. Royal name and personal name and title scarabs
form about 3–4% of the total corpus. The remainder shared a limited
range of design motifs that included c-scroll, s-scroll, lion, ibex,
human figure, cobra and various hieroglyphics. Because so many of
the design scarabs shared the same motif, it is difficult to imagine how
they functioned as seals for personal identification. However, there are
several ways in which these seals could be used even though they were
not completely distinctive. Design scarabs could have been used to seal
documents and jar stoppers where security rather than official
identification was needed. Secondly, they could be used by craftsmen
to distinguish the intended owner or patron. Such practice may
account for the number of stamped[1] loom weights found at Megiddo
(i.e., L. 4025, 4056nr and 4063). Scarabs themselves are found at
most Palestinian sites with Middle Bronze Age occupation. At the
same time, so few corresponding bullae have been recovered that the
ways in which these scarabs were utilized at different sites cannot yet
be documented. For the purpose of this study, scarabs found in a
domestic context have been classified as items pertaining to business,
including crafts, especially when found in association with weights or
tools. Of course, in other assemblages, their use as items of personal
adornment, jewellery or amulets, cannot be excluded.

Table 3.56. *Tell el-'Ajjul Middle Bronze Age Loci Stratum 3*

Locus	Area	Description	Levels (inches)
BB	B	Room	
BD	B	Room	
BE	B	Room	
BF	B	Room	

1. Another suggestion for the occurrence of stamp impressions on loom weights
is that they represent ownership and were impressed by the owner who made the
loom weights for his/her own use. However, such owners marks as seal impressions
imply high status. In such a case, it would not be surprising if the weights had been
made by a professional potter for a wealthy owner.

Table 3.56—*Continued*

Locus	Area	Description	Levels (inches)
BG	B	Room	
BH	B	Room	
BJ	B	Room?	
BK	B	Room	
BL	B	Room	
BM	B	Room	
BN	B	Room	
BO	B	Room	
BP	B	Room—Stratum 2?	
DA	D	Room	
DB	D	Room	
DC	D	Room	
DD	D	Room	
DE	D	Room	
DF	D	Room	
DJ	D	Room	
DK	D	Room	
DL	D	Room	
DM	D	Room	
DN	D	Room	
DO	D	Street	
DP	D	Room	
DR	D	Room	
DS	D	Room	
DT	D	Room	
EAN	E	Room	
EAO	E	Room	
EAQ	E	Oven	
EAR	E	Room	
EAU	E	Room	
EAV	E	Room	
EAW	E	Room	
EAX	E	Room	
EA	E	Room	
EB	E	Room	
EC	E	Room	
ED	E	Room	
EE	E	Room	
EF	E	Room	
EJ	E	Room	
EK	E	Room	
EL	E	Room	

Table 3.56—*Continued*

Locus	Area	Description	Levels (inches)
EM	E	Room	
EN	E	Room	
EQ	E	Room	
ER	E	Room	
ES	E	Room	
ET	E	Room	
EU	E	Room	
EW	E	Large room	
EY	E	Room	
EBC	E	Room	
EBD	E	Room	
EBE	E	Room—3 rooms with same letters	
EBF	E	Room	
EBH	E	Room—3 rooms with same letters	
EBJ	E	Room	
EBK	E	Room	
EBL	E	Room	
EBN	E	Room	
ECA	E	Room	
ECB	E	Room	
ECC	E	Room	
ECD	E	Room—later phase?	
GAA	G	Room	825–851
GAB	G	Room	830–860
GAC	G	Room	823–871
GAD	G	Undefined	873–917
GAG	G	Room	
GAH	G	Room?	870–884
GAJ	G	Room	849–936
GAL-GAN	G	Street	
GAE	G	Large Pit	768
GAO	G	Room	821–855
GAP	G	Room	839–870
GAR	G	Room	829–872
GAS	G	Undefined	813–867
GBA	G	Room	824–867
GBB	G	Room	831–876
GBC	G	Room	831–883
GBD	G	Alley	877–906
GBE	G	Room	814–884

Table 3.56—*Continued*

Locus	Area	Description	Levels (inches)
GBF	G	Room	825–863
GBG	G	Room	838–911
GBH	G	Room/Street	820–851
GBI	G	Room	803–867
GBJ	G	Undefined	805–899
GBK	G	Room	875–898
GBL	G	Room = GBK	863–887
GBM	G	Room	838–912
GBN	G	Undefined	upper phase levels
GBO	G	Room?	838–877
GBP	G	Room?	861–875
GBQ	G	Undefined	829–833
GBR	G	Room	871–890
GBS	G	Room	858–873
GBU	G	Undefined	804–858
GBV	G	Room	824–864
GBW	G	Room?	827–852
GBX	G	Large Pit	701–822
GBY	G	Undefined	
GBZ	G	Room?	811–874
GCA	G	Room	841–901
GCB	G	Room	870–898
GCC	G	Room	892–921
GCD	G	Room	872–939
GCE	G	Room	891–931
GCH	G	Room	833–933
GCL	G	Room?	869–913
GCM	G	Room	864–905
GCN	G	Room	870–899
GCO	G	Undefined	
GCP	G	Room?	957–937
GCQ	G	Room?	
GCR	G	Undefined	869–889
GDE	G	Room	869–900
GDF	G	Room	865–919
GDG	G	Room	885–937
GDH	G	Room	864–928
GDJ	G	Room	875–932
GDK	G	Room	872–930
GDL	G	Room	887–951
GDP	G	Room	868–906
GDR	G	Room	860–899

Table 3.56—*Continued*

Locus	Area	Description	Levels (inches)
GDS	G	Room	859–904
GDS	G	Room	909–946
GDT	G	Room	880–906
GDU	G	Room	816–870
GDV	G	Courtyard? and Pit	887–926
GDW	G	Room	893–936
GDY	G	Room	927–952
GDZ	G	Room	876–966
GEA	G	Room	883–962
GEC	G	Undefined	882–939
GED	G	Undefined	874–912
GEF	G	Room?	877–932
GEK	G	Undefined	882–941
GEL	G	Room	891–947
GEM	G	Undefined	925–933
GEN	G	Undefined	872–939
GEO	G	Room?	918–940
GER	G	Room	877–947
GET	G	Room	882–955
GFA	G	Room	892–918
GFB	G	Room	891–924
GFC	G	Room	888–929
GFD	G	Street	
GFE	G	Room	892–933
GFF	G	Room	867–907
GFG	G	Undefined	
GFP	G	Room	907–942
GFV	G	Room	865–940
GFW	G	Room	896–953
GFY	G	Room?	902–928
GFZ	G	Room	863–911
GGA, GGF, GDX	G	Large Pit	676–882
GGB	G	Undefined	900–937
GGC	G	Undefined	891–942
GGD	G	Room	887–936
GGE	G	Room?	894–941
GHF	G	Room	869–920
GHH	G	Undefined	861–933
GHJ	G	Undefined	875–918
GJM	G	Room?	927–967
GJO	G	Room	891–941

Houses and their Furnishings

Beth Shemesh (Map Reference 147/128)

The ancient site of Beth Shemesh is located in the Sorek valley, 20 km
west of Jerusalem. The town was built on a ridge extending into the
valley and occupied 2.8 hectares. Excavations at Beth Shemesh were
carried out during five seasons, 1928, 1929, 1930, 1931 and 1933 under
the direction of Elihu Grant of Haverford College (Grant 1934: 1).
Grant was assisted, during the 1929 season, by C. S. Fisher who
drew the plans of the various occupation levels (Grant 1932: 11). In
addition, Albright's work at Tell Beit Mirsim, beginning in 1926,
served as an important resource for Grant in his analysis of pottery
from the various strata of Beth Shemesh. However, like Albright,
Grant depended on architectural features to determine the stratigraphy
and phasing. In this method, loci were not named until a room or
other feature was identified. As a result, the location of artefacts was
frequently unclear both in horizontal and vertical specification (Grant
1933: 5-6). In spite of this weakness, many ceramic vessels and artefacts were assigned to each locus and even related to the floor level.
Some were known to be above, upon or under the floor or wall
foundations. With this information, certain activity areas can be
identified in the Middle and Late Bronze structures.

The earliest structural remains, uncovered in all areas, were those
from the Middle Bronze Age while the most recent structure was the
Byzantine monastery. In order to discuss, with some precision, the
structures from the Bronze Age, the excavated areas have been
grouped together by location and renamed: the western section (1928,
1929 and 1930 trenches), the central section (1933 trench), and the
eastern section (1931 trench).

Stratum V—Western Section (Fig. 36)
The excavations in the western section were carried out during three
seasons, the second lasting for five full months. This area extended
from the 1912 excavation of D. Mackenzie up to and beyond the western city wall. In several places, Grant reached bedrock (Stratum 6)
and his intention seemed to be to turn over the entire mound (1932:
41). Because he left standing the walls of later structures until he had
completely exposed the earlier stratum, it was difficult for him to
study the structural phases and transitions of each stratum. However,
he did distinguish a late Middle Bronze phase, above bedrock, that was

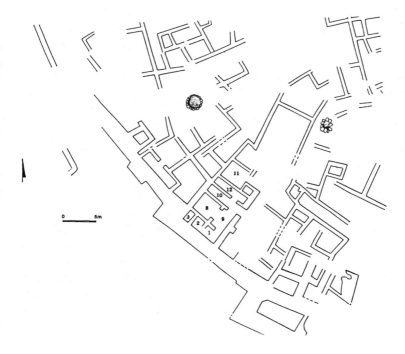

Figure 36. *Beth Shemesh Stratum V Western Section, after Grant 1933*

partially reused during the succeeding Late Bronze Age.

In the western section, the most coherent structure was a house built against the city wall near the south gate. This house, reused and enlarged in Stratum IV, does not appear to be completely preserved in Stratum V. Only rooms 1, 2, 3, 8, 9 and 10 (Fig. 36) can be identified with certainty as belonging to the house in its earliest phase (Grant and Wright 1939: 29). Additional Stratum V structures[1] were recognized, one to the northwest—L. 73, 74, 75, 79 (see Chapter 4, Fig. 65b). A series of rooms in the northeast may also have been part of Stratum V occupation (L. 161–93, see Chapter 4, Fig. 65c). However, these rooms were not distinguished from the Stratum 4 loci and no finds from these rooms were assigned to Stratum V.

Unfortunately for this analysis, the number of finds assigned to Stratum V in the western section are too few to determine the range of activities that occurred in these rooms (Table 3.57). The store jar from Room 9 of the southern house indicates food storage but does not confirm the exclusive function of Room 9 as a storeroom. While the shape and size of the rooms themselves may give some clue to their original function, any functional designations must remain tentative. Wright suggested that Room 10 served as a stairway because of its narrow shape. However, he also found evidence for three doorways into this room which makes it difficult to imagine where the stairs were located (Grant and Wright 1939: 29). Because the house remains were not completely preserved, comparison with other Middle Bronze houses is not helpful at this point.

Table 3.57. *Beth Shemesh Western Section Stratum V—*
Finds and Functional Classes

Locus	Finds	Functional Class
1	1 jug	food preparation/storage
9	1 narrow-neck jar	liquid storage
23	bone button	adornment
41	gold bead	adornment
	bronze toggle pin	adornment
41nr	glass bead	adornment

1. Rooms 73-79 were designated as a Stratum V, Middle Bronze Age structure on the basis of the similarity of construction techniques with those employed in the southern house, that is all major walls were two rows of stone thick. Repairs or additions to House 73-79 were built with single row walls (Grant and Wright 1939:30).

Stratum V—Central Section (Fig. 37)

The central section was located to the east of Grant's 1930 excavation area in the western section and north of Mackenzie's trench. Remains from the Middle Bronze Age were separated from the superimposed Late Bronze phases. A series of rooms, uncovered above bedrock, may not have been part of the same structure. Nor is it certain that these rooms constituted a complete building. In fact, the building techniques employed reflect two different styles of wall construction: what Grant called the typical Middle Bronze Age style of two row walls and the single stone thick walls which he assigned to the Late Bronze Age (1934: 1). The contemporaneity of these Stratum V rooms was based on their position beneath the earliest Late Bronze Age structures[1] and on their Middle Bronze Age ceramic corpus.

Only two rooms yielded assemblages diagnostic for domestic activities, L. 539A and 584, while a third was suggestive, L. 581 (Table 3.58). Although 90% of the finds from Room 539A were used in food preparation or consumption, the assemblage is not a strong tool kit when compared to the paradigm for these activities. The similarity coefficient is less than 100 (89.5 or 44.5%). On the other hand, the finds from Room 584 clearly indicate storage facilities with a similarity coefficient of 112 or 56%. Because the walls preserved in this area seem to reflect more than one phase, they may not constitute a complete room. As a result, contamination of the storage assemblage remains a distinct possibility.

The walls of the third room (L. 581) with evidence of domestic activity were not completely preserved (Fig. 37). Indeed, the finds themselves, 1 bowl, a cooking pot and a juglet, constitute such a small assemblage that they are not statistically significant. However, in themselves, they are all related to food preparation. Such activity is to be expected in view of the proximity of L. 581 to the other rooms where domestic activities were probably carried out.

Several other well preserved rooms were recorded (570, 579, 583, and 590). As can been seen (Table 3.58), the finds registered from each locus are too few for analysis. Taken together, the majority of finds, 77%, were related to food preparation or storage. The

---

1. The plans, as published, do not include elevations although it is certain that Fisher recorded numerous levels (see the greatly reduced plans in Grant 1929: 217, 219, 221). In view of this situation, comparison of levels by me was not possible.

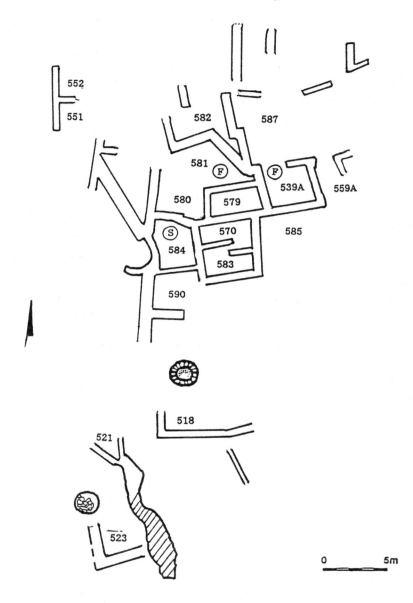

Figure 37. *Beth Shemesh Stratum V Central Section, after Grant 1934: Map IV*

remaining items were associated with personal adornment, lighting and various unknown activities.

The eastern section did not yield any complete rooms in Stratum V. As a result, only the rooms described above can be attributed to the Middle Bronze Age. Because no complete house was recovered, the arrangement of rooms and the distribution of activity areas cannot be described with certainty. What does seem apparent, is that there were no large courtyards where food preparation and other activities occurred together. As an example, Room 539A, which clearly functioned in a food preparation capacity, measured 3.4 × 3.0 m, a typical roofed room size. So too, the largest room in the western section, L. 8, was 3.0 × 3.0 m.

Wright's suggestion that Room 10 in the Western Section house was a stairway must be related to the possibility of a second storey. The width of the wall foundations certainly supports this possibility. In the western area, the walls of the southern house were c. 65 cm thick and in the central area they ranged from 75–100 cm. Such wide foundations could support at least two stories. This may account for the small number of artefacts recovered from the ground floor rooms. In the case of Room 539A, the upper level that collapsed on top of the Stratum V room may have been the upper storey. A jug, attributed to Stratum 4a, may have been part of the remains of such a room (Grant 1934: 25).

Table 3.58. *Beth Shemesh Central Section Stratum V—Finds and Functional Classes*

Locus	Finds	Functional Class
518	1 jar	storage
	1 whorl	textile production
523	1 bowl	food preparation/consumption
	stone-lined circle	unknown
539A	1 bowl	food preparation/consumption
	4 jugs	food preparation/storage
	1 vase	food preparation/storage
	1 toggle pin	adornment
551	1 cooking pot	food preparation
	clay stopper	lid
552	1 bowl	food preparation/consumption
	2 jars	storage
581	1 bowl	food preparation/consumption
	1 cooking pot	food preparation
	1 juglet	multipurpose

Table 3.58—*Continued*

Locus	Finds	Functional Class
583	1 jug	food preparation/storage
	flint blade	tool
584	1 wide-neck jar	dry storage
	jars	storage
	1 jug	food preparation/storage
	cooking pots	food preparation
	gaming board	recreation

The similarity coefficient for L. 584 is 112 or 56% when compared to the storage paradigm.

| 586 | 1 lamp | lighting |
| 587 | 1 jar | storage |

Table 3.59. *Beth Shemesh Middle Bronze Age Loci Stratum V*

Locus	Area	Description	Similarity Coeffficient
1	AA 29	Room	
2	AA 29	Room	
3	AA 29	Room	
8	AA 29	Room	
9	AA 29	Room	
10	AA 29	Stairway	
182	AB 30	Room	
183	AB 30	Room	
184	AB 30	Room	
483A		Undefined	
518		Room?	
523		Room?	
539A		Room	
549		Undefined	
551		Room?	
552		Room?	
556		Undefined	
559A		Undefined	
570		Room	
579		Room	
580		Room	
581		Room	
582		Room	
584		Room	112 or 56%
587		Undefined	
590		Room	

Additional Sites Based on Preliminary Publication

The Middle Bronze Age sites studied so far are those that have been extensively exposed to that level, such as Megiddo, or those sites where little or no subsequent occupation occurred. Such sites include Khirbet el-Meshash, Hazor, where only Late Bronze Age occupation overlaid the Middle Bronze houses, and Tell el-'Ajjul, where a similar situation existed. There are, however, numerous sites where Middle Bronze Age domestic structures have been excavated in limited areas revealing only a few rooms with domestic artefacts. Most of these excavated remains are published only in preliminary reports, as was Ta'anach, or in annual archaeological news and notes from the field. Because of the nature of this study, only sites with published artefacts and ceramic vessels can be utilized in functional and spatial analysis. Nevertheless, it is my concern to document the domestic structures referred to in the archaeological literature and comment on the extent of their preservation and their usefulness in understanding ancient houses.

Tell Ta'anach (Map Reference 170/214)

Ancient Ta'anach was located in the Jezreel Plain, 8 km southeast of Megiddo. The heavily fortified mound, now covering 4.5 hectares, includes the remains of occupation dating from the Early Bronze Age through the Persian period. Evidence for Roman and Byzantine occupation has been located at the base of the tell, while an Abbasid period fortress has been identified on the tell itself. Excavations were carried out by E. Sellin during 1902–1904, and, much later, by a joint American Schools of Oriental Research and Concordia Seminary expedition directed by Paul W. Lapp in 1963, 1966 and 1968. Structures dating to MB IIC and LB I were uncovered by both excavation projects, although it was Lapp who realized that the destruction at the end of MB IIC did not affect the whole site. The evidence for continuous occupation is even more important for understanding the history of this site and its subsequent destruction (Lapp 1969: 4-5).

MB IIC

The earliest Middle Bronze Age occupation excavated in the southwest quadrant of the tell included several rooms surrounding a larger room or courtyard. The walls of these rooms were only one stone thick, and probably did not support an upper storey. While several features are visible in the photograph (Lapp 1969: Fig. 15; no plan has yet been published), the details of these installations are lacking. Lapp suggested that these rooms were related to the West Building excavated by Sellin as service rooms of a large residence. Because of the limited publication, it is not possible to evaluate this judgment or determine whether these rooms could have been part of a distinct domestic structure.

A second phase of building was cut through the 0.8 m of fill that covered the earlier rooms. The walls of this new phase were two stones thick, considerably more substantial than the previous phase. Although Lapp judged the walls to have been constructed during the MB IIC period, he was equally certain that the features and artefact remains reflected LB I occupation. While domestic activities were indicated by various features within the rooms, Lapp again identified these rooms as part of a service quarter for the West Building (1969: 23).

To the south of the public quarters associated with the West Building was a series of structures located between a north–south street and the earlier MB IIC casemate fortifications along the west edge of the tell. Similar structures, east of the street, corresponded in their stratigraphic phasing to those on the west (MB IIC followed by two phases of LB I). Because the LB I phases were a rebuilding of earlier structures, Lapp preferred to date these rooms, including the so-called LB I Building (see below), to MB IIC–LB I (1969: 27). The structures themselves were classified by the excavator as an insula of workrooms or shops bounded by streets (1969: 25, 27, Fig. 17). Until a final publication appears, there is no way to substantiate this view or to compare the finds with those from clearly domestic structures.

The only other evidence of MB IIC occupation was found on the southern shoulder, below the Early Bronze Age fortifications. This consisted of one cave dwelling that contained a bench with several intact ceramic vessels. In front of this cave was a plastered floor with a jar burial that contained an infant under the floor (Lapp 1969: 30). Unfortunately, no vessels from this locus have been published and therefore it is not possible to determine whether they represent a domestic corpus or an industrial complex.

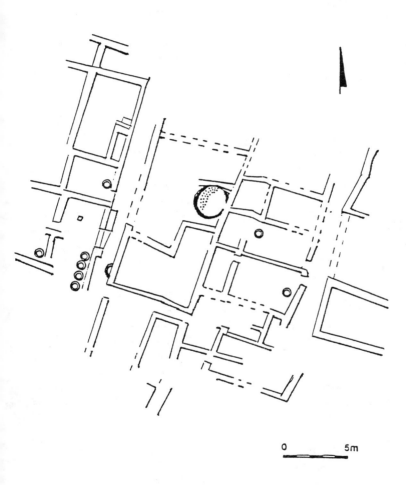

Figure 38. *Tell en-Nagila, after Amiran 1967: 43*

Tell Nagila (Map Reference 127/101)

Situated in the inner coastal plain, 28 km east of Gaza, Tell en-Nagila rises on the west bank of Nahal Shiqma. The tell is a square mound with rounded corners that covers 2.5 hectares. The only excavations at the site were directed by Ruth Amiran, assisted by A. Eitan, in 1962 and 1963. These excavations were sponsored by the Institute for Mediterranean Studies (R.A. Mitchell) (Avi Yonah: III, 894). The best preserved settlement on the tell dates to the Middle Bronze Age II period, Strata 11–7. Three strata, 9–7, share a similar plan and seem to represent three phases of one MB II stratum (Fig. 38). Although only a limited area of these strata was exposed in Area A, several blocks of houses were uncovered. The houses shared party walls and consisted of several small rooms and one larger room. Amiran identified the larger rooms as courtyards even though these rooms frequently contained pillar bases indicating that they had been roofed. She judged that the court was only partially roofed above the section of floor that was paved (Amiran and Eitan 1967: 43-44). Because detailed plans have not been published, no final judgment can be made concerning the consistent treatment of the floors and the relationship of the flagstone paving to the pillar bases.

Features within the houses included ovens, benches, pebble-lined depressions to hold vessels and plastered silos. A ceramic assemblage from a typical 'courtyard' included 5 narrow-neck storejars, 5 dipper juglets, 7 bowls and a cooking pot. These vessels were accompanied by flint blades and grinding stones (Amiran and Eitan 1967: 44). Actually, this assemblage compares very favourably with the paradigm for food preparation or consumption. The amount of storage represented by the jars may argue against an open court, but more examples are needed to confirm this view.

As we have already seen, the location of the oven in an enclosed area is not a foolproof indicator of a courtyard. Here, at Tell Nagila, six ovens were located immediately inside a doorway, one oven was near the back wall of a large room opposite the doorway, and another oven appears to have been placed in the corner of a room. It is possible that all of these locations were roofed rooms rather than courtyards.

Conclusions

House Walls

The houses of Middle Bronze Age Palestine, presented in this study, share a series of characteristics, both in architectural style and construction techniques, that are of interest in understanding ancient houses. Although few houses were recovered with their walls intact above the foundation level, it is generally assumed that the majority of Palestinian houses were built with mud brick walls on stone foundations (Aurenche 1977: 161). The width of these foundations is understood to be indicative of the strength of the walls and the number of possible stories in the house. While it has not been possible to gather information on wall foundation width for all sites, both because of excavation techniques and the style of the published plans, certain site reports provide data that demonstrate the range of widths typical of the Middle Bronze Age and the various construction techniques employed.

The most fragile house walls, those at Tell Ta'anach, were one stone wide and measured c. 40–50 cm thick. More typical were the walls at Hazor Area C that were two stones thick and measured 50–70 cm thick (Table 3.60). Walls of comparable thickness can be seen at Khirbet el-Meshash (Table 3.61), and in the houses of Strata E and D at Tell Beit Mirsim (Table 3.62), and the successive structures at Tel Mevorakh (Table 3.63).

Table 3.60. *Hazor Area C Stratum 3 Wall Thickness*

Wall Locus	Thickness in centimeters											
	35	40	45	50	55	60	65	70	75	80	90	100
6059						X						
6093						X						
6122						X						
6123								X				
6161								X				
6525								X				
6526								X				
6529						X						
6531						X						

Table 3.60—Continued

Wall Locus	Thickness in centimeters											
	35	40	45	50	55	60	65	70	75	80	90	100
6532						X						
6534			X									
6539			X									
6540					X							
6541			X									
6542		X										
6544							X					
6549					X							
6552											X	
6553							X					
6554					X							
6556							X					
6557										X		
6560					X							

Table 3.61. *Khirbet el-Meshash MB Wall Thickness*

Wall Locus	Thickness in centimeters											
	35	40	45	50	55	60	65	70	75	80	90	100
815				X	X	X	X	X				
808				X	X	X	X	X				
807				X	X	X	X	X				
Back Wall								X				
806						X						

Table 3.62. *Tell Beit Mirsim Wall Thickness—Selected Loci*

Wall Locus	Thickness in centimeters											
	35	40	45	50	55	60	65	70	75	80	90	100
Stratum G												
House									X			
Stratum D												
South House					X							
North House						X						
Patrician House												X+

Table 3.63. *Tell Mevorakh Wall Thicknesses—Selected Loci*

Wall Locus	Thickness in centimeters											
	35	40	45	50	55	60	65	70	75	80	90	100
Stratum 15											X	
Stratum 13					X							
Stratum 12					X							

Several conclusions can be drawn from these tables. It appears that the standard wall thickness for a house with one storey was approximately 50–70 cm whereas that for a two storey house, or prestige dwelling, was c. 0.7–1.0+ m. A mud brick wall 50 cm thick could probably sustain a second storey but comparable interior walls, appropriately spaced, would also have been necessary. A good example is the house in Stratum G at Tell Beit Mirsim. The interior walls were the same thickness as the exterior ones, 80 cm. In the main room, a row of pillar bases divided the 4.5 m width of the room and provided additional support for the ceiling and for rooms on the upper floor.

An interesting feature of the Middle Bronze Age house at Hazor Area C is the strength of the interior walls which were 70 cm thick whereas the external walls were 55–60 cm. The main room (L. 6205), 3.9 m wide, did not contain any sign of pillar bases. It has been suggested that this room served as a courtyard but the thickness of the walls along each side of this room suggests that it was roofed. Without the evidence of pillar bases, however, one cannot be certain that the upper floor was divided into rooms. The roof may have served as a terrace for work areas or summer sleeping quarters. The sturdy wall construction could easily have supported upper storey rooms over the smaller rooms on either side of Locus 6205 (L. 6191, 6192, 6103 and 6203). The preserved height of these walls, c. 0.2–1.1 m above the floors, makes it very clear that more than foundation levels are being considered here. Indeed, the use of stone walls above the floor level seems to have been more common in the regions where stones were plentiful and good soil was reserved for agriculture.

The Courtyard

A major transition in domestic architecture and spatial organization occurred during the Middle Bronze Age. Houses which had rooms with pillar supports, in one phase, were rebuilt along the same lines without pillars (see Tell Beit Mirsim above). Several factors could account for this change. It could indicate a difference in the type and availability of roofing materials, or the use of the roof as a terrace rather than as the floor of second storey rooms, or the elimination of the roof altogether and the transformation of the main room into an open court.

Wright suggests two categories of Middle Bronze Age houses, the horizontal house with all rooms on the ground floor, and tower houses with more than one storey. In the latter category, the ground floor served as a yard or court where cooking, storage and work areas were located. In these structures, the principal living rooms were located on the upper floor (Wright 1985: 292). Wright sees the Patrician house at Tell Beit Mirsim as a tower house with an upper storey of rooms that open onto a terrace above the main room (1985: 292). This interpretation does not consider the possibility that the main room on the lower floor was unroofed.

In order to evaluate these various alternatives, comparison of supposed Middle Bronze Age courtyards with the courtyards and living room areas of traditional style Near Eastern houses could be useful. In her study of village architecture in Iran, Watson presented plans of those houses she was allowed to enter. Each house had a major room which served as the main living room. The activities performed in this room included food preparation, consumption, storage and sleeping. Where there were two living rooms in one housing unit, one was used for cooking and the other for eating, entertaining and sleeping. Most of these houses were built beside a private courtyard, although, in some cases, the court was shared with another house (Houses 16 and 44). The largest courtyard (187 m^2) was shared by two families who had, between them, three living rooms. In order to understand the relationship of the courtyard as an activity area to the living room, I have compared the size of selected living rooms to those of their respective courtyards (Table 3.63). The ratio of courtyard space to living room is more than 2:1 for Houses 4, 8, 28 and 36. For the remaining houses the ratio is 3:1 (7, 13, 16, 17, 19, 20, 21, 23, 32). The size of these courtyards suggests the space necessary for their double function as work area and animal pen.

The size of possible courtyards in Middle Bronze Age houses tells a very different story (Table 3.65). First of all, the 'courtyard' is the largest room in the house, sometimes, it may be argued, the only large food preparation and consumption area, or likely living room; for example, the Patrician House and Hazor House 6205 (see Figs. 3, 27). In other cases, more than one large room can be identified in the same house, such as South House at Tell Beit Mirsim (Fig. 26). These large rooms, however, do not compare favourably in size with the courtyards at Hasanabad. At Hasanabad, the smallest courtyard was 75 m^2 (House 4) whereas at Tell Beit Mirsim the average small 'courtyard' was 27 m^2. The largest courtyard at Hasanabad, 225 m^2, overshadows Room 2, the largest walled space in the Patrician House at Tell Beit Mirsim, 79 m^2, and L. 6205 at Hazor, 28 m^2.

Another way of looking at these data is to compare the average size of all courtyards at Hasanabad with the possible courtyards from Middle Bronze Age houses. At Hasanabad, the average size was 130.4 m^2, whereas for Palestinian houses the average was 38.1 m^2. Excluding Room 2 of the Patrician House, which was significantly larger than other possible ancient courtyards, the average for Middle Bronze Age 'courtyards' was 32.9 m^2, very close to the average size of living rooms at Hasanabad (28.4 m^2).

This analysis cannot prove that all large rooms in Middle Bronze Age houses were roofed. What is suggested is that the function of these rooms or 'courtyards' was very different from the known courtyards at Hasanabad.

Table 3.64. *Hasanabad—Size of Courtyards and Living Rooms*

House	Room	Size (m)	Area (m²)
4	Courtyard	15 × 5	75
	Living room	8 × 4	32
7	Courtyard	10.5 × 7.5	78.7
	Living room-2	7.0 × 5.0	35
8	Courtyard	12.5 × 12.3	153.75
	Living room	7.5 × 2.5	19.5
13	Courtyard	20 × 7.5	
		15 × 5.0	225
	Living room	1.8 × 2.5	
	Aywan (iwan)	4.5 × 2.0	21
16	Courtyard	12 × 10	120
	Living room	5.5 × 3.0	
	Aywan	3.5 × 2.5	25.2
17	Courtyard	20 × 7	140
	Living room	8 × 3.2	25.6
19	Courtyard	13 × 10	130
	Living room	4 × 3	12

Table 3.64—*Continued*

House	Room	Size (m)	Area (m²)
20	Courtyard	10.2 × 12	125.4
	Living room-2	7.8 × 6	46.8
21	Courtyard	12 × 10	120
	Living room	5 × 3.0	
	Aywan	3 × 2	21
23	Courtyard	14 × 12	168
	Living room	9.8 × 2.5	22.4
28	Courtyard	22 × 8.5	187
	Living room-2	3.8 × 3	
		8.5 × 4	45.4
	Living room	9.0 × 4	36
32	Courtyard	12.5 × 7.5	93.7
	Living room	6.5 × 3.5	22.7
36	Courtyard		79.5
	Living room-2	9.3 × 3.5	32.5

Table 3.65. *The Size of the Largest Room in Selected Middle Bronze Age Houses*

Site	House/Locus	Size (m)	Area (m²)
Hazor	6205	7.0 × 4.0	28.0
	6199	5.4 × 4.0	21.6
Megiddo	5034	8.0 × 4.3	34.4
	5094	9.1 × 4.2	38.1
	3096N	6.8 × 4.8	32.6
	3046E	7.0 × 4.8	33.6
Tell Beit Mirsim	South 5-6	10.4 × 4.2	43.6
	East 1-7	7.9 × 4.0	31.6
	Patrician 2	12.1 × 6.6	79.8

Mean (not including Patrician House Room 2) = 32.9 m²

Functional and Spatial Analysis

While it is apparent that different activities would take place in court-yards depending on the season, Watson has documented the range of features and items of equipment related to the activities usually carried out in courtyards at Hasanabad. These features include open grain pits and a summer hearth associated with food preparation, a small water trough, a limestone slab for salt, mangers and hitches related to animal husbandry, and miscellaneous items such as a rock platform and water bag, various tools and a broom, and a drain (Watson 1979:

157-59). The most obvious conclusion from the data concerning courtyard size is that the small size of ancient 'courtyards' suggests that they functioned differently than those at Hasanabad.

The determination of activities carried out in the largest room of an ancient house is difficult, both because of the uncertainty regarding the identification of the room as a roofed area or as a courtyard, and because of the incomplete preservation of the functional tool kits. However, several examples of artefact assemblages can be cited: Hazor–Stratum 3, Locus 6205, included an oven and a mortar along with vessels and objects related to food preparation. In addition there were vessels for storage, and special or status type artefacts. At Tell Beit Mirsim, the largest room in South House (Stratum E) included such a diverse assemblage that it is difficult to identify one activity likely to have been performed there to the exclusion of others. There were ceramic forms associated with food preparation, consumption and storage along with jewellery and status items. Precisely because no one tool kit dominated the assemblage, the identification of this room with a living room, rather than an unroofed courtyard, is strongly suggested.

Another criterion for identifying ancient courtyard areas may be the presence of pits sunk in the floor. At Hasanabad, Watson noted that grain storage pits were located both in the living room (8 pits) and in the courtyard (3 pits). These pits were used to store unmilled grain surpluses (Watson 1979: 122-28). As a result of these observations, this feature in itself is no longer enough to identify an enclosed area of an ancient house as a courtyard.

On the basis of the analysis undertaken here, no unequivocal identification of an ancient courtyard has been made. The Middle Bronze Age houses did not include any features or artefacts that point to activities related to animal husbandry. The only activities represented in the artefact assemblages involved food preparation, storage and cooking. Miscellaneous personal possessions completed these assemblages. Other domestic activities, such as textile production, have been identified but were not located consistently in a particular space in ancient houses. In fact, this is an activity that can be moved depending on the season. A variety of tools and weapons have also been found. While these items may very well have been in secondary usage as household blades, no clear associations have been seen that would clarify their precise function in a discrete tool kit. Therefore, these weapons may have been personal possessions that were evidence of status, wealth or profession.

Finally, many small items related to recreation, adornment, cosmetic use and religious belief have been found randomly scattered throughout the ancient houses. Such finds have witnessed to the range of activities and interests of the inhabitants but have not made it possible to pinpoint the room or part of a room where such items were habitually used. In fact, the presence of such personal possessions and status items in the largest room suggests, very strongly, that these areas were roofed and served as a living room rather than an open courtyard, or that a living room was located on an upper storey. In either case, such rooms would have been roofed.

The location of a bin against the outside wall of a house could be indicative of the way in which animals, at least donkeys, were cared for. Two examples of such bins were identified: Hazor Area C, L. 6212 (Fig. 3) and Tell Nagila (Fig. 38). Numerous bins within houses have also been recognized but their location in interior rooms and their close association with food preparation/consumption assemblages suggest that these were used for food storage and not as mangers.

Chapter 4

LATE BRONZE AGE HOUSES

Introduction

Archaeological exposure of Late Bronze Age occupation levels is somewhat more extensive than for Middle Bronze Age remains. At certain sites, the Late Bronze structures were found immediately below top soil, such as at Hazor (the lower city), Tell el-'Ajjul and Tell el-Far'ah (S). The result, in these cases, is that numerous houses and other structures have been completely revealed. At the same time, the uppermost level also suffered the greatest damage by erosion and ploughing, increasing the possibility of contaminated strata. The advantage and limitations of such a situation affect the usefulness of the recovered data.

Many sites in this study with Middle Bronze Age occupation were also inhabited during the Late Bronze Age, but, in many cases, destruction or a gap in occupation separated the respective strata. The sites chosen for functional analysis are those with the most complete publication of Late Bronze Age remains. Other sites, published in a preliminary manner, are considered in a special section at the end of this chapter.

Table 4.1. *Sites with Late Bronze Age Strata*

Site	LB I	LB IIA	LB IIB
Hazor	XIV/2	XIII/1B	XIII/1A
Tell Abu Hawam	VA (1 2 3 4 5)		VB
Megiddo	IX	VIII	VIIB VIIA
Ta'anach	LB I		
Beth Shan	IX	VIII	VII VI
Tell el-Far'ah (N)		Niveau 4	
Aphek			12 11
Shechem	XIV	XIII	XII
Bethel		LB IIA	LB IIB

Table 4.1—*Continued*

Site	LB I				LB IIA	LB IIB	
Beth-shemesh	IVA				IVB		
Gezer	XVII				XVI	XV	XIV
Tell Batash	X	IX	VIII	VII		VI	
Ashdod					XVI	XV	XIV
Tel Mor	11	10			9	8	7
Lachish					VII	VI	
Tell el-Hesi	IIb-II				III	IVb-IV	
Tell Halif	X	IXB			IXA	VIII	
Tell Beit Mirsim	C1				C2	B1	
Khirbet Rabud					LB 2	LB 1	
Tell esh-Sheri'a	XII				XI	X	IX
Tell el-'Ajjul	City II						
Tell el-Far'ah (S)						Y	

Hazor (Map Reference 203/269)

Bronze Age occupation in the Lower City of Hazor began in the Middle Bronze period. The remains of late MB IIC domestic architecture were uncovered only in Area C (see above). More extensive Late Bronze Age occupation was uncovered in three areas, C, F and 210 (Yadin 1972: 28, 47). In both Areas C and F, the domestic remains were associated with cultic structures or shrines. Although few complete houses were fully exposed, the structural remains from these areas provide sufficient evidence for a study of Late Bronze Age houses at Hazor. In fact, Hazor has some of the best preserved and excavated examples of second millennium houses.

Area C

The excavation of Late Bronze Age strata at Hazor began in 1955 in Area C of the Lower City. Located in the southwest corner of the enclosure, this area abutted the earthen rampart (Yadin *et al.* 1958: 71). Built into the rampart itself was a one room structure, identified by the excavators as a shrine (L. 6136, see below). To the north and east, L. 6136 was surrounded by a cluster of buildings (Yadin *et al.* 1960: 95-96). These structures represent the latest strata of occupation

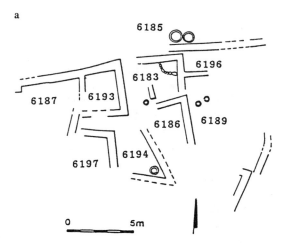

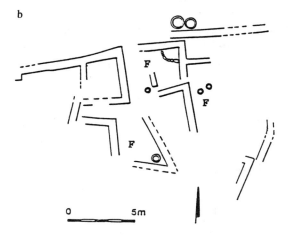

Figure 39. *Hazor Area C Stratum 2, after Yadin et al. 1960: Pl. CCVII*

in the Lower City, Strata 1A and 1B, both dated by the excavators to
LB II.[1]

Stratum 2 (Fig. 39). The remains of Stratum 2 were uncovered only
in the southeastern corner of Area C, above the Middle Bronze Age
houses. Although a small section of Stratum 3 wall line was reused in
this phase, the alignment of the major rooms was very different
(Yadin *et al.* 1960: 92). Indeed, Stratum 2, dated to LB I, was
separated from the Middle Bronze Age houses by a layer of debris. In
the same way, the plan of Stratum 1B showed no continuity with the
fragmentary remains of Stratum 2 (Yadin *et al.* 1958: 92).

The structures of Stratum 2 were not exposed sufficiently to reveal
complete building plans (Fig. 39). However, the pottery, objects and
features from these loci can be analysed in such a way that tool kits
reflecting various domestic activities are identifiable. Since the purpose of this study is to associate such tool kits with domestic architecture in order to specify activity areas and room arrangement, only
limited analysis of this Hazor stratum will be undertaken.

Based on a functional analysis of the ceramic vessels, objects and
features, 87% of the finds from Stratum 2 were related to food preparation, consumption and storage (Table 4.2). In view of the fact that
no finds were reported for three out of ten loci (Rooms 6187, 6193
and 6196), this is a very heavy concentration of finds associated with a
set of related activities. For example, Room 6183 had a similarity
coefficient of 143.8 or 71.9% when compared with the food preparation and consumption paradigm.

Table 4.2. *Hazor Area C Stratum 2—Finds and Functional Classes*

Locus	Finds	Functional Class
6183	5 bowls	food preparation/consumption
	3 kraters	food preparation/consumption
	1 cooking pot	food preparation
	2 narrow-neck jars	liquid storage
	1 loom weight	textile production
	basalt mortar	food preparation
	bin	storage/manger

---

1. Wood demonstrates that Hazor, Area C, Stratum 1A pottery is contemporary
with Gezer/Ashdod Stratum XV, LB IIB1. On this basis, he judges that Late Bronze
Age occupation ended earlier here than at some other sites (1985: 311).

Table 4.2—*Continued*

Locus	Finds	Functional Class

The similarity coefficient for L. 6183 is 143.8 or 71.9% when compared to the food preparation and consumption paradigm.

Locus	Finds	Functional Class
6185	6 bowls	food preparation/consumption
	1 krater	food preparation/consumption
	1 jar stand	storage
	oven	food preparation
	silo/bin	storage
6186	2 cooking pots	food preparation
	1 juglet	multipurpose
	1 jar stand	food preparation/storage
	stone tool	unknown
	bronze dagger	weapon
6189	2 bowls	food preparation/consumption
	1 krater	food preparation/consumption
	1 narrow-neck jar	liquid storage
	2 mortars	food preparation
6194	oven	food preparation
6197	1 bowl/chalice	food preparation/consumption
	1 bone whorl	textile production
6264	1 cooking pot	food preparation
	1 lamp	lighting

Several other areas were clearly associated with food preparation: L. 6194 and 6185 both contained ovens, and L. 6189 had two basalt grinding bowls *in situ*. A third grinding bowl was located in Room 6183. Food storage activities were represented in various loci by storejars. However, the main storage feature seems to have been the use of bins, one (L. 6033) was located in the corner of Room 6183, and a second was built beside the oven in L. 6185 (Yadin *et al.* 1958: 93). Because the walls were so poorly preserved in this area, one cannot determine whether these loci were all part of the same house. But the domestic character of the activities performed in these rooms is certain on the basis of the concentration of food preparation equipment. The only other activities suggested by the remaining finds from Stratum 2 were textile production (1 loom weight and 1 whorl) and lighting.

Strata 1B and 1A. During excavation, it was difficult to distinguish clearly the Late Bronze Age building phases in certain loci along the east side of Area C. As a result, the room assemblages of pottery and objects from Stratum 1B may be somewhat contaminated.[1] In view of this situation, the finds attributed to these strata must be handled cautiously. On the other hand, near the earthen embankment on the west, clear Stratum 1A floors were found in many places, separated from Stratum 1B surfaces by as much as 1 m of debris. Consequently, it remains the case that the domestic structures of Stratum 1B provide the best evidence of Palestinian Late Bronze Age domestic architecture.

The loci in Area C whose stratification cannot be firmly established, such as those in deep probes or soundings,[2] will not be considered in this study. Other loci which are not useful include surface loci,[3] and those that were cancelled during excavation.[4] In addition, certain loci were not closely related to any architectural features, such as fragments of cobbles outside of Building 6063. Such loci[5] were too far removed from the rooms under consideration to contribute meaningfully to a functional study of the nearest structures, even though they may, in themselves, have been part of a deliberate construction technique.[6]

Shrine 6136 (Fig. 40). Two structures in Area C need special consideration, L. 6136 and 6211.[7] Locus 6136 is a one room structure, 16.1 m², built into the east side of the earthen rampart. In Stratum 1B, this room had benches along each interior wall including the terrace wall (L. 6134) on the west. In the middle of the west wall was a niche,

---

1. Aware of the lack of clear stratification along the east side of the excavation area, the excavators indicate doubt concerning a sure attribution of pottery by marking the stratum number with an asterisk, see Yadin *et al.* 1960: Pls. 117, 118, 123.

2. These loci are L. 6008, 6009, 6014, 6029, 6030, 6040, 6051, 5056, 6082, 6087, 6110, 6127 and 6247. Cobbles in Probe Locus 6014 may relate to Stratum 2 or 3, see below.

3. Locus 6062 cannot be related to the phases under discussion.

4. See locus lists, Yadin *et al.* 1958: 93-8, Yadin *et al.* 1960: 119-26.

5. For example, L. 6001, 6009, 6015, 6020, 6021, 6029, 6036 and 6041. Locus 6020 was so disturbed by plowing that no architectural remains were preserved.

6. These cobbled areas should be regarded as deliberately constructed features, rather than natural stone accumulations. The use of pebbles and/or cobble layers has a long history as a construction technique for pavements, damp layers or as an ingredient in plaster floors (Aurenche 1981: 16).

7. Another one room structure, L. 6025, will be discussed in the analysis of Stratum 1A remains below.

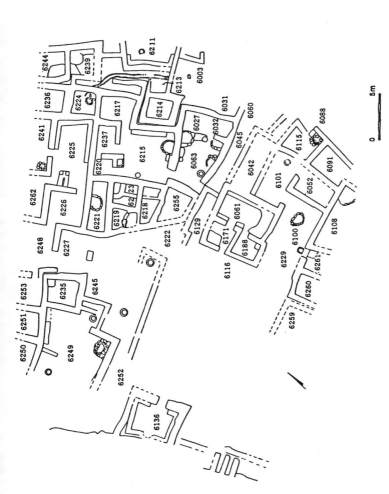

Figure 40. *Hazor Area C Stratum 1B, after Yadin et al. 1960: Pl. CCVIII*

L. 6142, and, in front of it, a roughly finished basalt slab (Fig. 42; Yadin *et al.* 1958: 87-90). These architectural elements clearly indicate that this was a special purpose structure and not a house.[1]

Two very distinct phases could be identified in the use history of this special room. The earlier phase, Stratum 1B, was that of its original construction. After a general destruction of Stratum 1B, Room 6136 and the niche were rebuilt (L. 6135) and many of its features reused (Fig 42). Because few artefacts were recovered from the earlier phase, it can be assumed that the most important objects were removed from the debris and employed in Stratum 1A, such as those found in Niche 6142 (1 basalt seated male figurine, 10 stelae and a lion orthostat). Because most of the ceramic vessels and artefacts were recovered from the later phase, which quickly succeeded the earlier one, only one assemblage has been compiled (Table 4.3). It is my view that this assemblage represents the tool kits characteristic of the activities performed in this unique structure during both strata.

Table 4.3. *Hazor Area C Stratum 1B-1A (L. 6135, 6136, 6142)—Finds and Functional Classes*

Locus	Finds	Functional Class
6136	20 bowls	food preparation/consumption
	8 chalices	food consumption/libation
	2 kraters	food preparation
	2 cooking pots	food preparation
	2 narrow-neck jars	liquid storage
	2 jugs	food preparation/storage
	2 juglets	multipurpose
	2 lamps	lighting
	bronze cymbals	music
	bronze bowl	special/status
	glass scepter	special/status
	2 basalt slabs	special/cultic
6142	1 jug	food preparation/storage
	items from 6135[2]	special/cultic

1. The loci connected with the shrine and its associated terrace walls that have been omitted from the loci under consideration include L. 6505, 6506, 6507, 6508, 6509, 6510, 6511, 6130, 6131, 6134, 6138, 6140, 6178, 6626.

2. The excavators assumed that many of the specialized items found in Stratum 1A loci were reused from Stratum 1B. There were some clear examples, that is the stelae found on the rampart outside the shrine, that demonstrated that this had indeed been the case (Yadin *et al.* 1958: 84-5).

Table 4.3—*Continued*

Locus	Finds	Functional Class
6135	2 bowls	food preparation/consumption
	1 juglet	multipurpose
	1 lamp	lighting
	dolerite macehead	weapon/status
	basalt disk with hole	unknown
	basalt statue	special/cultic
	10 stelae	special/cultic
	lion orthostat	special/cultic
	offering table	special/cultic
	stone phallus	special/cultic
	2 statuettes	special/cultic

A total of 69 artefacts and architectural features were recovered from Room 6136. Of these, 34% were specialized items that would be unlikely to appear in a domestic structure. The remaining 66% consisted of items that may have been used in a house. However, their numbers and association with such a large amount of special objects makes their ordinary functional classification questionable. The presence of cooking pots and kraters strongly implies food preparation but the number of bowls and chalices (30) far exceeds the number usually associated with a domestic context (10 or less). These everyday vessels could have been used for the preparation and consumption of a cultic meal or the care and feeding of the deity honoured in this cult room. While miniature vessels were found in the nearby domestic loci, none were reported for the cult room itself. This could imply that these vessels were used in the houses in a specialized function, possibly related to a continuation of the cult practised in Shrine 6136 (see Holladay 1987).

The excavators saw many parallels to the objects and ceramic vessels found in Room 6136 in the artefacts from Fosse Temples II and III at Lachish (Yadin *et al.* 1958: 85, 92). The contrast between the artefact corpus from the Hazor cult room with typical domestic assemblages confirms the designation of this building as a shrine (Yadin *et al.* 1960: 97).

A second unique structure (L. 6211), located along the eastern edge of the excavation area, was a broad room style building open on one side (Fig. 40). Because this structure was only one room and was not completely enclosed, it does not seem useful to include it in a study of house types. In fact, the finds consisted of unused ceramic vessels (Yadin *et al.* 1960: 104-106) and a bronze standard (Pl. 181) which suggest that this room served as a shop or specialized storeroom.

Stratum 1B (Figs. 40, 41). The remains of Stratum 1B were sufficiently well preserved to reveal the plan and features of six different structures, although only one (Building 6063) was completely excavated. Many walls were preserved to a height of 0.50 –0.70 m. In a few cases, a wall remained standing 1 m or more (the west wall of L. 6221). As a result, the location of doorways could clearly be seen where they existed. The problem of rooms without doorways will be discussed below.

House 6063 (Figs. 40, 41). In Stratum 1B, Building 6063 had two phases. During the latest phase, the central unit consisted of Rooms 6063, 6032, 6027, 6215, 6220, 6237 and 6217 (Fig. 40). The main entrance from Lane 6045 was into Room 6063, identified by the excavator as a workshop on the basis of its installations and finds. The installations included a shelf, a large bin, two rectangular installations and a circular structure. The generic labels assigned to these features indicate that their function was not immediately apparent. Perrot, the excavator of this area, suggested that the circular structure was an oven, and that one of the rectangular features was the base for a potter's wheel because an upper thrust bearing was found inside (Yadin *et al.* 1958: 77; Pl. 87 item 24). The number and variety of installations in this room are unusual. It may be that more than one activity is represented.

Room 6063 also contained a variety of ceramic vessels and objects that could identify this room as either a centre of food preparation or a craft and industry area. Indeed, certain objects were used in both types of activity areas; for example, basalt bowl grinders, pestles, saddle querns and funnels. Only the presence of artefacts exclusive to an activity can specify an area that contains such finds, since it is unlikely that these two activities would have occurred in the same space. Such functionally specific items would include a potter's wheel thrust bearing, forming tools or a potter's jar on the one hand, and, on the other hand, cooking pots,[1] baking trays and an oven. This is

1. Yassine lists a cooking pot in the ceramic assemblage of L. 6063 (Yassine 1974: 70) although no such vessel is listed in the Plates of Yadin *et al.* 1958, nor is

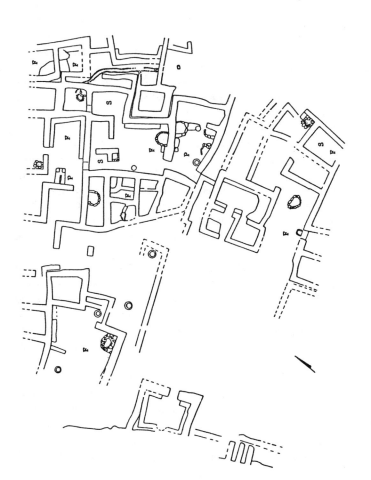

Figure 41. *Hazor Area C Stratum 1B, spatial distribution*

precisely the case with regard to Room 6063 which contained a potter's wheel and Room 6215, to the north, which included cooking pots, store jars and jugs in an assemblage that was very similar to that of L. 6063 (Table 4.4) but lacked a potter's wheel.[1]

In an attempt to determine more precisely the activities performed in L. 6063, comparison can be made with the typical paradigms of both food preparation and/or consumption and pottery production. The similarity coefficient for food preparation yielded 122 or 61% and that for pottery making 95 or 47.5%. Because only one potter's wheel was found along with a collection of food preparation items, that wheel, along with the numerous bins and shelves, results in only a weak fit when compared to the tool kit for a pottery production area. To the best of my knowledge, the rooms adjoining L. 6063, on the east (L. 6027 and 6032), do nothing to support this functional interpretation. Both rooms were stone paved, in contrast to the beaten earth floor of L. 6063, and contained few finds: a cooking pot in L. 6032, and 1 bowl and a juglet in L. 6027 (Table 4.4). At this distance from the oven, the cooking pot could have been either in storage or secondary use. Both vessels in L. 6027 could have served a variety of functions and have been found in association with both storage and craft activities.

The position of an oven near an entrance is a common feature in houses at Hazor (see Stratum 3 above and Area F below). At the same time, the presence of the oven is not necessarily an indicator of the location of other food preparation activities. While extensive activity related to food preparation and consumption was usually performed in the main living room space, the cooking itself could have been done elsewhere.

Room 6215, the largest room in House 6063, measured 5.0 × 5.4 m and seems to have served as the main living room. The variety of ceramic vessels, objects and installations (Table 4.4) testifies to a multi-functional use of space. The occurrence of storage vessels in front of the bench along the east wall suggests that the bench served as a shelf. The large number of these vessels (13) in contrast to the small

one mentioned in the text (Yadin *et al.* 1958: 77). The suggestion that a smashed 'cooking pot and a storejar were found on the masonry debris in the opening between' L. 6215 and 6063 may be the basis for his inclusion of the cooking pot in L. 6063 although this is not clear on the basis of the excavator's discussion (Yadin *et al.* 1960: 99).

number of reported bowls (4) weakened the comparison of the total room assemblage with the paradigm for food preparation and/or consumption. The similarity coefficient is 102 or 51%. While this assemblage is not a typical tool kit of any one activity, it clearly testifies to the multifunctional character of this living room area.

So far, the evidence for Building 6063 demonstrates that it was indeed a domestic structure. The finds from the small rooms surrounding Locus 6215 support this judgment. Room 6220, which opened directly onto Room 6215, was found full of smashed pithoi[1] and must have functioned as a storeroom. The distribution pattern of artefacts in a storeroom is considerably more homogeneous than that of food preparation or craft areas, making identification of the use of space, in this case, much easier. Typically, few other finds were reported: 1 clay 'button', 1 smashed store jar and a basalt grinding bowl (Yadin *et al.* 1960: 99).

The assemblage from a second storeroom (L. 6217) was somewhat less homogeneous (Table 4.4). Here 5 pithoi, a stone lid, 1 bowl and 1 jar were recorded along with a potter's wheel, a flat stone and a funnel. This assemblage has a similarity coefficient of 135 or 67.5% when compared to the storage paradigm. In the northwest corner of L. 6217, there was a small partition wall which may have served to support a pithos or store jar. That this low partition was associated with pottery production (Yadin *et al.* 1960: 99-100), has yet to be demonstrated. The fact that an upper potter's wheel and a flat stone were found in the room is insufficient, in itself, to support the identification of a pottery production area here. An ethnographic study of Cypriot potters by Gloria London found that potter's wheels were kept in storage during the season when pots were not in production.[2] The flat basalt stone may be related instead to food preparation activities, especially if the pithoi contained dried legumes or grains. The last of the three small rooms, L. 6237, was found empty, except for a bone handle(?) and a few sherds near the door into the main living room, L. 6215. Locus 6237 may have contained something that was completely perishable, such as grain, wool or fuel (see Chapter 5 below, Tell Hadidi).

Five rooms with no direct access to house 6063 (L. 6221, 6219,

---

1. See p. 66 n. 1. Despite the excavator's affirmation that all pottery was published, no finds were illustrated for this room (L. 6220) except for the 'button'.

2. Personal communication by Gloria London, July 1987, 'Amman, Jordan.

6223, 6218, 6255) could, nevertheless, have been part of this same complex (Fig. 40). Because the walls of Room 6221 remained standing to a height of 1.5 m above floor level and 0.8 m above the street without any opening, it is apparent that this was a basement room entered from above. Its function is less certain because the finds were quite disparate—a flat basalt stone, a small weight, a perforated stone, and a krater spout fragment surrounded a large paved bin (Table 4.4). No mention was made in the published report of the contents of the bin. It could have served equally well for food storage or for industrial purposes such as pottery production.

From what we have seen so far, it is evident that room function can only be identified when all activity areas are recognized. The meager evidence from a room such as L. 6219, which contained one bowl, some charcoal ash and an unidentified oval feature, does not clarify either the activities of this room or the function of those adjoining it (Table 4.4). South of the partition wall formed by this oval feature and a large monolith were ashes and signs of a high heat conflagration (Yadin *et al.* 1960: 100). While it is probable that this area was used for domestic or industrial purposes, it is always possible that an accidental fire damaged the room.

The finds from Room 6223, immediately to the east, may provide additional evidence of room function and arrangement. Here, a bin was built into the corner where the doorway to Room 6221 had been blocked. Further divided by a partition wall, the room contained bowls, kraters, cooking pots and a jar—finds definitely related to food preparation (Table 4.4). Analysis of this assemblage yields a similarity coefficient of 165 or 82.5%, a close comparison for a room without an oven. By contrast, the finds from Loci 6218 and 6255 were too fragmentary to contribute to our understanding of these rooms.

Table 4.4. *Hazor Area C Stratum 1B—Finds and Functional Classes*

Locus	Finds	Functional Class
House	1 bowl	food preparation/consumption
6063	1 chalice	food consumption
	3 kraters	food preparation
	1 pithos	dry storage
	1 narrow-neck jar	liquid storage
	2 pyxides	special/cosmetic
	1 miniature bowl	special/cultic
	bone whorl	textile production

Table 4.4—*Continued*

Locus	Finds	Functional Class
	basalt grinder	food preparation
	basalt mortar	food preparation
	potter's wheel	pottery production
	oven	food preparation
	3 bins	multipurpose
	2 shelves	multipurpose

The similarity coefficient for L. 6063 is 122 or 61% when compared to the food preparation and consumption paradigm and 95 or 47.5% when compared to the pottery production paradigm.

6027	1 bowl	food preparation/consumption
	1 juglet	multipurpose
6031	2 kraters	food preparation/consumption
6032	1 cooking pot	food preparation
6215	2 bowls	food preparation/consumption
	1 miniature bowl	special/cultic
	1 krater	food preparation/consumption
	2 cooking pots	food preparation
	1 pithos	dry storage
	3 narrow-neck jars	liquid storage
	1 wide-neck jar	dry storage
	6 jugs	food preparation/storage
	2 juglets	multipurpose
	stone whorl	textile production
	round basalt stone	multipurpose
	basalt pestle	food preparation
	conical stone	unknown
	1 bin	multipurpose
	2 shelves	storage/multipurpose
	2 benches	multipurpose
	pit and perforated stone	storage/refuse

The similarity coefficient for L. 6215 is 102 or 51% when compared to the food preparation and consumption paradigm.

6217	1 bowl	food preparation/scoop
	5 pithoi	dry storage
	1 narrow-neck jar	liquid storage
	1 strainer	multipurpose
	jar stopper	storage
	potter's wheel	pottery production
	basalt stone/mortar	food preparation

The similarity coefficient for L. 6217 is 135 or 67.5% when compared to the storage paradigm.

| 6220 | smashed pithoi | storage |

Table 4.4—*Continued*

Locus	*Finds*	*Functional Class*
	smashed jars	storage
	1 button	adornment
6237	carved bone	unknown
Side Rooms		
6218	1 bowl	food preparation/consumption
6219	1 bowl	food preparation/storage
	bin?	unknown
	ashes	heavy burning
6221	1 krater	food preparation/consumption
	round flat stone	food preparation?
	perforated stone	weight?
	clay weight	business
	bin	storage
6223	3 bowls	food preparation/consumption
	2 kraters	food preparation/consumption
	2 cooking pots	food preparation
	1 narrow-neck jar	liquid storage
	partition wall	unknown
	bin	storage

The similarity coefficient for L. 6223 is 165 or 82.5% when compared to the food preparation and consumption paradigm.

6255	jar stand	food preparation/storage
	sherds	multipurpose
	round flat stone	food preparation?

In summary, it can be said that House 6063 was a medium sized house (central section alone—79.6 m^2) with food preparation and storage facilities, along with a pottery workshop, on the ground floor. Whether the side rooms (L. 6221–6255) were actually part of the same house remains unclear. What is certain is that House 6063 had distinct food storage areas within the main unit as well as a multifunctional food preparation area. In view of the amount of storage in the main room, L. 6215, it is quite possible that this room was roofed, even though the excavators described it as a courtyard (Yadin *et al.* 1960: 98). Such an interpretation does not take into account the fact that the floor level was considerably below that of the street (0.7–0.8 m), making drainage of an open court a real problem. This was especially true in the last phase of occupation when the entry to Room 6224 and the drain in that room was blocked. In addition, the remains of a Stratum 2 wall, reused in the western part of L. 6215, could have functioned as a pillar base, while the benches could have served as beds. On the other hand, it is possible that there were living quarters and reception rooms on an upper storey which would also have provided access to the lower rooms on the west side. In this case, the total area of the house would be increased significantly, to a maximum of 243.2 m².

It is possible, in view of the food preparation area located in L. 6223, that the side rooms (L. 6221–6255) were a separate house (Yassine 1974: 70-73; Pl. 8 figs. 4, 5). However, two factors seem to reduce the likelihood of their use as a distinct house: first, there was no room large enough for sleeping quarters, unless the roof was used or a second storey existed here, and second, there is little evidence of communication from one room to another on the ground floor level.

House 6225 (Figs. 40-41). Rooms with evidence of the usual domestic activities can be identified in all other Area C houses excavated in part only. To the north of Building 6063, elements of the food preparation and pottery production tool kits occurred together in Room 6225. The range of finds included potter's wheel upper and lower thrust bearings,[1] a basalt grinding bowl and a cooking pot. The remaining artefacts and features (Table 4.5) could be associated with either activity and both probably occurred in the same room, although tool kits, sufficiently complete to be tested by the coefficient of similarity, cannot be reconstructed.

In its final phase, L. 6225, which originally had opened into House 6063, was part of a separate house to the north which probably included L. 6226, 6262, 6241, 6236 and 6224 (Fig. 40). On the east side of this complex, rooms with features comparable to the side rooms of House 6063 can be identified: L. 6244 contained a large corner bin and a food preparation assemblage and L. 6239 had a bin and 2 shelves (Table 4.5). Although Room 6244 was only partially excavated and did not contain an oven, comparison with the food preparation paradigm yielded a 108.8 or 54.4% similarity. The small assemblage from Room 6239 was less diagnostic, although the architectural features make it clear that this was, at one time, a storeroom. A similarity coefficient of only 113.4 or 56.7% reflects the small

---

1. Yassine lists 9 potters' wheels for L. 5225 (*sic*). However, only one pair of wheels are recorded by the excavators for L. 6225. See Yadin *et al.* 1960: 127, 9 (Yassine, 1974: 89).

number of jars in this assemblage. It should be noted that both these rooms contained one sherd each of a painted storejar showing an ibex. These could well be fragments of the same jar broken before the rooms were abandoned or fallen from an upper floor.

The integrity of these rooms with the rest of House 6225 is questionable because of the double wall between them and Rooms 6236 and 6224. The few finds from these neighbouring loci are inadequate to explain their precise function (Table 4.5) or to demonstrate their relationship to the rooms in question. Two rooms on the north (L. 6241 and 6262) that were surely part of Building 6225 were exposed in a very limited area (Fig. 4.40). No finds were reported for Room 6262; only a fragment of carved basalt and a cistern or pit[1] were attributed to Room 6241. In view of the well stratified refuse in this 'cistern' (L. 6243), which included material from both Strata 3 and 2, it seems likely that it was built in an earlier period and improved and reused by the inhabitants of Stratum 1B.

The main entrance of Building 6225 was from Street 6248, on the west, into Room 6226. The activities performed here seem to be a continuation of those of the main room (L. 6225), although the finds (2 bowls, 1 baking tray, 1 pyxis, a disk; Table 4.5) do not form a particularly strong example of a food preparation tool kit with a similarity coefficient of only 122 or 61%.

Table 4.5. *Hazor Area C Stratum 1B—Finds and Functional Classes*

Locus	Finds	Functional Class
House 6225	1 krater	food preparation/consumption
	1 cooking pot	food preparation
	1 narrow-neck jar	liquid storage
	basalt bowl	food preparation
	2 potter's wheels	pottery production
	loom weight?	textile production
	clay mask	special/cultic
	pillar base/mortar	food preparation?
	3 benches	multipurpose
6224	1 bowl	food preparation/consumption
	1 miniature vessel	special/cultic
	bin	storage

1. The precise way in which this feature (L. 6243) functioned in Stratum 1B is not certain. The rim of the cistern was stone lined and protruded 20 cm above the floor indicating that it was not intended as a sump to drain Room 6241.

Table 4.5—*Continued*

Locus	Finds	Functional Class
	drain	drainage
6226	2 bowls	food preparation/consumption
	1 pyxis	special/cosmetic
	1 baking tray	food preparation
	disk	unknown

The similarity coefficient for L. 6226 is 122 or 61% when compared to the food preparation and consumption paradigm.

6236	1 bowl	food preparation/consumption
	stone slab	unknown
6239	1 bowl	food preparation/storage
	2 narrow-neck jars	liquid storage
	1 jug	food preparation/storage
	weight	business
	2 benches	multipurpose
	1 bin	storage

The similarity coefficient for L. 6239 is 113.4 or 56.% when compared to the storage paradigm.

6241	carved basalt	decoration
	cistern/pit	water supply/refuse
6244	2 bowls	food preparation/consumption
	1 narrow-neck jar	liquid storage
	1 baking tray	food preparation
	basalt bowl	food preparation
	bin	storage

The similarity coefficient for L. 6244 is 108.8 or 54.4% when compared to the food preparation and consumption paradigm.

House 6249 (Figs. 40, 41). Food preparation and storage activities can also be identified in Courtyard 6249 (6 × 6 m) to the west of House 6225. Here, there were two ovens, a bench, 2 basalt grinding bowls, a bowl, a krater, a cooking pot and a jug (Table 4.6). A silo, so called by the excavators, stood in the southwest corner of this large court. Because the 'silo' had a central stone slab at a higher level than the surrounding stonework, it is more consistent to call it a bin. Its function as a receptacle for food storage or as a manger must remain uncertain (Yadin *et al.* 1960: Pl. 207). Due to the presence of this multifunctional feature and a bench, the similarity coefficient is only 96 or 48% when compared to the food preparation/consumption paradigm.

The relationship of Court 6249 to the surrounding rooms is confused due to the lack of connecting doorways. In the southeast corner, two parallel walls suggest a stairway that led into L. 6235 from above. Such an approach would have been necessary in its final phase because the entrance from the street (L. 6248) into this room had been blocked and a corner bin built in its place. While no recognizable tool kit was recovered from Room 6235 (Table 4.6), the size, shape and features of this room show many similarities to L. 6239 and 6244. The same can be said of L. 6250, 6251 and 6253 to the north where limited exposure of these rooms and the small corpora of finds makes further analysis impossible.

Table 4.6. *Hazor Area C Stratum 1B—Finds and Functional Classes*

Locus	Finds	Functional Class
House 6249	1 bowl	food preparation/consumption
	1 krater	food preparation/consumption
	1 cooking pot	food preparation
	1 jug	food preparation/storage
	2 basalt bowls	food preparation
	2 ovens	food preparation
	1 bench	multipurpose
	corner bin?	manger/storage

The similarity coefficient for L. 6249 is 96 or 48% when compared to the food preparation and consumption paradigm.

6235	1 bowl	food preparation/consumption
	1 jug	food preparation/storage
	cylinder seal	business
	female figurine	special/cultic
	armour scale	weapon
6250	6 bowls	food preparation/consumption
	2 chalices	food consumption
	1 juglet	multipurpose
6251	1 store jar	storage
	perforated stone	multipurpose
6253	2 jar stands	support
	sherd with hole	unknown
Area 6100	1 bowl	food preparation/consumption
	1 cooking pot	food preparation
	1 narrow-neck jar	liquid storage
	1 juglet	multipurpose
	2 baking trays	food preparation
	bronze arrowhead	weapon
	silo?	storage?

Table 4.6—*Continued*

Locus	Finds	Functional Class
	mortar?	food preparation

The similarity coefficient for L. 6100 is 105 or 52.5% when compared to the food preparation and consumption paradigm.

Locus	Finds	Functional Class
6229	3 bowls	food preparation/consumption
	1 chalice	food consumption
	1 krater	food preparation/consumption

Open Area 6100 (Figs. 40, 41). In an early phase of Stratum 1B, L. 6100 and 6229 served as a central courtyard for the buildings to the north, east and south. Rooms 6061, 6101, 6052 and 6261 all opened onto this area at one time. During the last phase of Stratum 1B, only House 6101 retained an entrance onto L. 6100. Uncovered in L. 6100 and 6229 were a silo (or hearth), an assemblage of vessels used for food preparation, and another, unnamed installation, possibly a mortar (Table 4.6). Altogether, the similarity coefficient for this tool kit in comparison with the paradigm for food preparation or consumption is 105 or 52.5%. Interestingly enough, the only oven, apart from the silo/hearth in L. 6100, was in Room 6101, near the entrance to inner Room 6115. The width of L. 6101 was such, 2.5 m, that it is most likely that it was a roofed room. The tradition of ovens located in roofed space as well as in open courtyards seems now to be well established.

House 6101 (Figs. 40, 41). The full extent of House 6101 cannot be known due to the limits of excavation and the subsequent disturbance of the site in this area. In addition, there are not enough finds reported to present a convincing analysis of the activity areas of most rooms in complex 6101 (Table 4.7). At the same time, parallels in construction techniques with other Stratum 1B houses, certain features and room arrangement indicate that this complex was also a house; notice the oven in L. 6101, the silo and shelf in L. 6115 and paved Room 6042.

The only room with a diagnostic assemblage was L. 6091. Its relationship to House 6101 is not clear because it was only partially excavated. The finds represent two domestic tool kits, food preparation and storage. By comparison with the food preparation/consumption paradigm, the similarity coefficient is 102 or 51%. This comparison results from the large number of storage vessels included in the assemblage.

House 6108 (Figs. 40, 41). Several buildings (6108 and 6259) were located along the south side of Open Area 6100/6229. Because the exposure of these structures was so limited, little can be said concerning their plan or function. Two rooms contained corner bins, L. 6108 and 6261, along with items representing domestic activities, such as food preparation, textile production and business (Table 4.7). The reported finds, however, are too few for analysis.

Table 4.7. *Hazor Area C Stratum 1B—Finds and Functional Classes*

Locus	Finds	Functional Class
House 6101	oven	food preparation
6052	1 pithos	dry storage—Stratum 1A?
	miniature bowl	special/cultic
	button	adornment
	installation?	unknown
6091	3 bowls	food preparation/consumption
	3 pithoi	dry storage
	1 narrow-neck jar	liquid storage
	1 miniature bowl	special/cultic
	1 baking tray	food preparation
	basalt bowl	grinder

The similarity coefficient for L. 6091 is 102 or 51% when compared to the food preparation and consumption paradigm.

6115	1 krater	food preparation/consumption
	1 narrow-neck jar	liquid storage
	silo	storage
	shelf	storage
House 6108	1 bowl	food preparation/consumption
	1 baking tray	food preparation
	loom weight	textile production
	clay weight	business
	corner bin	storage
6261	corner bin	storage
House 6061	1 bowl	food preparation/consumption
	1 juglet	multipurpose
	1 scarab	business/adornment
	3 benches	multipurpose
	1 shelf	storage
6171	shelf	storage
6188	2 warped bowls	special?
	1 pyxis	special/cosmetic
	corner shelf	storage

Building 6061 (Figs. 40, 41). To the north of Open Area 6100/6229 was a square building with three rooms (L. 6061, 6171, 6188). The size and shape of this structure varied considerably from the other houses in Area C. Its location, facing Shrine 6136, and unique appearance should be clues to its function. The rooms, themselves, contained benches, shelves, and stone-paved areas. But no apparent function can be discerned. While the finds do not represent typical domestic tool kits, neither do they clarify the original function of this building (Table 4.7). At this stage in this study, no conclusion can be made concerning Building 6061.

Stratum 1A (Fig. 42). The latest excavated stratum, 1A, was not sufficiently well preserved to reveal a clear architectural plan. Its walls and floor surfaces had been damaged by ploughing and few remained intact. What did remain showed no continuity with the plan of Stratum 1B, although the Stratum 1A builders reused certain walls and surfaces of the earlier stratum where possible (Yadin *et al.* 1958: 76). This seemed to be the case particularly along the east edge of the excavated area. On the west, near the earthen embankment, clear Stratum 1A terrace walls and platforms were found in association with Shrine 6136.

Although the shrine was evidently used during this phase, no complete houses appear to have been in use nearby. Only a few scattered domestic assemblages can be identified. A series of ovens (L. 6025, 6116), located against the east side of Platform 6041, were found without any other items from the food preparation tool kit (Fig. 42). One oven (6025) was inside a heavy walled room (0.7 m thick) while the other appeared to be in an open area outside the room (6116). To the north, Street 6227 had been converted into a room with an oven and an assemblage that has a similarity coefficient of 122 or 61% when compared with the food preparation paradigm (Table 4.8). Nearby, in L. 6245 and 6249, there were compatible assemblages although the architectural space in which these items were used cannot be reconstructed.

On the other hand, a quite complete food preparation/consumption tool kit, except for an oven, was found to the southeast of the series of ovens. This assemblage was near the stone paving (6072) above the silo/hearth in Area 6100. This locus was now separated from L. 6229 by a partition wall (Fig. 42). The similarity coefficient of the

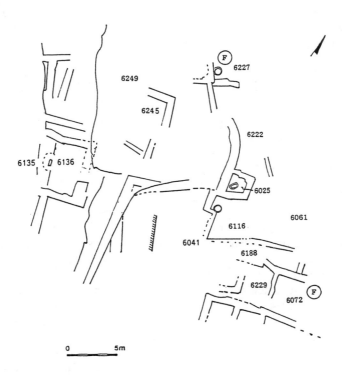

Figure 42. *Hazor Area C Stratum 1A, after Yadin et al. 1960: Pl. CCIX*

assemblage from L. 6072 is 121.7 or 60.8%. Because of the slope of the lower city at this point, the eastern part of this locus has been disturbed and its perimeter destroyed.

No other loci in the domestic area produced sufficient finds for analysis. As we have seen, activities related to food preparation were carried out in certain loci. Whether these activities were related to the cult practiced in Shrine 6136 or related to domestic occupation cannot be determined.

In order to see whether the houses of Area C were typical of Hazor during the Late Bronze Age we will look briefly at Area F where other housing complexes have been reported.

Table 4.8. *Hazor Area C Stratum 1A—Finds and Functional Classes*

Locus	Finds	Functional Class
6003	3 bowls	food preparation/consumption
	1 chalice	food preparation/consumption
	2 kraters	food preparation/consumption
	2 store jars	storage
	3 juglets	multipurpose
6035	1 krater	food preparation/consumption
	basalt vessel	food preparation
6061	miniature bowl	special/cultic
	jar stand	food preparation/storage
	bronze needle	textile production
6025	oven	food preparation
6116	oven	food preparation
6227	1 bowl	food preparation/consumption
	1 krater	food preparation/consumption
	1 juglet	multipurpose
	1 jar stand	food preparation/storage
	oven	food preparation
	installation	unknown

The similarity coefficient for L. 6227 is 122 or 61% when compared to the food preparation and consumption paradigm.

6245	1 bowl	food preparation/consumption
	1 bilbil	multipurpose
6249	3 bowls	food preparation/consumption
	2 kraters	food preparation/consumption
	baking trays	food preparation
6072	1 bowl	food preparation/consumption
	1 krater	food preparation/consumption
	1 cooking pot	food preparation
	1 miniature vessel	special/cultic

Table 4.8—*Continued*

Locus	Finds	Functional Class
	1 pithos	dry storage
	1 narrow-neck jar	liquid storage
	bronze arrowhead	weapon

The similarity coefficient for L. 6072 is 121.7 or 60.8% when compared to the food preparation and consumption paradigm.

Area F

The Late Bronze Age strata uncovered in Area F of the Lower City were judged, at first, to be compatible with those found in Area C. However, the excavator, Jean Perrot, noted that while 1A walls and floors were clearly preserved in a few places, in general, the 1B walls were reused and, in some cases, the 1B floor itself had been removed by the Stratum 1A inhabitants. In addition, the pottery was so homogeneous that it could not be used to distinguish discrete strata (Yadin *et al.* 1960: 128-30*). Because two distinct strata can only be distinguished in a few instances, most finds appear to represent phase 1A. Indeed, it seems more appropriate to identify these strata as construction phases of Stratum 1 on the grounds that the structures of 'Stratum' 1B were not completely destroyed and replaced.

House 8039 (Figs. 43, 44). In Area F, the terrain slopes steeply from west to east. To compensate for this slope, the ancient inhabitants built terraces on which they constructed their buildings. The most complete structure is Building 8039, located on the second terrace from the western edge of the excavation area (Fig. 43). On the east side of this complex, Room 8015 was built on the slope down to the third terrace with the result that its floor level was below that of the rest of the house. As is clear from the plan, there was only one entrance into this room and there can be no doubt that it was an integral part of Building 8039. The finds indicate that L. 8015 may have served as a storeroom although the assemblage is not a strong representative of the storage tool kit. Due to the lack of large store jars, there was only a similarity coefficient of 74 or 37% when compared to the storage paradigm (Table 4.9). The presence of a storage bin may account for the imbalance in this assemblage.

The overall plan of this large complex (House 8039) includes two entrances, one on the south into L. 8016, and one on the north into

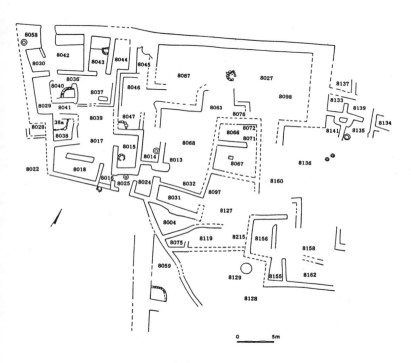

Figure 43. *Hazor Area F Stratum 1B, after Yadin et al. 1960: Pl. CCX*

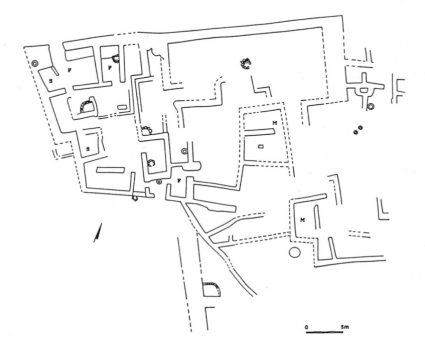

Figure 44. *Hazor Area F Stratum 1B, spatial distribution*

L. 8042. The excavators identified three courtyards, L. 8039 on the south, separated by a bench or partition wall from L. 8037, and L. 8042. An analysis of finds to determine the kind of activities conducted in these rooms indicate that L. 8039 and 8042 were most probably food preparation areas containing bowls, jars, jugs, a cooking pot and a pestle (Table 4.9). The finds in 'Court' 8037, however, characterize it as a storeroom—2 pithoi, benches/shelves and a 'button'. However, with so few finds it is statistically impossible to test whether such a pattern of finds is meaningful.[1] Its location and the probable traffic pattern seem to militate against its exclusive use as a storeroom.

The finds in Room 8030, however, do indicate a storeroom—2 store jars, 2 jugs, a bowl and a chalice (Table 4.9). This assemblage has a similarity coefficient of 131 or 65.5%. The same can be said for L. 8038 where the similarity coefficient is 128 or 64%. However, the location of an orthostat in the entrance makes it difficult to imagine how this room was used. In contrast, three paved rooms (L. 8018, 8041 and 8029) contained too few finds to identify their proper function. The same was true for the paved rooms of Area C. It is clear, however, that grinding, possibly related to food preparation activities, was carried out in the corridor (L. 8017 west) formed by the northwest wall of L. 8018 and the southeast wall of L. 8038. Here were the remains of grinding bowls and pestles (Yadin *et al.* 1960: 134).

One basement room, L. 8059 (in the northwest corner), included an oven as did Vestibule 8025. In view of similar arrangements in Area C, it is now apparent that ovens were frequently placed in rooms near an entrance or in an area separated from other rooms, such as a basement room.

The size of L. 8042 (4.9 × 5.2 m) does not necessitate its identification as a courtyard unless wood was very sparse in the region when this structure was built. The features and finds recorded for this locus (Table 4.9) seem to indicate that it served as a food preparation area next to the oven in Room 8058. Perrot judged that these finds, too few for statistical analysis, were preserved on an upper floor and therefore assigned them to a later phase, Stratum 1A (Yadin *et al.* 1960: 144).

---

1. The fact that these pithoi were covered by a stone layer led Yadin to attribute these vessels to Stratum 1B (Yadin *et al.* 1960: 134) although Perrot understood the floor level of L. 8037 to be a Stratum 1A feature because of the presence of complete vessels (Yadin *et al.* 1960: 129*).

Two neighbouring rooms (L. 8043, 8044) that opened onto 'Court' 8037 contained finds compatible with the function of L. 8042, although the emphasis seems to have been on storage (Table 4.9). Another feature which could have had the same function was corner Bin 8040. The result of this distribution indicates that there was a series of rooms that included features, such as bins, silos, shelves/platforms, and finds that were all intended for use in food preparation and storage. No unequivocal evidence for other activities or crafts was reported.

House 8068 (Figs. 43, 44). A second complex with comparable architectural features and similar room arrangement was House 8068. Located on the third terrace, this house had fewer than three finds per room (Table 4.9). The only exception was Room 8024, which shared Vestibule 8025 with House 8039 during its final phase. The finds from L. 8024 included 2 store jars, 2 pilgrim flasks, a mortar, bowl and miniature bowl. This corpus, along with its close proximity to an oven, fits the pattern of a food storage and preparation area. By analysis, it has a similarity coefficient of 156.1 or 78% in comparison to the storage paradigm.

Locus 8068 was larger (6 × 10 m) than the main rooms (L. 8037-8039) in House 8039 (4.3 × 11 m), and probably functioned as a central courtyard. Because this area was so close to the surface, few of the finds and features in the court itself and little of the surrounding rooms to the north and east were preserved. Indeed, the total extent of Building 8068 remains unclear.

Several rooms (L. 8003-8004, 8075 and 8119), located southeast of House 8068, were associated with L. 8127. In addition, there was an entrance from L. 8127 into Room 8031 located immediately south of Courtyard 8068. Because of the poor state of preservation, the integrity of this building as a separate house cannot be ascertained. It cannot even be known, with certainty, whether Rooms 8066 and 8067 were part of this same structure or belonged, instead, to Building 8136, further north. Beyond that, little evidence for the range of activities performed in 'House' 8127 can be presented due to the paucity of reported finds (10 items from all loci, Table 4.9).

House 8136 (Figs. 43, 44). Another complex of rooms was located on the fourth terrace, in the southeast corner of the excavated area. Here, a few small rooms to the south of L. 8136 were poorly preserved,

L. 8155, 8156, 8158 and 8162. The distance between L. 8136 and these rooms makes their association in the same house questionable. Unfortunately, the only published find from these rooms, a clay crucible in Room 8156, does little to demonstrate the range of activities performed here or the possible association of these rooms with other loci. However, the presence of a second crucible at L. 8071 in Room 8066 does indicate a certain amount of metallurgical activity in this area. The only other evidence of activity areas in 'House' 8136 is a group of 3 basalt bowls used for grinding and a bronze needle, all in L. 8136 (Table 4.9). Because the perimeter walls of this locus have not yet been exposed, its total dimensions cannot be determined[1].

House 8139 (Figs. 43, 44). On the fifth terrace, the remains of another house were partially uncovered. Because of the limited exposure of this structure, its plan cannot be reconstructed. So too, the few reported finds do not reveal the expected activity areas. Although finds from three loci were published (L. 8135, 8137 and 8139), only those from L. 8137 were typical of the assemblages that have been studied so far: these consist of 1 flask and 1 basalt bowl (Table 4.9). The remaining finds were atypical: a figurine, an arrowhead, an oversize krater and a giant cooking pot. Only further excavation of Area F can clarify the function of these rooms.

Table 4.9. *Hazor Area F Stratum 1—Finds and Functional Classes*

Locus	Finds	Functional Class
8004	1 flask	liquid storage
	conical weight	business
8011	2 alabaster vessels	special/status
8013	1 flask	liquid storage
8015	1 chalice	food consumption
	1 jug	dry storage
	1 juglet	multipurpose
	1 stirrup jar	liquid storage
	limestone disk	unknown

1. The Late Bronze I remains have not yet been published although a description of the palace located here during Stratum 2 was promised for Yadin *et al.* 1961. It appears that the large stones, reused in Houses 8039, 8068 and 8136, were from this palace. Without the plan of the underlying building, and with the disturbance of Stratum 1A by ploughing, the complete plans of Houses 8068 and 6136 cannot be reconstructed.

Table 4.9—*Continued*

Locus	*Finds*	*Functional Class*
	silo/bin	storage

The similarity coefficient for L. 8015 is 89.6 or 44.8% when compared to the storage paradigm.

Locus	*Finds*	*Functional Class*
8016	carved basalt	decoration
8017	1 bowl	food preparation/consumption
	pestles	food preparation
	grinding stones	food preparation
8018	1 bowl	food preparation/consumption
	1 narrow-neck jar	liquid storage
8019	1 cooking pot	food preparation
	1 baking tray	food preparation
	clay drain pipes	drainage
	basalt bowl	food preparation
	oven (L. 8023)	food preparation
8020	alabaster vessel	special/status
8024	2 bowls	food preparation/consumption
	1 pithos	dry storage
	1 narrow-neck jar	liquid storage
	1 jug	food preparation/storage
	2 flasks	liquid storage
	basalt mortar	food preparation

The similarity coefficient for L. 8024 is 156 or 78% when compared to the storage paradigm.

Locus	*Finds*	*Functional Class*
8025	oven	food preparation
8030	1 bowl	food preparation/consumption
	1 chalice	food consumption
	1 pithos	dry storage
	1 narrow-neck jar	liquid storage
	2 jugs	food preparation/storage

The similarity coefficient for L. 8030 is 131 or 65.5% when compared to the storage paradigm.

Locus	*Finds*	*Functional Class*
8031	1 bowl	food preparation/consumption
	1 chalice	food consumption
8032	bronze axe	tool
	perforated stone	weight?
	carved basalt	decoration
8036	1 stirrup jar	liquid storage
	corner bin	storage
8037	2 pithoi	dry storage
	clay button	adornment/textile production
	basalt table slab	multipurpose
	2 benches	multipurpose

Table 4.9—*Continued*

Locus	Finds	Functional Class
8038	2 narrow-neck jars	liquid storage
	1 stirrup jar	liquid storage
	basalt grinder	food preparation
	orthostat	special/pillar base

The similarity coefficient for L. 8038 is 128 or 64% when compared to the storage paradigm.

Locus	Finds	Functional Class
8039	2 bowls	food preparation/consumption
	basalt pestle	food preparation
8041	1 bowl	food preparation/consumption
8042	1 krater	food preparation/consumption
	1 cooking pot	food preparation
	1 flask	liquid storage
	basalt basin	trough?
	platform	multipurpose
8043	1 bowl	food preparation/consumption
	1 narrow-neck jar	liquid storage
	bronze lion weight	business
	platform and bin	storage?
8044	2 basalt bowls	food preparation
	shelf?	multipurpose
8045	basalt bowl	food preparation
8046	1 cup and saucer	special/cultic
	bench	multipurpose
8047	1 lamp	lighting
8058	oven	food preparation
8059	1 bowl	food preparation/consumption
	kernos	cultic
8063	1 baking tray	food preparation
8066	2 pithoi	dry storage
	basalt bowl	food preparation
8067	2 bowls	food preparation/consumption
	1 lamp	lighting
	jar stand	support
	orthostat	special/pillar base
8068	clay wheel	unknown
	basalt statue	cultic
8071	2 drain pipes	drainage
	clay crucible	metallurgy
8075	1 bowl	food preparation/consumption
8097	1 lamp	lighting
8124	1 narrow-neck jar	liquid storage
8135	1 krater	food preparation/consumption

Table 4.9—*Continued*

Locus	Finds	Functional Class
	1 cooking pot	food preparation
8136	3 basalt bowls	food preparation
	bronze needle	textile production
8137	1 flask	liquid storage
	1 basalt bowl	food preparation
8139	1 figurine	cultic
	arrowhead	weapon
8156	clay crucible	metallurgy

Area 210: Stratum 2 (Fig. 45)

The limited excavation in Area 210 restricted the exposure of the domestic structures belonging to the Middle and Late Bronze Ages. In Stratum 2, Yadin identified L. 2004 as a courtyard that opened onto surrounding rooms. The courtyard had a beaten earth floor, except for the southeast corner which was paved (1972: 50). The finds recorded for L. 2004 consist of bowls, a chalice, cooking pots, a storejar and a possible lid (Table 4.10). This assemblage is a firm example of a food preparation or consumption tool kit with a similarity coefficient of 179.2 or 89.6% when compared to the paradigm.

Area 210: Stratum 1B (Fig. 46)

Above the courtyard house, a new floor plan was constructed in Stratum 1B. Two rooms were exposed (Yadin 1972: 50). The finds from Room 2002 can be classified as a storage tool kit (Table 4.11) with a similarity coefficient of 157.3 or 78.6%. The assemblages published for Area 210 clearly demonstrate that the traditional pattern for the use of space in domestic structures was consistent throughout the Lower City. Further excavation here might be very useful because of the noticeable lack of evidence for typical domestic crafts in Areas C and F, such as textile production, as well as for business and trade.

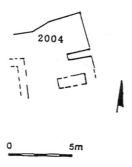

Figure 45. *Hazor Area 210 Stratum 2, after Yadin 1972: Fig. 10*

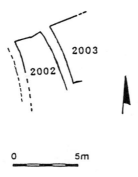

Figure 46. *Hazor Area 210 Stratum 1B, after Yadin 1972: Fig. 10*

Table 4.10. *Hazor Area 210 Stratum 2—Finds and Functional Classes*

Locus	Finds	Functional Class
2004	7 bowls	food preparation/consumption
	1 chalice	food consumption
	3 cooking pots	food preparation
	1 narrow-neck jar	liquid storage
	1 lid?	food preparation

The similarity coefficient for L. 2004 is 157.3 or 78.6% when compared to the food preparation and consumption paradigm.

Table 4.11. *Hazor Area 210 Stratum 1B—Finds and Functional Classes*

Locus	Finds	Functional Class
2002	2 bowls	food preparation/consumption
	8 pithoi	dry storage
	2 jugs	food preparation/storage
	1 baking tray	food preparation

The similarity coefficient for L. 2002 is 179.2 or 89.6% when compared to the storage paradigm.

House Plan. What is apparent from this discussion of domestic structures in Areas C and F is that the houses at Hazor were large, irregularly shaped complexes that included multipurpose activity areas and monopurpose storage facilities. For the most part, the storage rooms were smaller than the food preparation and living areas and were located away from the main entrance. Such a location may have been an attempt to store food stuffs far from the light. The treatment of the floors in storage rooms seems to have been consistent: all were of beaten earth. This leaves open the question of the function of the rooms with stone-paved floors. In Area C, it could be that these rooms were used to store clay for the pottery industry. However, the same style of floor treatment occurred in Area F where no evidence of pottery production was reported. Several of these rooms were found to be empty, or with few finds. Not one such room contained an identifiable artefact tool kit.

Another alternative for the storage needs of the pottery industry in Area C can be seen in the large number of bins and installations, especially those in the basement rooms of House 6063. It is assumed that the pottery industry represented in these structures was related to the small shrine set into the west side of the earthen embankment and to the shop (L. 6211) located to the east of the houses.

Also characteristic of the houses in Areas C and F is the large number of rooms in each house. Although few complete houses were fully exposed, it is clear from Houses 6063 and 8039 that the total number of rooms could be as many as 10–14. This number reflects only the ground floor plan and does not take into account the rooms on an upper storey that would have been necessary to enter basement rooms from above. Thus, the plans themselves seem to indicate a complex social organization of extended families. This pattern is closer in style to what was found at Ugarit than what appears to be typical at other Palestinian sites.[1]

An important feature of the artefact assemblages from the houses at Hazor is the paucity of Egyptian goods. The contrast between Hazor, with no reported scarabs from the houses, and Tell el-'Ajjul, where one or more scarabs were found in almost every room, is striking. Only a few Egyptian items were found in the entire site, and then mostly in tombs.[2] The same contrast can also be seen closer at hand where the finds and the architecture at Beth Shan reveal heavy Egyptian presence. These observations support Weinstein's view that there is little if any Egyptian pottery found at Hazor (1981: 22), thereby indicating the range of the Egyptian empire during LB IIB. This apparent independence of Hazor may be a sign that it was more closely related to the Syrian states to the north. Indeed, the similarity of house size with examples from Ugarit points in the same direction.

Table 4.12. *Hazor Area C Stratum 2 Loci*

Locus	Square	Description	Similarity Coefficient
6183	M4	Room	143.8 or 71.9%
6185	N5	Undefined	
6186	M3	Undefined	
6187	L5	Room	
6189	N3	Undefined	
6193	M4-5	Room	
6194	M3	Room	
6196	N4	Room	
6197	L3-4	Undefined	

1. Compare the size of house at Ugarit (10×23 m, each of 2 stories) described by Callot (1983) with House 8039 at Hazor (10×23 m) and Stratum 8 house at Tell Batash (9×10 m; see below).

2. A scarab of Thutmosis IV was reported from Tomb 8144-5 as well as a stopper in the shape of the head of Hathor from Tomb 8112 in Area F (Yadin 1972: 45-46).

Table 4.13. *Hazor Area C Stratum 1B Loci*

Locus	Square	Description	Similarity Coefficient
6003	O5	Fragments of Paving	
6027	N5	Paved floor of Room	
6031	N4	Undefined Area	
6032	N4	South part of Locus 6027	
6042	M4	Paved Floor of Room	
6045	N4	Lane	
6047	N3	Floor	
6052	M3	Room	
6060	N4	Stone Paving	
6061	L4	Room	
6063	M5	Room?	122 or 61.0%(FP/C)
			95 or 47.5% (P)
6088	N2	Undefined Area	
6091	M2	Room	102 or 51.0%
6100	L3	Open Square	105 or 52.5%
6101	M3	Courtyard	
6108	L2	Room/Courtyard	
6115	N3	Room	
6116	K4	Courtyard(?)	
6129	L5	Room	
6171	L4	Room	
6188	K4	Room	
6213	O6	Undefined Area	
6214	N6	Room	
6215	M6	Room/Courtyard	102 or 51%
6217	N7	Room	135 or 67.5%
6218	L6	Room	
6219	L6	Room	
6220	M7	Room	
6221	L7	Room	
6222	K6	Undefined Area	
6223	L6	Room	165 or 82.5%
6224	N7	Room	
6225	M7	Room/Courtyard	
6226	L7	Room	122.0 or 61%
6227	K7	Undefined Area	
6229	K3	Undefined Area	
6235	J7	Room	
6236	N8	Room	
6237	M7	Room	
6239	O7	Room	113.4 or 56.7%
6241	M8	Room	

Table 4.13—*Continued*

Locus	Square	Description	Similarity Coefficient
6244	O8	Room	108.8 or 54.4%
6245	J7	Undefined Area	
6248	K8	Undefined Area	
6249	H7	Room	96.0 or 48%
6250	H8	Room	
6251	J8	Room	
6252	H6	Undefined Area	
6253	J8	Room	
6255	L5	Room	
6259	J3	Room	
6260	K3	Room	
6261	K2	Room	
6262	L8	Room	

Table 4.14. *Hazor Area C Stratum 1A Loci*

Locus	Square	Description	Similarity Coefficient
6022	L5	Fragments of floor	
6025	K5	Room	
6027	N5	Raised floor	
6034	M4	Raised corner of L. 6042	
6035	N3	Stone paving	
6045	N4	Lane	
6049	L4	Floor	
6052	M3	Room	
6061	L4	Floor	
6072	L3	Stone paving	121.7 or 60.8%
6084	L2	Layer of cobbles	
6108	L2	Room/Courtyard	
6116	K4	Courtyard	
6136	G5-6	Shrine	
6188	K4	Undefined Area	
6222	K6	Undefined Area	
6227	K7	Undefined Area	122.0 or 61%
6229	K3	Undefined Area	
6240	J6	Undefined Area	
6245	J7	Undefined Area	
6249	H7	Courtyard	

Table 4.15. *Hazor Area F Stratum 1B Loci*

Locus	Square	Description	Similarity Coefficient
8003	L3	Triangular Room	
8004	L3	Triangular Room	
8013	L5	Paving in L. 8068	
8014	L5	Room	
8015	L5	Room	74.0 or 37%
8016	L5	Passage	
8017	J5	South part of L. 8039	
8018	J5	Paved Room	
8022	H5	Street	
8024	K4	Room	156.1 or 78%
8025	K4	Room	
8027	O7	Platform	
8028	H6	Room	
8029	H7	Paved Room	
8030	H8	Paved (?) Room	123 or 61.5%
8031	L4	Paved Room	
8032	L4	South part of L. 8068	
8036	J7	Room	
8037	J7	North part of L. 8039	
8038	J6	Room	128 or 64%
8038a	J6	Bin	
8039	J6	Court	
8040	J7	Bin	
8041	J6	Passageway	
8042	J8	Court?	
8043	K7	Room	
8044	K8	Room	
8045	L8	Room	
8046	K7	Room	
8047	K6	Room	
8058	H9	Room?	
8059	L2	Undefined	
8063	N6	Undefined	
8066	N5	Room	
8067	N4	Room	
8068	M5	Court	
8071	O5	Drain Pipes	
8072	N5	Bin	
8075	L2	Room	
8076	N6	Undefined	
8087	M7	Undefined	
8097	M4	Court	

Table 4.15—*Continued*

Locus	Square	Description	Similarity Coefficient
8098	P6	Undefined	
8119	M3	Paved Room	
8127	N3	Court	
8128	N1	Undefined	
8129	N1	Depression	
8133	Q6	Room	
8134	R5	Room	
8135	Q5	Room	
8136	P4	Court?	
8137	Q6	Room	
8139	Q6	Room	
8141	P5	Bin	
8155	O2	Paved Room	
8156	N2	Paved Room	
8158	O2	Court	
8160	O4	Court	
8162	P1	Paved Room	
8163	N3	Undefined	
8215	N2	Undefined	

The initial discovery of Altar 9001 pointed to cultic activities in Area F. The loci connected with the altar and its supporting terrace have not been included.

The loci above designated as 'undefined area' were included because of their close proximity to clearly defined structures.

Table 4.16. *Hazor Area 210 Stratum 2 and Stratum 1B Loci*

Locus	Square	Description	Similarity Coefficient
Stratum 2			
2004	A1	Courtyard?	157.3 or 78.6
Stratum 1B			
2002	A1	Room	179.2 or 84.6%
2003	A1	Room	

Megiddo (Map reference 167/221)

Late Bronze Age occupation at Megiddo has been uncovered in several excavation areas, AA in the north, BB in the east and CC in the south. The exposure of domestic architecture, however, was limited to Areas BB and CC (Loud 1948: Figs. 401-403). The structures in Area

AA, on the other hand, were monumental. Here were the city wall, the gate complex and an administrative complex (Loud 1948: Figs. 382-84). However, the finds from the Area AA 'palace' can serve as a useful control for better understanding the range of artefacts commonly used in ancient houses.

Late Bronze Age phases include Strata VIII–VIIA in Area AA, Strata IX–VIIA in Area BB, and Strata VIIB–VIIA in Area CC. Serious stratigraphic problems continue to plague those who try to understand the history of occupation at Megiddo and correlate its strata. It seems clear that the palace of Stratum IX, located in Area AA, belonged to the end of the MB IIC period (Kenyon 1969: 58; Gonen 1987: 89). As we have seen above, the paucity of finds from this building precluded detailed functional analysis of artefact distribution.[1] In view of an apparent gap in occupation,[2] no LB I structures from Area AA have been identified. The most coherent group of early Late Bronze Age buildings was located in Area BB, southeast of the foundations of Temple 2048.

Stratum IX Area BB SE (Fig. 47)

Houses uncovered in the southeast section of Area BB, between the temple and the city wall, show continuity during Strata IX–VIIB (Kenyon 1969: 49). From the plans, it is clear that these houses were rebuilt, first in Stratum VIII, and then in Stratum VIIB (Figs. 47-49). The remains from Stratum VIIB, however, were more fragmentary. The published report did not describe these buildings in any detail, leaving one to guess the nature of the wall construction and features. However, the restored plan can be supplemented by photographs which offer a partial view of the construction materials and plan of these Late Bronze Age houses during excavation.

The typical house appears to have been somewhat square with a central hall or court surrounded by rooms on all sides. Houses shared

1. I, therefore, must depend on the refined stratigraphical reassessment attempted by others who have studied the pottery from the tombs as well as the architecture. Consensus has not yet been reached however, see Davies versus Kenyon and Tufnell, concerning Stratum VIII (Davies 1986: 56-7), and Gonen versus Dothan, on the inclusion of Stratum VIIA in the Late Bronze Age (Gonen 1987: 96).

2. Kenyon notes only one Stratum VIII feature with similarities to a Stratum IX architectural element along with a serious gap in the pottery sequence from these two strata (1969: 58-59).

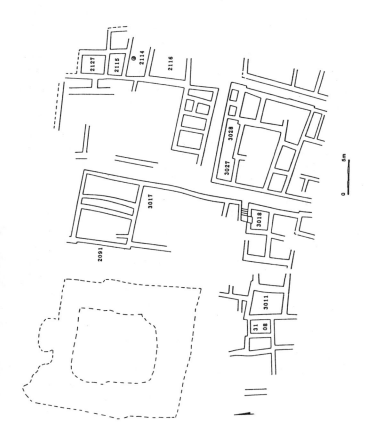

Figure 47. *Megiddo BB SE Stratum IX, after Loud 1948: Fig. 401*

party walls and a straight wall along the street. Benches, silos, ovens and thick-walled store rooms and/or stairwells can be recognized, especially in the one complete house east of the north–south street (Fig. 47).

Even with the excavation techniques and recording methods employed during the 1930s, it is evident that the Area BB houses at Megiddo differed from those found at Hazor. First of all, the Megiddo houses were much more regular in shape and, although they shared party walls, there was no intrusion of the rooms of one house into the space of its neighbour. Their total size was approximately 10 × 11 m or 11 × 13 m, whereas the houses at Hazor measured c. 10 × 20 m (Building 8039, Area F) or c. 10 × 13 m (Building 6063, Area C).

Table 4.17. *Megiddo Area BB Stratum IX—Finds and Functional Classes*

Locus	Finds	Functional Class
2091	1 bowl	food preparation/consumption
	1 lamp	lighting
	figurine fragment	special
	game piece	recreation
2091Erm	1 bowl	food preparation/consumption
	weaving tool	textile production
	1 scarab	business/adornment
	figurine head	special
	faience bead	adornment
	arrowhead	weapon
2114	oven	food preparation
2127W	4 jugs	food preparation/storage
	2 juglets	multipurpose
	1 toggle pin	adornment
	1 spearhead	weapon
3017W	1 jug	food preparation/storage
3018E	toggle pin	adornment
3018S	1 baking tray	food preparation
	bichrome jug?	food preparation/storage
	1 bead	adornment
3018W	1 flask	storage
	2 lamps	lighting
3027E	1 krater	food preparation/consumption
3028rm	flint blade	tool
	bone inlay	special/status

For Stratum IX, 14 floors were shown on the plan of which 6 were intact (Loud 1948: 401). If incomplete pottery vessels had been published from find spots such as these,[1] it might have been possible to reconstruct functional tool kits. However, the published report referenced all finds to 6 locus numbers among the 50 rooms excavated (Fig. 47) and recorded only 29 items and 1 oven (Table 4.17). As a result, no detailed functional analysis is possible. With the small corpus of ceramic vessels and objects that has been published, only the range of domestic activities, spread across all loci, can be identified. These activities included food preparation, storage,[2] textile production, and the possession of weapons, jewellery, games and status items, including fragments of figurines. At the same time, no complete tool kit of any one of these activities can be recognized, making it impossible, by my criteria, to identify living rooms and store rooms.

Table 4.18. *Megiddo Area BB Stratum VIII—Finds and Functional Classes*

Locus	Finds	Functional Class
2094	2 juglets	multipurpose
	1 scarab	business/adornment
	1 pendant	adornment
	burnishing tool	pottery production
2094N	1 lamp	lighting
	ivory bowl lid	special/cosmetic
2099N	1 lamp	lighting
	1 jar stand	food preparation/storage
2104N	scarab ring	business/adornment
2110E	1 narrow-neck jar	liquid storage
	1 jug	food preparation/storage
3000S	1 narrow-neck jar	liquid storage
3000W	ivory disk	unknown
3000nr	stud/rivet	unknown
3001	1 jug	food preparation/storage
3001N	1 jug	food preparation/storage
3002	2 jugs	food preparation/storage
3002N	1 bowl	food preparation/consumption

1. As in the Middle Bronze Age strata, it is not clear what area was constituted by a given locus number; a room, part of a room, a paved floor or an unpaved area. In fact, all objects found within the debris contained in a room received the same locus number. This means that a locus group may represent more than one coherent assemblage.

2. The small number of published pottery vessels is evidence of selectivity. Actually, it seems that more than one occurrence of common types were not noted.

Table 4.18—*Continued*

Locus	Finds	Functional Class
3003	alabaster jug	special/status
3003nr	1 jug	food preparation/storage
3004E	1 jug	food preparation/storage
3007	1 jug	food preparation/storage
3016W	1 juglet	multipurpose
3018Wrm	bronze needle	textile production
	flint chisel	tool
	bronze knife	cutting
	2 arrowheads	weapon
	bronze dagger	weapon
	bronze spearhead	weapon
	bronze fitting	unknown

Stratum VIII Area BB SE (Fig. 48). The houses of Stratum VIII reused the walls of the earlier structures with certain changes in interior layout. However, no complete houses can be reconstructed with certainty. While more locus numbers (12 versus 5) were assigned to individual rooms, the finds reported for each locus were few. As a result, no tool kits could be assembled from the widely scattered finds, although certain artefacts indicate a slightly different range of domestic activities (Table 4.18). For example, a burnishing tool may be suggestive of pottery production, a small ivory container may point to cosmetic use, and a collection of bronze tools and weapons in L. 3018Wrm, may indicate a storeroom (see Tell Batash, below). The remaining finds include bowls, jars, jugs, juglets and lamps.

Stratum VII Area BB SE (Fig. 49). The houses of Stratum VIIB continued the architectural tradition of Stratum VIII although there were some changes in alignment.[1] No complete houses and few intact rooms have been assigned to this stratum. In addition, so few locus numbers (6) were published that it is difficult to talk about the arrangement of rooms and courtyards in these structures.

The finds reported for Stratum VIIB were so limited (a total of 22 items) that the normal range of domestic activities was not fully represented. Only one assemblage contained sufficient items to

---

1. Only one sentence that describes these structures was included in the published report (Loud 1948: 104).

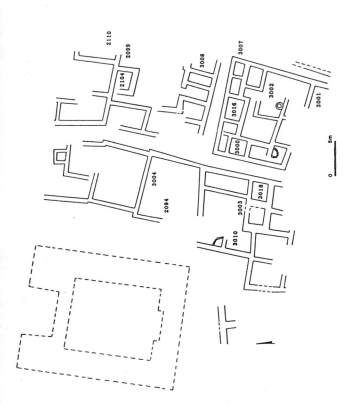

Figure 48. *Megiddo BB SE Stratum VIII, after Loud 1948: Fig. 402*

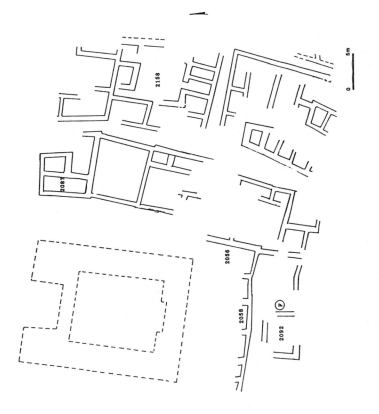

Figure 49. *Megiddo BB SE Stratum VIIB, after Loud 1948: Fig. 403*

identify a functional tool kit, L. 2092E (Table 4.19). Here, food preparation/consumption was well represented, with a similarity coefficient of 127 or 63.5% when compared to the paradigm, although the extent of the locus itself and the presence or absence of an intact floor remains unknown.

Stratum VIIA Area BB SE. Although the date of Stratum VIIA is disputed by scholars,[1] there is consensus that it fell in the Late Bronze period (Gonen 1987: 97; Kenyon 1969: 53). The Stratum VIIA structures were built above a thick debris layer, evidence of the destruction of Stratum VIIB. In spite of the fact that the earlier phase was extensively destroyed, a few walls were reused by the Stratum VIIA builders. So little of the later buildings has been preserved that no complete houses can be recognized. Indeed, the finds from Stratum VII were assigned to both Strata VIIB and VIIA (Table 4.19) making it extremely difficult to determine the activity areas and date of the respective phases.

Building 2090, a new structure in Square 15 N, was not an ordinary house (Loud 1948: Fig. 404). The wall foundations were 1.4 m thick, approximately twice that of a typical domestic structure. Because no finds were reported for this building, comparison with other buildings cannot be undertaken.

Table 4.19. *Megiddo Area BB Stratum VII—Finds and Functional Classes*

Locus	Finds	Functional Class
2056E	2 chalices	food consumption
	1 juglet	multipurpose
	1 lamp	lighting
2058S	alabaster pulley?	unknown
2087E	1 whorl	textile production
	2 bronze fragments and cloth	metallurgy
	bronze axe	tool
2092E	2 bowls	food preparation/consumption
	1 chalice	food consumption
	2 kraters	food preparation/consumption
	2 juglets	multipurpose

1. Kenyon had dated Stratum VIIA to the 14th century BC, after a gap in occupation following the destruction of Stratum VIIB—Area BB—by Thutmosis III (1969: 53, 59) whereas Gonen located this stratum in the 12th century BC (1979: 96, 97).

Table 4.19—*Continued*

Locus	Finds	Functional Class
	1 cup and saucer	special/cultic
	1 scarab	business/adornment
	1 bead	adornment
	bronze bowl	special/status

The similarity coefficient for L. 2092E is 127 or 63.5% when compared to the food preparation and consumption paradigm.

Locus	Finds	Functional Class
2092W	1 scarab	business/adornment
2092nr	human figurine	special/cultic

Stratum VIIB–VIIA Area CC (Figs. 50, 51). To the south, a second domestic area was uncovered in Area CC. Here the remains of the 13th century houses of Stratum VIIB were poorly preserved and receive little mention in the published report (Loud 1948: 113). Fragments of walls, patches of pavement, ovens and silos—possibly from a later stratum—are all that was recovered. Attempts to identify individual houses from the plan are made more difficult by the lack of verbal description of individual rooms and of the precise location of vessels and objects found in the debris (see p. 263 n. 1).

The houses appear to have been linked by party walls but the streets separating them into blocks are difficult to discern.[1] The architectural remains, themselves, seem to support the hypothesis that the houses in Area CC were similar in plan to those of Area BB during Stratum VIII. Ideally, a study of the artefact assemblages would allow us to organize a group of loci into a typical household complex. However, the close overlay of Strata VIIB, VIIA and VI increased the possibility of artifact contamination from one stratum to another. As a result, it is difficult to guarantee contemporaneity of all items listed for a particular locus.

Stratum VIIB Area CC (Fig. 50). Only 14 loci were assigned to Stratum VIIB, approximately one locus to each housing unit. These loci were, in all probability, uncovered beneath the Stratum VIIA floor level and, as a result, considered to be Stratum VIIB. Exposure of the earlier phase, in its entirety, was not completed. Therefore,

1. No indication of construction techniques and materials can be discerned from the schematic drawings of house walls. Such information may have been helpful in distinguishing discrete housing units.

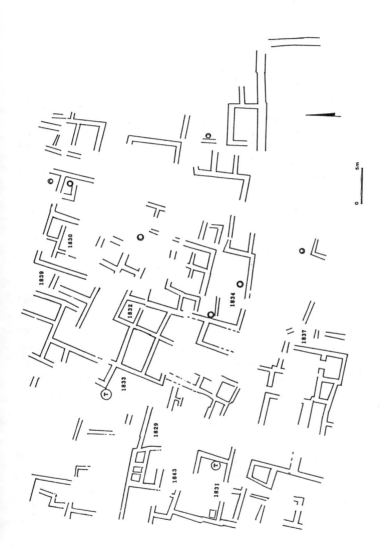

Figure 50. *Megiddo CC Stratum VIIB, after Loud 1948: Fig. 409*

only one composite plan could be published (Loud 1948: Pl. 409).

A much larger number of finds was recorded for each Area CC locus than for similar room loci in Area BB. Few assemblages reflect, however, the typical domestic tool kits of food preparation and storage. A total corpus of vessels related to food preparation and consumption consisted of 24% of all finds (Table 4.20). Only 4 narrow-neck store jars and 1 wide-neck jar indicate the storage of liquid and dry food stuffs. Here again, this may be due to the paucity of ceramic vessels included in each assemblage. For comparison, it is important to keep in mind that the ratio of pottery to objects in this stratum of Area CC is 31:69 whereas the ratio at Beth Shemesh, Area C, Stratum IVa is 71:29.

What is distinctive about the finds in Area CC is the number and diversity of artefacts, especially those related to textile manufacture and the possession of status items. Although few complete tool kits can be isolated, several craft activities were clearly represented. Whorls, spindles or both were located in L. 1829, 1831, 1831E (in the southwestern part of the excavated area), and in L. 1833N (to the northwest of L. 1829). This last corpus, including 2 bronze awls, represents 16.6% of all finds for Stratum 7B. The assemblage from Room 1833N is the closest parallel to the textile manufacture paradigm that has been found, having a similarity coefficient of 189 or 94.5%. Another corpus that can be compared with the paradigm for textile manufacture is that from L. 1831E, which has a similarity coefficient of 149 or 74.5%. The remaining distribution of items related to textile manufacture did not form clusters large enough for analysis.

No clay loom weights were identified although several stone rings were registered. Because these have not been drawn or photographed, it is difficult to assess the likelihood that they functioned as weights. Other categories of artefacts consist of jewellery, which accounts for 15% of the total finds, and bronze tools and a steatite mould for jewellery manufacture, which is 12%.

While no small weights were reported, business activities may be evidenced by the presence of stamp, scarab and cylinder seals (9.5% of the finds). It is always possible that such items served as jewellery, but this seems more likely for scarabs, which may have been treasured as amulets, than for stamp or cylinder seals.

Table 4.20. *Megiddo Area CC Stratum VIIB—Finds and Functional Classes*

Locus	Finds	Functional Class
1829	1 krater	food preparation/consumption
	1 jug	food preparation/storage
	cup and saucer vessel	special/cultic
	1 rhyton?	special
	1 whorl	textile production
	1 stamp seal	business/adornment
	1 scarab	business/adornment
	bronze animal figure	special/cultic
	3 beads	adornment
	limestone object	unknown
	alabaster flask	special/status
	bronze ring/chain	unknown
	bronze handle	container
1829N	bronze blade	tool
1830	1 bowl	food preparation/consumption
	2 scarabs	business/adornment
	1 jar stopper	storage
1830E	1 jug	food preparation/storage
	1 juglet	multipurpose
	beads	adornment
	limestone object	unknown
	1 arrowhead	weaponry
	limestone macehead	weaponry
1831	1 bowl	food preparation/consumption
	1 narrow-neck jar	liquid storage
	1 pyxis	special/cosmetic use
	1 spindle	textile production
	1 scarab	business/adornment
	mould	metallurgy
	1 arrowhead	weaponry
1831E	2 narrow-neck jars	liquid storage
	2 spindles	textile production
	4 whorls	textile production
	1 cylinder seal	business/adornment
	1 bead	adornment
	limestone object	unknown
	quartz object	unknown
	diorite statuette	status/cultic
	stone ring	weight?
	clay disk	unknown
	bone inlay	special/status

Table 4.20—*Continued*

Locus	Finds	Functional Class

The similarity coefficient for L. 1831E is 149 or 74.5% when compared to the textile manufacture paradigm.

Locus	Finds	Functional Class
1832	1 bowl	food preparation/consumption
	statue base	special/cultic
	1 bead	adornment
	toggle pin?	adornment
	bronze object	unknown
	bronze nail	tool
1832E	1 scarab	business/adornment
1833	1 scarab	business/adornment
1833N	1 flask	liquid container
	3 whorls	textile production
	1 needle	textile production
	1 grinder	food preparation
	beads	adornment
	limestone ring	weight?
	bronze awl	multipurpose
	bone inlay	special/status
	horn object	unknown

The similarity coefficient for L. 1833N is 189 or 94.5% when compared to the textile manufacture paradigm.

Locus	Finds	Functional Class
1833W	1 bowl	food preparation/consumption
1834	1 chalice	food consumption
	1 krater	food preparation/consumption
	1 narrow-neck jar	liquid storage
	2 beads	adornment
	1 pendant	adornment
	1 finger ring	adornment
	alabaster vessel	special/status
	bronze awl	multipurpose
	stone axe	tool
	arrowhead	weapon
1839	1 scarab	business/adornment
	2 grinders	food preparation
1843N	1 wide-neck jar	dry storage
	clay tripod?	unknown
	finger ring	adornment

Stratum VIIA Area CC (Figs. 51a, b). Contrary to expectation, analyses of artefact groups assigned to Stratum VIIA, do not clearly

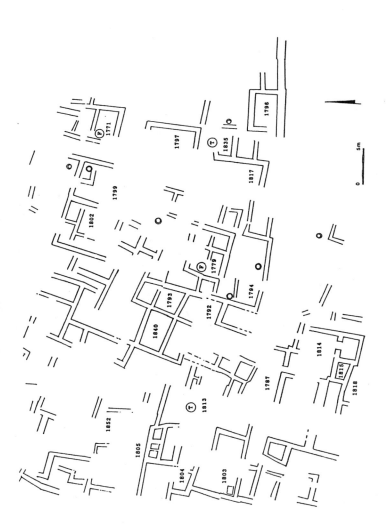

Figure 51a. *Megiddo CC Stratum VIIA, after Loud 1948: Fig. 409*

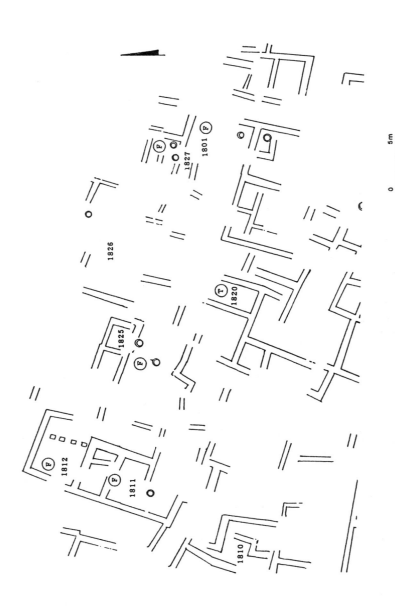

Figure 51b. *Megiddo CC Stratum VIIA, after Loud 1948: Fig. 409*

distinguish the various functions expected for each house. For example, only two assemblages are adequate for analysis in comparison with the food preparation paradigm, Loci 1771N and 1811N. The similarity coefficient for L. 1771N is 132.7 or 66.8% and for 1811N, 162 or 81%. These figures indicate tool kits with a strong representation of food preparation vessels. On the other hand, the fact that 15 ovens and 18 grinders were noted, while only 1 cooking pot was reported, clearly points to a serious imbalance in the recording of ceramic vessels. The result is that only these two clearly defined assemblages, among a possible 15 housing units, can be reassembled. However, several other loci can be designated as food preparation areas when stone bowls and grinding stones are associated with the ovens drawn on the plans (Fig. 51). These include a concentration of 4 ovens and 8 stone bowls or grinders in L. 1779, 1801 and 1827 (Table 4.21). A second concentration of 2 ovens and 1 grinder was located south of Room 1825, while 5 grinders were reported for L. 1812W. Ovens and grinders occurred individually in other loci but no clear functional associations could be established with other finds from the same locus.

It was surprising that no concentration of storage equipment, jars and jugs was located. This is extremely rare for an area of domestic structures. Storejars did occur with bowls, mortars, tools, jewellery, weaponry and spindle whorls. Indeed, a similar diversity of finds in L. 1840 (Table 4.21) indicates a multipurpose area with some food preparation activity. However, in each functional category, the finds were so few that no satisfactory comparison to tool kit paradigms could be attempted. Nevertheless, it is precisely such assemblages, indicating multifunctional areas, that are our best evidence for the location of living rooms.

The inclusion of whorls and/or spindles, needles, weapons and tools in many Stratum VIIA loci, indicates extensive craft activity. Some rooms may have been used exclusively as workshops even though the floor plan of the house showed no modification (see Tell Beit Mirsim, Stratum D). In three loci (L. 1813, 1820 and 1835N) the distribution of finds reflects the production of textiles (Table 4.21). Although each assemblage is small, the diversity of finds is such that comparison with the textile manufacture paradigm is possible. The results yield a similarity coefficient for L. 1813 of 160 or 80%, that for L. 1820 of 190 or 95%, and that for L. 1835N of 160 or 80%.

Two other categories of finds point to functions which cannot be specified: weapons and natural resources. These finds (19) comprised about 8% of the total finds (366) and were distributed evenly throughout the area. Because so few assemblages can be functionally identified, it is unclear whether these items were in primary or secondary use. Although the original function of the weapons is clear, they may have been reused in the houses, in food preparation or craft activities. Sharp blades would be especially useful in textile production where tough fibres required separation or cutting.

Only 13 tools were assigned to this large domestic area. Two, of special interest, were agricultural tools, a plough point (L. 1771N) and a hoe (L. 1779). The lumps of metal, stone and clay, on the other hand, may have been used in a variety of crafts and industries including jewellery making, metallurgy and the production of status goods.

In spite of this evidence of craft activity, few measuring weights were recorded, and only 11 seals (scarab, cylinder and stamp) were found.[1] While it is possible that weights were not essential to the textile industry as it was practised in this section of the city, other crafts certainly made use of weights. This is another case in which an artefact imbalance appears in the published archaeological record.

The presence of status goods, jewellery and cosmetic items confirms the basic function of the buildings in Area CC. It is certain, both from the finds and the architectural plan, that a large concentration of houses occupied the southern part of the city at the end of the Late Bronze Age. What has been most useful for our purposes is that the finds in Area CC reflect the great diversity of possessions and equipment utilized by ancient city dwellers and kept in their homes. The association of food preparation and textile manufacturing items with items of female adornment and with personal possessions possibly belonging to women may reflect women's work areas. This seems to be the case for L. 1787, 1792, 1793W, 1797W, 1801, 1803S, 1805N, 1812, 1812S, 1812W, 1813, 1817, 1818, 1820, 1820S and 1820W (Table 4.21). However, in terms of understanding the location and relationship of activity areas in the domestic setting, spatial analysis of artefact distribution has not been as useful as expected in view of the large number of finds. While other types of analysis may be more

1. The fact that the total number of seals recorded for Area CC comprised only 3% of the finds leads one to suspect that many such small and marketable items may have been 'lost' during excavation.

fruitful, this particular study has been hindered by the lack of clearly assigned locus numbers and the small percentage of published pottery forms.

Table 4.21. *Megiddo Area CC Stratum VIIA—Finds and Functional Classes*

Locus	Finds	Functional Class
1771N	4 bowls	food preparation/consumption
	1 amphora	liquid storage
	1 flask	liquid storage
	2 spindles	textile production
	3 beads	adornment
	1(?) bronze bowl	special/status
	plough point	agriculture
	spear point	weapon

The similarity coefficient for L. 1771N is 132.7 or 66.8% when compared to the food preparation and consumption paradigm.

Locus	Finds	Functional Class
1779	2 beads	adornment
	bronze hoe(?)	agriculture
1779N	1 zoomorphic rhyton	special/status
	1 whorl	textile production
	zoomorphic figurine	special/cultic
	2 grinding stones	food preparation
	ivory funnel	multipurpose
	2 beads	adornment
	clay lump	unknown
	1 axe	tool
	iron ring	tool
	bronze dagger	weapon
	horn fragment	unknown
1779W	1 whorl	textile production
	bronze dagger	weapon
1787	2 whorls	textile production
	ivory bowl lid	special/cosmetic
	stamp seal	business
	1 scarab	business/adornment
	1 amulet	adornment/cultic
	1 bracelet	adornment
	3 beads	adornment
	1 pin head	adornment
	bronze object	unknown
	alabaster object	unknown
	faience bowls	special/status
	glass jug	special/status
	arrowhead	weapon

Table 4.21—*Continued*

Locus	Finds	Functional Class
	ivory disk	unknown
1792	1 bowl	food preparation/consumption
	1 amphora	liquid storage
	1 whorl	textile production
	stone bowl	food preparation
	1 bead	adornment
	bronze object	unknown
	bronze ring/chain	tool
	weight	business
1792S	1 jug	food preparation/consumption
	2 beads	adornment
	alabaster vessel	special/status
	bronze nail?	tool
	bronze ring/chain	tool
	weight	business
	arrowhead	weapon
1792W	1 lamp	lighting
	glass bead	adornment
	armour scale	weapon
1793	1 krater	food preparation/consumption
	jar stopper	storage
	drain pipe	drainage
1793E	1 whorl	textile production
1793N	1 needle	textile production
	bronze object	unknown
	bronze knife	tool
1793W	2 whorls	textile production
	1 bead	adornment
	toggle pin	adornment
	bronze awl	tool
	bronze axe	tool
	javelin point	weapon
	unknown object	unknown
1794	1 jug	food preparation/storage
	1 bead	adornment
1794N	3 whorls	textile production
	arrowhead(?)	weapon
1794S	1 bowl	food preparation/consumption
	1 jug	food preparation/storage
1794W	1 whorl	textile production
	1 bead	adornment
1796	1 jar	food storage

Table 4.21—*Continued*

Locus	Finds	Functional Class
	drain pipe	drainage
	grinding stone	food preparation
	bone awl	multipurpose
	unknown object	unknown
1796N	1 scarab	business/adornment
	1 amulet	adornment/cultic
	bronze knife	tool
	iron hook	tool
1797	1 jug	food preparation/storage
	1 pyxis	special
	ivory ornament	adornment?
	unknown object	unknown
1797W	1 bowl	food preparation/consumption
	1 flask	liquid storage
	1 rhyton	special/cultic
	2 whorls	textile production
	1 glass bead	adornment
	beads	adornment
	unknown object	unknown
1801	1 bowl	food preparation/consumption
	1 needle	textile production
	basalt grinder	food preparation
	2 basalt bowls	food preparation
	1 amulet	adornment/cultic
	bronze ring/chain	adornment/tool
	perforated stone	tool/weight
1803E	stamp seal	business/adornment
	1 amulet	adornment/cultic
1803S	1 whorl	textile production
	1 amulet	adornment/cultic
	2 finger rings	adornment
1805	1 weight	business
1805N	1 needle	textile production
	1 scarab	business/adornment
	1 amulet	adornment/cultic
	1 glass bead	adornment
	bronze object	unknown
	1 arrowhead	weapon
1810	1 krater	food preparation/consumption
1810S	1 jug	food preparation/storage
1810W	1 krater	food preparation/consumption
1811E	1 krater	food preparation/consumption

Table 4.21—*Continued*

Locus	Finds	Functional Class
	1 pyxis	special
1811N	1 bowl	food preparation/consumption
	1 chalice	food consumption
	1 cooking pot	food preparation
	1 jar	food storage
	1 flask	liquid storage
	beads	adornment

The similarity coefficient for L. 1811N is 162 or 81% when compared to the food preparation and consumption paradigm.

1812	1 bowl	food preparation/consumption
	1 flask	liquid storage
	kohl stick	cosmetic
	clay object	unknown
	2 arrowheads	weapon
	bone handle	unknown
1812E	1 amulet	adornment/cultic
1812S	drain pipe	drainage
	2 whorls	textile production
	1 needle	textile production
	1 scarab	business/adornment
	toggle pin	adornment
	arrowhead	weapon
	ivory handle?	unknown
	horn	unknown
1812W	1 flask	liquid storage
	1 scarab	business/adornment
	1 animal figurine	special/cultic
	5 basalt bowls	food preparation
	1 amulet	adornment/cultic
1813	1 bowl	food preparation/consumption
	4 whorls	textile production
	1 needle	textile production
	1 amulet	adornment/cultic
	bronze weight	business
	arrowhead	weapon

The similarity coefficient for L. 1813 is 160 or 80% when compared to the textile manufacture paradigm.

1813N	bronze knife	tool
1814	1 stirrup jar	liquid storage
	limestone knob?	unknown
	2 spindles	textile production
	1 scarab	business/adornment

Table 4.21—*Continued*

Locus	Finds	Functional Class
	2 basalt bowls	food preparation
	2 amulets	adornment/cultic
	4 beads	adornment
	bronze pin head	adornment
	3 alabaster vessels	special/status
	ivory hand	special/cultic
	ostrich egg	special/status
1814fl	1 scarab	business/adornment
	1 pendant	adornment
	1 bead	adornment
	1 disk	unknown
1814S	1 stamp seal	business/adornment
	1 bead	adornment
1814W	1 bowl strainer	food preparation
	loom weight	textile production
1815W	1 jug	food preparation/storage
1817	1 narrow-neck jar	liquid storage
	1 whorl	textile production
	1 scarab	business/adornment
	female plaque	special/cultic
	jar stopper	storage
	3 beads	adornment
	3 pendants	adornment
	metal rings	adornment/metallurgy
	dagger pommel	weapon
1817S	cup and saucer vessel	special/cultic
	1 needle	textile production
	beads	adornment
	bone inlay	special/status
1817W	1 bowl	food preparation/consumption
	bowl sherds	food preparation/consumption
	cup and saucer vessel	special/cultic
	wall bracket	architectural feature
	3 whorls	textile production
	ivory bowl	special/cosmetic
	stone bowl	food preparation
	gold pin head?	adornment
	clay ram's horn	unknown
	bone inlays	special/status
1818	3 bowls	food preparation/consumption
	1 bilbil	liquid storage
	1 kernos	special/cultic

Table 4.21—*Continued*

Locus	Finds	Functional Class
	1 jar stand	food preparation/storage
	ivory container	special/cosmetic
	ivory comb	cosmetic
	1 cylinder seal	business/adornment
	faience scarab	business/adornment
	faience figurine	special/cultic
	2 amulets	adornment/cultic
	4 beads	adornment
	faience pendant?	special/adornment
	bronze fibula	adornment
	gold fragments	metallurgy
	alabaster jug	special/status
1820	1 loom weight	textile production
	2 whorls	textile production
	1 needle	textile production
	2 beads	adornment
	toggle pin	adornment
	ivory object	unknown
	bronze nail	tool

The similarity coefficient for L. 1820 is 190 or 95% when compared to the textile manufacture paradigm.

Locus	Finds	Functional Class
1820E	1 juglet	multipurpose
	1 whorl	textile production
	1 bead	adornment
	1 arrowhead	weapon
1820S	1 whorl	textile production
	spinning bowl	textile production
	1 cylinder seal	business/adornment
	1 faience bead	adornment
	beads	adornment
	toggle pin	adornment
1820W	1 bowl	food preparation/consumption
	1 jar	storage
	2 whorls	textile production
	1 scarab	business/adornment
	limestone stopper	storage
	faience amulet	adornment/cultic
	2 beads	adornment
	crystal pendant	adornment
	gold earring	adornment
	toggle pin	adornment
	1 arrowhead	weapon

Table 4.21—*Continued*

Locus	Finds	Functional Class
	cone/horn	weight/unknown
1825E	1 pyxis	special
	1 whorl	textile production
	2 amulets	adornment/cultic
	bronze bracelet	adornment
	1 weight	business/adornment
	armour scale	weapon
1825N	1 jar	storage
1825S	1 bowl	food preparation/consumption
	1 juglet	multipurpose
	1 flask	liquid storage
	1 spindle	textile production
	2 whorls	textile production
	zoomorphic figurine	special/cultic
	1 grinder	food preparation
	faience vessel	special/status
	bronze ring/chain	tool
1826	alabaster vessel	special/status
1826E	1 cylinder seal	business/adornment
1827	cup and saucer vessel	special/cultic
1827E	figurine fragment	special/cultic
1827S	1 bowl	food preparation/consumption
	1 flask	liquid container
	1 jar stand	food preparation/storage
	3 whorls	textile production
	3 basalt grinders	food preparation
	2 beads	adornment
	toggle pin	adornment
	fish bone	unknown
	limestone object	unknown
	burnishing tool	pottery production
	weight	business
	bronze spearhead	weapon
	bronze spear butt	weapon
	bone inlay	special/status
1835	1 jar	storage
	2 clay drain pipes	drainage
	ivory game board	recreation
1835N	1 chalice	food consumption
	1 juglet	multipurpose
	1 jar stand	food preparation/storage
	4 whorls	textile production

Table 4.21—*Continued*

Locus	Finds	Functional Class
	3 needles	textile production
	1 scarab	business/adornment
	zoomorphic figurine	special/cultic
	1 bead	adornment
	1 pin head?	adornment
	1 bronze awl	tool
	bronze ring/chain	unknown/tool
	2 bone objects	unknown
	limestone object	unknown
	clay disk	unknown

The similarity coefficient for L. 1835N is 160 or 80% when compared to
the textile manufacture paradigm.

Locus	Finds	Functional Class
1835S	2 wide-neck jars	dry storage
	2 bowls	food preparation/consumption
1840	2 narrow-neck jars	liquid storage
	2 beads	adornment
	1 finger ring	adornment
	armour scale	weapon
1852	1 scarab	business/adornment

Stratum VIII Area AA (Fig. 52). Area AA presents a sharp contrast
to Areas BB and CC. Here, a monumental building was founded in
Stratum VIII and rebuilt and redesigned in Strata VIIB and VIIA
before its final destruction. It is clear from the 21 × 12 m courtyard
and 2 m thick walls (Loud 1948: 25) that this building was a public or
royal building rather than a private dwelling. Such walls could support
at least one, and possibly two, upper stories (Gonen 1987: 89).

The Stratum VIIB floors were built immediately above those of
Stratum VIII. In some cases, the Stratum VIII floor was reused in the
subsequent phase. As a result, it was difficult for the excavators to
distinguish, in every instance, the finds from these phases and to
recover the remains of Building 2041 in Stratum VIII. Thus, not one
room in the 'palace' produced a complete functional tool kit and the
assemblages themselves were small, 2–5 items. Only two rooms are of
interest, L. 3100 and 3102. In Room 3100, a hoard of 53 status items,
including lapis lazuli and gold jewellery, gold vessels, ivory objects,
seals, weapons and gold foil fragments, was found under the floor
(Loud 1948: 173). No paradigm has been designed for this type of
assemblage, but we could give it an arbitrary coefficient of 199 or

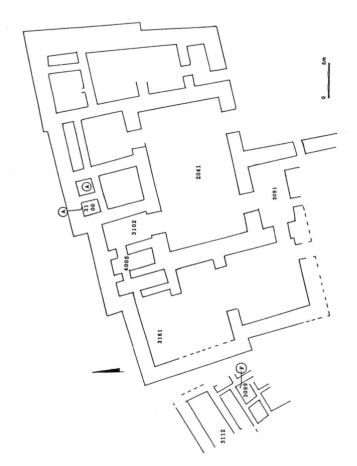

Figure 52. *Megiddo AA Stratum VIII, after Loud 1948: Fig. 382*

99.5% because it is a coherent group of special objects. A smaller assemblage, located in 3100E, included beads, scarabs and an ivory plaque (Table 4.22).[1]

In L. 3102, a room to the north of Courtyard 2041, were 2 bowls, 3 jugs, a spearhead and an armour scale. While not constituting a complete tool kit, or even one that could be compared to a functional paradigm, these finds suggest food preparation or consumption activities. Without additional material from surrounding loci, it is impossible to determine the likelihood that this assemblage was representative of the activities carried out in this room. In any 'palace' there should be certain functional tool kits that overlap with activities represented in typical houses, as well as assemblages of unique items. This was, indeed, the case in Building 2041.

In Area AA, west of the 'palace', a second building was partially exposed. The walls, c. 65 cm thick, were those of a typical house, as were the finds. An assemblage from Room 3099, and surrounding loci, included 5 bowls, 1 jar, 4 jugs and 1 scarab. The similarity coefficient of this corpus when compared to the food preparation paradigm is 138 or 69%. Because the remainder of this building was unexcavated, its identification as a house must remain tentative.

Table 4.22. *Megiddo Area AA Stratum VIII—Finds and Functional Classes*

Locus	Finds	Functional Class
3091W	2 bowls	food preparation/consumption
	1 jug	food preparation/storage
	1 lamp	lighting
	1 cup and saucer vessel	special/cultic
3099nr	1 scarab	business/adornment
3099N	4 bowls	food preparation/consumption
	4 jugs	food preparation/storage
3099Nfl	1 bowl	food preparation/consumption
3099S	1 jar	storage

The similarity coefficient for L. 3099N, 3099Nfl, and 3099S is 138 or 69% when compared to the food preparation and consumption paradigm.

3100	2 cylinder seals	business/adornment
	26 beads	adornment
	1 scarab ring	business/adornment
	2 gold headbands	adornment

1. Another unidentified ivory object was also found. From the photograph it could be a funnel or lid (Loud 1948: 287, 4).

Table 4.22—*Continued*

Locus	Finds	Functional Class
	9 gold rosettes	adornment
	gold foil fragments	metallurgy
	gold bowl	special/status
	stone and gold jars	cosmetic use
	gold objects, ivory disk and chain	special/adornment
	2 twin gold heads	adornment?
	ivory figurine head	special/cultic
	ivory wand	special/ceremonial
	5 paste objects	unknown
	sandstone whetstone	tool/ceremonial
	spear/arrowhead	weapon
	blunt arrowhead	weapon

The similarity coefficient for L. 3100 is 199 or 99.5% when assigned an arbitrary value.

Locus	Finds	Functional Class
3100E	2 scarabs	business/adornment
	beads	adornment
	ivory plaque	special/status
	ivory object	unknown/lid?
3100S	bronze chain	unknown
3102	2 bowls	food preparation/consumption
	3 jugs	food preparation/storage
	spear/arrowhead	weapon
	armour scale	weapon
3161	1 jug	food preparation/storage
	zoomorphic vessel	special/cultic
	1 gold rosette	adornment
4005N	animal figurine	special/cultic
	1 chisel	tool

Stratum VIIB Area AA (Fig. 53). The 'palace' was redesigned in Stratum VIIB but its character as a monumental building was maintained. In fact, all loci excavated in this area were of the same architectural style, thick-walled rooms and courts. The finds in this stratum are much more numerous than in the previous phase (Table 4.23). Locus 2131, with 45 items, seems to have served as a kitchen and storeroom to the west of the gate complex. In fact, Room 2131 may have been part of the service wing of the 'palace'. The assemblage from this locus has a similarity coefficient of 141 or 70.5% when

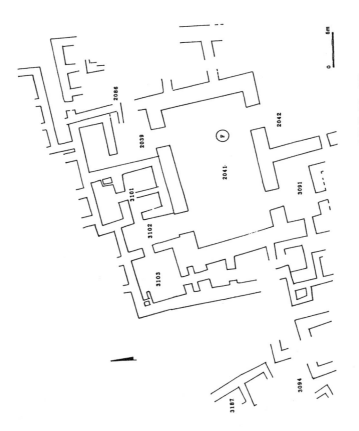

Figure 53. *Megiddo AA Stratum VIIB, after Loud 1948: Fig. 383*

compared to the food preparation paradigm. The only obvious item not represented is cooking pots.

In the 'palace' proper, jewellery and status goods (27 items), weapons and cultic objects seem to predominate. Contrary to expectation, no clearly administrative tool kits could be recognized. For example, from the large court (L. 2041, 2041E and 2041W) came a typical assemblage of food preparation equipment (3 bowls, a chalice, 4 jars, a bowl scoop[1] and a grinding bowl). Again, no cooking pots were recorded. Thus this tool kit has a similarity coefficient of only 109 or 54.5% when compared to the food preparation paradigm, even though no other types of activity were adequately represented by the artefact assemblage (Table 4.23). The remaining artefact groups were too small or contained items so disparate that no other functional clusters can be recognized.

Table 4.23. *Megiddo Area AA Stratum VIIB—Finds and Functional Classes*

Locus	Finds	Functional Class
2039	1 bowl	food preparation/consumption
	2 chalices	food consumption
	1 lamp	lighting
	2 cup and saucer vessels	special/cultic
	1 jar stand	food preparation/storage
	1 needle	textile production
	1 scaraboid	business/adornment
	2 amulets	adornment/cultic
	4 beads	adornment
	faience ring	adornment
	inlay fragment	special/status
	model shrine	cultic
2041	1 wide-neck jar	dry storage
	1 whorl	textile production
	1 scarab	business/adornment
	1 basalt bowl	grinding
	1 amulet	adornment/cultic
2041E	1 chalice	food consumption
	1 narrow-neck jar	liquid storage
	1 bowl scoop	multipurpose/storage

1. The bowl scoop seems to have been a special item manufactured during this period for the 'palace' as all occurrences were found here. The same may also be said of the 7 cup-and-saucer vessels. Only 3 such vessels were found in Area CC and 1 in Area BB.

Table 4.23—*Continued*

Locus	Finds	Functional Class
	1 amulet	adornment/cultic
	1 bead	adornment
	bronze hook	tool
	1 spear butt	weapon
	3 bowls	food preparation/consumption
2041W	2 narrow-neck jars	liquid storage

The similarity coefficient for L. 2041, 2041E, and 2041W is 109 or 54.5% when compared to the food preparation and consumption paradigm.

Locus	Finds	Functional Class
2042	funnel bowl	special/cultic
	1 scarab	business/adornment
2086	1 krater	food preparation/consumption
	1 wide-neck jar	dry storage
	1 jug	food preparation/storage
	kohl stick	cosmetic use
	faience vessel	special/status
2086E	1 flask	liquid storage
	zoomorphic figurine	special/cultic
2131	19 bowls	food preparation/consumption
	1 chalice	food consumption
	1 goblet	food consumption
	1 krater	food consumption
	3 narrow-neck jars	dry storage
	2 jugs	food preparation/storage
	2 juglets	multipurpose
	1 flask	liquid storage
	2 pyxides	special
	3 lamps	lighting
	5 cup and saucer vessels	special/cultic
	1 bowl scoop	multipurpose/storage
	1 clay lid	storage
	1 alabaster lid	special/status
	2 clay drain pipes	drainage

The similarity coefficient for L. 2131 is 141 or 70.5% when compared to the food preparation and consumption paradigm.

Locus	Finds	Functional Class
2131N	2 scarabs	business/adornment
	1 buckle	adornment
	1 mould	metallurgy
2131nr	1 scarab	business/adornment
3091	2 bowl scoops	multipurpose/storage
	carnelian bead	adornment
	gold earring	adornment
3094E	potter's? bowl	pottery production?

Table 4.23—*Continued*

Locus	Finds	Functional Class
3101lt	2 bowls	food preparation/consumption
	1 lamp	lighting
	ivory plaque	special/status
3101rt	ring/chain fragment?	unknown/tool
3102	1 bowl	food preparation/consumption
	1 bowl scoop	multipurpose/storage
	bronze hand fragment	special/cultic
	bronze bracelet	adornment
3103	1 bowl	food preparation/consumption
3103S	2 bowls	food preparation/consumption
3103W	1 bowl	food preparation/consumption
	1 bowl scoop	multipurpose/storage
3152	1 whorl	textile production
3163	game piece	recreation
3187	1 needle	textile production
	1 scarab	business/adornment
	toggle pin	adornment
	bronze blade	tool
3187fl	bronze pendant	adornment
	bronze snake	special/cultic
	spearhead	weapon

Stratum VIIA Area AA (Fig. 54). While Stratum VIIA saw a complete rebuilding of the northern area of the city, continuity of architectural style and function is evident.[1] This is in contrast to the complete change of architectural plan and style in the succeeding phase, Stratum VIB. Thus, it can be assumed that there was continuity of population from Stratum VIIB to VIIA (Avi-Yonah 1977: III, 847).

In the 'palace' proper, two assemblages can be functionally identified, that for L. 3061 and that for L. 3073. Room 3061 and its surrounding loci (E and N) represent a strong food preparation tool kit.

---

1. Debate among scholars concerning the dating of this stratum continues. Gonen (1987: 96) locates the beginning of Stratum VIIA firmly in the Late Bronze Age. On the other hand, Dothan assigns all ceramic vessels of Late Bronze style to Stratum VIIB in order to account for the presence of Philistine sherds in Stratum VIIA. In some cases, she even assigns certain loci (i.e., L. 3043), on the basis of their finds, to the earlier stratum (1982: 70-72). Davies follows Dothan in this regard affirming that she has 'shown' that the LB pottery belonged to VIIB (1986: 66). In my opinion, evidence for such a judgment is nowhere apparent.

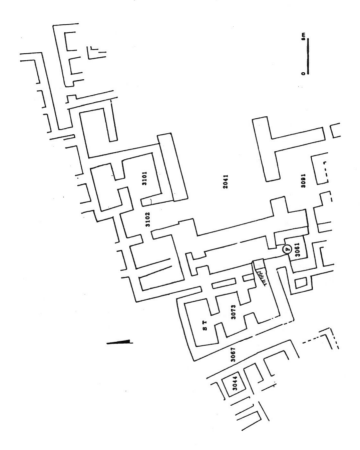

Figure 54.   *Megiddo AA Stratum VIIA, after Loud 1948: Fig. 384*

The only cooking pot reported for Area AA was found here (Table 4.24). The similarity coefficient is 118 or 59%. The relationship of the activities performed in this room to the rest of the building is not clear because the vestibule (L. 3185) of the 'treasury' (L. 3073), which was to the north was found empty, and all rooms to the south remain unexcavated.

The 'treasury' itself (L. 3073) consisted of three basement rooms which contained a wealth of status items, obviously in storage (Table 4.24). Here again we could assign an arbitrary similarity coefficient of 199 or 99.5% to such a unique assemblage. While the debate concerning the date of this hoard continues to occupy scholars, little can be said concerning the function of surrounding rooms in the 'palace' due to the paucity of reported finds. The only other functionally meaningful assemblage (3073N) was found in the debris from earlier structures, probably dug up during the construction of the basement rooms.

What is clear from this brief study of Area AA is that the finds vary in quantity, quality and concentration from those reported for typical domestic structures in Areas BB and CC. While it is not possible to say what specific activities were performed in the 'palace', other than food preparation and special storage capacity, the contrast of this building, in its functional tool kits, with typical Late Bronze Age houses is apparent.

Table 4.24. *Megiddo Area AA Stratum VIIA—Finds and Functional Classes*

Locus	Finds	Functional Class
3043	2 bowls	food preparation/consumption
	1 jug	food preparation/storage
	1 juglet	multipurpose
	1 lamp	lighting
	zoomorphic vessel	special/cultic
	wall bracket	decoration
	bronze bowl	special/status
3044W	1 bowl	food preparation/consumption
	1 axe	tool
3061	2 bowls	food preparation/consumption
	1 cooking pot	food preparation
3061E	3 bowl scoops	multipurpose/storage
3061N	4 bowls	food preparation/consumption
	1 amphora	storage
	1 flask	liquid storage
	1 lamp	lighting

Table 4.24—*Continued*

Locus	*Finds*	*Functional Class*
	1 cup and saucer vessel	special/cultic
	1 axe	tool
	1 dagger	weapon
3061W	alabaster lid	cosmetic use?

The similarity coefficient is 118 or 59% for L. 3061, 3061E, and 3061W when compared to the food preparation and consumption paradigm.

3067	1 pendant	adornment
3073	2 bowls	food preparation/consumption
	1 krater	food preparation/consumption
	2 cup and saucer vessels	special/cultic
	diorite jar	status
	basalt bowl/lid	status
	2 amulets	adornment/cultic
	17 gold beads	adornment
	3 necklaces	adornment
	7 pendants	adornment
	2 earrings	adornment
	faience button?	adornment
	alabaster object	status
	2 alabaster vessels	status
	ostrich egg fragment	status
	382 ivory pieces	status
	fitting and socket	decoration
	5 arrowheads	weapon
	7 spearheads	weapon
	slate? inlays	status

The similarity coefficient is 199 or 99.5% when assigned an arbitrary value.

3073E	1 scarab	business/adornment
3073N	3 bowls	food preparation/consumption
	1 krater	food preparation/consumption
	1 jug	food preparation/storage
	1 cup and saucer	special/cultic
	2 alabaster lids	status
	4 alabaster vessels	status
3073S	1 bowl	food preparation/consumption
	female figurine	cultic
3098	2 bowls	food preparation/consumption

Table 4.25. *Megiddo Area BB Stratum IX Loci*

Locus	Square	Description
2061	O13	Undefined
2091	N14	Undefined
2091Erm	N14	Room
2114	N15	Room
2115	N15	Room
2116	O15	Room
2127	N15	Room?
2127W	N15	Room?
3011	O14	Room
3017W	N14	Room?
3018E	O14	Room
3018S	O14	Room
3018W	O14	Room
3019	O13-14	Room
3027E	O14-15	Room
3028rm	O15	Room
3108	O13-14	Pit?

Table 4.26. *Megiddo Area BB Stratum VIII Loci*

Locus	Square	Description
2094	N-O14	Room
2094N	N14	Room
2099N	N15	Room?
2104N	N15	Room
2110E	N15	Room?
3000S	O14	Room
3000W	O14	Street
3000nr	O14	Room?
3001	O15	Room
3001N	O15	Room
3002	O15	Room
3002N	O15	Room
3003	O14	Room
3003nr	O14	Room
3004E	N14	Room
3007	O15	Undefined
3008	O15	Room
3010	O15	Drain
3016W	O15	Room
3018Wrm	O14	Room

Table 4.27. *Megiddo Area BB Stratum VII Loci*

Locus	Square	Description	Similarity Coefficient
2056E	O14	Undefined	
2058S	O13-14	Undefined	
2087E	N14	Room	
2092E	O13	Room	127 or 63.5%
2092W	O13	Undefined	
2092nr	O13	Room	
2158	N-O15	Room	

Table 4.28. *Megiddo Area CC Stratum VIIB Loci*

Locus	Square	Description	Similarity Coefficient
1829	R9	Room?	
1829N	R9	Undefined	
1830	R10	Room?	
1831	S8	Room	
1831E	S8	Room	149.0 or 74.5%
1832	R9	Room	
1832E	R9	Room	
1833N	R9	Room?	189.0 or 94.5%
1833W	R9	Undefined	
1834	S9	Room	
1837	S9	Room?	
1839	R10	Room?	
1843	R8	Room?	

Table 4.29. *Megiddo Area CC Stratum VIIA Loci*

Locus	Square	Description	Similarity Coefficient
1771N	R10	Room	132.7 or 66.8%
1779	S9-10	Room	
1779W	S9-10	Room	
1787	S9	Street?	
1792	R-S9	Room	
1792S	S9	Room	
1792W	R-S9	Room?	
1793	R9	Room	
1793E	R9	Room	
1793N	R9	Room	
1793W	R9	Room	
1794	S9	Room	

Table 4.29—*Continued*

Locus	Square	Description	Similarity Coefficient
1794N	S9	Room	
1794S	S9	Undefined	
1794W	S9	Room	
1796	S10-11	Room	
1796N	S10	Undefined	
1797	R10	Room	
1797W	R10	Undefined	
1799	R10	Room	
1801	R10	Room?	
1802	R10	Room?	
1803E	S8	Room	
1803S	S8	Room	
1804	R8	Room	
1805	R8	Room?	
1805N	R8	Undefined	
1810	R8	Room	
1810S	R8	Room?	
1810W	R8	Undefined	
1811E	Q9	Room	
1811N	Q9	Room	162 or 81%
1812	Q9	Room	
1812E	Q9	Room	
1812S	Q9	Room	
1812W	Q9	Room	
1813	R9	Floor	160 or 80%
1813N	R9	Undefined	
1814	S9	Room	
1814fl	S9	Floor	
1814S	S9	Room	
1814W	S9	Room	
1815	S9	Room	
1817	S10	Room?	
1817S	S10	Undefined	
1817W	S10	Undefined	
1818	S9	Undefined	
1820	R9	Room	190 or 95%
1820E	R9	Room?	
1820S	R9	Room	
1820W	R9	Room	
1825E	Q9	Undefined	
1825N	Q9	Undefined	
1825S	Q9	Undefined	

Table 4.29—*Continued*

Locus	Square	Description	Similarity Coefficient
1826	Q9-10	Floor	
1826E	Q10	Undefined	
1827	Q10	Room	
1827E	Q10	Room	
1827S	Q10	Undefined	
1835	S10	Room	
1835N	S10	Undefined	160 or 80%
1835S	S10	Room	
1840	R9	Room	
1852	R9	Undefined	

Table 4.30. *Megiddo Area AA Stratum VIII Loci*

Locus	Square	Description	Similarity Coefficient
3091	L7-8	Room	
3091W	L7	Room	
3099nr	L6	Room	
3099N	L6	Room	
3099Nfl	L6	Room	
3099S	L6	Room	138 or 69% for all L. 3099.
3100	K7	Room	
3100E	K7	Room	
3100S	K7	Room	
3102	K7	Room	
3112	K-L6	Room	
3113	K6	Room?	
3161	K7	Floor	
4005N	K7	Room	

Table 4.31. *Megiddo Area AA Stratum VIIB Loci*

Locus	Square	Description	Similarity Coefficient
2039	K8	Room	
2041	K-L7-8	Room	
2041E	K8	Room	
2041W	K-L7	Room	109 or 54.5% for all L. 2041.
2042	L8	Room	
2086	K8	Undefined	

Table 4.31—*Continued*

Locus	Square	Description	Similarity Coefficient
2086E	K8	Undefined	
2131	J8	Room	141 or 70.5%
2131N	J8	Room	
2131nr	J8	Room?	
3091	L7-8	Room	
3094E	L6	Undefined	
3101lt	K7	Room	
3101rt	K7-8	Room	
3102	K7	Room	
3103	K7	Room	
3103S	K7	Room	
3103W	K7	Stairs?	
3152	J-K9	Room	
3163	J9	Room?	
3187	K6	Room	
3187fl	K6	Floor	

Table 4.32. *Megiddo Area AA Stratum VIIA Loci*

Locus	Square	Description	Similarity Coefficient
3043	L6-7	Floor	
3044W	K6	Room	
3061	L7	Room	
3061E	L7	Room	
3061N	L7	Room	
3061W	L7	Room	118 or 59% for
3067	K6	Street	all L. 3061.
3073	K-L7	Basement rooms	
3073E	K-L7	Room?	
3073N	K7	Undefined	
3073S	L7	Room?	
3091	K7	Room	
3101	K7	Room	
3102	K7	Room	

Beth Shan (Map Reference 197/212)

During the ten seasons of excavation by the University Museum of the University of Pennsylvania on the mound of Beth Shan, domestic structures were uncovered around the two Egyptian style villas, House 1500 and House 1700, and around the temple (James 1966: Fig. 9). In fact, two phases of Level VI were identified; Level VI and Late Level VI (James 1966: 13). Because the villas will be considered in the discussion of the 'Residencies', this analysis will focus on the remaining structures.

North Area (Fig. 55)

Along the north side of House 1700, a series of rooms was cleared by FitzGerald in 1933 and assigned to Level VI. As James has shown, the stratigraphy at the edge of the tell where these structures were located is very difficult to reconstruct (1966: 13).[1] As a result, it is not certain that these rooms were contemporary, although it is probable. At the same time, their relationship to one another, and the boundaries of individual houses cannot be determined.

Because of the small number of finds published,[2] only two rooms lend themselves to functional analysis, L. 1721 and 1728. Here, however, the assemblages consist entirely of objects (no ceramic vessels were reported)[3] with the result that no recognizable paradigm can be assigned. What can be said about these rooms is that either they functioned as storerooms for tools and weapons, or that they were the focus of various craft-related activities (Table 4.33). For each locus, items of personal adornment were also reported. Because of the method of excavation and recording, it is not possible to determine to what extent these items were deposited or lost at random. And, in themselves, they do not help to clarify the function of these assemblages.

An oven in Room 1729, contiguous to both L. 1721 and 1728, may indicate food preparation. Nevertheless, without additional evidence, this designation must remain tentative because the oven may have been used for other purposes. A chisel and a dagger were found in L. 1732, immediately south of Room 1721. The ceramic vessel associated with these objects (1 beer jar, Table 4.33) does not fall into a distinct functional assemblage and therefore adds nothing to our understanding of these rooms.

On the other hand, a structural device noted during excavation does

---

1. This is due in part to the fact that so few elevations were recorded by the original excavators. See James's comment regarding the earlier phase of Level VI (1966: 14).

2. Many pottery vessels, especially those badly smashed, were not drawn by the expedition (James 1966: 13).

3. This is not to say that none were found!

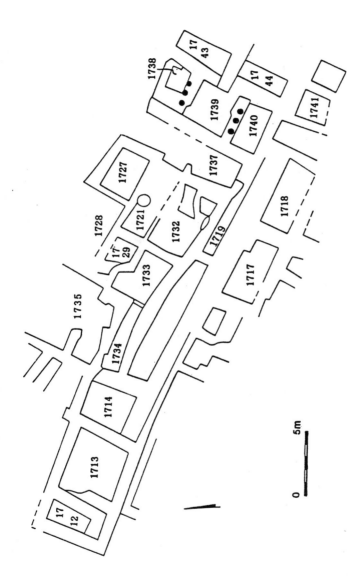

Figure 55. *Beth Shan Level VI north end, after James 1966: Fig. 76, 1*

add some information about these rooms. In L. 1732, 2 post holes
with remains of charred wood were identified as pillars supporting the
ceiling. Similarly, in Rooms 1738 and 1740, pillar recesses were
observed in the makeup of interior walls. It was assumed that these
supports were intended to strengthen the walls (James 1966: 14). In
fact, these supports may be evidence that these rooms were the lower
floor of a multistoried building.[1]

Table 4.33. *Beth Shan Level VI North—Finds and Functional Classes*

Locus	Finds	Functional Class
1714	2 flasks	liquid storage
1721	1 bead	adornment
	1 toggle pin	adornment
	1 whetstone	tool
	1 chisel	tool
	2 bronze blades	tool
	1 plough	agricultural tool
	1 arrowhead	weapon
	1 dagger	weapon
1728	bronze tweezers	multipurpose
	faience scaraboid	business/adornment
	bead spacer	adornment
	2 whetstones	tool
1729	oven	food preparation
1732	1 beer jar	liquid storage
	1 chisel	tool
	bronze dagger	weapon
	post holes and wood	pillars
1733	1 bowl	food preparation/consumption
	1 stirrup jar	liquid container
	stamp seal	business
1737	1 arrowhead	weapon
1738	1 bead	adornment
1740	1 krater	food preparation/consumption
	1 lamp	lighting
1741	1 bead	adornment
1744	1 bead	adornment

1.   While FitzGerald clearly identified a later phase of his Level VI, it is not possible in this study to analyse the finds from this phase. Complete building plans and
elevations do not exist for these rooms (James 1966: Fig. 77) making it impossible to
distinguish the finds from this phase. Nor is it possible to discover whether the upper
phase identified by FitzGerald was an upper story of the lower phase buildings.

South Side (Fig. 56)

To the south of the Egyptian style houses there was a small temple surrounded by a courtyard and several clusters of rooms. Because these rooms shared party walls, it is difficult to distinguish individual houses. Indeed, most structures are incomplete due to erosion along the edge of the tell in this area, and the pit (L. 1139) dug into Level VI from above. Nevertheless, several activity areas can be identified.

To the east of the temple, two house complexes were divided by a north–south street. To the east of the street (L. 1203), an east–west alley (L. 1199) formed the southern boundary of complex 1201. Locus 1201 is one of the few intact rooms in this house. While only 4 items were registered for this room, it contained an oven and was probably a major living area. The remaining finds form no recognizable functional assemblage (Table 4.34), although the model bread was probably used in association with the temple. In fact, Locus 1206, which was destroyed along its north end, yielded a more coherent assemblage consisting of a basalt grinder, 2 storejars, a krater and a corner bin (Table 4.34). In spite of the small number of recorded finds, this locus has a similarity coefficient of 112 or 56% in comparison with the storage paradigm. The remaining rooms of this complex were small and without significant finds (Table 4.34). There was, however, a spindle whorl reported for L. 1209. While this is not significant in itself, the fact that there were 7 other items associated with textile production distributed in other loci surrounding the temple indicates that there was a concentration of this craft in this area.

Between the temple and Street 1203 was a second complex, House 1200, also destroyed along its north side. Three rooms (L. 1200, 1202 and 1195) can be assigned, with some certainty, to the same house (Fig. 56). The finds from these rooms point to a variety of domestic activities: food preparation, storage, textile production and business or trade. In addition, an Egyptian inscribed lintel and an alabaster jar indicate status and wealth.

It is not clear whether other rooms further south, such as L. 1196 and 1197, belonged to House 1200. The finds recovered from Room 1196 clearly testify to its function as a storeroom (Table 4.34). Five jars, which one would expect to hold liquids, contained sesame seeds. The similarity coefficient for this room when compared to the storage paradigm is 152 or 76%. On the other hand, no such clear picture can be gained from Room 1197 where the reported assemblage included

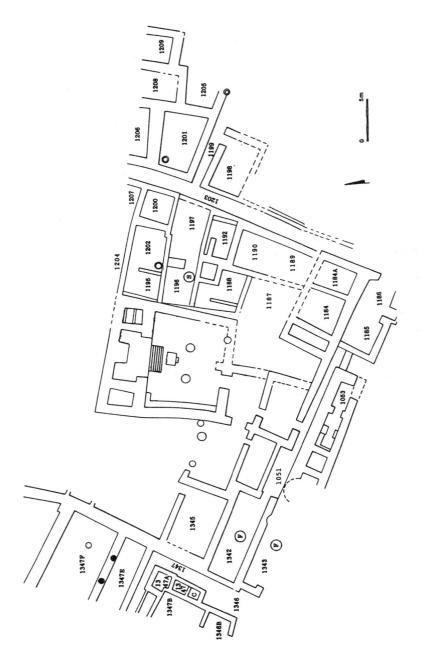

Figure 56.   *Beth Shan Level VI south end, after James 1966: Fig. 77*

items involved in food preparation, textile manufacture, personal adornment and business (Table 4.34) without forming any clusters related to the tool kits under discussion in this study.

Additional rooms that shared a party wall on the south (L. 1188, 1192) also reflect typical domestic activities. The assemblage for Room 1192 is too diverse to be compared with any one paradigm; it included items related to food preparation, along with a baking stone (James 1966: 18), textile production and personal adornment (Table 4.34). The three finds recorded from Room 1188, to the west, were too few to be meaningful.

Further south, in Locus 1189, a paved floor was found covered with flint tools and animal bones. It is not clear from the description or the published plan whether this locus was a room or an open court where food preparation or activities related to the temple took place. No vessels or objects from the surrounding rooms have been reported, leaving the true function of L. 1189 uncertain.

Two phases of occupation were discerned in the rooms to the south of the temple. It may be that the confusion of surfaces in these rooms accounts for the small number of registered finds (4 items from 10 loci). To the west of L. 1051 was a series of three rooms (L. 1342, 1343, 1345) which are in sharp contrast to the rooms studied so far (Fig. 56). The contrast, both in size and content, may confirm the suspicion that these rooms do not form an ordinary domestic structure. The largest assemblage was registered for Room 1342, a total of 30 items. The next largest assemblages, from rooms to the east of the temple, were those of L. 1195 and 1196, each with 10 items.[1]

Table 4.34. *Beth Shan Level VI South—Finds and Functional Classes*

Locus	Finds	Functional Class
1044	1 bead	adornment
1053	spinning bowl	textile production
	alabaster pyxis	special/cosmetic
1060	iron knob	decoration?
1185	1 chalice	food consumption
	2 kraters	food preparation/consumption
	1 jar	storage
	1 flask	liquid storage

1. This does not include the other assemblages from the parallel rooms, L. 1343 and 1345.

Table 4.34—*Continued*

Locus	Finds	Functional Class
	spinning bowl	textile production
	basalt bowl	food preparation
	grain	food storage
1186	1 krater	food preparation/consumption
	2 narrow-neck jars	liquid storage
	1 jug	food preparation/storage
	2 flasks	liquid storage
	1 kernos	special/cultic
	3-leg mortar	food preparation
1187	bronze axe	tool
1188	1 jug	food preparation/storage
	1 whetstone?	uncertain
	bronze blade	tool
1189	flint implements	tool
	bones	food preparation
1192	1 bowl	food preparation/consumption
	2 kraters	food preparation/consumption
	1 jug	food preparation/storage
	1 scarab	business/adornment
	baking stone	food preparation
1194	perforated stone	weight
1195	1 bowl	food preparation/consumption
	1 jug	food preparation/storage
	1 juglet	multipurpose
	spinning bowl	textile production
	1 amulet	adornment/magic
	1 buckle	adornment
	1 whetstone	tool
	alabaster jar	special/status
	1 weight	business
	lintel fragment	architectural feature
1196	1 krater	food preparation/consumption
	5 narrow-neck jars	storage
	2 jugs	food preparation/storage
	model bread	special/cultic
	sesame	food storage

The similarity coefficient for L. 1196 is 152 or 76% when compared to the storage paradigm.

1197	1 jug	food preparation/storage
	1 juglet	multipurpose
	1 needle	textile production
	1 scarab	business/adornment

Table 4.34—*Continued*

Locus	Finds	Functional Class
	basalt bowl	food preparation
	1 bead	adornment
	2 alabaster pyxides	special/cosmetic
1198	1 juglet	food preparation/consumption
1199	1 krater	food preparation/consumption
	1 amphora	liquid storage
	1 rivet	tool
1200	1 weight	business
1201	1 juglet	multipurpose
	1 cylinder seal	business/adornment
	model bread	special/cultic
	1 spearhead	weapon
	oven	food preparation
1202	1 narrow-neck jar	liquid storage
	1 flask	liquid storage
	1 bead spacer	adornment
1203	1 flask	liquid storage
	1 needle	textile production
	bronze fragment	broken tool?
	bronze point	weapon
	1 arrowhead	weapon
1204	jewellery mould	metallurgy
1205	alabaster cover	special/cosmetic
	alabaster pyxis—unfinished	vessel production
1206	1 krater	food preparation/consumption
	2 narrow-neck jars	liquid storage
	female figurine	special/cultic
	3-leg mortar	food preparation

The similarity coefficient for L. 1206 is 112 or 56% when compared to the storage paradigm.

1209	1 whorl	textile production
	1 bead	adornment
1342	6 bowls	food preparation/consumption
	3 kraters	food preparation/consumption
	3 narrow-neck jars	liquid storage
	1 amphora	liquid storage
	4 jugs	food preparation/storage
	1 juglet	multipurpose
	2 kernoi	special/cultic
	2 scarabs	business/adornment
	bronze figurine	special/cultic
	2 amulets	adornment/cultic

Table 4.34—*Continued*

Locus	Finds	Functional Class
	1 bead	adornment
	2 alabaster pyxides	special/status
	carved limestone	architectural feature
	stone and holes	libation?
	animal bones	food consumption
	carbonized grain	food storage
	shells	food consumption/special

The similarity coefficient for L. 1342 is 125.6 or 62.8% when compared to the food preparation and consumption paradigm.

Locus	Finds	Functional Class
1343	4 bowls	food preparation/consumption
	2 kraters	food preparation/consumption
	1 narrow-neck jar	liquid storage
	1 jug	food preparation/storage
	1 flask	liquid storage
	1 whorl	textile production
	1 spatula	textile production
	model bread	special/cultic

The similarity coefficient for L. 1343 is 148 or 74% when compared to the food preparation and consumption paradigm.

Locus	Finds	Functional Class
1345	1 jug	food preparation/storage
	1 amulet	adornment/cultic
	2 beads	adornment
	1 bead spacer	adornment
	alabaster duck	special/status
	model bread	cultic
	2 arrowheads	weapon
1347	1 bowl	food preparation/consumption
	1 juglet	multipurpose
	1 bead	adornment
	ivory duck head	special/status
	weight	business
	carved limestone	architectural feature
	stone and holes	unknown

At least two distinct tool kits seem to be represented in L. 1342: food preparation/consumption and cultic activity. While no cooking pots were reported, the total assemblage has a similarity coefficient in comparison to the food preparation paradigm of 125.7 or 62.8%. The presence of carbonized grain in one of the storejars led James to the conclusion that this locus served as a storeroom (1966: 17). Such a judgment cannot be supported by comparison with the storage paradigm because of the great diversity of vessels and objects associated with other activities. A second possible tool kit consists of 2 kernoi, 1 figurine, several amulets and a clay object with 2 depressions and internal channels[1]. The presence of the bronze figurine is not unique to this locus. However, its association with other items, such as the kernoi, and possibly the pyxides (Table 4.34), indicates a concentration of special or cultic objects in this room. If these items related to cultic activity had constituted the total assemblage for this locus, I could have assigned an arbitrary similarity coefficient of 199 or 99.5%. The remaining vessels would then have a similarity coefficient of 158 or 79% when compared to the food preparation and consumption paradigm.[2]

The rooms on either side, L. 1343 and 1345, each contained a model bread but no other clearly cultic objects. In Room 1343, food preparation is well represented by an assemblage with a similarity coefficient of 148 or 74%. Again, no cooking pots, oven or baking area was mentioned for this locus. By contrast, the finds from Room 1345 do not fall into any coherent tool kits, and James notes that this locus was not described in the original publication.

The rooms surrounding the temple seem to fall into two categories: those on the east were typical of domestic architecture in size and artefact remains, while those on the south and west were larger, contained more objects related to cultic activity and were probably associated with functions taking place in the temple courtyard.[3] At the same time, it is not possible to determine the plan of a typical domestic unit at Beth Shan since doorways were not indicated. Publication of earlier strata, promised by McGovern (1986: 14), may facilitate such study.

1. James classified this item as an object involved in some type of industry. However, no evidence to support this judgment is offered (1966: 17) nor were any other craft-related objects reported.

2. The analysis of such an assemblage would be best served by multivariate analysis which is outside the design of this study.

3. L. 1347 was assigned to 6 different rooms making analysis of the reported finds for functional assemblages impossible.

Table 4.35. *Beth Shan Late Bronze Age Loci Level VI*

Locus	Square	Description	Similarity Coefficient
1053	Q8	Room	
1184	R9	Room	
1184A	R9	Room	
1185	R9	Room	
1186	R9	Room	
1188	R8	Room	
1189	R9	Room?	
1192	R8	Room	
1195	R8	Room	
1196	R8	Room	152.0 or 76%
1197	R8	Room	
1198	R8-9	Room	
1199	R8	Street	
1200	R8	Room	
1201	R8	Room	
1202	R8	Room	
1203	R8-9	Street	
1204	R8	Undefined	
1205	S8	Room	
1206	R8	Room	112.0 or 56%
1207	R8	Undefined	
1208	S8	Room	
1209	S8	Room	
1224	R7	Room	
1282	R7-8	Room	
1342	Q8	Room	125.7 or 62.8%
1343	Q8	Undefined	148.0 or 74.0%
1345	Q8	Room	
1346	Q8	Passageway	
1346B	Q8	Room	
1347	Q8	Passageway	
1347A	Q8	Room	
1347B	Q8	Room	
1347C	Q8	Room	
1347E	Q8	Room	
1347F	Q8	Room	

Locus	Square	Description	Phase
1712	Q7	Room	Lower Level
1713	Q7	Room	Lower Level

Table 4.35—*Continued*

Locus	Square	Description	Phase
1714	Q-R7	Room	Lower Level
1717	R7	Room	Lower Level
1718	R7	Room	Lower Level
1719	R7	Room?	Lower Level
1721	R7	Room	Lower Level
1727	R7	Room	Lower Level
1728	R7	Room?	Lower Level
1729	R7	Room	Lower Level
1732	R7	Room	Lower Level
1733	R7	Room	Lower Level
1734	R7	Room	Lower Level
1737	R7	Room	Lower Level
1738	R7	Room	Lower Level
1739	R7	Room	Lower Level
1740	R7	Room	Lower Level
1741	R7	Room	Lower Level
1743	R7	Room	Lower Level
1744	R7	Room	Lower Level

Table 4.36. *Beth Shan 1500 House and 1700 House Loci*[1]

Locus	Square	Description	
1584	Q7	Court	1700 House
1585	Q7	Court	1700 House
1583	Q7	Room	
1586	Q7	Room	
1587	Q7	Room	
1588	Q7	Room	
1592	Q7	Room	
1599	Q7	Room	
1701	Q7	Room	
1702	Q7	Room	
1703	P7	Court	
1704	P-Q6-7	Room	
1705	P6-7	Room	
1706	P6	Room	
1707	P7	Room	

1. See below—discussion of Governors' Residencies.

Table 4.36—*Continued*

Locus	Square	Description
1709	P7	Room
1710	P7	Room
1711	P7	Room
1715	R7	Room
1716	R7	Room

Ashdod (Map Reference 117/129)

A city of the Philistine Pentapolis, Ashdod was located 4 km east of the Mediterranean. The tell consists of an acropolis and a lower city with a total area of approximately 37.5 hectares (90 acres).[1] Modern excavations were begun in 1962 under the direction of Moshe Dothan with the assistance of D.N. Freedman. More than seven seasons of excavation have been carried out. As a result of these excavations, evidence of occupation from the Middle Bronze Age to the Byzantine period has been documented (Avi-Yonah I, 1975: 105, 107). Late Bronze Age domestic remains at Ashdod were uncovered only in Area B. Here, one building with four LB phases was exposed. The phases that are important for this study are Strata 3 and 2 (Dothan and Freedman 1967: Pls. 3, 4).

Stratum 3 (Fig. 57)
With Stratum 3, a new building was constructed with an orientation different from that of earlier structures. This rectangular building, including Rooms 529, 507 and 535 which were added on the south,[2] measured c. 12 × 17 m The walls which surrounded the three southern rooms were 1.2 m thick while the exterior walls to the north were only 60–65 cm thick. The reason for this discrepancy is

1. It is not clear from the description whether the area of the lower city included the 20 acres of the acropolis. In addition, the lower city was severely damaged by modern ploughing so that its original parameters are not known.

2. Three rooms on the east (L. 539b, 538b, 547b) appear to have had several occupation phases. However, it is not at all certain that the earlier phase was simultaneous with Stratum 3. Because excavation further east was left incomplete, the extent of the complex of buildings of Stratum 2 remains unknown, leaving the question of the relationship of these rooms to the main house unclear.

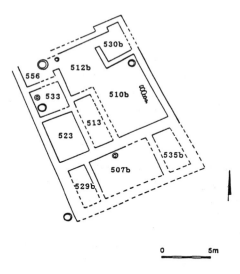

Figure 57. *Ashdod Stratum 3, after Dothan and Freedman 1967: Pl. 4*

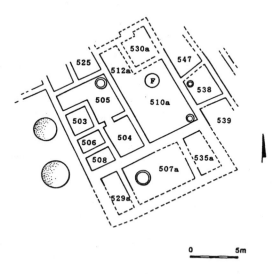

Figure 58. *Ashdod Stratum 2, after Dothan and Freedman 1967: Pl. 3*

unknown. All walls were of mud brick on stone foundations. According to the excavators, most of these walls were destroyed below floor level so that no doorsills were preserved (Dothan and Freedman 1967: 74). From the published plan (Dothan and Freedman 1967: Pl. 4), evidence for only two doorways was preserved, one into L. 512b from L. 530b, and another from L. 512b into L. 556 (Fig. 57).

The floors were made of beaten earth and features within the rooms included ovens and a bench. Although these features were identified as having a domestic function, the excavators interpreted this structure as a public building. The reason for this judgment is the small amount of pottery and objects recovered from the Stratum 3 building (Table 4.37). Only 2 vessels were reported for all the loci (more than 10 rooms)! It seems significant to me that those vessels were common domestic forms related to food preparation and consumption, a bowl and a krater. In fact, the Ashdod building is not excessive in size for a private house (15.4 × 11.2 m) when compared to those at Hazor (10 × 13 m and 10 × 20 m). The thickness of the walls (c. 65 cm, Fig. 57) of the main part of the house do not seem to support the view of the excavators that this structure was similar to the Residency at Tell Far'ah (S) (200 cm thick, Fig. 76) or to the public buildings at Megiddo (c. 230 cm thick, Fig. 53) (Dothan and Freedman 1967: 75).[1] Unfortunately, artefact analysis to support the view that this structure at Ashdod was a private house cannot be attempted with so few finds.

Table 4.37. *Ashdod Stratum 3—Finds and Functional Classes*

Locus	Finds	Functional Class
507b	oven	food preparation
510b	oven	food preparation
513	1 bowl	food preparation/consumption
	1 krater	food preparation/consumption
533	2 ovens	food preparation
556	bench	multipurpose
	oven	food preparation

1. The public building at Megiddo, Area AA, Stratum VIII measured 47 × 33 m, significantly larger than this structure at Ashdod.

Stratum 2 (Fig. 58)

When the Stratum 3 building was remodelled, several small rooms were created on the west side (L. 503, 506 and 508). In addition, Rooms 547a, 538a and 539a were added outside the east wall (Dothan and Freedman 1967: 77). Because of the limits of the excavation area, it is not certain that these rooms were an integral part of the main building. There could have been a second structure further east that shared a party wall. In either case, the oven in Room 538a would have been located in an interior room, not uncommon for a second millennium house.

The reported finds from the Stratum 2 building were more numerous than those of the previous phase. For example, an assemblage of 15 items is reported from Room 510a. The assemblage consists of bowls, a cooking pot, jars and jugs, a jar stand and an oven (Table 4.38). Such finds are sufficient for functional analysis and yield a similarity coefficient of 150 or 75% when compared to the food preparation paradigm. Included in the assemblage were a spindle whorl and a miniature jug, evidence of the multifunctional character of this locus. In view of the fact that L. 510a was the largest room in the house, it probably served as the living room. As we have seen repeatedly, the presence of an oven in the largest interior space does not necessarily imply that this room was unroofed.

Although no other assemblage was large enough for analysis, the finds from Rooms 503, 505 and 506, consisting of bowls, kraters, cooking pots and an oven (Table 4.38), clearly indicate that food preparation was carried out in several parts of the house. Such a distribution of activity areas could reflect a situation where the location of cooking was changed with the season or where cooking was done on a large scale for an extended family or group. We have already seen a similar pattern of more than one oven in the same house at Hazor in both the Middle and Late Bronze Age strata. These houses typically had 10–14 rooms, and were comparable to this building at Ashdod.

Other domestic activities are reflected in the presence of whorls, the top of a bow drill, and the lid of a cosmetic dish. In view of the fact that the second phase of this building can be shown to have served a domestic function, it is likely that it was also a house in Stratum 3. Further excavation to the east may uncover additional houses, thereby making possible further comparisons. However, these excavations at Ashdod have been concluded.

Table 4.38. *Ashdod Stratum 2—Finds and Functional Classes*

Locus	Finds	Functional Class
503	1 bowl	food preparation/consumption
	1 cooking pot	food preparation
505	3 bowls	food preparation/consumption
	2 kraters	food preparation/consumption
	faience lid	cosmetic use?
	1 whorl	textile production
	oven	food preparation
506	2 cooking pots	food preparation
	1 whorl	textile production
507a	1 bowl	food preparation/consumption
	1 lamp	lighting
	wall bracket	decoration
	pommel/bow drill	tool
	silo	storage/refuse
510a	4 bowls	food preparation/consumption
	1 krater	food preparation/consumption
	1 cooking pot	food preparation
	1 jar	storage
	2 jugs	food preparation/storage
	1 juglet	multipurpose
	1 bilbil	liquid storage
	miniature vessel	special
	jar stand	storage
	1 whorl	textile production
	oven	food preparation

The similarity coefficient for L. 510a is 150 or 75% when compared to the food preparation and consumption paradigm.

Locus	Finds	Functional Class
512	1 kylix	food consumption
525	1 bowl	food preparation/consumption
	1 jug	food preparation/storage
	2 flasks	liquid storage
534a	krater sherd?	food preparation/consumption?
	1 krater	food preparation/consumption
538a	oven	food preparation

Table 4.39. *Ashdod Stratum 3 Loci*

Locus	Square	Description
507b	J19	Room
510b	J1-20	Court?
512b	H1	Room

Table 4.39—*Continued*

Locus	Square	Description
513	H-J20	Room
523	H20	Room
529b	H19	Room
530b	J1-2	Room
533	G-H20	Room
535b	K19-20	Room
556	G1	Room

Table 4.40. *Ashdod Stratum 2 Loci*

Locus	Square	Description	Similarity Coefficient
503	GH-20	Room	
504	H-J20	Room	
505	H1	Room	
506	H20	Room	
507a	J19	Room	
508	H19	Room	
510a	J1-20	Court?	150 or 75%
512a	H1	Room	
525	H1	Room	
526	G1	Room	
529a	H19	Room	
530a	J1-2	Room	
535a	K19-20	Room	
538	K1	Room	
539	K20	Room	
547	J-K1	Room	

Tel Batash (Map Reference 1416/1326)

In the Shephelah, between Beth-shemesh and Khirbet el-Muqanna (Tel Miqne), is the site of Tel Batash. The mound, located on the southern bank of the Sorek River, is a square tell that covers 2.25 hectares (5.6 acres). The shape of the tell and its orientation to the points of the compass indicate that it was first occupied in the Middle Bronze Age (Kelm and Mazar 1983: 56). Ten seasons of excavations, under the archaeological direction of Amihai Mazar, have been carried out since 1977. Domestic architecture has been uncovered in the Late Bronze and Iron Age strata, VIII–II.

Stratum VIII (Fig. 59)

Two Late Bronze Age houses were uncovered in Area B, one in Stratum VIII and its successor in Stratum VII. Although both houses date to LB IIA (14th century), a difference in room arrangement is apparent (see below). In the Stratum VIII house, four rooms occupied the ground floor: an entryway, L. 494; a large roofed hall on the east, L. 475; and twin rooms on the west, L. 492 and 467. Both of these smaller rooms, along with the entryway, appear to have served as storerooms. They contained a total of 33 jars, 15 jugs, 19 bowls and 16 cooking pots (Table 4.41). Such a functional identification is based on the assumption that the cooking pots were in storage rather than part of current food preparation activities. The presence of such a large number of bowls is also unusual unless they were being used as lids or scoops. Taken individually, Entryway 494 has a similarity coefficient of 137 or 68.5% and Room 492 of 146.8 or 73.4% when compared to the storage paradigm, whereas Room 467 has a coefficient of only 125 or 62.5%. In fact, this latter room is closer to the food preparation paradigm, due to the large number of cooking pots and yields a similarity coefficient of 152 or 76% when compared to that paradigm. Indeed the number of vessels found in these storerooms is markedly higher than the number of vessels found, for example, at Hazor in Room 6217 which contained 5 or 6 pithoi and 1 jug.

The same types of ceramic wares (Table 4.41) were found in the large hall (L. 475) but in smaller numbers (Kelm and Mazar 1985: 98, Table 2). Nevertheless, Room 475 may have functioned as the primary food preparation area. It had a similarity coefficient of 148 or 74% in comparison to the food preparation and consumption paradigm. Other activities that were carried out in this room cannot yet be ascertained because none of the small finds have been published to date. However, on the basis of its location in the house and its size in relation to other rooms, L. 475 probably served as the main living room

The fact that there were so many vessels in the storerooms has led the excavators to suggest that the Tel Batash house belonged to a local ruler rather than an individual family (Kelm and Mazar, 1982: 13), and indeed it does bear some similarities to the Late Bronze Age 'government house' excavated at Aphek (Kochavi 1978, 1981). The one significant caveat is the size of the Tel Batash building, c. 9 × 9 m, not including the entryway (L. 194). While it is possible that there

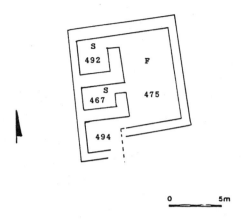

Figure 59: *Tel Batash Stratum VIII, after Kelm and Mazar 1985: Fig. 8*

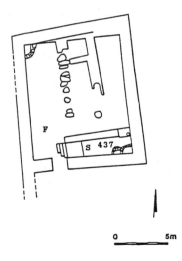

Figure 60. *Tel Batash Stratum VII, after Kelm and Mazar 1982: Fig. 9*

was an upper storey, this building is still well within the size range of typical Late Bronze Age houses.

Table 4.41. *Tel Batash Area B Stratum VIII—Finds and Functional Classes*

Locus	Finds	Functional Class
467	11 bowls	food preparation/consumption
	14 cooking pots	food preparation
	19 jars	storage
	9 jugs	food preparation/storage
	2 juglets	multipurpose
	2 other	unknown

The similarity coefficient for L. 467 is 152 or 76% when compared to the food preparation and consumption paradigm.

475	5 bowls	food preparation/consumption
	4 cooking pots	food preparation
	4 jars	storage
	4 jugs	food preparation/storage
	1 juglet	multipurpose
	3 other	unknown

The similarity coefficient for L. 475 is 148 or 74% when compared to the food preparation and consumption paradigm.

492	8 bowls	food preparation/consumption
	3 kraters	food preparation/consumption
	1 chalice	food consumption
	2 cooking pots	food preparation
	14 jars	storage
	6 jugs	food preparation/storage
	1 juglet	multipurpose
	1 other	unknown

The similarity coefficient for L. 492 is 146.8 or 73.4% when compared to the storage paradigm.

494	2 bowls	food preparation/consumption
	4 jars	storage
	3 jugs	food preparation/storage

The similarity coefficient for L. 494 is 137 or 68.5% when compared to the storage paradigm.

Stratum VII (Fig. 60)

The Stratum VII house, built above the walls of the earlier structure, was very different in plan. To the right of the main entrance was a stairway leading to the second floor. The ground floor area was divided into three parallel rooms separated by pillars. The area under the stairs, L. 437, contained finds that indicate that it was used as a storeroom; the finds included jars containing carbonized grain, a jug with almonds in their shells and a group of fused metal weapons, as vell as a large bilbil (Table 4.42). The similarity coefficient of this assemblage in comparison to the storage paradigm is 156 or 78%.

In the westernmost room of the ground floor area,[1] smashed bowls, jars and cooking pots (Table 4.42) testify to food preparation activities. Although the details of ceramic ware forms, objects and features have not been published for these loci, the evidence from this assemblage seems to be in contrast to the view of the excavators who judged that the ground floor of this house served as a cellar and storage area (Kelm and Mazar 1982: 11).

In the debris above the fallen ceiling of this same western room, the excavators recovered more than 50 beads, 5 cylinder seals and 2 Egyptian scaraboid seals. Such finds point to the upper floor as the living quarters and reception rooms of the family (Kelm and Mazar, 1982: 11-12). This evidence for an upper storey corresponds well with the construction techniques employed to build this house. The outer walls were 1.2 m thick and had reinforced corners (Kelm and Mazar 1982: 9). Such strong walls were unusual for private dwellings in this period where the more typical wall was less than 0.8 m thick.

The architectural style of the Stratum VII pillared house with its tripartite division and cobbled floor was an example of Late Bronze Age domestic architecture that anticipated similar features in Iron Age pillared buildings, such as the tripartite shrines at Tell Qasile, and the ubiquitous 'four room house' (Kelm and Mazar 1985: 98). Unlike Iron Age houses, however, there was no positive evidence that animals were stabled in the house at Tell Batash.

Strata VI–V

Above the burnt remains of the Stratum VII house was built a square structure with four rooms. Assigned to the Late Bronze Age, the plan of this 'house' recalls Building 6061 at Hazor (see above) and several square buildings at Tell Abu Hawam (Hamilton 1934).[2] However, to date, no details of the finds have been published (Kelm and Mazar 1982: 14). As a result, it is impossible to recognize activity areas in

1. Assignment of individual items to specific loci and complete plans with locus numbers have not yet been published.

2. A special study of these square structures will be undertaken when the recent work of J. Balensi at Tell Abu Hawam is available to me.

this building and confirm its identification as a house.

In Stratum V, the building in Area B was reconstructed and functioned as a house. Ovens and rubbish pits were located nearby. This phase of occupation involved a major cultural change evidenced not only by the ovens and pits but also by Philistine pottery. No detailed presentation of the finds from this house has been published to date (Kelm and Mazar 1982: 14). However, its presence in Area B confirms the continuity of domestic architecture in this area of the city.

Table 4.42. *Tel Batash Area B Stratum VII—Finds and Functional Classes*

Locus	Finds	Functional Class
314	flagstone paving	multipurpose
315	bowls	food preparation/consumption
411	cooking pots	food preparation
412	jars	storage
413	pyxis	special/cosmetic
428[1]	zoomorphic vessel	special/cultic
	maceheads	weapon
	spearheads	weapon
	arrowheads	weapon
	chisels	tool
	cobbled floor	multipurpose
437	5 jars	dry storage
	1 jug	food preparation/storage
	1 bilbil	liquid storage
	grain	stored food
	almonds	stored food
	fused arrowheads	weapon
	bronze objects	tool
438	cobbled floor	multipurpose
439		
Upper Storey	50 glass beads	adornment
	5 cylinder seals	business/adornment
	2 scarabs	business/adornment

1. Assignment of individual items to specific loci has not yet been published.

Table 4.43. *Tel Batash Late Bronze Age Loci, Stratum VIII*

Locus	Square	Description	Similarity Coefficient
467		Room	152.0 or 76.0%
475		Room	148.0 or 74.0%
492		Room	146.8 or 73.4%
494		Room	137.0 or 68.5%

Table 4.44. *Tel Batash Late Bronze Age Loci, Stratum VII*

Locus	Square	Description
314		Part of room
315		Part of room
411		Room
412		Part of room
413		Room
428		Part of room
437		Room
438		Room
439		Stairway

Table 4.45. *Tel Batash Late Bronze Age Loci, Stratum VI*

Locus	Square	Description
442		Room
448		Room

Table 4.46. *Tel Batash Late Bronze Age Loci, Stratum V*

Locus	Square	Description
313		Room
408		Room

Beth Shemesh (Map Reference 147/128)

Extensive remains from the Late Bronze Age were uncovered in the excavations of Beth Shemesh by Elihu Grant during the five season Haverford Expedition (Grant 1934: 1). These remains were primarily domestic and were found in all three main excavation areas.[1] Several

1. I assigned Grant's excavation trench from the 1928-1930 seasons to the

occupation phases were encountered in each area. As mentioned above (Chapter 3), Grant's field methods and recording system were not sufficiently refined to deal adequately with the subtle stratigraphy present at this site (1934: 2, 5). Nevertheless, approximately 500 registered items were assigned room numbers (see Tables 4.47–4.51). With such a corpus, it is possible to undertake a certain amount of spatial and functional analysis with regard to the activities of the ancient inhabitants at Beth Shemesh.

Central section (Figs. 61–63)

In the central section or trench, Grant distinguished two phases of Late Bronze occupation, Stratum IVA (LB I) and Stratum IVB (LB II). The architectural remains consisted primarily of stone foundation walls, floors and various installations, such as silos, bins, ovens and a metal smelting furnace (Grant, Stratum IVB). The published plans lead one to suspect that there were, in fact, three phases, two within LB II. For our purposes the later phases will be distinguished as Stratum IVB and IVC (Grant, Stratum IVB). Without elevations (Grant 1934: Map III), however, it is impossible to test this theory.[1]

Stratum IVA (Fig. 61)

The most complete structure recovered in the central section was a large house in Stratum IVA (L. 530–570). This was evidently an imposing structure in its day (Grant 1934: 22-26). The wall foundations, both interior and exterior, were built of two rows of large stones and measured 1.0 m thick. Such walls could easily have supported a second storey, and were so well built that they were reused in subsequent phases (see below, Stratum IVB).

On the ground floor were 6 rooms, a corridor or stairway (L. 532) and a vestibule (L. 596). All attempts to identify the activities performed in these rooms is hampered by the flaws in the recording system which did not consistently distinguish the various phases in each room. For example, no finds were reported for Rooms 537 and 570; all ceramic vessels reported for Room 530 appear to belong to Stratum IVB; and only one artefact, a spindle whorl, was assigned to

'western section', the 1931 trench to the 'eastern section' and the 1933 trench to the 'central section'.

1. See above, Chapter 3, Beth Shemesh, p. 204 n. 1. Stratum IVC consists of the loci assigned by Grant to Stratum IVB, L. 477-489.

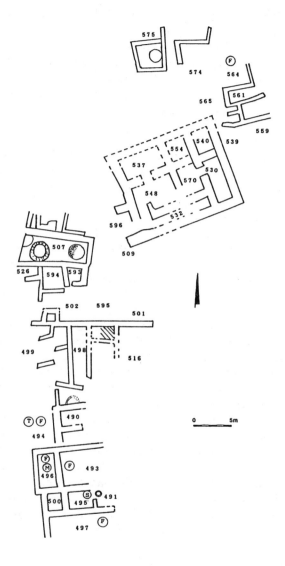

Figure 61. *Beth Shemesh Stratum IVA Central Section, after Grant 1934: Map IV*

L. 532 (Grant 1934: 26). All remaining assemblages, those for Rooms 540, 548 and 554, are too limited for statistical analysis (Table 4.47). These finds represent, however, the typical range of activities seen in other Late Bronze Age loci at Beth Shemesh, such as food preparation and consumption, storage, harvesting, business and adornment.

To the west of this fine house were the partial remains of a second building, some of whose walls were also two stones thick (Fig. 61). The largest room, L. 507, contained a plastered press, a grain storage pit, an assortment of bowls, a lamp, some beads and a faience vessel (Table 4.47). Such an assemblage does not univocally represent a particular tool kit, nor does it clarify the function of the 'press'. While the surrounding rooms contained some interesting objects (a clay axe with cuneiform inscription in L. 526; and, in L. 594, a bowl covering a skull) these finds did not add to my understanding of the activities carried out in Room 507 or in the complex of rooms as a whole.

A second well built house (L. 490–500), located in the southwest corner of the excavation area, was only partially preserved. The foundations combined single row and double row stone walls.[1] Additional walls remaining from the earlier phase were discovered under the phase IVB lime pavement in Room 493. The same pavement was also recovered in Room 496. Unfortunately, the reported finds were not clearly associated with their find spot. As a result, the assemblages assigned to Stratum IVA may be contaminated with items in use during IVB. All that can be attempted here is a general understanding of the activities carried out in this structure during the Late Bronze Age.

For the most part, the finds from this house were quite numerous and representative of typical domestic tool kits. The assemblage reported for Room 493 consisted of an almost complete food preparation tool kit, including bowls, cooking pots and a jar (Table 4.47). The similarity coefficient for this assemblage is 150 or 75% when compared to the food preparation and consumption paradigm. Such an assemblage, along with its size in relation to the surrounding rooms, suggests that L. 493 served as a living room. A similar assemblage

1.   House 490-500 is drawn on Grant 1934: Map III, and both phases were assigned to Phase IVA (but see Wright's assertion that this house was originally built in the earliest phase and reused before the construction of the smelting complex) (Grant and Wright 1939: 35).

was that from Locus 494.[1] In this case, however, there were no cooking pots and another activity, namely textile production, was indicated by the presence of several spindle whorls. Even so, the similarity coefficient to the food preparation paradigm was still strong, 146 or 73%. The same two activities, food preparation and textile production, evidenced by the presence of loom weights, were reflected in the assemblage from Room 495. However, the presence of a jar along with a large amount of wheat and chaff (Grant 1934: 33) indicated that this room functioned primarily as a storage area. Indeed, the presence of a stone mortar, reused in the north wall, suggests that this room had a history of use as a grain storeroom. It is possible that at the time the house was abandoned, the loom weights were also in storage.

Multiple activity areas were also in evidence among the finds of Room 496. Here were tool kits that clearly represent both food preparation and metallurgy (Table 4.47). The similarity coefficient to the food preparation paradigm cannot be calculated because of the absence of numbers for cooking pots and jars in the assemblage. While the remaining finds do not form a recognizable tool kit, they point to metal smelting activity in the area. The deep, thick-walled pot or jug certainly does not belong to the typical food preparation assemblage and was probably used, instead, in association with the fragments of bitumen and copper found in this room.

Two other rooms were not completely preserved, L. 491 and 497. Nevertheless, each contained items which indicate domestic activities. The only oven found inside this house was located in Locus 491. Nearby was a limestone gaming board, one of two found in Late Bronze Age strata. In Locus 497, there was a well defined food consumption assemblage consisting of bowls, jugs and a bilbil. As we have seen in other rooms of this house, textile production must have been a common activity. Here, too, was a spindle whorl, along with a bronze arrowhead. While it is not certain that L. 497 was a room within the house, it is clear from the finds that it was closely associated with the oven in L. 491 and the activities carried out in the rest of the house.

1. It is not certain that this locus was integral to the house itself. However, because it shared the activities represented by the artefact assemblages in the house and was located immediately north of Room 496 and west of Rooms 490, it has been included in this discussion.

In addition, the house was bounded on the north by a complex of rooms, L. 490, 498, 499 and 516, that also appears to have been used during two phases, IVA and IVB (Figs. 61, 62).[1] Locus 490 consisted of twin rooms that could have been part of the original house since these rooms also had two-row stone foundation walls and were paved with a pebble and lime floor (Grant 1934: 34). Finds reported for this locus included 4 bowls, a hearth against the north wall and a grain storage silo (Table 4.47).

The Stratum IVA walls of L. 498, 499 and 516 were, by contrast, one stone row thick. No clear plan can be reconstructed to determine room arrangement or assure that these rooms were part of House 490–500 during this first Late Bronze phase. The finds indicate clearly, however, that this was a domestic area (Table 4.47), although it is not certain that these assemblages can be assigned exclusively to Phase IVA.

A group of rooms with similar wall construction, L. 561–565, was partially preserved to the northeast of the large house (Fig. 61). The finds from Room 564 have a similarity coefficient of 129 or 64.5% in comparison to the food preparation paradigm, while the assemblage from L. 565 does not form a well balanced tool kit (Table 4.47). The assemblage does, however, reflect domestic activities and contained bowls, a krater, a flask and a hoe. An isolated room to the north of the house, L. 575, functioned as a food storeroom. Besides a grain silo, it contained a large jar and olive pits (Grant 1934: 16). This room could have been part of another structure beyond the northern limit of excavation.

Table 4.47. *Beth Shemesh Central Section Stratum IVA—*
Finds and Functional Classes.

Locus	Finds	Functional Class
490	4 bowls	food preparation/consumption
	1 jug	food preparation/storage
	hearth	food preparation/heat
491	gaming board	recreation
	oven	food preparation
493	4 bowls	food preparation/consumption
	cooking pots	ʰood preparation

1.   The walls of this complex to the north of House 490-500 were drawn partly on Grant 1934: Map III and partly on Map IV.

Table 4.47—*Continued*

Locus	Finds	Functional Class
	1 narrow-neck jar	liquid storage
	lamps	lighting
	sickle blade	harvesting
	zoomorphic vessel	special/cultic

The similarity coefficient for L. 493 is 150 or 75% when compared to the food preparation and consumption paradigm.

Locus	Finds	Functional Class
494	1 bowl	food preparation/consumption
	2 kraters	food preparation/consumption
	1 jar	storage
	1 jug	food preparation/storage
	1 whorl	textile production

The similarity coefficient for L. 494 is 146 or 73% when compared to the food preparation and consumption paradigm.

Locus	Finds	Functional Class
495	3 bowls	food preparation/consumption
	1 jar	storage
	tweezers	multipurpose
	loom weights	textile production
	wheat	food storage
496	3 bowls	food preparation/consumption
	chalice	food consumption
	cooking pots	food preparation
	jars	storage
	2 amphora	storage
	2 juglets	multipurpose
	1 flask	liquid storage
	1 lamp	lighting
	1 deep pot	special
	1 funnel	multipurpose
	1 finger ring	adornment
	bitumen fragments	tool making?
	copper fragment	metallurgy
	1 horn(?) tool	unknown
	1 arrowhead	weapon
497	4 bowls	food preparation/consumption
	1 goblet/mug	food consumption
	2 jugs	food preparation/storage
	1 bilbil	liquid storage
	1 whorl	textile production
	1 arrowhead	weapon
500	1 lamp	lighting

Table 4.47—*Continued*

Locus	Finds	Functional Class
501	2 jars	storage
	2 jugs	food preparation/storage
507	bowls	food preparation/consumption
	1 lamp	lighting
	2 beads	adornment
	faience vessel	special/status
509	bowls	food preparation/consumption
	jars	storage
	1 jug	food preparation/storage
	1 bilbil	liquid storage
	hearth	heat/cooking
516	1 jug	food preparation/storage
	plaque fragment	special/cultic
526	cuneiform tablet	special
532	bone whorl	textile production
539	1 krater	food preparation/consumption
	2 jugs	food preparation/storage
540	1 bowl	food preparation/consumption
	sickle blade	agriculture
548	1 bowl	food preparation/consumption
	1 jug	food preparation/storage
554	1 bowl	food preparation/consumption
	1 jar	storage
	1 bilbil	liquid storage
	1 scarab	business/adornment
559A	1 jar	burial
564	2 bowls	food preparation/consumption
	1 krater	food preparation/consumption
	2 jars	storage
	2 juglets	multipurpose
	1 flask	liquid storage
	1 female plaque	special/cultic

The similarity coefficient for L. 564 is 129 or 64.5% when compared to the food preparation and consumption paradigm.

565	4 bowls	food preparation/consumption
	1 krater	food preparation/consumption
	1 flask	liquid storage
	1 hoe	tool
575	1 jar	storage
	olive pits	produce
	silo	grain pit

Table 4.47—*Continued*

Locus	Finds	Functional Class
594	1 bowl	covered skull
	1 jug	food preparation/storage
	1 juglet	multipurpose
596	1 krater	food preparation/consumption

The number and form of ceramic vessels has been estimated on the basis of Grant's description in the text (1934) and his illustration of various items (Grant and Wright 1938). Exact numbers cannot be expected as he frequently mentioned 'sherds of bowls, chalices, jars, and open dishes' (Grant 1934: 33) without any further specification.

Stratum IVB (Fig. 62a)

House 490–500, in the southwest corner of the excavation area was reused in Stratum IVB. A pavement, much like that in Rooms 496 and 493 of Stratum IVA, extended under the smelting furnace, constructed in Stratum IVC (Grant and Wright 1939: 35, 40), which truncated the house walls that extended further east.[1] The few finds definitely related to Phase IVB are insufficient to constitute complete functional tool kits. Because it is possible, and even likely, that the finds assigned by me to Phase IVA belonged in part to Phase IVB, it seems consistent with the evidence to affirm that the domestic activities of food preparation and storage probably continued to characterize these rooms (Tables 4.47, 4.48). Typical Late Bronze II ceramic forms were attested for Phase IVB, for example, the pyxis and stirrup jar in Room 493 (both dated by Wright to Stratum IVA—earlier than the smelting installation; Grant and Wright 1939: 40).

Underlying the smelting complex were Rooms 504, 505 and 480. While only one cooking pot was reported from L. 505, a large assemblage of 20 items was assigned to L. 480. The majority of these items reflect food preparation and consumption, with a similarity coefficient of 136 or 68%. This room, also paved with lime, may have been used in both Phases IVB and IVC (Grant 1934: 41-42).

1. The latest occupation phase, including the smelting furnace, was labelled Stratum IVB by the excavator (Grant 1934: Map III).

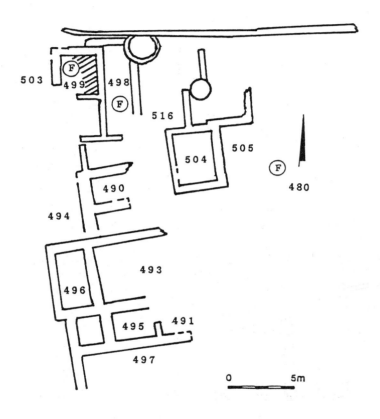

Figure 62a. *Beth Shemesh Stratum IVB Central Section (south part), after Grant
1934: Map III*

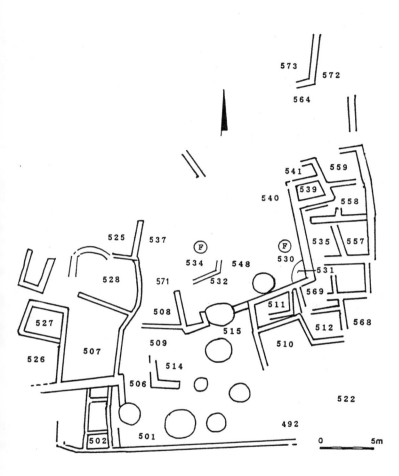

Figure 62b. *Beth Shemesh Stratum IVB Central Section (north part), after Grant 1934: Map III*

The rebuilding of L. 499, to the northwest, was evident in the construction of new foundation walls, a stone-paved floor and oven. The finds (Table 4.48), which were tentatively assigned to Phase IVA (see above), could have been associated with these features as part of a food preparation area. The similarity coefficient for this locus to the food preparation paradigm is 138 or 69%. It appears that the house, of which this room was a part, lay further west and was not completely excavated.[1] Locus 498, on the other hand, was now associated with L. 516, to the east. Although only one jug and a female plaque were reported for L. 516, Room 498 yielded an assemblage of 10 items that reflect food preparation activities (Table 4.48). The similarity coefficient for this tool kit is 130 or 65% when compared to the food preparation and consumption paradigm.

An east–west wall separated these houses from the grain storage silos that were to the north (Fig. 62b). The transition from storage bins to silos took place in Stratum IV. That the silos were used to store grain is confirmed by the wheat chaff that remained in the bottom (Grant and Wright 1939: 40-41). Many silos were stone lined and most appear to date to the end of Stratum IVB-C, as Stratum III walls cross over them, for example, those in L. 530 and 515 (Grant and Wright 1939: 41).

These silos were surrounded on the west, north, and northeast by rooms with domestic functions. No complete houses were distinguished even though many rooms were paved with stone or lime. For the most part, it was evident that the rooms assigned to this phase were above the Phase IVA remains. Therefore, the recorded finds can be discussed as evidence for activities during Phase IVB.

No characteristic tool kits were identified from the rooms to the west of the silos (L. 502, 503, 507, 513, 525, 526, 527, 528, 544, 545, 593; Fig. 62). In fact, only 17 items were reported for these loci (Table 4.48). Of these, 77% were associated with food preparation or storage. The remaining 23% reflected textile production, harvesting and other unspecified tasks.

To the north of the silos was a partially preserved room, L. 508. Here, two occupation phases were discovered above the large house of Stratum IVA, the lower was numbered L. 571 and the upper (see

---

1. It seems that Grant had difficulty connecting his earlier excavations in the western section with those in the central trench, especially along the balk line which he described as the west scarp (Grant 1934: 32).

Stratum IVC), L. 508 (Grant 1934: 30). Only one bowl was registered for this locus (Table 4.48). Bowls and lamps, along with one spindle whorl, were collected from the debris of L. 571 (Table 4.48). Further north in L. 537, 2 cooking pots, 2 seals and a bead were registered. Such finds do not form a functional tool kit but do indicate the range of typical domestic activities in this area.

Further east, the walls of House 530–570 were reused and a series of smaller rooms were built, L. 510–559, 568–569. While the wall lines do not often constitute coherent architectural units, it is apparent that this was a heavily occupied area during the Late Bronze Age. As it is, only two poorly preserved rooms yielded assemblages that can be identified as recognizable tool kits, L. 534 and 530 (Table 4.48). The similarity coefficient to the food preparation paradigm for L. 534 is 132 or 66%. In addition, this room contained the second of two game boards found in these Late Bronze strata (Grant 1934: 26).

A stone pavement and hearth (L. 531) had been laid over the lower walls of Room 530. During this same occupation phase, a grain silo was built at the west end of the new room (Grant 1934: 27). On the assumption that the finds registered for this locus represent Phase IVB, the artefact assemblage and hearth together correspond well to the food preparation paradigm with a similarity coefficient of 142 or 71%. Two lamps and 2 bilbils were discarded in the hearth (L. 531). While these items do not specifically support food preparation or consumption activities, they are not inconsistent with a multipurpose domestic area.

Of the remaining rooms (L. 510, 511, 512, 535, 539, 540, 541, 548, 557, 558, 559, 568 and 569) none contained published assemblages adequate for analysis. There were a total of 20 items, 75% of which were directly related to food preparation or storage. For example, these rooms contained 2 cooking pots, a silo and a quantity of peas and almonds (Grant 1934: 22, 26). The finds which may have had other functions included whorls, blades, and a scraper (Table 4.48).

To the north of this complex of rooms were the remains of several, even more poorly preserved structures (L. 564–577). Only one locus, 572, yielded a meaningful assemblage (Table 4.48). The large number of jars and jugs results in a similarity coefficient of 123 or 61.5% in comparison with the storage paradigm. This is one of the few loci that could be compared to this paradigm. It appears, in this phase, that the use of silos for grain storage reduced the number of jars employed for this purpose,[1] in contrast to the Middle Bronze Age levels.

Table 4.48. *Beth Shemesh Central Section Stratum IVB—*
Finds and Functional Classes

Locus	Finds	Functional Class
480	4 bowls	food preparation/consumption
	3 kraters	food preparation/consumption
	cooking pots	food preparation
	2 jars	storage
	3 jugs	food preparation/storage
	2 juglets	multipurpose
	1 pyxis	special
	1 lamp	lighting
	2 whorls	textile production
	1 figurine	special/cultic

The similarity coefficient for L. 480 is 136 or 68% when compared to the food preparation and consumption paradigm.

Locus	Finds	Functional Class
488	1 jug	food preparation/storage
490	1 jug	food preparation/storage
492	2 bowls	food preparation/consumption
	1 jar	storage
	1 stirrup jar	liquid storage
	plaque	special/cultic
	1 bead	adornment
	1 rattle	special
	1 chisel	tool
	sickle blade	harvesting
	2 arrowheads	weapon
493	1 bowl	food preparation/consumption
	1 pyxis	special
	1 stirrup jar	liquid storage
497	1 goblet/mug	food consumption
498	4 bowls	food preparation/consumption
	1 jar	storage
	1 jug	food preparation/storage
	1 blade	tool
	2 sickle blades	agricultural tool
	1 arrowhead	weapon
499	3 bowls	food preparation/consumption

1. It is also apparent that the recording system employed by Grant did not register large numbers of rim sherds which may have significantly increased the number of vessels reported for each assemblage.

Table 4.48—*Continued*

Locus	Finds	Functional Class
	1 miniature bowl	special/cult
	1 krater	food preparation/consumption
	1 juglet	multipurpose
	1 scarab	business/adornment
	1 blade	tool
	oven	food preparation

The similarity coefficient for L. 499 is 138 or 69% when compared to the food preparation and consumption paradigm.

Locus	Finds	Functional Class
500	1 krater	food preparation/consumption
501	1 bowl	food preparation/consumption
502	2 bowls	food preparation/consumption
	1 goblet/mug	food consumption
	1 sickle blade	agricultural tool
503	1 bowl	food preparation/consumption
	1 chalice	food consumption
	flint scraper	tool
505	1 cooking pot	food preparation
507	1 jug	food preparation/storage
508	1 bowl	food preparation/consumption
510	2 blades	tool
511	1 cooking pot	food preparation
	1 jug	food preparation/storage
512	1 cooking pot	food preparation
513	1 chalice	food consumption
	1 bilbil	liquid storage
	1 whorl	textile production
514	1 earring	adornment
515	bowls	food preparation/consumption
	1 jug	food preparation/storage
	1 pyxis	special/cosmetic
	grain pit	storage
522	1 jar	storage
525	1 amulet	adornment/cultic
528	3 bowls	food preparation/consumption
	2 stirrup jars	liquid storage
530	2 bowls	food preparation/consumption
	cooking pots	food preparation
	1 jug	food preparation/storage
	1 juglet	multipurpose
	1 flask	liquid storage
	1 bilbil	liquid storage

Table 4.48—*Continued*

Locus	Finds	Functional Class
	1 lamp	lighting
	hearth	heat/cooking

The similarity coefficient for L. 530 is 142 or 71% when compared to the food preparation and consumption paradigm.

Locus	Finds	Functional Class
531	2 bilbils	liquid storage
	2 lamps	lighting
533	1 bowl	food preparation/consumption
	1 krater	food preparation/consumption
534	1 bowl	food preparation/consumption
	2 cooking pots	food preparation
	1 flask	liquid storage
	1 bilbil	liquid storage
	sickle blade	agricultural tool
	game board	recreation

The similarity coefficient for L. 534 is 132 or 66% when compared to the food preparation and consumption paradigm.

Locus	Finds	Functional Class
535	2 bowls	food preparation/consumption
	peas	stored food
	flint scraper	tool
537	2 cooking pots	food preparation
	1 scarab	business/adornment
	1 stamp seal	business/adornment
	1 bead	adornment
541	3 bowls	food preparation/consumption
	1 whorl	textile production
	1 blade	tool
548	1 bowl	food preparation/consumption
	1 jug	food preparation/storage
	silo	grain storage
553	4 bowls	food preparation/consumption
558	1 bowl	food preparation/consumption
	1 jug	food preparation/storage
	1 bilbil	liquid storage
571	bowls	food preparation/consumption
	lamps	lighting
	1 spindle whorl	textile production
	almonds	food product
572	1 bowl	food preparation/consumption
	1 krater	food preparation/consumption
	3 jars	storage
	jugs	food preparation/storage

Table 4.48—*Continued*

Locus	Finds	Functional Class
	1 bilbil	liquid storage
	mask fragment	special/cultic

The similarity coefficient for L. 572 is 123 or 61.5% when compared to the storage paradigm.

Locus	Finds	Functional Class
573	sickle blade	agricultural tool
575	1 jar	storage
	olive pits	stored food
	silo	grain storage

Stratum IVC (Fig. 63)

The latest structures in the central excavation area are assigned to Stratum IVC. Support for this phase division is found in the stratigraphy of L. 480 and 505 which both had two construction phases during the Late Bronze Age (Grant 1934: 31, 41-42) and by the presence of a plaster floor like that in Rooms 496 and 493 that ran under the oval furnace of Phase IVC (Grant and Wright 1939: 40).[1]

The construction techniques employed in the Phase IVC complex differ from the typical house walls of Phase IVB. Most walls are two stones thick, c. 80–90 cm, and are closer in style to the walls of Phase IVA. In addition, several 'rooms' appear to have functioned as smelters and it appears that this industrial quarter was used for metallurgy (Grant 1934: 41).

The presence of ash along with vent holes (for tuyères?) in the cubicles of L. 477 and the ash and slag in the oval furnace of L. 479 strongly suggest extensive smelting activities (Grant and Wright 1939: 38-39). However, few other tools were represented in the assemblages from the rooms in this complex (Table 4.49). Instead, some good examples of food preparation and storage tool kits were reported. The most complete assemblage was found in L. 487, a large area north of the smelting complex. In association with a pot sunk into a stone pavement were items representing food storage, textile production and personal adornment. Taking the ceramic vessels as a separate assemblage would yield a similarity coefficient of 148.6 or 74.3% when compared to the storage paradigm.

The distribution of cooking pots (L. 479, 482, 483 and 487) along

1. The Phase IVB plaster was assigned by Wright to the same phase as L. 508, a stone pavement that ran over the Large House of Stratum IVA.

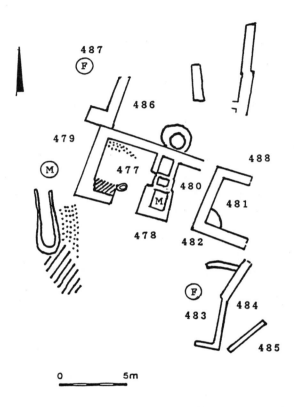

Figure 63. *Beth Shemesh Stratum IVC Central Section, after Grant 1934: Map III*

with the typical cooking oven in L. 477 is also a strong indicator of food preparation activities. Although Room 481 contained a corner hearth, the artefact assemblage of 1 bowl, 1 jug, 1 whorl and an amulet does not help to clarify how such a feature was used. The presence of cooking pots near the hearth in L. 530 (Phase IVB) is suggestive but not conclusive that these hearths were used to cook food.

Another strong food preparation tool kit was reported for L. 483, south of the smelting complex (Table 4.49). The similarity coefficient is 134 or 67% when compared to the food preparation and consumption paradigm. Included in this assemblage, were a bronze chisel, which probably served a variety of uses, and a clay plaque. Altogether, in Stratum IV, there were 3 plaques, 1 figurine and 1 rattle recorded, all from apparently domestic loci.

Complete tool kits for the remaining loci of Phase IVA are lacking and cannot be reassembled from the excavator's description (Table 4.49). The total number of reported items from these loci (L. 478–489), not including L. 477, 479 and 487, is 44, of which 71.4% are related to food preparation and storage, and the remaining 28.6% include items of personal adornment and tools. In addition, the rooms surrounding the smelting complex were poorly preserved and no coherent plan can be reconstructed (Fig. 63). Similarities between the Late Bronze smelting complex and the oval furnace of Stratum 3 were noted by the excavator (Grant 1934: 41).

Table 4.49. *Beth Shemesh Central Section Stratum IVC—*
Finds and Functional Classes

Locus	Finds	Functional Class
477	1 bowl	food preparation/consumption
	1 jar	storage
	blades	tool
	1 whorl	textile production
	oven	cooking
	furnaces	smelting
	ash	debris
	platform	unknown
478	1 bowl	food preparation/consumption
	1 krater	food preparation/consumption
	2 jugs	food preparation/storage
	1 bilbil	liquid storage
	amulet	adornment/cultic
	blades	tool

Table 4.49—*Continued*

Locus	Finds	Functional Class
479	2 bowls	food preparation/consumption
	cooking pots	food preparation
	3 jugs	food preparation/consumption
	furnace	smelting
	ash and slag	debris
481	1 bowl	food preparation/consumption
	1 jug	food preparation/storage
	1 whorl	textile production
	hearth	heat/cooking
482	1 cooking pot	food preparation
	2 jars	storage
	1 jug	food preparation/storage
	1 whorl	textile production
	amulet	adornment/cultic
483	2 bowls	food preparation/consumption
	1 krater	food preparation/consumption
	1 cooking pot	food preparation
	2 jars	storage
	1 plaque	special/cultic
	1 chisel	tool

The similarity coefficient for L. 483 is 134 or 67% when compared to the
food preparation and consumption paradigm.

484	2 bowls	food preparation/consumption
	1 chalice	food consumption
	1 jar	storage
485	1 bowl	food preparation/consumption
	2 jars	storage
486	2 bowls	food preparation/consumption
	2 jugs	food preparation/storage
	1 lamp	lighting
	1 button?	adornment
	1 bead	adornment
487	1 bowl	food preparation/consumption
	1 cooking pot	food preparation
	5 jars	storage
	2 jugs	food preparation/storage
	1 juglet	multipurpose
	1 pyxis	special/cosmetic
	1 stirrup jar	liquid storage
	1 button?	adornment
	1 plaque	special/cultic
	3 earrings	adornment

Table 4.49—*Continued*

Locus	Finds	Functional Class
	2 beads	adornment
	shuttle	textile production
	loom(?) weight	textile production?
	2 whorls	textile production
	sickle blade	agricultural tool

The similarity coefficient for L. 487 is 148.6 or 74.3% when the ceramic vessels alone are compared to the storage paradigm.

Locus	Finds	Functional Class
488	bowls	food preparation/consumption
	1 stirrup jar	liquid storage
	1 juglet	multipurpose
489	1 jar	storage
	1 awl	multipurpose
	1 knife	cutting
	oven	food preparation
508	krater/jug?	food preparation/storage
	2 chisels	tool
	1 blade	tool

Eastern Section

An area of 36 squares east of the central trench and north of the Byzantine monastery was excavated in 1931. The same major strata were identified that had been uncovered in the other areas of the mound, Byzantine Period, Iron Age, and Middle and Late Bronze Age. The reporting for this area seems to be much less complete than for the central and western sections. This is seen most clearly in Stratum V, where only a few wall fragments were assigned to the Middle Bronze Age.[1]

Stratum IV (Fig. 64a, b)

Only one Late Bronze Age occupation level was discerned during excavation. While several complete rooms were preserved, no recognizable structures could be reconstructed. Incomplete rooms, missing doorways, and lack of description makes it impossible to discuss room arrangement in these houses. The published finds are also unsatisfactory. A total of 14 items were recorded (Table 4.50), of which 6 were related to food preparation or storage, 4 were containers (bilbils)

---

1. These remains were so scattered that illustration is not useful.

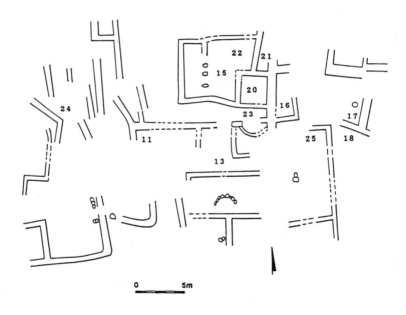

Figure 64a.   *Beth Shemesh Stratum IV Eastern Section (north part), after Grant and Wright 1938: Pl. XXVI*

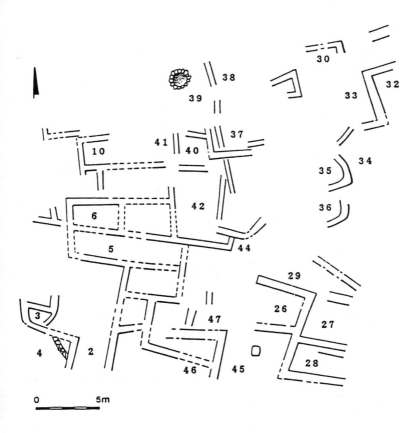

Figure 64b. *Beth Shemesh Stratum IV Eastern Section (south part), after Grant and Wright 1938: Pl. XXVI*

whose purpose has been very controversial,[1] and 3 were miscellaneous. Because of the small numbers involved, no statistical analysis on a room by room basis is possible. In fact, there is no way to ascertain that these finds were not random. The only secure assemblage was the four bilbils in L. 23.

Table 4.50. *Beth Shemesh Eastern Section Stratum IV—*
Finds and Functional Classes

Locus	Finds	Functional Class
16	1 bowl	food preparation/consumption
	1 amulet	adornment/cultic
17	bronze finger ring	adornment
22	1 bowl	food preparation/consumption
	1 vase	food preparation/storage
	1 lamp	lighting
23	4 bilbils	liquid storage
24	1 jug	food preparation/storage
25	1 spouted bowl	food preparation/consumption
26	1 krater	food preparation/consumption
46	bone bead	adornment

Western Section—Stratum IV (Figs. 65a, b, c)
The largest coherent excavation area, worked in 1928, 1929 and 1930, included houses immediately inside the western city wall and certain tombs and structures outside the wall. In this western section, almost 200 loci were identified. However, not all rooms discussed in the report appear on the plan (Grant 1932: Map II). In the south, the large Stratum V house, built against the wall, was reused and enlarged by walls with one row of stones. Sadly enough, no finds were attributed to these Stratum IV rooms, making functional analysis of this structure impossible.

The total number of finds reported for the entire western section (107) is less than one artefact per room[2] (Table 4.51). Of these finds,

1. The use of bilbils as trade containers for opium has been difficult to confirm because so many vessels have been reused (Merrillees 1974: 32-34).

2. The excavator mentioned the numerous pottery baskets collected during the excavation of particular areas. It is clear from these references that only whole, restorable pieces or special diagnostic sherds were published. The vast majority of ceramic remains were not counted or reported in more than a very general way, referring to types published in the *Corpus of Palestinian Pottery* for ware forms and imported wares (e.g. Grant 1934: 33).

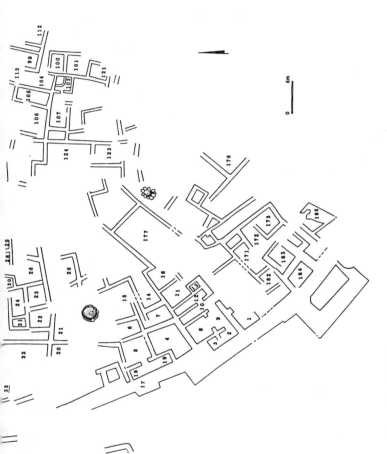

Figure 65a. *Beth Shemesh Stratum IV Western Section (south part), after Grant 1933*

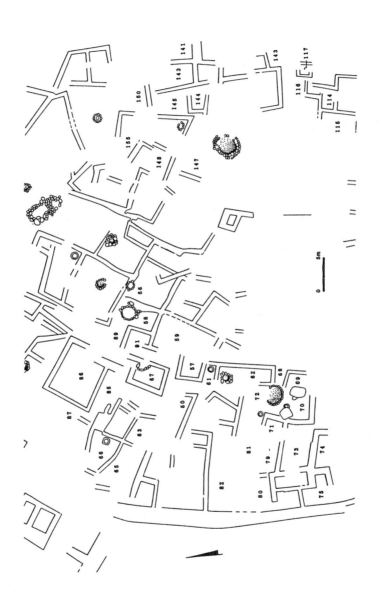

Figure 65b. *Beth Shemesh Stratum IV Western Section (middle part), after Grant 1933*

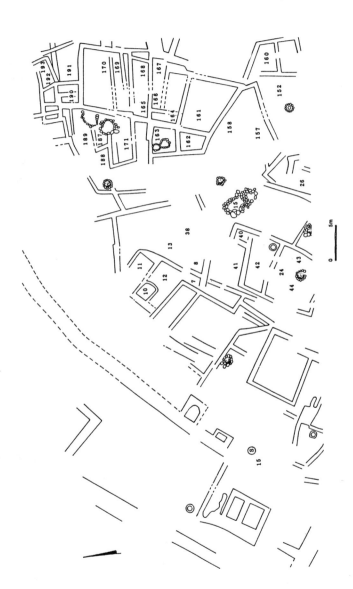

Figure 65c. *Beth Shemesh Stratum IV Western Section (north part), after Grant 1933*

83% can be related to food preparation or storage. Tools, scarabs and spindle whorls account for 15% of the assemblage and multipurpose items represent 2%. The function of only one room, L. 15, can be identified with certainty.[1] In this room, the brick walls collapsed on 10 gallons of wheat (see Tell Hadidi, Chapter 5, below), 2 bowls, 1 cooking pot and 1 store jar. Such an assemblage could be assigned an arbitrary similarity coefficient to the storage paradigm of 199 or 99.5% since it can hardly have served any other purpose.

Table 4.51. *Beth Shemesh Western Section Stratum IV—*
Finds and Functional Classes

Locus	Finds	Functional Class
15	2 bowls	food preparation/consumption
	1 cooking pot	food preparation
	1 jar	storage
	wheat	food storage

The similarity coefficient for L. 15 is 199 or 99.5% when assigned an arbitrary value.

Locus	Finds	Functional Class
20	1 scarab	business/adornment
22	1 bowl	food preparation/consumption
22-sub	1 milk bowl	food preparation/consumption
25	1 scarab	business/adornment
31	1 bowl	food preparation/consumption
	1 krater	food preparation/consumption
38	1 jug	food preparation/storage
43	2 cooking pots	food preparation
44	1 cooking pot	food preparation
45	1 krater	food preparation/consumption
	2 whorls	textile production
50	javelin point	weapon
	shells	adornment?
51	2 bowls	food preparation/consumption
55	3 bowls	food preparation/consumption
	1 bilbil	liquid storage
55-above	1 bowl	food preparation/consumption
55S-sub	2 chalices	food consumption

1. This room (L. 15) was drawn on the Stratum III plan but is surely Stratum IV. Indeed, Wright was certain that this room belonged to Stratum IVA rather than IVB (Grant and Wright 1939: 38), although it is difficult to make this distinction on the basis of the published report; see Grant 1932: 20, Fisher's description of his excavation of the grain room and Grant 1932: 44 where Grant mentions the later western wall passing over Stratum IV Room 86, leaving L. 15 outside the wall.

Table 4.51—*Continued*

Locus	Finds	Functional Class
56	1 jug	food preparation/storage
56-above	1 juglet	multipurpose
57	2 cooking pots	food preparation
58	1 bowl	food preparation/consumption
	1 krater	food preparation/consumption
58-above	1 bowl	food preparation/consumption
61-sub	macehead	weapon
62	1 chalice	food consumption
	alabaster kohl pot	cosmetic use
	button	adornment
62W	2 bowls	food preparation/consumption
63	1 jar	storage
63-sub	6 bowls	food preparation/consumption
	1 chalice	food consumption
	3 cooking pots	food preparation
63-above	1 bowl	food preparation/consumption
64	6 bowls	food preparation/consumption
	1 jug	food preparation/storage
64-sub	1 bowl	food preparation/consumption
	2 kraters	food preparation/consumption
64-above	1 bowl	food preparation/consumption
66	1 bowl	food preparation/consumption
	1 krater	food preparation/consumption
	3 amulets	adornment/cultic
	bronze punch	tool
	animal weight	business
64-above	1 flask	liquid storage
68	2 cooking pots	food preparation
	1 jug	food preparation/storage
69	3 cooking pots	food preparation
73	1 bowl	food preparation/consumption
	1 cooking pot	food preparation
	jug and mixed hoard	metallurgy/theft
74	1 bowl	food preparation/consumption
75-sub	1 bowl	food preparation/consumption
	2 chalices	food consumption
78	1 cooking pot	food preparation
79	1 krater	food preparation/consumption
80	1 chalice	food consumption
83	1 cooking pot	food preparation
84	1 krater	food preparation/consumption
85-sub	1 bowl	food preparation/consumption

Table 4.51—*Continued*

Locus	Finds	Functional Class
	1 cooking pot	food preparation
86 above	2 bowls	food preparation/consumption
86E	1 jug	food preparation/storage
	1 bilbil	liquid storage
86W	4 bowls	food preparation/consumption
	1 krater	food preparation/consumption
87	2 bowls	food preparation/consumption
	1 krater	food preparation/consumption
87W	ivory seal	business/adornment
91	1 chalice	food consumption
101	1 krater	food preparation/consumption
	1 jug	food preparation/storage
103	1 krater	food preparation/consumption
107	1 jug	food preparation/storage
107SW	javelin point	weapon
108	1 bowl	food preparation/consumption
	2 chalices	food consumption
113	1 juglet	multipurpose
116	1 bowl	food preparation/consumption
	1 juglet	multipurpose
117	1 juglet	multipurpose
144	faience vessel	special/status
152	1 jug	food preparation/storage
161	6 bowls	food preparation/consumption
	1 jug	food preparation/storage
	1 juglet	multipurpose
	1 lamp	lighting
	1 whorl	textile production
	1 javelin point	weapon
162	1 pyxis	special
	1 lamp	lighting
165N	1 chalice	food consumption
168	diorite vessel	special/status
169	1 scarab	business/adornment
174	1 amulet	adornment/cultic
187	1 jug	food preparation/storage
	1 pyxis	special/cosmetic

Cooking pots were also found in Rooms 43, 44, 57, 63-sub, 68, 69, 73, 78, 83 and 85-sub. It is interesting to note that all these vessels were located in the north central part of the western section (Fig. 65c), an area with several ovens (L. 61, 39) and food storage silos or bins

(L. 58, 72) (Grant 1932: 39). In addition, there were several special rooms, such as Room 40 which had a plaster floor sealed against the base of the walls. This room could have served as a grain storage area (Grant 1932: 46) as there was no drain or sign that water was used in this locus.

Next door, in Room 42, there was a stone basin filled with a powdery substance (Grant 1932: 39). A similar feature was uncovered in Room 66. While a variety of finds were also recovered from L. 66 (Table 4.51), no one functional tool kit can be identified. As a result, the purpose of the stone basins must remain unknown. Other features which probably served as presses were located in Room 69–70. These features consisted of two circular stone slabs, each with a bowl on one side (Grant 1932:41). The only other finds associated with the presses were 3 cooking pots. However, such an assemblage does not clarify the function of the stone installations.

Conclusion

Beth Shemesh Stratum IV was characterized by a wealth of domestic structures. These houses filled the town from the southern gate to the Byzantine monastery in the east. The construction techniques varied from double row to single row walls but all houses were joined, sharing party walls. Complete house plans and room arrangement are difficult to reconstruct, both because of the excavation techniques employed at the time and the paucity of reported finds. Further study of the original plans and notebooks may yet yield a more complete picture of domestic life at Beth Shemesh.

Table 4.52. *Beth Shemesh (Central Section) Stratum IVA Loci*

Locus	Square	Description	Similarity Coefficient
490		2 Rooms	
491		Room	
493		Room-2 phases	150 or 75%
494		Undefined	146 or 73%
495		Room	
496		Room	
497		Undefined	
498		Room	
499		Room-2 phases	
500		Room	
501		Undefined	
502		Undefined	
504		2 Rooms	

Table 4.52—*Continued*

Locus	Square	Description	Similarity Coefficient
505		Room	
507		Room	
509		Undefined	
516		Undefined	
526		Room	
530		Room	
532		Stairway?	
537		Room	
539		Undefined	
540		Room	
548		Room	
554		Room	
559		Undefined	
561		Room	
564		Room?	129 or 64.5%
565		Undefined	
570		Room	
574		Room?	
575		Room and silo	
593		Room	
594		Room	
595		Undefined	
596		Undefined	

Table 4.53. *Beth Shemesh (Central Section) Stratum IVB Loci*

Locus	Square	Description	Similarity Coefficient
480		Room	136 or 68%
488		Undefined	
490		2 Rooms	
491		Room	
492		Undefined	
493		Room-2 phases	
494		Undefined	
495		Room	
496		Room	
497		Undefined	
498		Room	
499		Room-2 phases	138 or 69%
500		Room	
501		Undefined	

Table 4.53—*Continued*

Locus	Square	Description	Similarity Coefficient
502		2 Rooms	
503		Undefined	
506		Undefined	
507		Room	
509		Undefined	
510		Room	
511		Room	
512		Room	
513		Room	
514		Room	
515		Undefined	
516		Room	
517		Room	
522		Undefined	
525		Undefined	
526		Room	
527		Room	
528		Room	
530		Undefined	142 or 71%
531		Fireplace	
532		Undefined	
534		Room?	132 or 66%
535		Room	
537		Undefined	
538		Undefined	
539		Room	
540		Room?	
541		Room	
544		Room?	
545		Room	
548		Undefined	
553		Undefined	
557		2 Rooms	
558		Room	
559		Room	
564		Undefined	
568		Undefined	
569		Room	
571		Room	
572		Undefined	123 or 61.5%
573		Room?	

Table 4.54. *Beth Shemesh (Central Section) Stratum IVC Loci*

Locus	Square	Description	Similarity Coefficient
477		2 Rooms	
478		Undefined	
479		2 Rooms	
481		Room	
482		Undefined	
483		Room?	134 or 67%
484		Undefined	
485		Undefined	
486		Room	
487		Room?	148.6 or 74.3%
488		Undefined	
489		Undefined	
508		Pavement in room?	

Table 4.55. *Beth Shemesh (Eastern Section) Stratum IV Loci*

Locus	Square	Description
2	Y38-39	Room?
3	Y38	Room
4	Y38	Undefined
5	X38-39	Room
6	X38-39	Room
10	W38-39	Room
11	U41	Room?
13	U41-42	Room
15	T40	Room
16	T-U42	Room
17	U43	Room
18	U43	Undefined
20	T42	Room
21	T42	Room?
22	T42	Room
23	U42	Room?
24	U40	Undefined
25	U42	Undefined
26	Y40	Room
27	Y40	Room?
28	X-Y40	Room
29	X40	Undefined
30	W40	Undefined
32	W41	Room?

Table 4.55—*Continued*

Locus	Square	Description
33	W40	Undefined
34	W40	Undefined
35	W40	Room?
36	W40	Room?
37	W40	Undefined
38	W40	Undefined
39	W39	Undefined
40	W39	Room
41	W39	Room
42	W-X39	Room
44	X40	Undefined
45	Y40	Room
46	Y39	Room?
47	Y39	Room?

Table 4.56. *Beth Shemesh (Western Section) Stratum IV Loci*

Locus	Square	Description	Similarity Coefficient
1	AA29	Room	
2	AA29	Room	
3	AA29	Room	
4	AA29	Room	
5	Z 28	Room	
6	Z 29	Room	
7	Z 29	Room	
8	AA29	Room	
9	AA29	Room	
10	AA29	Room	
11	AA29	Room	
12?	AA29	Room	
13	AA29	Room	
14	Z 29	Room	
15	Z 29	Room	199 or 99.5%
16	Z 29	Room	
17	Z 28	Room	
18	Z 28	Room	
19	AA28	Room	
20	Y 28	Undefined	
21	Y 28	Undefined	
22	Y 28	Room	
23	Y 29	Room	

Table 4.56—*Continued*

Locus	Square	Description	Similarity Coefficient
24	X 29	Room	
25	Y 29	Room	
26	Y 29	Room	
28	X 29	Room	
29	X 29	Undefined	
30	X 29	Room	
31	Y 28	Room	
32	Y 28	Undefined	
33	Y 27	Undefined	
37	S28-29	Room	
40?	T 29	Room	
41	S-T29	Room	
42	T 29	Room	
43	T 29	Room	
44	T 29	Room	
46	U 30	Room	
48	U 30	Room	
50	U 30	Room	
51	U 30	Room	
52	U 29	Room	
53	V 29	Room	
54	V29-30	Room	
55	V 29	Room	
56?	U 29	Room	
57	V 28	Room	
58	U 29	Room	
59	U 28	Undefined	
60	V 27	Undefined	
61	V 28	Room	
62	V-W28	Room	
63	U 27	Room	
65	U 27	Room	
66	U 27	Room	
67	U 28	Room	
68	W 28	Room?	
69	W 28	Room	
70	W27-28	Room	
71	W 27	Room	
72	W 28	Room	
73	W 27	Room	
74	X 27	Room	
75	W-X26	Room	

Table 4.56—*Continued*

Locus	Square	Description	Similarity Coefficient
79	W 27	Undefined	
80	W 26	Room	
81	W 27	Undefined	
82	V 26-7	Undefined	
85	U27-28	Room	
86	T 28	Room	
87	T 27	Undefined	
89	U28-29	Room	
91	U 28	Room	
99	W-X32	Room	
100	X 32	Room	
101	X 32	Room	
103	X 32	Room	
104	X 32	Room	
105	X 32	Room	
106	X 31	Room	
107	X 31	Room	
112	W 33	Room	
113	W 32	Room	
114	W 32	Room	
115	W 32	Undefined	
116	W 32	Undefined	
117	W 32	Room	
121	Y 32	Room	
123	Y 31	Room	
124	X-Y31	Room	
126	Y 30	Room	
141*	U 32	2 Rooms	
143*	U 32	Room	
143*	V 32	Undefined	
144	U 32	Room	
145	U 32	Room	
147	U-V31	Undefined	
148	U 31	Room?	
150	U 31	Undefined	
155	T-U31	Room?	
152	T 31	Room	
157	T 31	Undefined	
158	S 31	Undefined	
160	T32	Room	
161	S31-32	Room	
162	S 31	Room	

Table 4.56—*Continued*

Locus	Square	Description	Similarity Coefficient
163	R-S31	Room	
164	R 31	Room	
165	R 31	Room	
166	R 31	Room?	
167	R 32	Room?	
168	R 32	Room	
169	R 32	Room	
170	Q-R32-31	Undefined	
171*	R 31	Room?	
187	R 31	Room	
188	R 30-31	Room	
189	Q 31	Undefined	
190	Q 31	Undefined	
191	Q 32	Room	
192	Q 32-31	Room	
193	Q 32	Room	
171*	AA-AB30	Room	
172	AA-AB30	Room	
173	AB 31	Room	
176	AA31-32	Undefined	
177	Z 30	Room	
182	AB 30	Room	
183	AB 30	Room	
184	AB 30	Room	
185	AB 31	Room	

Tell El-'Ajjul (Map Reference 093/097)

The two major occupation levels excavated inside the city were separated in almost all areas by a distinct ash layer. While cultural and architectural continuity was evident in the reuse of some wall lines and in the gradual transformation of ceramic ware form styles, the transition from Middle Bronze to Late Bronze Age had occurred. This transition was distinguished by Petrie himself during his excavations in 1931–1934. The Late Bronze Age remains, identified as the upper city, were found in several densely occupied areas, A, E, T and G.

Area A (Fig. 66)

The structures of Area A, in the southwest corner of the site, were excavated in 1931 during Petrie's first season. Three streets (AA, AN, AT) and 2 alleys bordered the blocks of buildings. The houses themselves shared party walls on one or more sides and cannot be distinguished easily. Where one would expect some indication of separate units, the plans are deceiving (Petrie 1931: Pl. LIV); exterior walls appear thinner than interior walls, and the thickest walls are frequently pierced by doorways. Establishing artefact groups that reflect the finds from a possible discrete housing unit is thereby tentative.

Rooms AC and AQ form part of a small structure south of Street AN and its intersection with Street AA (Fig. 66). Two other rooms in the same building are unlettered. What is significant about these rooms is the number of reported artefacts (Table 4.57), a total of 48 items. Several functional tool kits can be recognized in these assemblages, specifically food preparation, consumption and storage. When the total assemblage is compared to the food preparation/consumption paradigm, the similarity is not very strong due to the great variety of artefacts: for Room AC it is 116 or 58% and for Room AQ, 128 or 64%. However, when the items most likely to have been used together in one activity are evaluated, the similarity to the food preparation and consumption paradigm is stronger: AQ = 158 or 79%, when 1 needle, a spatula, 4 scarabs, a toggle pin and a macehead are put in a separate assemblage.[1] Other activities were not as clearly represented in the assemblage of Room AQ. Scarabs and toggle pins continued to be common finds. The relationship of the limestone macehead with other finds reported for Room AQ is uncertain. Although weapons were frequent finds, their use as symbols of authority or as tools of the trade cannot be distinguished. This is especially true of maceheads.

Across the alley in Room AJ (Fig. 66) were the remains of several smashed storejars. When comparing the reported finds from Tell el-'Ajjul with other sites, the paucity of storejars is very noticeable. Few rooms exclusively used for storage can be identified. The other finds

---

1. The overlapping of two or more tool kits in the same locus requires multivariate analysis which is beyond the scope of this study. Consistent use of Robinson's coefficient of similarity requires that all finds from a particular locus be included in the tool kit that is to be compared to the paradigm. The presence of large numbers of scarabs at Tell el-'Ajjul makes comparison especially difficult.

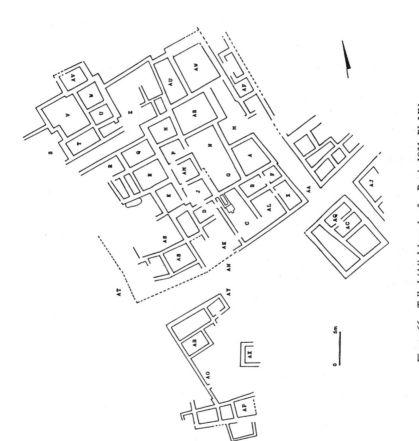

Figure 66. *Tell el-'Ajjul Area A, after Petrie 1931: Pl. LIV*

included in the assemblage of Room AJ do not significantly weaken this identification. While the bowl and chalice are usually associated with food consumption, it is not unusual for a bowl to be used as a scoop. Although no other functional tool kit can be clearly recognized (Table 4.57), this assemblage does not compare well to the storage paradigm (74.2 or 37.1%) because of the number of scarabs. If the scarabs alone were assigned to an economic tool kit, the remaining finds would compare more favourably to the storage paradigm with a similarity coefficient of 118 or 59% (see p. 361 n. 1, below).

Several factors may account for the lack of recognizable store rooms. One is definitely the method of excavation and preservation of ceramic remains, especially sherds. Another factor may be the storage practices of the ancient inhabitants themselves. Were there storage facilities in each house? Were there, instead, communal storage areas which Petrie did not uncover? What was the function of the numerous pits cut into the bedrock—were they all located under the floor? While some of these pits were clearly dug before the houses were built (the house walls go over the pits), this is certainly not the situation in every case. By the time of the Late Bronze Age buildings, several of the pits had been reused as graves. This means that their possible function as grain pits in the Middle Bronze Period (Petrie 1931: 5) did not continue into the later phase. There could, of course, be another option, such as the grain room at Beth Shemesh, but Petrie made no mention of carbonized grain.

The major building complex of the Late Bronze Age in Area A probably included more than one house (Fig. 66). Petrie himself identified one unit as Rooms A, G, N, AB, H, P, AM and J (1931: 5). The doorway in room J led into Rooms D, Y and C. While no clear entrance from street AA had been recorded—Petrie mentioned a broken down entry into Room A (1931: 6)—there can be no doubt about the doorway between Rooms J and D; the wall remained standing more than 2 m high along with the lintel formed of two mud bricks (Petrie 1931: Frontispiece).

The artefact assemblages from this large house do not represent distinct functional tool kits but are suggestive of a range of domestic activities (Table 4.57). Storejars were found in several rooms, J and P, while other rooms (AM and C) contained jugs or juglets. In this study, juglets have usually been classified as multipurpose vessels. However, in those cases where a juglet was associated with a storejar or a jug, it could have served as a dipper and would, therefore, contribute to a storage tool kit. In other rooms, the association of a juglet or jug with bowls, chalices, kraters or cooking pots would contribute to a food preparation or consumption tool kit. This is precisely the situation in Rooms G, N and H.

Because each assemblage was small (2–8 items) and contained diverse artefacts ranging from bowls to weapons, distinct functional clusters were infrequent. In Room C, however, 50% of the artefacts were probably related to textile production: 2 needles, a spindle and bronze tweezers. A large hearth was also located in this room although the artefact assemblage seems to reflect a living room devoid of food preparation or consumption activities.

In contrast, 47 items were reported for Room F (Table 4.57), the smallest room in a complex to the south of House A–J. In this assemblage, several functional tool kits can be identified, such as food preparation, consumption and storage. The tool kit representing storage is especially strong, 26 items, even though the large number of jugs and juglets seems unusual. A similarity coefficient for all items is only 94 or 47%. Clearly, the expected storage assemblage does not appear at Tell el-'Ajjul. In this particular room (F), the jugs may have been used in the place of jars. Additional items of personal adornment and cosmetic use, along with tools, weapons and status items complete this assemblage. In Room B, which connected with F, were 1 jug, 2 juglets and a jar stand, also closely related to storage activities. The other rooms in this small complex seemed to be at functional variance with B and F. Room X was a plastered bathroom which yielded no artefacts save a javelin point, and Room; AL contained 3 random items: a double vessel, a scarab and a macehead. The broken wall between Room AL and Room C makes it impossible to determine whether these four southern rooms were a distinct house or part of the larger complex.

Actually, the small size of Room F poses a serious problem for understanding how this domestic unit functioned. It was the only room which yielded the typical domestic tool kits of food consumption and storage. However, because of its size (2 × 2 m) and the number of finds, it is not likely that food preparation and consumption activities could have been carried out in this room. This leaves two possibilities: either this room served as a storeroom for all the items in the assemblage, or many items fell into the room from an upper storey. In the latter case, it would be possible that Rooms F, B, AL and X were a distinct house with a living room on the upper storey. The mud brick walls, made of hard yellow clay, were 55–65 cm thick (Petrie 1931: 5), sufficient to support an upper storey. On the other hand, if House B–X represents a complete unit, its small size (42 m²) contrasts sharply with the rambling room arrangement of House A–J (c. 176 m²) next door.

A second complex to the west, Rooms AS–R, was poorly preserved. Only two rooms contained useful assemblages, AS and K. The designation AS was assigned to two rooms and, as a result, there is no way of distinguishing the assignment of artefacts to one room or the other. One activity dominated the assemblage, food preparation and consumption (Table 4.57). Although an oven was cut into the north wall of Room AS, it is not clear that the oven was actually in the same room as the assemblage.

A fairly typical storage assemblage, located in Room K, yielded a similarity coefficient of 102 or 51%. The relationship of this room to House AS–R is not certain because the only preserved doorway is into Room J. Of the remaining rooms (E, Q and R), no functional tool kits can be identified due to the small number of finds (Table 4.57). Room Q, however, did include a larger than normal number of scarabs (8). The only other reported find, a bone toggle pin, does not clarify the function of the scarabs in this context (see above).

While the total artefact corpus from Rooms AV–Z (Fig. 66) included only 21 items (Table 4.57), the dominant tool kit was that of food preparation and consumption. The similarity coefficient for the corpus, as a whole, is 110.1 or 55%. The similarity, as usual, is weakened due to the presence of scarabs. Room Z, which contained a cooking pot, krater, 2 jugs and 3 bowls, was the best single food preparation/consumption assemblage of the complex with a similarity coefficient of 153 or 76.5%.

The relationship between the rooms in this house to one another is very uncertain due to lack of reported doorways. This is especially true of Rooms AU and AW, further east. It cannot be determined whether they were related to House A–J or AV–Z, or to Shrine AF. The finds from Room AW are typical of food consumption and reception activities, with a similarity coefficient of 129 or 64.5% when compared to the food preparation and consumption paradigm, and are very suitable for the large size of this room (4.6 × 5.8 m) which may have served as a living room.

The last complex of rooms that can be assigned to the Late Bronze Age stratum (AP–AY) was poorly preserved (Fig. 66). Only two assemblages are of interest to this study, that for Room AR and for Locus AO. In Room AR, the finds can be classified in three basic tool kits, food preparation, craft and industry, and business or adornment. Because of this plurality of tool kits, Robinson's coefficient of similarity cannot be used to evaluate this assemblage. The tools and needle may all have been used in textile production but this cannot be affirmed univocally because we know so little about the way in which blades were used in ancient crafts and industries. The remaining functional class is a group of 5 scarabs used either as seals or amulets.

The finds from Locus AO were functionally very mixed. They included jewellery, a figurine, tools, bowls, 1 jug and pieces of bone inlay. Whether the figurine was associated with the small shrine room to the east of Locus AX, or with Room AY, plastered in the same manner as shrine room AF, is unknown. At the far end of the complex was a row of three small rooms, of which only one was designated, AP. The range of items reported for Room AP reflects storage activities, although the number is too few for comparison with the storage paradigm. In fact, it is unlikely that this room was indeed part of the same complex as the rooms further north (Rooms AO and AR) in view of the difference in alignment.

Table 4.57. *Tell el-'Ajjul Late Bronze Area A—Finds and Functional Classes*

Locus	Finds	Functional Class
A	1 krater	food preparation/consumption
	2 scarabs	business/adornment
AB	1 jug	food preparation/storage
	2 bronze needles	textile production
	bronze tweezers	multipurpose
	1 scarab	business/adornment
	bone toggle pin	adornment
	chain link?	special/tool
	bone inlay	special/status
AC	7 bowls	food preparation/consumption
	2 miniature vessels	special/cultic
	4 jugs	food preparation/storage
	6 juglets	multipurpose
	1 pyxis	special

Table 4.57—*Continued*

Locus	Finds	Functional Class

The similarity coefficient for L. AC is 116 or 58% when compared to the food preparation and consumption paradigm.

Locus	Finds	Functional Class
AE	1 bowl	food preparation/consumption
AF	1 storejar	storage
	3 jugs	food preparation/storage
	1 flask	storage
	gold earrings	adornment
	alabaster vessel	special/status
AG	1 pyxis	special/cosmetic
	iron knife	tool
AH	1 bowl	food preparation/consumption
AJ	1 bowl	food preparation/consumption
	1 chalice	food consumption
	3 storejars	storage
	6 scarabs	business/adornment
	knob	special
	tool?	unknown

The similarity coefficient for L. AJ is 74.2 or 37.1% when compared to the storage paradigm.

Locus	Finds	Functional Class
AK	1 bowl	food preparation/consumption
	1 krater	food preparation
	1 storejar	storage
	1 jug	food preparation/storage
	1 juglet	multipurpose
	amulet	special/cultic
AL	special vessel	unknown
	1 scarab	business/adornment
	macehead	weapon
AM	2 jugs	food preparation/storage
	toggle pin	adornment
	alabaster jug	special/status
	bone inlay	special/status
AN	1 bowl	food preparation/consumption
	alabaster vessel	special/status
AO	2 bowls	food preparation/consumption
	1 jug	food preparation/storage
	male figurine	special/cultic
	1 scarab	business/adornment
	toggle pin	adornment
	tool?	unknown
	chisel	tool
	bone inlay	special

Table 4.57—*Continued*

Locus	Finds	Functional Class
	ostrich beads	adornment?
AP	1 bowl	food preparation/consumption
	1 storejar	storage
	1 jug	food preparation/storage
	alabaster vessel	special/status
	bronze arrowhead	weapon
	bronze spearhead	weapon
AQ	10 bowls	food preparation/consumption
	1 goblet	food preparation/consumption
	1 krater	food preparation/consumption
	1 cooking pot	food preparation
	1 jug	food preparation/storage
	2 juglet	multipurpose
	1 pyxis	special/cosmetic
	1 vase	food preparation/storage
	1 copper needle	textile production
	bone tube spatula	special/cosmetic
	4 scarabs	business/adornment
	toggle pin	adornment
	2 bronze knives	tool
	limestone macehead	special

The similarity coefficient for L. AQ is 128 or 64% when vessels only are compared to the food preparation and consumption paradigm.

AR	2 bowls	food preparation/consumption
	2 cooking pots	food preparation
	krater/cooking pot	food preparation/consumption
	2 jugs	food preparation/storage
	1 juglet	multipurpose
	1 bronze needle	textile production
	5 scarabs	business/adornment
	alabaster vessel	special/status
	bronze tool?	unknown
	bronze chisel	tool
	double hook	tool
	bronze blade	tool
	copper arrowhead	weapon
AS	1 bowl	food preparation/consumption
	1 krater	food preparation/consumption
	1 storejar	storage
	1 jug	food preparation/storage
	1 juglet	multipurpose
	clay strainer	food preparation/multipurpose

Table 4.57—*Continued*

Locus	Finds	Functional Class
	1 scarab	business/adornment
AW	4 bowls	food preparation/consumption
	1 chalice	food consumption
	jug	food preparation/storage
	1 juglet	multipurpose
	1 scarab	business/adornment
	alabaster vessel	special/status
	bronze dagger	weapon

The similarity coefficient for L. AW is 129 or 64.5% when compared to the food preparation and consumption paradigm.

Locus	Finds	Functional Class
AX	1 cylinder seal	business/adornment
	1 scarab	business/adornment
B	1 jug	food preparation/storage
	2 juglets	multipurpose
	1 jar stand	storage
	1 scarab	business/adornment
	alabaster vessel	special/status
	bone inlay	special
C	1 jug	food preparation/storage
	2 bronze needles	textile production
	bronze tweezers	multipurpose
	1 cylinder seal	business/adornment
	1 scarab	business/adornment
	1 spindle	textile production
	alabaster vessel	special/status
D	1 bowl	food preparation/consumption
	bronze dagger	weapon
E	2 bowls	food preparation/consumption
F	7 bowls	food preparation/consumption
	2 storejars	storage
	1 amphora	storage
	10 jugs	food preparation/storage
	9 juglets	multipurpose
	1 flask	storage
	3 bilbils	storage
	1 pyxis	special/cosmetic
	2 whorls	textile production
	kohl stick	special/cosmetic
	bone tube spatula	special/cosmetic
	gold earrings	adornment
	2 toggle pins	adornment
	gaming piece—die	special/recreation

Table 4.57—*Continued*

Locus	Finds	Functional Class
	tool?	unknown
	chisel	tool
	2 arrowheads	weapon
	dagger pommel	weapon

The similarity coefficient for L. F is 94 or 47% when compared to the storage paradigm.

Locus	Finds	Functional Class
G	2 bowls	food preparation/consumption
	1 chalice	food consumption
	1 juglet	multipurpose
	silver ring	adornment
	bone inlay	special/status
H	2 bowls	food preparation/consumption
	1 jug	food preparation/storage
	2 alabaster vessels	special/status
J	3 bowls	food preparation/consumption
	1 storejar	storage
	alabaster vessel	special/cosmetic
K	3 storejars	storage
	1 jug	food preparation/storage
	1 juglet	multipurpose
	tweezers	multipurpose
	1 scarab	business/adornment
	basalt mortar	food preparation
	2 toggle pins	adornment

The similarity coefficient for L. K is 102 or 51% when compared to the storage paradigm.

Locus	Finds	Functional Class
N	2 bowls	food preparation/consumption
	1 jug	food preparation/storage
	1 buckle	adornment
	bronze blade	tool
	bronze dagger	weapon
	1 narrow-neck jar	liquid storage
P	1 vase	food preparation/storage
	1 juglet	multipurpose
	bronze needle	textile production
	bronze adze	tool
Q	8 scarabs	business/adornment
	bone toggle pin	adornment
R	2 jugs	food preparation/storage
S	1 jug	food preparation/storage
	1 juglet	multipurpose
	1 scarab	business/adornment

Table 4.57—*Continued*

Locus	Finds	Functional Class
T	1 bowl	food preparation/consumption
	1 jug	food preparation/storage
	1 juglet	multipurpose
	2 scarabs	business/storage
U	1 bowl	food preparation/consumption
	1 juglet	multipurpose
	1 scarab	business/adornment
V	1 krater	food preparation
W	1 scarab	business/adornment
X	javelin point	weapon
Y	decorated sherd	unknown
	1 scarab	business/adornment
Z	3 bowls	food preparation/consumption
	1 krater	food preparation
	1 cooking pot	food preparation
	2 jugs	food preparation/storage
	special vessel	special

The similarity coefficient for L. Z is 153 or 76.5% when compared to the food preparation and consumption paradigm.

Area E (Fig. 67)

In Area E, north of Area A, were several units of housing divided into blocks by major east–west and north–south streets. Immediately east of Street EAA was the best preserved block. The most promising house plan includes Rooms EAB–EZ. The largest room, EAD (4.8 × 8 m), contained three ovens but little else (Table 4.58). Indeed, the only food preparation vessel forms from these rooms were 1 jug (EAD) and 1 bilbil (EAG). The paucity of finds and the lack of reported doorways makes the analysis of houses in Area E very difficult.

Loci EAE, EDJ and EDK may have been a street or a communal courtyard shared by the houses on either side. Only one blade was attributed to these loci, providing little information concerning any activities carried out here. The house on the north side, Rooms EAF–EDG, yielded only 13 items, of which 3 were gaming pieces (Table 4.58). Such a corpus does not allow for functional analysis of individual rooms. To the east of the main street, a second block of rooms, EAA–EZ was built immediately west of Area T structures. The Area E rooms contained 2 scarabs and 1 cylinder seal. Again, a

Houses and their Furnishings

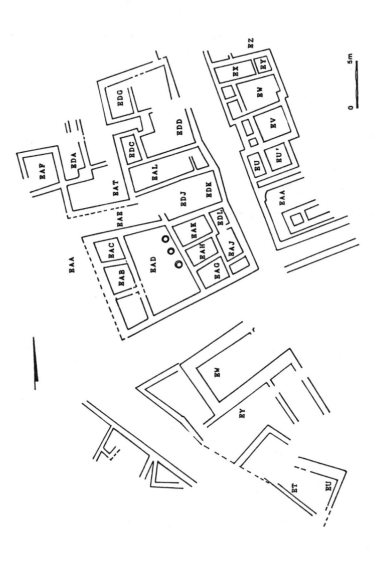

Figure 67. Tell el-'Ajjul Area E, after Petrie 1934: Pl. LXII

corpus too limited for analysis. A small room west of Room EV was paved with shells. Unfortunately, no contents were reported which might clarify its function. This fact may indicate that it had been used as a bath. The arrangement of rooms in this complex varies from the houses further west, making the identification of EAA–EZ as a house rather tentative.[1]

Table 4.58. *Tell el-'Ajjul Late Bronze Area E—Finds and Functional Classes*

Locus	Finds	Functional Class
EAD	1 jug	food preparation/storage
	1 scarab	business/adornment
EAE	blade	tool
EAF	1 jug	food preparation/storage
	1 whorl	textile production
	gaming piece—die	special/recreation
EAG	1 bilbil	container
EAL	1 juglet	multipurpose
	1 whorl	textile production
	?? lead roof roller	unknown
	dagger	weapon
	blue paste cylinder	unknown
EDC	tube	unknown
EDD	alabaster vessel	special
	dagger	weapon
EDG	2 gaming pieces	special/recreation
EDQ	1 jug	food preparation/storage
EK	1 blade	tool
EV	2 scarabs	business/adornment
EZ	1 cylinder seal	business/adornment

Area T (Figs. 68a, b)

Extending east and south around the erosion channel were several housing units designated Area T. Excavated in 1934 by Petrie, these houses yielded too few artefacts for a room by room functional analysis. However, to the west of Street TAN–TDH, several discrete room groups were preserved.

One such room group included Rooms TB–TP (Fig. 68a). Room TO was a large room (4.0 × 6.6 m), surrounded by a smaller one. No

---

1. Equally tentative is any attempt to understand the structures to the south of the east-west street, Rooms EW-EU (Fig. 67). Because no finds were recorded for these loci, they will not be considered in this study.

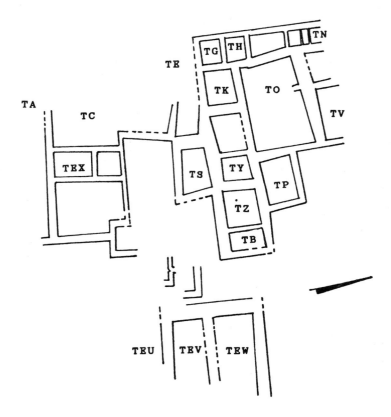

Figure 68a. *Tell el-'Ajjul Area T, after Petrie 1934: Pl. LXIII*

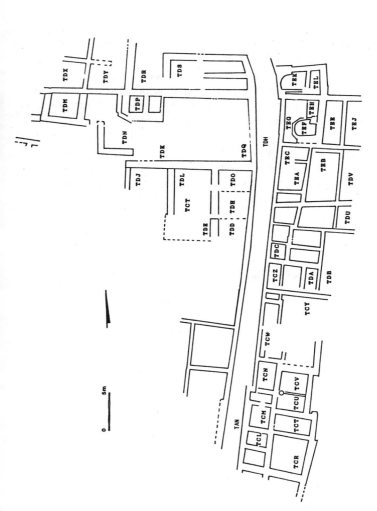

Figure 68b. *Tell el-'Ajjul Area T, after Petrie 1934: Pl. LXIII*

domestic artefact assemblages were reported. The tentative identification of this structure as a house is based primarily on room arrangement, wall thickness, and the similarity of the few artefacts that were found with those recorded for other houses (Table 4.59).

A second room group, TEX–TS, was less well preserved. Only one juglet was reported for these rooms. It is not clear whether Room TC, to the west, was part of this complex. Petrie identified this locus as a bath, even though the finds reported for it (1 bowl, a goblet, a jar and a scarab) suggest the possible location of food preparation, consumption and storage activities (Table 4.59). A second bath (unlettered) with a plaster floor was partially preserved west of Room TEV. Because of its state of preservation, it is not possible to determine its relationship to the surrounding buildings.

A large complex of rooms (TEU–TCT, Figs. 68a, 68b), some with stone wall foundations, were located between the bath and Street TAN–TDH. The thick walls of these rooms (0.9–1.0 m), along with their size and shape, suggest a multistoried structure. As it turned out, many loci yielded little in the way of artefacts. Rooms TEU, TEV, TEW, TDM, TDN, TDJ, TDR and TDS were reportedly empty. Large rooms, such as TDX, TDY and TDZ, contained only scarabs and fragments of bone inlay. Two very small rooms, one labelled TDP, also contained scarabs, along with an alabaster vessel. The plan of this large complex suggests a public building with a large piazza rather than domestic structures.[1] The doorways into the central space, TDN–TDQ, were very narrow (0.8 m). While such entrances may not have been suitable for a market area, the narrow rooms of Locus TDS do suggest public storerooms.

Six rooms with stone foundation walls (TDD–TDO) extended south along Street DTH. The finds from these loci reflected, in some cases, more than one phase (i.e. TCT and TDH[2]) making the identification of activity areas very tentative. The corpus from Room TDH is so small, three items, that it is statistically useless (Table 4.59). The finds from Room TCT are confused by the fact that two rooms were assigned the same letters. While elevations may be useful to distinguish discrete

1. The well in TDQ, indicated on the plan (Petrie 1934: Pl. LXIII), appears to have been related to the later phase of this complex.

2. This room was assigned the same letters as the street, TDH. There is no certain way of distinguishing the finds from these loci. For the purposes of this study, it is assumed that the finds were located in the room.

loci in other situations, they are not helpful in assigning artefacts to precise loci in Area T.[1] The assemblage assigned to Locus TCT contained vessels used for food preparation, consumption and storage, while in Room TDL, next door, there were 2 whorls and a dagger. While all these artefacts were typical of domestic structures at Tell el-'Ajjul, the regular shape and 1 m thick walls of the rooms in this complex, as well as their proximity to loci TDN–TDQ, argues strongly that they were part of the public complex.

Along the east side of Street TAN–TDH, there were a series of houses that shared party walls, TCL–TEK (Fig. 68b). The artefacts cited for these rooms are not significantly more numerous than was the case in other parts of Area T. In fact, most loci contained only a scarab and one other random find, such as a weapon, vessel or whorl (Rooms TCL, TCM, TCY, TDA, TDB, TDC, TDK, TDV and TEB). The omnipresence of scarabs probably suggests more their ability to be lost or misplaced than about the functional designation of their find spots at Tell el-'Ajjul. The number of tools and weapons that could have been reused as tools (8), along with 6 whorls may indicate a certain amount of textile manufacture in this group of dwellings. Several grinders and pounders, probably used in food preparation, were reported for Rooms TEC, TCG and TEK. However, they were not associated with any other food preparation objects or vessels. Two rooms that may have served that purpose (TCU and TCV) contained a stone vessel, 1 juglet, 2 jugs and 3 scarabs. Whether the food preparation tool kit from Room TCT belonged to the room with that designation in this same house must remain uncertain because of the presence of another locus with the same name in complex TDD–TDO,[2] to the northwest (Fig. 68b).

1. All the finds from Rooms TCL–TEK were given elevations high above the wall levels indicated on the plan (Petrie 1934: Pl. LXIII). Whether these finds are at all useful for determining activity areas remains doubtful.

2. Locus TCT in complex TDD–TDO must be a mistake on the original plan (Petrie 1934: Pl. LXIII) because all other rooms west of Street TAN–TDH are TD loci.

Table 4.59. *Tell el-'Ajjul Late Bronze Area T—Finds and Functional Classes*

Locus	Finds	Functional Class
TC	1 bowl	food preparation/consumption
	1 goblet	food preparation
	1 wide-neck jar	dry storage
	1 scarab	business/adornment
TG	disk/wheel	unknown
TH	1 scarab	business/adornment
TK	1 scarab	business/adornment
	dagger	weapon
TN	2 toggle pins	adornment
	dagger	weapon
TO	whorl	textile production
TV	dagger	weapon
	dagger pommel	weapon
TY	large tweezers	tool
	awl and bone handle	multipurpose
TCL	1 blade	tool
TCM	1 scarab	business/adornment
TCN	1 goblet	food preparation/consumption
	whorl	textile production
TCP	1 narrow-neck jar	liquid storage
	3 scarabs	business/adornment
TCT	1 bowl	food preparation/consumption
	1 krater	food preparation
	1 wide-neck jar	dry storage
	1 scarab	business/adornment
TCU	1 jug	food preparation/storage
	1 whorl	textile production
	3 scarabs	business/adornment
	stone vessel	special/status
TCV	1 jug	food preparation/storage
	1 juglet	multipurpose
TCY	1 scarab	business/adornment
TDA	1 scarab	business/adornment
	javelin point	weapon
TDB	dagger pommel	weapon
TDC	1 scarab	business/adornment
	dagger	weapon
TDH	1 jug	food preparation/storage
	1 whorl	textile production
	1 scarab	business/adornment
TDK	3 scarabs	business
	saw	tool

Table 4.59—*Continued*

Locus	Finds	Functional Class
TDL	2 whorls	textile production
	dagger	weapon
TDP	2 scarabs	business/adornment
	alabaster vessel	special/status
TDU	1 wide-neck jar	dry storage
	1 scarab	business/adornment
TDV	1 scarab	business/adornment
TDX	2 scarabs	business/adornment
	bone inlay	special/status
TDY	1 scarab	business/adornment
TDZ	3 scarabs	business/adornment
TEA	1 bowl	food preparation/consumption
TEB	1 scarab	business/adornment
	horse bridle piece	riding
TEC	3 scarabs	business/adornment
	basalt mortar	food preparation
	javelin point	weapon
TEG	granite socket	door socket
	2 scarabs	business/adornment
	2 basalt bowls	food preparation
TEH	2 bone inlay	special/status
TEK	2 scarabs	business/adornment
	limestone pestle	food preparation
	1 awl	multipurpose
TEL	1 whorl	textile production
TEX	1 juglet	multipurpose

Attempts to isolate individual houses and study their arrangement are severely limited because so few doorways were plotted. At certain points, walls perpendicular to the street are common to more than one room. This feature is the only clue for identifying discrete houses, and it remains far from certain. Future excavations at Tell el-'Ajjul would certainly be valuable in view of the extensive occupation at this site.

Area G (Figs. 69a, b)

Without a final plan of all excavated areas, it is not possible to determine the exact location of Area G in relation to the other domestic areas. However, it is clear that the lower level was separated from the upper by a thick destruction layer. For example, the preserved top of the wall in Room GAO was 855 inches in the earlier phase and the

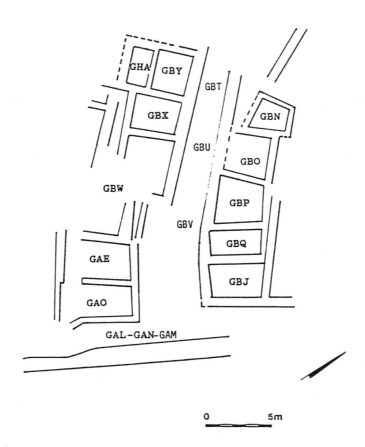

Figure 69a. *Tell el-'Ajjul Area G (south part), after Mackay 1952: Pl. XXXV*

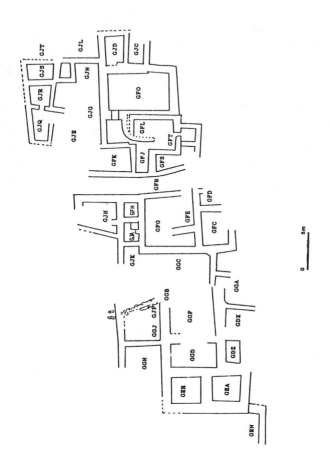

Figure 69b. *Tell el-'Ajjul Area G (north part), after Mackay 1952: Pl. XXXV*

foundation of the later wall was 889 inches, c. 90 cm difference. The thick debris layer accounts for the fact that the wall alignment differs considerably in the upper level even though Street GAL–GAN remained in use and the wall along the southeast had been built up (Mackay 1952: 27). A second street, GAR–GBT, ran perpendicular, separating the structures that lined it on either side.

Three distinct buildings can be distinguished in this group. Along the south side of Street GAR–GBT were located two structures of quite different construction. The walls of Rooms GAO–GBW (east room) were c. 50 cm thick while those of Rooms GBW (west room)–GBY measured 60–85 cm Because the finds from all these rooms were so scanty, a total of 3 items, no analysis to determine room function is possible. Only one small room, Locus GHA (1.5 × 2.8 m), had an assemblage worthy of note. It included a scarab, 2 awls, 1 fish-hook and 1 bronze dagger (Table 4.60).

Room GBW (west room) was identified by the excavator as a bath-room because of the partial remains of a pebble floor (Mackay 1952: 27). The size of this room (3.3 × 4.0 m), and the treatment of the floor, varied considerably from the rooms previously identified as bath rooms. In fact, its closest parallel is the room with the shell pavement in Area E, west of Room EV, where the floor was covered with large clam shells. The same treatment had been given to a bench at the entry of the shrine in Area A, near Room AF, and a second bench located outside a smaller shrine near Room AX. All of these shell pavements were uncovered in Late Bronze Age levels and were associated with the use of water, or some other liquid. Of these, only the very small room west of L. EV was identified as a bath by the excavator (see above). Another room (GFK) with a stone-paved floor was located to the northwest in a house along Street GFR (Fig. 69b). However, Room GFK measured 3.0 × 5+ m, significantly larger than the typical bath room. Whatever the function of the stone pavement in Room GBW, the overall plan and purpose of this thick-walled structure remains unknown.

On the north side of Street GAR–GBT was a group of five rooms with poorly aligned walls that may reflect more than one phase (Fig. 69a). From two rooms, GBO and GBP, a corpus of only three items was recorded: 1 bracelet, a flint drill point and a jug (Table 4.60), too few for an identifiable tool kit. Because the walls were severely denuded in this area, no complete building plan could be recovered.

As a result, the type of dwelling represented by these rooms remains uncertain.

Further west were a series of rooms with walls of *terre pisé* (GEA, GER, GGD, GDZ, Fig. 69b). Because of the difficulty of excavating such walls and ascertaining their exact dimensions, they appear on the plan to have been very thick, c. 1.5 m (Mackay 1952: Pl. XXXIV). In fact, these walls appear to be a reuse of the earlier construction along the south side of the square pit (GGA, Fig. 35). Because the later phase of these walls is founded c. 1.5 m above the floor of the earlier rooms, one could almost suspect that these rooms were the upper storey of the earlier house. To the north, however, the pit had been filled in and new structures built in its place, Rooms GDX, GGA and GGF (Fig. 69b). There were no recorded finds that could clarify the function of these rooms. A stone-lined drain ran west from L. GGF–GGB and passed under the wall of L. GGL. It seems that the drain served to take water away from the new loci built above the square pit. Unfortunately, the lack of finds from these loci makes it impossible to identify, with certainty, this area as a courtyard.

To the north, bordering the south side of Street GFR was another complex that included Rooms GFC–GJH (Fig. 69b). Because of the limits of the excavated area, it is not clear that Room GFC was part of the same house as GJA. Three rooms in this structure contained more than two artefacts, GFC, GFH and GJA. Although no assemblages were large enough to be compared with the functional paradigms, the finds in Locus GFC were typical of a domestic inventory, 1 jug, 1 needle, 2 weights and an arrowhead (Table 4.60). The same can be said for L. GJA which also contained a jug, scarab, goblet, stone vessel, weapons and a bronze disk. No particular tool kit is represented by such a corpus, but it is typical of artefacts and vessels reported for Tell el-'Ajjul. Room GFH yielded another stone vessel, a dagger and a whorl. Also recorded for this complex were 5 awls that could have been used with the needle and whorl in textile production. Other domestic tool kits were missing.

To the north of Street GFR was another complex, L. GFK–GFT. The rooms in this building were very irregular in size and shape (Fig. 4.69b). The largest assemblage of reported finds, from L. GFL, included elements of several functional tool kits, food preparation, textile manufacture and business (Table 4.60). Finds from the surrounding rooms were all associated with these functions but insufficient in number to indicate that a particular activity occurred in any one room. The size of L. GFO (4.8 × 8.0 m) would support its identification as a courtyard. However, the finds reported from this locus (1 bowl and a weight) do not, in themselves, confirm this judgment. In the few remaining rooms to the north and west of GFO, only random finds were recognized (Table 4.60). However, there were several tools, weapons, and a potter's wheel thrust bearing. The inclusion of tools and weapons, possibly in secondary use, throughout these rooms provides some indication of the range of activities, mostly domestic and craft related, that may have taken place in these Late Bronze Age houses.

Table 4.60. *Tell el-'Ajjul Late Bronze Area G—Finds and Functional Classes*

Locus	Finds	Functional Class
GAE	haematite weight	business
GAH	toggle pin	adornment
GAO	javelin point	weapon
GAT	bronze needle	textile manufacture
GBA	1 bowl	food preparation/consumption
GBO	bronze bracelet	adornment
	flint drill point	tool
GBP	1 jug	food preparation/storage
GBW	1 scarab	business/adornment
GER	plumb bob	tool
GFC	1 jug	food preparation/storage
	1 needle	textile manufacture
	2 haematite weights	business
	bronze arrowhead	weapon
GFD	1 scarab	business/adornment
GFE	2 awls	multipurpose
GFH	1 whorl	textile manufacture
	alabaster juglet	special/status
	bronze dagger	weapon
GFJ	1 whorl	textile manufacture
	1 scarab	business/adornment
	bronze dagger	weapon
GFK	1 krater	food preparation
	1 scarab	business/adornment
GFL	1 bowl	food preparation/consumption
	1 jug	food preparation/storage
	clay strainer	food preparation
	1 needle	textile manufacture
	1 scarab	business/adornment

Table 4.60—*Continued*

Locus	Finds	Functional Class
	clay mask	special/cultic
	1 awl	multipurpose
	haematite weight	business
	2 maceheads	weapon
GFO	1 bowl	food preparation/consumption
	haematite weight	business
GFS	bone whorl	textile manufacture
	1 scarab	business/adornment
GHA	1 scarab	business/adornment
	2 awls	multipurpose
	1 fish hook	fishing
	bronze dagger	weapon
GJA	1 goblet	food preparation/consumption
	1 jug	food preparation/storage
	1 scarab	business/adornment
	alabaster vessel	special/status
	2 javelin points	weapon
	bronze disk	unknown
GJB	1 bowl	food preparation/consumption
	1 jug	food preparation/storage
GJC	1 scarab	business/adornment
	plumb bob	tool
GJD	1 whorl	textile manufacture
	2 scarabs	business/adornment
	chisel	tool
	bronze dagger	weapon
	javelin point	weapon
GJE	1 bowl	food preparation/consumption
GJH	2 scarabs	business/adornment
	3 bronze awls	multipurpose
GJJ	1 bowl	food preparation/consumption
	2 scarabs	business/adornment
GJQ	1 scarab	business/adornment
GJS	toggle pin	adornment
	basalt potter's wheel	pottery production

Table 4.61. *Tell el-'Ajjul Area A Stratum 2 Loci*

Locus	Area	Description	Similarity Coefficient
A	A	Room	
B	A	Room	
C	A	Room	
D	A	Room	
E	A	Room	
F	A	Room	94 or 47%
G	A	Room	
H	A	Room	
J	A	Room	
K	A	Room	102 or 51%
M	A	Room	
N	A	Room	
P	A	Room	
Q	A	Room	
R	A	Room	
S	A	Room	
T	A	Room	
U	A	Room	
V	A	Room	
W	A	Room	
X	A	Bathroom	
Z	A	Room	153 or 76.5%
AA	A	Street	
AB	A	Room	
AC	A	Room	116 or 58%
AF	A	Room	
AJ	A	Room	74.2 or 37.1%
AK	A	Room	
AL	A	Room	
AM	A	Room	
AN	A	Street	
AO	A	Room	
AP	A	Room	
AQ	A	Room	128 or 64.0%
AR	A	Room	
AS	A	Room (large)	
AS	A	Room (small)	
AT	A	Street	
AU	A	Room	

Table 4.61—*Continued*

Locus	Area	Description	Similarity Coefficient
AV	A	Room	
AW	A	Room	129 or 64.5%
AX	A	Room	
AY	A	Street	

Table 4.62. *Tell el-'Ajjul Area E Stratum 2 Loci*

Locus	Area	Description
EAA	E	Room—also Street locus
EAB	E	Room
EAC	E	Room
EAD	E	Room
EAE	E	Room
EAF	E	Room
EAG	E	Room
EAH	E	Room—also Street locus
EAJ	E	Room
EAK	E	Room
EAL	E	Room
EAT	E	Room

[Stratum 2 Rooms with same letters]

Locus	Area	Description
EU		
EU'		
EV		
EW		
EX		
EY		
EZ		
EDA	E	Room
EDC	E	Room
EDD	E	Room
EDG	E	Room
EDJ	E	Room
EDK	E	Room
EDL	E	Room
EDM	E	Room
EDN	E	Room

Table 4.63. *Tell el-'Ajjul Area G Stratum 2 Loci*

Locus	Area	Description	Levels (inches)
Southern Rooms			
GAE	G	Room	868–911
GAO	G	Room	874–927
GAL-GAN	G	Street	
GBJ	G	Room	863–913
GBN	G	Room	913–928
GBO	G	Room	896–921
GBP	G	Room	891–924
GBQ	G	Room	883–912
GBW[1]	G	Room	891–934
GBX	G	Room	891–934
GBY	G	Room	893–945
GHA	G	Room	886–938
Northern Rooms			
GHF	G	Room	896–940
GHH	G	Room	921–952
GHJ	G	Room	921–952
GEN	G	Room	928–952
GER	G	Room	945–970
GFC	G	Room	916–956
GFD	G	Room	916–955
GFE	G	Room	946–970
GFG	G	Room	915–982
GFH	G	Room	931–989
GFJ	G	Room	921–983
GFK	G	Room	934–996
GFL	G	Room	917–943
GFO	G	Room	921–977
GFR	G	Street	
GFS	G	Room	943–979
GFT	G	Room	907–967

1. There are two rooms labeled GBW. The western room, with its curving stone foundation, was almost completely preserved, while the eastern room was poorly preserved. There is, however, a problem in understanding the relationship of finds labelled GBW to the western room because the section drawing indicates Room GBX to the west of GBU (Pl. V) although section line 7-8 goes through Room GBW (west) (Pl. XXXV).

Table 4.64. *Tell el-'Ajjul Area T Stratum 2 Loci*

Locus	Area	Description
TA	T	Undefined
TB	T	Room
TC	T	Bath
TE	T	Undefined
TG	T	Room
TH	T	Room
TK	T	Room
TN	T	Room
TO	T	Room
TP	T	Room
TS	T	Room
TV	T	Room
TY	T	Room
TZ	T	Room
TCE	T	Room
TCF	T	Room
TCL	T	Room
TCM	T	Room
TCN	T	Room
TCP	T	Room
TCR	T	Room
TCT	T	Room
TCU	T	Room
TCV	T	Room
TCW	T	Room
TCY	T	Room
TCZ	T	Room
TDA	T	Room
TDB	T	Room
TDC	T	Room
TDD	T	Room
TDE	T	Room
TDE	T	Room
TDH	T	Room—also Street locus
TDJ	T	Room
TDK	T	Room
TDL	T	Room
TDM	T	Room
TDN	T	Room
TDO	T	Room
TDP	T	Room
TDQ	T	Room

Table 4.64—*Continued*

Locus	Area	Description
TDR	T	Room
TDS	T	Room
TDU	T	Room
TDV	T	Room—2 rooms same letters
TDX	T	Room
TDY	T	Room
TDZ	T	Room
TEA	T	Room
TEB	T	Room
TEC	T	Room—2 rooms same letters
TEE	T	Room
TEF	T	Room
TEG	T	Room
TEH	T	Room
TEJ	T	Room
TEK	T	Room
TEL	T	Room
TEU	T	Room
TEV	T	Room
TEW	T	Room
TEX	T	Room

Additional Houses with only Preliminary Publication

At several Palestinian sites, Late Bronze Age houses have been completely exposed, as at Tell Abu Hawam and Tell Beit Mirsim, or partially uncovered, as at Ta'anach, Tel Halif, and Bethel (see detailed discussion below). Several of these sites have been published only in a preliminary fashion without complete artefact assemblages. As a result, spatial/functional analysis is not possible for these sites to the same extent as for those with more complete documentation. As has been shown repeatedly in this study, few site reports indicate the total quantity of ceramic vessels. Rather, a selection of ware form types is illustrated from an unreported total corpus making it virtually impossible to use statistics with any degree of certainty. In the following sites, the situation is even more tenuous. Nevertheless, it was considered important to include these structures in this study for the sake of completeness. Future publication may shed more light on the character of these domestic structures and make comparison with other sites easier.

Tell Ta'anach

The joint expedition of the American Schools of Oriental Research and Concordia Seminary documented the continuity of occupation from MB IIC to LB I in two areas of the southwest quadrant. One area, immediately south of the West Building, has been described above. It included the MB IIC walls with LB I occupation remains in the rooms formed by these walls. In this second MB IIC phase, the walls were two stones wide, considerably more substantial than the construction from the earlier phase. Although the rooms and courtyard formed by these walls contained domestic installations, they have been interpreted, in preliminary publications, as service quarters for the West Building (Lapp 1969: 25). Without additional publication of the plans and finds it is not possible to suggest an alternative function.

To the south, and extending 15 m eastward from the last phase of the MB IIC casemate fortification, was an area of Late Bronze Age structures. Rebuilt on the same lines as the previous MB IIC structures these rooms were located on both sides of a north–south street. The street itself underwent at least six repavings (Lapp 1967: Fig. 9). A similar sequence of construction techniques from single stone thick walls to two stone thick walls was observed. The later LB I Building, uncovered in the 1966 season, was interpreted as a series of small rooms which may or may not have had a unified plan and function (Lapp 1967: 16). The rooms of this complex varied greatly in size (1.1 × 1.4 m versus 2.6 × 3.5 m). Two small rooms with plastered floors (Rooms 3 and 4) could have served as storerooms while Room 2 contained a stone-lined cistern (Lapp 1967: Fig. 8). To date, no finds that might indicate room function have been published. The interpretation of the excavator remains our only source of information.

Tel Halif (Map Reference 1373/0879)

The site of Tel Halif (Khirbet Khuweilifeh) lies along the route from Hebron to Gaza where the Judaean hills overlook the Shephelah and the coastal plain, at its juncture with the Negev. Excavations by the Lahav Research Project, under the direction of Joe D. Seger, began in 1976 and are continuing. Occupation from the Early Bronze Age to

the Modern Arab period has been identified. To date, the only significant second millennium domestic architecture has been uncovered in
Field 1, Stratum 9.

Stratum 9B (Fig. 70)
Uncovered in Stratum 9B was a well built house, constructed above
meagre occupational remains that dated to the MB IIC–LB IA transition. Deep packed clay foundations supported stone and mud brick
walls that were 80–100 cm thick. A large (6.0 × 6.5 m) hall or court
was surrounded by rooms on all sides (Jacobs 1987: 69).[1] In the
exposed area, three phases were discerned. The ceramic and artefact
remains date to the final phase. So far, only a sample of the finds have
been published (Table 4.65) making it difficult to assign functional
classification to the various activity areas.

The main room (L. 10042) did contain finds which pointed to a
variety of domestic activities associated with food preparation, such as
mortars, querns, storejars, bowls and kraters (Jacobs 1987: 74). The
specific function of the central depression and the two bins remains
unclear. Nevertheless, on the basis of the relative size of this room
and the artefact assemblage, it is probably safe to suggest that it served
as the living room

The oven in Room B clearly indicates the location of cooking
although much of the food preparation in the form of grinding and
storage was carried out in the main room. When a second oven in
Room B was constructed in the doorway to Room A, a change took
place in the use of Room A. The excavators suggest that it was subsequently used for refuse collection. This judgment is based on the finds
which included beads, pottery sherds, stone tools and bone artefacts
along with ashes from the oven (Jacobs 1987: 72).

The existence of an upper storey is indicated by the remains of a
stairway in the main room and the timber framing in the south wall of
Room G (Jacobs 1987: 72-74). Because so much of the house remains
unpublished, it is not possible, with Jacobs, to compare it to other
Egyptian style houses of the Late Bronze Age. What is clear, so far, is

---

1. Jacobs's collection of parallel house plans (Tell el-Far'ah [S], Amman,
Gerizim, Ur and Ugarit) perpetuates the uncritical view that the 'central courtyard'
house is identical to the 'Amarna style' house.

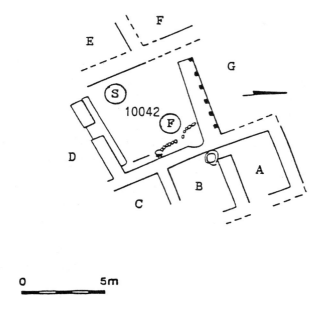

Figure 70. *Tel Halif Stratum 9, after Jacobs 1987: Fig. 2*

that the building did function as a house, with food preparation activities and several other activity areas both on the ground floor and on an upper storey. When excavation of this building was completed in 1983, it measured c. 16 × 16 m (Jacobs 1985: 4).[1]

1. Jacobs mentions only one parallel to the timber framing in the south wall of Room G, Kuntillet 'Ajrud (1987: 73). In an earlier publication, he had thought that it was not represented in Palestine at all (1985: 4). Oren refers to Building 410 at Tel Masos which its excavator, Kempinski, has described as having massive pillars integrated in the walls (Oren 1984: 48). In addition, Wall 958a at Shechem, Strata XX-XIX, had pillar bases along one side.

Table 4.65. *Tel Halif Stratum 9B—Finds and Functional Classes*

Locus	Finds	Functional Class
A	cobbled area	unknown
B	oven	food preparation
C		
D		
E		
F		
G		
10042	3 bowls	food preparation/consumption
	1 spouted krater	food preparation
	3 cooking pots	food preparation
	2 jars	storage
	2 jugs	food preparation/storage
	1 vase	food preparation/storage
	blades	tool
	saddle quern	food preparation
	2 mortars	food preparation
	2 bins	grain? storage
	pillar base	roof support
	basin	unknown
	bench	multipurpose
	lined pit	unknown

Table 4.66. *Tel Halif Stratum 9A—Finds and Functional Classes*

Locus	Finds	Functional Class
10041	beads	adornment
	scarabs	business/adornment
	stamp seal	business

Stratum 9A

After the destruction of the final Stratum 9B phase, the house was rebuilt in LB IIA. No plan of the house during this phase has been published and only a few finds (beads and seals) have been mentioned. The final report should provide a considerable amount of additional material concerning building techniques, artefacts and ceramic vessels from this interesting building.

Bethel (Map Reference 172/148)

The site of ancient Bethel was located on a spur of the Judaean hills 17 km north of Jerusalem. Excavations at the site were carried out by W.F. Albright and J.L. Kelso in 1934, on behalf of Pittsburgh Theological Seminary and the American Schools of Oriental Research. After World War II, excavations were resumed under Kelso in 1954 and continued in 1957 and 1960.

Late Bronze Age occupation at Bethel was represented by remains of the LB II period only. No bichrome ware was recovered in the debris although two Late Bronze building phases were distinguished in Areas I (A) and II (B) (Kelso 1968: Pl. 3, 120). In both areas, what appeared to be domestic architecture consisted of well built, flat stone foundations, flagstone or thick plaster floors and stone-lined drains (Kelso 1968: 28). Unfortunately, the excavation areas were so limited that not one complete building was revealed (Figs. 71, 72). Yassine has reconstructed one house by extending the walls on both sides and by duplicating the rooms that were exposed in Area I (A), showing a central room with smaller rooms on all four sides (1974: Pl. XII, item 2). While this plan cannot be proven, it certainly represents a likely room arrangement.[1]

The function of discrete activity areas within House A is more difficult to ascertain due to the excavation and reporting methods employed. This becomes apparent when the ceramic vessels and artefacts are assigned to their locus groups (Table 4.66). No balanced tool kits can be identified although food preparation and consumption items predominate (72%). The large number of cooking pots reported for this structure (10) confirms its primary function as a house. However, their distribution was more scattered than one would expect. Cooking pots were found outside the main entrance (L. 60), in the main room (L. 54, 55), as well as in the side rooms (L. 52, 58, 63). The only other find reported for the main room was a bowl (L. 55). Nevertheless, this room was the largest in the building and appears to have been centrally located in relation to the surrounding rooms. In view of its location, it probably served as the living room.

---

1. Although two phases of occupation were distinguished during excavation, the plans are so poorly reproduced that the layout of the respective rooms and features can barely be recognized (Kelso 1968: Pl. 3).

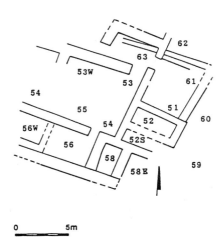

Figure 71. *Bethel LB Area 1, after Kelso 1968: Pl. 3*

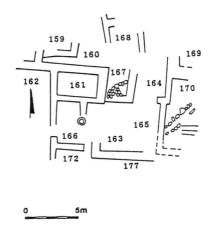

Figure 72. *Bethel LB Area 2, after Kelso 1968: Pl. 3*

In a small side room, L. 58, and in L. 58N (not on the plan, Kelso 1968: Pl. 3), 25 bowls were uncovered. The exact function of this concentration remains unclear although these vessels may have been in storage. On the other hand, evidence of food storage was minimal (L. 52, 58, 63, 1 jar each). Remaining artefacts point to textile production, cosmetic use and adornment—typical domestic activities.

The second domestic structure, in Area II (B) (Fig. 72), was poorly preserved and only partially exposed. Only one complete room (L. 161) was uncovered, revealing both construction phases. This structure was characterized by a series of stone-lined drains and flat stone walls. One such wall, found collapsed in L. 162, seemed to have had 19 courses of stone and stood to c. 2.5 m (Kelso 1968: 29). Such a wall may indicate that the ground floor walls were built completely of stone.[1] Unfortunately, nothing in the room arrangement of this building necessitates its identification as a house. At the same time, the artefacts reported were too few to contribute further to an understanding of its function (Table 4.67).[2]

Table 4.67. *Bethel Area 1—Finds and Functional Classes*

Locus	Finds	Functional Class
51	2 bowls	food preparation/consumption
	1 juglet	multipurpose
52	1 bowl	food preparation/consumption
	1 cooking pot	food preparation
	1 jar	storage
	1 whorl	textile production
	scarab	business/adornment
	2 bronze knives	cutting
	bone handle	tool?
52N	2 bowls	food preparation/consumption
	1 juglet	multipurpose
52SE	1 cooking pot	food preparation
54	1 cooking pot	food preparation

1. For a comparable construction technique, see House A at Ugarit (Callot 1983: 15). A systematic study of the relationship between geographical setting, local topography and building materials would be very useful in understanding the development and variety of construction techniques.

2. Because it is not possible to locate with precision the artefacts designated as Sub 162, for example, such finds have not been included in the Table of Finds and Functional Classes. In fact, only two items fell into this category, one flask and one cooking pot.

Table 4.67—*Continued*

Locus	Finds	Functional Class
55	1 bowl	food preparation/consumption
	1 cooking pot	food preparation
56	lead bar	metallurgy
	astragalus bone	recreation
57	bone cylinder	unknown
58	13 bowls	food preparation/consumption
	1 krater	food preparation/consumption
	1 cooking pot	food preparation
	1 jar	storage
	sistrum handle	special/music
	macehead	weapon
58N	12 bowls	food preparation/consumption
	1 cooking pot	food preparation
	1 juglet	multipurpose
58S	stag horn	unknown
60	3 bowls	food preparation/consumption
	2 cooking pots	food preparation
	2 juglets	multipurpose
	toggle pin	adornment
60W	1 bowl	food preparation/consumption
61	basalt bowl	grinding
	gaming piece	recreation
	arrowhead	weapon
62	2 whorls	textile production
	2 beads	adornment
	bone handle	tool?
	dagger handle	weapon
63	2 cooking pots	food preparation
	1 jar	storage
	kohl stick	cosmetic use
	3 beads	adornment

Table 4.68. *Bethel Area 2—Finds and Functional Classes*

Locus	Finds	Functional Class
161	bone inlay	special/status
164	bone handle	tool?
166	1 jar	storage
	clay knob	unknown
	oven	food preparation
172	1 whorl	textile production
	arrowhead	weapon

Tell Beit Mirsim (Map Reference 141/096)

During four seasons of excavations at Tell Beit Mirsim, Late Bronze Age occupation was uncovered in the southeast sector and assigned to Stratum C. Albright identified two phases, C1 (the earlier) and C. However, it is clear from his plan that at least three phases were exposed (Albright 1938: Pl. 52). The excavator himself asserted that the distinction between C1 and C was very difficult to discern because of the frequent rebuilding of partially destroyed buildings (Albright 1932: 38). In addition, many walls suffered denudation, or were robbed in antiquity for building materials. Several rooms, built up against the line of the earlier city wall, were later covered by the Late Bronze Age fortifications constructed during the second phase of Stratum C (Albright 1938: 63). As a result, it is not clear from Albright's plan to which house or houses these rooms belonged (1938: Pl. 52).

Attempts to better understand the function of specific rooms and clarify the room arrangement of individual structures, is frustrated by the fact that few artefacts were assigned locus or room numbers.[1] While isolated sherds, valuable as chronological indicators, were registered, insufficient numbers were preserved for understanding the functional character of the buildings exposed in this stratum. One can only assume, on the basis of room size and shape, that these buildings were indeed private houses.

Only one possible house was reconstructed by Albright (Fig. 73). It consisted of a large room (8.0 × 8.6 m) and three rooms along the east side, each c. 3.0 × 2.4 m A long room along the north side of the main room was poorly preserved. Since no pillar bases were found in the main room, Albright clearly envisioned a house with a courtyard and surrounding rooms (1938: 63-64). However, no parallels for this house can be discerned among the remaining rooms illustrated on the plan of Stratum C (1938: Pls. 52, 56).

---

1. Most ceramic vessels and artefacts from Stratum C were assigned to 'debris'; see the register of finds (Albright 1932). As a result, no database could be assembled to form artefact clusters for individual loci.

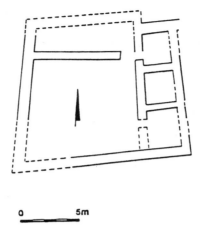

0 —————— 5m

Figure 73. *Tell Beit Mirsim Stratum C, after Albright 1938*

Tell Abu Hawam (Map Reference 152/245)

Tell Abu Hawam, at the foot of Mount Carmel, was the location of a harbour town on the south bank of the Kishon River. Although today it is 1 km from the present coastline, excavations of a sea wall along the west side of the town show that it was originally built directly on the shore. The extent of the mound was 1.5 hectares (3.6 acres) when it was surveyed by P.L.O. Guy in 1923.

Exploratory probes were undertaken in 1929 by L.A. Mayer and N. Makhouly and in 1930 by D.C. Baramki (Balensi 1985: 65). Excavations on the mound were carried out by R.W. Hamilton during two seasons, 1932–1933, during which he identified five strata of occupation. Further clarification of the Late Bronze Age settlement was undertaken by E. Anati in 1963 (Avi-Yonah 1975: I, 9-10). A major publication and revision project, undertaken by V. Hankey, E. Oren and J. Balensi, began in 1972 because 75% of the finds from Hamilton's excavations (including 90% of the Cypriot imports) remained unpublished (Balensi 1985: 66, 70, n. 1). In terms of this study, the provenience information for pottery and objects published for the earliest stratum (V), Late Bronze Age, is not specific enough to provide a basis for functional analysis of artefact assemblages.[1]

What remains useful for this study are the plans of the structures themselves (Fig. 74). While traces of Middle Bronze Age occupation were attested by artefacts and pottery, the earliest architectural remains date to the Late Bronze Age. Hamilton distinguished three phases of Late Bronze Age occupation. Recent analysis of the excavation material indicates that there were in fact five phases comparable to Megiddo IX–VIIb (Balensi 1985: 67). To date no plans of these phases have been published aside from the composite plan of Hamilton (1935: Pl. XI).

It is disappointing that Hamilton's description of the fortified Late Bronze Age town was so superficial. One can only suggest that certain buildings in Stratum V (such as 52, 54–55, 56, 59, 60, 61 and 66) served a domestic purpose. Building 61 had a square plan which reappeared in Stratum IV Buildings 36, 41, 44 and 45 (Hamilton 1935: Pl. 11). This plan recalls the square Building 6061 at Hazor, Area C. Indeed, all of the square buildings are comparable in size (c. 36–42 m²).

Features in these Late Bronze Age buildings included a well in Building 56, numerous ovens revetted with sherds, and silos of stone rubble construction (Hamilton 1935: 13). The wall foundations of the houses themselves were built of stone with rubble fill.

The most impressive building of Stratum V (c. 18 × 22 m), located in the southwest corner of the town, was House 63–65 (Fig. 74). Although only the east and north sides were preserved, Harif has suggested a reconstruction based on a comparison with Mycenaean megaron style houses. He identified rooms 63–65 as storerooms opening onto a central corridor. A larger room to the west, partially destroyed before excavation, may have had the form of a megaron unit (Harif 1974: Fig. 2). Balensi has suggested, more recently, that Building 66, which was constructed over the ruins of Room 65, had a system of latrines comparable to the Ashlar Building at Enkomi IIIa (1985: 68). These two Aegean parallels support the suggestion that Mycenaeans lived at Tell Abu Hawam and used some of the 700 imported Aegean vessels currently unpublished.[2] It is hoped that the

---

1. Without recourse to the museum collections where these artefacts are kept, it is not possible to compile database assemblages. Hamilton assigned some finds to particular rooms and others to excavation squares—each 225 m².

2. Balensi refers to a study of Aegean wares from Tell Abu Hawam by Vronwy Hankey and E. French (Balensi 1985: 71, n. 11).

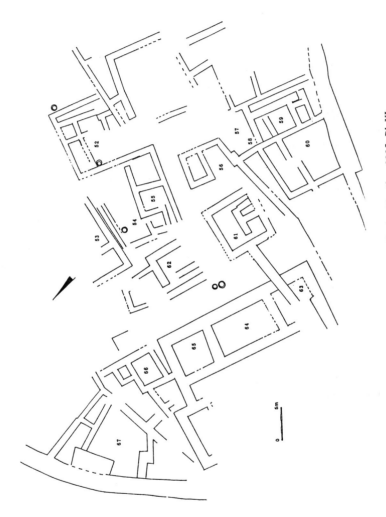

Figure 74. *Tell Abu Hawam Stratum V, after Hamilton 1935: Pl. XI*

present revision of Hamilton's work will enable a future re-evaluation of the houses at Tell Abu Hawam and an analysis of their activity areas.

Governors' Residencies

Evidence for Egyptian presence and control of Canaan during the time of the 18th–19th Dynasties can be seen in the material culture of many LB II Canaanite sites. Egyptian style ceramic vessels, alabastra, stelae, statuary, inscriptions and architectural features have been found from Tell el-Farah (S) to Beth Shan in the north (Weinstein 1981: 19-21). Egyptian style architecture was also recognized in the plan of temples dedicated to Egyptian deities, forts and large houses, variously identified as administrative buildings, or residencies.

Six residency buildings seem to have served domestic and/or administrative functions.[1]

1. Strata X–IX residency at Tell esh-Sheri'a (Avi-Yonah 1978; Oren 1982, 1984).
2. Tell el-Farah (S) residency and adjoining building (Petrie 1920; Macdonald, Starkey and Harding 1932).
3. Tell el-Hesi (Bliss 1898).
4. Building 480 at Khirbet el-Meshash (Fritz and Kempinski 1983).
5. Stratum X-12 fortified palace at Aphek (Kochavi 1981).
6. Buildings 1500 and 1700 at Beth Shan (James 1966). (Oren 1984: 42; Weinstein 1981: 18).

Several construction techniques employed in these buildings witness to Egyptian influence. For example, in many cases, the foundations were of brick rather than stone, exterior walls were 1.5–2.0 m thick, and T-shaped stone thresholds were employed.

---

1. Several buildings which have been described in a very preliminary fashion will not be considered in this study. These include Palace IV at Tell el-'Ajjul, and the migdol of Level 7 at Beth Shan (Weinstein 1981: 18). Oren reconstructed Building JF at Tell Jemmeh as a 15 × 15 m square, with rooms surrounding an open court (1984: 46; Fig. 2:5). Because the double row of rooms on one side of the central hall is very uncharacteristic of Egyptian houses and because the current excavator has redated the building to the Philistine period (Avi-Yonah 1976: II, 546), this house will not be included in this analysis.

The building plan that is usually compared to the Egyptian style structures in Canaan is that of an Amarna style house or villa (Oren 1984: Fig. 3). While these houses varied somewhat in plan, depending on their size, certain features were common to the majority of such houses. Each house had a central hall with one or more pillars supporting the roof, thus allowing for a clerestory (Peet and Woolley 1923: 5-6). In several houses, Petrie located a divan (low, raised bench), hearth and lustration slab in the central room, along with a decorated niche or false door. The main entrance to the house was usually through a northwest corner vestibule that led into the loggia, a rectangular room along the north side of the house that may have served for entertaining guests (Crocker 1983: 58). Entrance into the central hall was from the loggia (1894: 20-22).

On either side of the central hall were series of rooms that served for storage, while one such room held the stairway to the upper storey or roof. Behind the central hall were the private quarters of the family. In exceptionally large houses, there might even be a second pillared hall.[1] The bathroom and master bedroom, with a bed niche, were located in the private quarters. Additional sleeping quarters may have been on the upper storey (Petrie 1894: 21-22).

In the most prestigious homes, food preparation activities were frequently located in a separate building detached from the main house. Outside ovens, granaries and kitchens have been preserved, enabling their identification by excavators. However, in the house of the Vizier Nakht, the supposed location of the kitchen, banquet rooms and offices was on the upper storey (Peet and Woolley 1923: 7-9). In more modest houses, of course, these rooms were located on the ground floor near the storerooms to the side of the central hall.

In harmony with the topography of Akhetaten (Tell el-Amarna), major wall foundations of mud brick were laid in trenches and the interior space was leveled with soil. On this filling, a floor of tiles or unbaked bricks was laid which was then plastered with mud and painted. When the floor was finished, the interior walls were built (Peet and Woolley 1923: 5-6).

Because many of the inhabitants of Akhetaten were involved with government bureaucracy, their homes also served, to a certain extent, as administrative centres. As a result, the houses may have included

---

1. Crocker's analysis showed that 93% of the largest 10% of Amarna houses had a second square room with the same fittings as the Central Hall (1983: 60).

offices and working areas for administrative personnel. At the same time, this city was the national capital with certain areas specifically designated for official purposes, such as the Palace and the Records Office complex (Pendlebury 1951: 122-23).

The discovery of certain Egyptian style structures in Canaan has led archaeologists and historians to the identification of such structures as Residencies of Egyptian Governors. While certain construction techniques, such as brick foundations, could be employed in areas with topography similar to Amarna, such as the southern coastal plain, other techniques had to be employed elsewhere.

Because these structures share certain structural and functional characteristics, they will be considered as a group. This is not to say that these 'Residencies' all functioned in the same manner. In fact, their precise function has yet to be tested. Previous studies have focused primarily on structural similarities. This is due, of course, to the excavation methods employed in the earliest recovery of Amarna style houses in Canaan. The excavators of Tell el-Far'ah (S) (1929–1930) and those at Beth Shan (1921–1933) did not distinguish the finds on the floors from those in the debris layers, and in some cases, did not assign locus numbers to the finds. This makes it exceedingly difficult to reconstruct locus groups of ceramic vessels and objects that might constitute tool kits of domestic or administrative activities. Even those sites which have been excavated more recently, such as Tell esh-Sheri'a, Aphek and Tel Mor, have not published complete plans or object registers, let alone the quantity and type of ceramic vessels from each locus.[1]

Tell esh-Sheri'a (Map Reference 119/088)

Tell esh-Sheri'a,[2] located on the north bank of Nahal Gerar in the western Negev, lies between Tell Halif, to the east, and Tell el-'Ajjul, to the west. The remains of the ancient city, covering 1.6 hectares (3.8 acres), forms a steep-sided, horseshoe-shaped mound. Evidence from a sounding indicated that occupation on the tell began in the Middle

---

1. This is in contrast to the handy chart published by R.H. Dornemann (1981: 32, Table 1) in which the number and type of all vessels from the Tablet House are listed, see below.

2. The name of this site is variously spelled Tell esh-Shari'a and Tel Sera' (Avi-Yonah 1978: IV, 1059; Oren 1982: 156).

Bronze Age and continued through the Persian period. Evidence of other periods, notably Chalcolithic, Early Bronze, Roman and Byzantine, was revealed by ceramic and architectural remains on the eastern slope of the tell and on the south side of the wadi (Avi-Yonah 1978: IV, 1059). The top of the tell was occupied by a Muslim cemetery, a fragmentary mosaic floor and several installations from the Mameluke period.

Excavations have been carried out by Eliezer Oren for the Archaeological Division of Ben Gurion University of the Negev between 1972–1978. In Area A, Late Bronze Age structural remains were encountered in Strata 12–9. Public and cultic buildings have been reported from Strata 12–10, but, to date, no plans have been published. Only the 'Governor's Residency', from Stratum 9, has been discussed in some detail (Oren 1978, 1982, 1984).

Stratum 9 (Fig. 75)
One building in Area A (906), on the east side of the tell, has been partially exposed and identified as the seat of the Egyptian governor (Oren 1984: 41). This identification is based on a comparison of Building 906 with other large, Late Bronze Age houses in Canaan that share a certain similarity in plan to Amarna style houses, such as those at Beth Shan, Tell el-Farah (S),[1] and to residencies, comparable to the buildings at Aphek, Khirbet el-Meshash, Tell el-Hesi and Tell Jemmeh.[2] Support for such a comparison is strengthened by the plethora of Egyptian type vessels and objects reported from the Tell esh-Sheri'a house (see below).

Because Building 906 was not completely exposed, at the time of publication, the ground plan remains somewhat conjectural. It is assumed by the excavator that the building was square and measured c. 22×22 m (Oren 1984: 39; cf. 25×25 m, Oren 1982: 166). The basic plan consisted of a central court or hall with pillar bases, surrounded by small rooms and a paved area in the north. While this

---

1. Oren compares the 'residency' at Tell esh-Sheri'a to all the Amarna style houses and residencies without recognizing any significant differences (1984: Fig. 2; 39, 41). As will be shown below, the houses at Beth Shan and Tell el-Farah (S) were indeed comparable to Amarna style houses while the other 'residencies' were built on a somewhat different plan.

2. The style of these 'residencies' needs to be considered separately from the Amarna style houses.

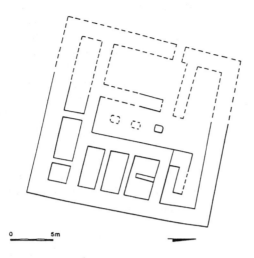

Figure 75. *Tell esh-Sheri'a, after Oren 1984: Fig. 2*

room arrangement is not at all clear from the composite plans (Avi-Yonah 1978: IV, 1062; Oren 1982: 164), a reconstructed plan (Fig. 75) is presented in the most recent publication (Oren 1984: Fig. 2.1).

The finds from this structure have been published only in a preliminary fashion, assigning no locus or room numbers to individual vessels or objects (Oren 1984: Figs. 4–7). While it is of interest that many vessels were Egyptian in style, such as the beer jar, straight sided bowls, drop-shaped jars, and high-necked cups, it is their function that must be considered here. Unfortunately, no clear indication of total quantity has been reported. Nevertheless, some idea of the relative proportion of vessels may be assumed on the basis of the published corpus, even though it is not possible to distinguish the respective functions of these two areas because there has been a mixing of vessels from the upper and lower floors (Oren 1984: 39). A comparison of the corpus (Table 4.69) to the functional paradigms employed in this study indicates a similarity coefficient of 160 or 80% to the food preparation and consumption tool kit. This is surprising in view of the fact that nearly a dozen bowls were inscribed in hieratic Egyptian with administrative information pertaining to tax gathering (Oren 1984: 41). If these bowls were subtracted from the corpus, the coefficient would be somewhat lower. We must recognize, however, that the numbers given in the publication are not necessarily representative of the total finds (Table 4.69).

Two other assemblages were reported in summary fashion (Oren 1982: 166). The first is a collection of bronze objects, all found in the same room. Included here was a staff with a sceptre-like loop or crook which could have represented the official status of the occupant of this house. In addition, there were 2 small copper ingots which suggest, along with the cobalt blue pigment, that supplies for the production of metal objects (i.e. weapons) and Egyptian style pottery may have been under the control of the 'Resident'.[1]

The judgment of the excavator that there was at least one upper storey is supported by the thickness of the outer walls (1.5–2.0 m) and the evidence of a fallen ceiling complete with wooden beams and collapsed mud brick (Oren 1984: 39). In fact, such thick walls could have supported two upper stories but this would be unusual for an Egyptian style house. Those at Amarna had thinner exterior walls (c. 50–75 cm).[2]

There were, however, several Egyptian building techniques employed in the construction of this residence. The foundations, as well as the walls, were built of mud brick. Because of the location of Tell esh-Sheri'a in the southern coastal plain, this similarity of construction methods may say more about the topography of the site than about the cultural tradition of the builders. It will be important to compare this feature, where possible, with other Egyptian style Late Bronze Age houses from other sites where stone wall foundations would be expected.

Table 4.69. *Tell esh-Sheri'a Stratum 9—Finds and Functional Classes*

Locus	Finds	Functional Class
906	12 bowls	food preparation/consumption
	1 goblet	food consumption
	2 kraters	food preparation/consumption
	3 cooking pots	food preparation
	1 store jar	liquid storage

1. During its last phase, the palace of Pylos was in control of all metal supplies, as indicated in the Pylos tablets (Chadwick 1958: 110-11).
2. Examples of wall thicknesses at Amarna include the house of Panhesy, 52 cm, and the house of Nakht, 75 cm (Peet and Woolley 1923).

Table 4.69—*Continued*

Locus	Finds	Functional Class
	1 amphora	liquid storage
	2 jugs	food preparation/storage
	2 juglets	multipurpose
	1 flask	liquid storage
	3 various jars	liquid storage
	1 lamp	lighting
	2 lids/funnels	food preparation
	cup and saucers	special/cultic
	1 alabaster pot	special/status
	2 scarabs	business/adornment
	1 ostracon	business

The similarity coefficient for L. 906 is 160 or 80% when compared to the food preparation and consumption paradigm.

Room?	bronze objects	miscellaneous
	bronze staff	administrative
	copper mini-ingots	votive/metallurgy
Room?	cobalt pigment	glass making?
	scarabs	business/adornment
	seals	business/adornment

Tell el-Far'ah (S) (Map Reference 100/076)

The site of Tell el-Far'ah (S) is located 24 km south of Gaza, near the west bank of Wadi Shellaleh (Nahal Besor). The identification of this mound with Sharuhen has been accepted by many scholars (Avi-Yonah 1978: IV, 1074), although studies by Stewart (1974: 62-63) and Weinstein (1981: 6) challenge it. The mound itself is severely eroded; nevertheless, the occupational debris covers approximately 6.6 hectares (15.8 acres).

Tell el-Far'ah (S) was excavated by Sir Flinders Petrie and his associates under the name Beth Pelet during 1928 and 1929 (Petrie 1930; Macdonald, Starkey and Harding 1932). At the north end of the site, four phases of Middle and Late Bronze Age dwellings were uncovered. The most interesting building in the two upper phases is the Residency which follows the plan and setting of an Amarna style villa (Fig. 76).

Two phases of this building, discerned by Petrie during excavation, are reflected in the wall levels recorded on the plans (Petrie 1930: Pls. LII, LIV). The mudbrick foundations of this house extended four to six feet below floor level (362 feet 3 inches to 368 feet 2 inches). The upper walls were either of brick or pressed earth and brick scraps, coated with plaster. Just above floor level, Petrie observed that the wall line projected or receded slightly.[1] Among the interior features, two styles of door frame were distinguished; for the smaller entryways, wooden door frames were embedded in plaster, and for the main entrances, wooden posts were erected in front of brick doorways (Petrie 1930: 17).

Although Petrie observed fallen ceiling beams covering the ground floor rooms, only a few luxury items (for example, the ivory box from Room YC) were recovered.[2] Based on Petrie's own excavations at Amarna, room function and arrangement can be determined, in some instances, on the basis of the plan typical of such houses. The Stratum 1 Residency (Fig. 76) included a stairway leading to the porch (YM) which opened into a vestibule (YP). The loggia (YV) led into the central hall (YR) which had a plastered floor. The long parallel rooms on the south (YH, YK, YL) may have been storerooms, although no finds were reported that support this suggestion. Stairs leading up to the roof or second storey were located in the southwest corner, Room YE (Macdonald *et al.* 1932: Pl. 69). In the final excavation season, a bedroom with raised brick platform (unlettered on plan; see Fig. 76) and a bathroom with stairs leading to a plastered water tank were exposed to the north of the central hall (Macdonald *et al.* 1932: 28). In addition, Macdonald identified a wine cellar (YS) containing 45 large storejars.[3]

1. Such construction peculiarities may be due to an attempt to employ the techniques used in building an Amarna style house in Egypt. As we have seen above, the usual practice was to construct the foundation walls up to a certain height at which point the substructure was filled in with dirt to support the floors. The upper walls and floors were then constructed. Such a method might account for the slight misalignment observed at Tell el-Far'ah (S). The use of this construction method might indicate the presence of Egyptian building engineers as this was not the method commonly employed in Canaan where foundations of ordinary domestic structures were less deep and the upper walls were a true continuation.

2. The excavations at Gerar and Beth Pelet added many forms to the Corpus of Palestinian Pottery (Duncan 1930).

3. While these jars may be represented in CPP, there were no ware forms assigned to this locus number (Macdonald *et al.* 1932: Pl. 89).

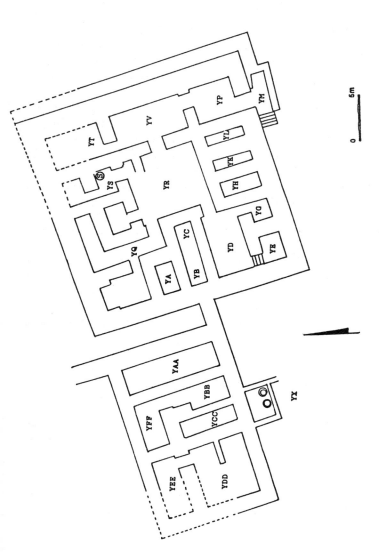

Figure 76.   *Tell el-Far'ah (S), after MacDonald 1932: Pl. LXIX*

Table 4.70. *Tell el-Far'ah (S) Stratum 1—Finds and Functional Classes*

Locus	Finds	Functional Class
YAA	3 kraters	food preparation/consumption
YEE	4 bowls	food preparation/consumption
	1 jug	food storage
YZZ	4 bowls	food preparation/consumption
	1 jug	food preparation/storage
YS	45 jars	liquid storage
YXa	12 bowls	food preparation/consumption
	2 kraters	food preparation/consumption
	2 narrow-neck jars	liquid storage
	2 juglets	multipurpose

The similarity coefficient for L. YXa is 151 or 75.5% when compared to the food preparation and consumption paradigm.

YXb	15 bowls	food preparation/consumption
	5 kraters	food preparation/consumption
	3 narrow-neck jars	liquid storage
	1 jug	food preparation/storage
	2 flasks	liquid storage
	2 stirrup jars	liquid storage

The similarity coefficient for L. YXb is 131.8 or 65.9% when compared to the food preparation and consumption paradigm.

The Residency had a subsidiary building (YAA–YFF) which probably served as a kitchen or office wing but Starkey and Harding provide no details (1932: 29). The finds reported from this structure were recovered from Rooms YAA and YEE (Table 4.70).[1] While neither assemblage constitutes a functional tool kit, all the finds point to food preparation. Other tool kits, such as food storage or administrative activities, should have been represented in view of the large size of this building (22 × 19 m).

The courtyard with its cobblestone pavement, flagstone path and gateway reflects the Egyptian tradition of a large compound surrounding the main house. The numerous finds recovered from the courtyard (Table 4.70) are attributed by Wood to the squatter occupation that followed the abandonment of the Residency. Wood is operating on the assumption that 'domestic pottery would not have been in use on the cobbled entrance court, nor in the open area south of the west

---

1. The vessels from these rooms have been classified by T. Dothan as Philistine pottery (1982: 27-28). This residency, built in the latest phase of LB IIB, continued in use into the Philistine period, possibly as late as the early 11th century BC.

extension' (Wood 1985: 456-57). While this is generally true, certain domestic activities may have been performed out of doors depending on the season. Wood's contention that these finds represent a squatter settlement is problematic because of the lack of cooking pots. This same factor is problematic in view of the proximity of several ovens (2) located in the walled area outside the subsidiary building.

It is important, therefore, to test the assemblage of ware forms from the courtyard for integrity as a functional tool kit as well as for its chronology as a post-Residency corpus. While the pottery finds do not constitute complete tool kits because of the lack of cooking pots, they strongly suggest food preparation or consumption. The similarity coefficient of Courtyard YXa is 151 or 75.5% and that of Courtyard YXb is slightly less, 131.8 or 65.9% when compared to the food preparation and consumption paradigm. Such a comparison, of itself, cannot prove that these finds are not the result of squatter occupation although we might expect more in the way of grain storage pits to accommodate the need for storage facilities. Thus, we seem to be left with the opinion of the excavators that these finds represent the latest phase of the Residency and not a subsequent occupation (Macdonald *et al.* 1932: 30).

The earlier phase of the Residency (ZA–ZV), constructed on the same basic plan, provided evidence to show that its foundation walls were reused in the later phase. While no finds uncovered from the floors of this phase were published with locus numbers, the room arrangement is so typical of an Egyptian house that the function of many rooms can be surmised. For example, the entrance to the house was in the southeast corner (ZP) and led into the loggia (ZV). To the west was the central hall (ZR) with store rooms on the south (ZG, ZK, ZL). The private quarters were along the west side of the house (ZA–ZF), with additional storerooms (ZS, ZT) to the north of the central hall. No evidence for a stairway was represented on the plan of this phase (Petrie 1930: Pl. LIV).

Excursus

Below this impressive house were the remains of several smaller structures. Here again two phases were represented (Fig. 77a, b). While no complete house plans were exposed due to the limited area of excavation, some features, objects and ceramic vessels were recovered and a register was published (MacDonald 1932: Pl. 89). The

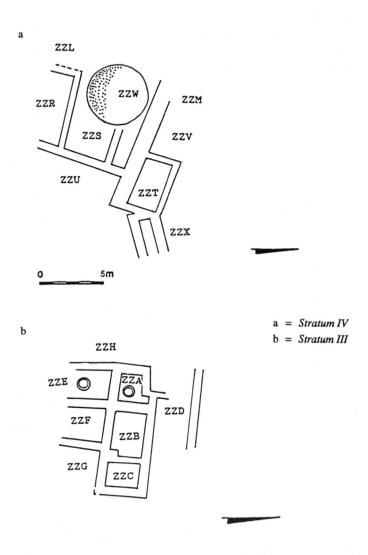

a = *Stratum IV*
b = *Stratum III*

Figure 77: *Tell el-Far'ah (S), after MacDonald 1932: Pl. LXVI*

pottery forms indicate that the lower phase dated to the Middle Bronze period and the upper phase to the Late Bronze Age. The registered finds that were assigned to precise loci were predominantly bowl forms. It is disappointing that many vessels and most objects were not assigned to specific loci (Macdonald *et al.* 1932: 83-88, Pl. LXXIII), making it impossible to identify any functional tool kits from the assemblages reported (Table 4.71).

Table 4.71. *Tell el-Far'ah (S)—Finds and Functional Classes*

Locus	Finds	Functional Class
ZZA	5 bowls	food preparation/consumption
	1 flask	liquid storage
ZZG	8 bowls	food preparation/consumption
	2 kraters	food preparation/consumption
ZZM	1 bowl	special/status
ZZR	2 bowls	food preparation/consumption
	1 krater	food preparation/consumption
ZZS	7 bowls	food preparation/consumption
ZZT	5 bowls	food preparation/consumption
	1 krater	food preparation/consumption
	2 juglets	multipurpose
ZZU	1 bowl	food preparation/consumption
	1 jar	storage

Table 4.72. *Tell el-Far'ah (S) Stratum I Loci*

Locus	Level (feet)	Description	Similarity Coefficient
YA	369.3	Room	
YB	368.7	Room	
YC	368.3	Room	
YD	368.5	Room	
YE	368.2	Stairs	
YF		Room	
YG		Room	
YH		Room	
YK		Room	
YL		Room	
YM	368.5	Porch	
YP	368.3	Vestibule	
YQ		Room	
YR	368.11	Central Hall	
YS	369.6	Room	

Table 4.72—*Continued*

Locus	Level (feet)	Description	Similarity Coefficient
YT	370.3	Stairs	
YV	369.2	Loggia	
YXa	361.0	Courtyard	151 or 75.5%
YXb	364.1	Courtyard	131 or 65.9%
YAA	367.1	Room	
YBB		Room	
YCC		Room	
YDD	367.8	Room	
YEE		Room	
YFF	370.4	Room	

Table 4.73. *Tell el-Far'ah (S) Stratum II Loci*

Locus	Level (feet)	Description
ZA	358.10	Room
ZB		Room
ZD	358.4	Room
ZE	360	Room
ZF	357	Room
ZG	355.4	Room
ZK	357.9	Room
ZL	361.5	Room
ZP	355.3	Vestibule?
ZQ		Room
ZR	355.7	Central Hall
ZS		Room
ZT		Room
ZV	355.8	Loggia

Table 4.74. *Tell el-Far'ah (S) Stratum III Loci*

Locus	Level	Description
ZZA		Room
ZZB		Room
ZZC		Room
ZZD		Undefined
ZZE		Room
ZZF		Room
ZZG		Room
ZZH		Undefined

Table 4.75. *Tell el-Far'ah (S) Stratum IV Loci*

Locus	Level	Description
ZZL		Undefined
ZZM		Undefined
ZZR		Room
ZZS		Room
ZZT		Room
ZZU		Undefined
ZZV		Undefined
ZZW		Pit
ZZX		Undefined

Tell el-Hesi (Map Reference 124/106)

The site of Tell el-Hesi is located on the west bank of Wadi Hesi (Nahal Shiqmah), 26 km east-northeast of Gaza in the Coastal Plain. Hesi consists of two distinct zones, the tell or acropolis, and the lower city. The acropolis, cut on the east by the wadi, rests on a natural sand dune and rises a total of 38 m above the stream bed. The top of the acropolis covers only 0.3 hectares (0.7 acres) while the earliest EB level was 1.6 hectares (4 acres). At this stage it formed part of the lower city which was 10.4 hectares (25 acres).

Well known as the site where Petrie tested his theory of pottery chronology in 1890, Hesi was subsequently excavated during four seasons by F.J. Bliss, 1891–1893. A multidisciplinary project was begun at Tell el-Hesi by John Worrell, L.E. Toombs, L.E. Stager and W.J. Bennett, Jr in 1970. Under the direction of D.G. Rose (1975–1981) and V.M. Fargo (1983), the Joint Archaeological Expedition to Tell el-Hesi continued for eight seasons.

No extensive Late Bronze Age occupation was exposed on the acropolis by the Joint Expedition.[1] One structure excavated by Bliss, in City IV (Fig. 78), has been identified by certain archaeologists as an Egyptian style residency (Oren 1984: 46-47) or citadel (Avi-Yonah 1976: II, 517). Although Bliss described several Egyptian building

---

1. A series of Late Bronze occupational surfaces, complete with grinding querns, ashes, botanical remains, Bichrome ware and a variety of objects was excavated by me in 1981. Unfortunately, little architecture was uncovered because the exposed area was limited to a 1 m probe.

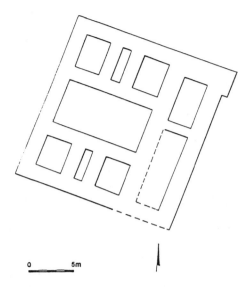

Figure 78. *Tell el-Hesi City IV, after Bliss 1894: 72*

techniques employed in the construction of this building, such as
foundations laid on a layer of sand, and the exclusive use of mud brick
for these foundations (1894: 73-74), the plan of this structure is quite
different from an Amarna style house. It is clear from the study of
782 Amarna houses by P.T. Crocker that room size, shape and
location were intimately connected with function. The square, or
almost square, central hall was not a status symbol, as was a second
loggia, but was a necessity in every house no matter how poor (1983:
60). It is precisely this room which is lacking in the City IV building
at Tell el-Hesi. In addition, while the plan shows great symmetry, the
size and shape of the rooms are not at all comparable to the Tell el-
Far'ah residency. Indeed, the Tell el-Hesi building shows greater
similarity to the structure at Tell esh-Sheri'a.

Functional analysis based on the reported finds for City IVb–IV
should not be attempted. Bliss was completely aware that he was excavating debris because he noted that the walls of the public building
were preserved, in every case, 'below the level of the original doorsills' (1894: 71). The published pottery and objects are drawn from
both phases of Stratum IV, a total of 15 feet of debris (Bliss 1894: 83-

84). Identification of this building must remain uncertain. Nevertheless, it seems most likely that however it functioned, it was not an Amarna style house.

Khirbet el-Meshash (Map Reference 146/069)

To the northeast of the Roman-Byzantine fort at Khirbet el-Meshash, Y. Aharoni discovered an Iron Age I settlement of 5 hectares (c. 12 acres). Excavations of this settlement by a joint German–Israeli team under the direction of V. Fritz and A. Kempinski, continued for several seasons (1972–1975). One house (480) from Area C Stratum 2 (the earlier phase) is usually included in studies of Egyptian style buildings in Canaan (Fig. 79). The house itself was almost square, 15 × 14 m with a rectangular central room divided lengthwise by a row of pillars. The exterior walls were c. 1.2 m thick, suggesting the possibility of an upper storey. Fritz himself compared House 480 to House P 49.2 at Tell el-Amarna (1981: Figs. 10, 11) although the difference in plan is striking. This difference is based not so much on room arrangement as on the size and shape of the rooms. At Amarna the central room was almost square as were many of the smaller, surrounding rooms. Secondly, except for the loggia and private quarters opposite, the rectangular side rooms were usually perpendicular to the sides of the central room. This was not the case with House 480; large rectangular rooms were parallel to three sides of the broadroom central hall. In fact, its closest parallel is the building at Tell esh-Sheri'a and not the Residencies at Beth Shan and Tell el-Far'ah (S), as Fritz has claimed (1981: 66-67).

The finds from the earliest phase of House 480 do not significantly clarify its function. Only one room (L. 483), interpreted by Fritz as a partially subterranean storeroom (1981: 66), can be analysed (Table 4.76). While this assemblage surely fits the pattern of a storeroom tool kit, the similarity coefficient of 137 or 68.8%, when compared to the storage paradigm, is only a moderately close fit. This is due to the number of kraters and chalices that were part of this corpus.

No other room had sufficient published finds for functional analysis. It is interesting to note, however, that a cooking pot was recovered from Room 492, the innermost room in the house, beside Storeroom 483.

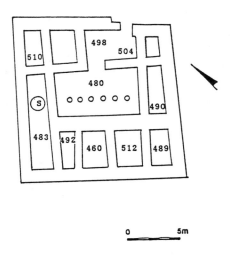

Figure 79. *Khirbet el-Meshash, after Oren 1984: Fig. 2*

Table 4.76. *Khirbet el-Meshash Stratum 2—Finds and Functional Classes*

Locus	Finds	Functional Class
483	2 chalices	food consumption
	2 kraters	food preparation/storage
	1 spouted krater	food preparation/storage
	2 narrow-neck jars	liquid storage
	2 pithoi	dry storage
	1 jug	food preparation/storage
	2 juglets	multipurpose
	1 flask	liquid storage
	1 lamp	lighting

The similiarity coefficient for L. 483 is 137 or 68.8% when compared to the storage paradigm.

492	1 cooking pot	food preparation
498	1 bowl	food preparation/consumption
	1 juglet	multipurpose

Aphek (Map Reference 143/168)

The site of Tell Ras el-'Ain is generally considered to be the location of ancient Aphek-Antipatris. Situated near the sources of the Yarkon River, 16 km east of the Mediterranean sea, this site was occupied from the Early Bronze Age to the Byzantine period. The area of the tell, while not reported by the excavator, appears to have been approximately 14.7 hectares (c. 35 acres).

Tell Aphek was first surveyed by Albright in 1923. Some time later, in 1934–1935,[1] J. Ory undertook a salvage excavation at Aphek; a second salvage expedition under the direction of A. Eitan took place in 1961 (Kochavi 1981: 76). The current excavations, under the direction of Moshe Kochavi, began in 1972. Within the perimeter formed by the Turkish fort, the Canaanite period citadel has been uncovered. It consists of a series of Middle Bronze Age 'palaces' and a Late Bronze Age 'Governor's Residency'.

Building 1104 (Fig. 80)

The building uncovered in Stratum X-12, called the governor's palace, measured 14 × 16 m and had foundation walls 1.4–1.5 m thick. Such thick walls were certainly designed to support upper stories. From this, it is clear that the rooms and stairway preserved on the ground floor represent only a small part of the total structure. However, the building was destroyed in a major fire with the result that many artefact remains from the upper storey were preserved along with those that were *in situ* on the ground floor (Kochavi 1981: 79).

Evidence for the activities which took place in the various rooms of the 'palace' is minimal due to the type of reports published to date. The plans lack locus numbers and scale, the pottery studies do not indicate the quantity of vessels per locus but only the types; and no complete list or drawings of artefacts have appeared.

Two observations can, however, be made: (1) Building 1104 was not typical of domestic structures discussed in this study, nor was it built on the plan of an Amarna style house; and (2) Building 1104, as reported, did not employ Egyptian style construction techniques (Oren 1984: 49). There are, however, several architectural elements that are

---

1. The dates of this first salvage operation are variously given, 1934–35 (Kochavi 1981: 76) and 1935–36 (Avi-Yonah 1975, I: 70*).

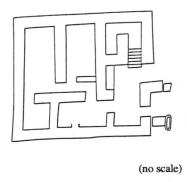

(no scale)

Figure 80. *Aphek Governor's Residency, after Kochavi 1981: 78*

of interest in understanding ancient construction techniques. These include the fact that stone-paved areas were uncovered both outside the building and in rooms that were obviously roofed. Secondly, the walls of the ground floor were built of stone, whereas those of the upper floor were of mud brick with a ceiling made of wooden beams (Kochavi 1978: 14).[1] One interesting feature, a stone basin outside the entrance, could have served as a manger for the animals bearing goods to be stored in this building.

The interpretation of this structure, by the excavator, as an administrative building seems quite plausible (Kochavi 1978: 14), although it is far from certain. Analysis of the artefacts will not be possible until the final reports are complete.

Beth Shan (Map Reference 197/212)

The imposing tell of Beth Shan is evidence that an important ancient city was located here, 7.5 km south of the Sea of Galilee, between the Jezreel Valley and the fords of the Jordan River. This strategic

1. The interpretation of this building in 1978 included a courtyard on the north with direct access to the stairway that led to the second floor (Kochavi 1978: Fig. 5). However, no mention of this courtyard was made in subsequent publications.

position was at the junction of major north–south and east–west roads. A perennial source of water, the Wadi Jalud (Nahal Harod), formed the border along the north side of the tell. While the area of the ancient city is not reported, the Roman period city of Scythopolis covered 8.6 hectares (20.6 acres).

The site was excavated in 10 three-month seasons by the University Museum of the University of Pennsylvania during 1921–1933. Directors of the project included C.S. Fisher and A. Rowe, assisted by G. FitzGerald. Occupation on the mound and in the surrounding area extended from the Neolithic to the Arab period. No complete published reports of the Middle and Late Bronze strata have been issued to date, although groups of objects from tombs and temples have been reported.

Levels IX–VII were dated to the Late Bronze period with certain structures continuing into Level VI at the beginning of the Iron Age. A restudy of the excavated Iron Age material at the University Museum by F. James makes it possible to analyse two Egyptian style houses (1500, 1700) along with the other domestic architecture from Level VI.[1]

House 1500 (Fig. 81)

The Egyptian style houses were named House 1500 and House 1700. Both were constructed in an early phase of Level VI. In a later phase, the rooms were redesigned and divider walls erected which destroyed the original layout. It is precisely the original plan that is of interest in this study. House 1500, the better preserved of the two, will serve as the model for understanding House 1700.

The key to the plan of House 1500 was the discovery of seven T-shaped doorsills still *in situ* (James 1966: 8). The mudbrick walls were 2 m thick with foundations extending c. 2 m below the sills (James 1966: 10). Although some rooms were not well preserved, the basic room arrangement can be reconstructed. Comparable to the houses at Tell el-Amarna, House 1500 had a central hall (L. 1586) with two pillar bases and a libation area. Because of the number of reported finds for this room, it is possible to get some idea of the tool kits common to this important domestic space. In fact, several tool kits are suggested: food consumption, textile manufacture, personal

1. A similar study is promised by P. McGovern of the Late Bronze Age, Strata IX-VII (1986: 14).

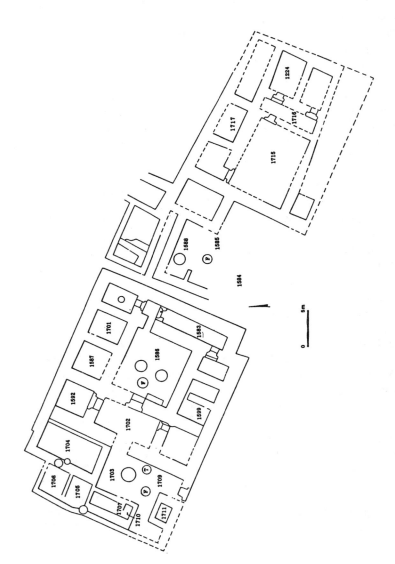

Figure 81.   *Beth Shan Level VI, 1500 House and 1700 House, after James 1966: 9*

adornment and business. The only tool kit complete enough for analysis from L. 1586 is food preparation and consumption (Table. 4.77) which has a similarity coefficient of 107 or 53.5%. No oven or cooking pots were reported for this locus and, as a result, the assemblage is not a very strong example of a food preparation or consumption tool kit.

Evidence of activity areas in the surrounding rooms is weak; few ceramic vessels and small finds were reported. Nor is it clear that the finds registered for Level VI were not contaminated by those from the second phase, Late Level VI (Table 4.77). To the east of the central hall (L. 1583), only one vessel, a large krater type jar (diameter = 35 cm), was reported. While this could have served for food storage, it could also have been used in the bathroom which is usually located, along with the bedroom, in this part of an Egyptian house.

In the rooms on the north and south sides of the central hall, storage and food preparation activities are to be expected. In the case of House 1500, 1 storejar and 1 stopper were reported for Room 1587 on the north and 2 bowls, 2 lids and a bronze awl for Room 1599 on the south.[1] One bowl, a cooking pot and 2 spinning bowls, found in Room 1589, reflect both food preparation and textile production although neither tool kit is well represented (Table 4.77). It is not clear whether these finds reflect activities performed in this room, located at the front of the house, or were related to the finds from the courtyard (L. 1703 and 1709).

The designation of L. 1703 and 1709 as a courtyard in front of the main entrance to House 1500 is suggested by James to account for the presence of Room 1704 which was built against an extension of the north wall of the main house (1966: 11). What seems out of place in this reconstruction is the presence of another doorsill in the southeast corner of L. 1709 (James 1966: Fig. 77). Although food preparation and textile production activities are clearly indicated for these loci (Table 4.77),[2] the plan of the house is not without problems.

Clearly the Amarna style houses in Canaan employed Egyptian

1. James notes that FitzGerald had difficulty separating the walls in these southern rooms (1966: 10-11). It is possible that the bricks he discovered were part of a stairway, a customary feature in this location.

2. The similarity coefficient of L. 1703 + 1709 as a food preparation/consumption assemblage is only 122.3 or 61.1% because of the small proportion of bowls reported. It is likely that many more were represented in the form of sherds which were not counted.

building techniques modified by Canaanite traditions and the require-
ments of the local topography. This can be seen most frequently in the
location of food preparation and cooking areas. The courtyards that
surrounded the large houses at Akhetaten, containing granaries, a
bakery, a workshop, stables and a chapel, were not reproduced in the
restricted confines of Palestinian tells. As a result, food preparation
and cooking activities were carried on in the houses or, in certain
seasons, out of doors. It appears that this was the case at Beth Shan, as
well as at Tell el-Far'ah (S) where a large assemblage of food preparation vessels and equipment were recovered from the paved courtyard (see above). A similar arrangement of cooking areas in front of
a house with a central hall has been identified at Tel Halif (see above).

Another difference between House 1500 and the typical Egyptian
style house is the location of the main entrance. In almost all Egyptian
houses there was a vestibule or porch that led into an anteroom. This
in turn led into the loggia whose broad sides constituted the front wall
of the house on the one hand and the main entrance to the central hall
on the other (Peet 1923: 5-6). At Beth Shan, the entrance appears to
have been directly into the broad wall of the loggia (L. 1702; Fig.
81). It would be interesting to know the elevations and construction
details of Room 1704 which was located in the space customarily
reserved for the vestibule.[1]

House 1700 (Fig. 81)
The plan of House 1700 is difficult to reconstruct because of the poor
condition of the remaining walls. Severely disturbed by later construction, it is not even certain that the building was completely
exposed (James 1966: 12). Indeed, James was of the opinion that the
central hall itself had not been cleared. The finds reported from
L. 1715 were so few that no functional study can be attempted:
1 basalt grinding bowl and a clay duck's head. Actually, these may be
random finds not related to the usual activities performed in that room
(Table 4.75).

On the other hand, the location of storage and food preparation
activities can be readily located in L. 1584, 1585 and 1588. Here, a

---

1. No elevations were published on the plans by the original excavators or by
James (1966: 9, Fig. 77), although it is clear from her discussion of the rooms to the
west of House 1500 that such elevations were preserved in the excavation records
(1966: 10-11).

large assemblage of bowls, cooking pots and various kinds of storejars indicate multiple activities. The similarity coefficient for a storage assemblage is 149 or 74.5%. While juglets are lacking from this assemblage, the large number of beer jars, flasks, storejars and a stirrup jar make the identification certain. Unfortunately, it is not equally clear whether this area consists of roofed rooms or an open court. James has suggested further excavation to clarify the room arrangement of this important house. One can only concur with this suggestion.

Table 4.77. *Beth Shan Level VI House 1500—Finds and Functional Classes*

Locus	Finds	Functional Class
1583	1 wide-neck jar	food preparation/storage
1586	4 bowls	food preparation/consumption
	1 chalice	food consumption
	1 beer jar	consumption/storage
	2 narrow-neck jars	liquid storage
	1 jug	food preparation/storage
	2 juglets	multipurpose
	1 lamp	lighting
	1 cup and saucer	special/cultic
	1 stirrup jar	liquid storage
	1 spinning bowl	textile production
	ivory comb	special/cosmetic
	1 cylinder seal	business/adornment
	figurine fragment	special/cultic
	1 bead	adornment
	1 pendant	adornment
	3 inscribed jambs	architectural feature

The similarity coefficient for L. 1586 is 107 or 53.5% when compared to the food preparation and consumption paradigm.

Locus	Finds	Functional Class
1586SW	1 bead	adornment
1587	1 jar	storage
	1 jar stopper	storage
	2 inscribed jambs	architectural feature
1589	1 bowl	food preparation/consumption
	1 cooking pot	food preparation
	3 spinning bowls	textile production
1591	bronze blade	tool
1599	2 bowls	food preparation/consumption
	2 stone lids	storage
	1 bronze awl	multipurpose
1702	jasper bead	adornment

Table 4.77—*Continued*

Locus	Finds	Functional Class
	looped pin head	adornment
	bronze nail head?	tool?
1703	1 bowl	food preparation/consumption
	1 krater	food preparation/consumption
	1 jar	storage
	4 beer jars	liquid storage
	1 lamp	lighting
	1 cup and saucer	special/cultic
1707	1 bowl	food preparation/consumption
	1 narrow-neck jar	liquid storage
	1 cup and saucer	special/cultic
1709	1 bowl	food preparation/consumption
	1 cooking pot	food preparation
	2 narrow-neck jars	liquid storage
	1 beer jar	liquid storage
	1 bilbil	liquid storage
	1 lamp	lighting
	1 spinning bowl	textile production
	female plaque	special/cultic
	1 jar stopper	storage
1711	1 narrow-neck jar	liquid storage

Table 4.78. *Beth Shan Level VI House 1700—Finds and Functional Classes*

Locus	Finds	Functional Class
1584	1 krater	food preparation/consumption
	2 narrow-neck jars	liquid storage
	1 glass scaraboid	business/adornment
1585	1 bowl	food preparation/consumption
	1 krater	food preparation/consumption
	2 cooking pots	food preparation
	2 jars	storage
	3 beer jars	liquid storage
	1 amphora	liquid storage
	3 flasks	liquid storage
	1 pyxis	special/cosmetic
	2 cup and saucer vessels	special/cultic
	1 stirrup jar	liquid storage
1588	1 chalice	food consumption

The similarity coefficient for L. 1584, 1585, 1588 is 149 or 74.5% when compared to the storage paradigm.

Table 4.78—*Continued*

Locus	Finds	Functional Class
1715	basalt bowl	food preparation
	duck figurine	special/status
1717	1 bowl	food preparation/consumption
1717W	2 scarabs	business/adornment

Level VII (Fig. 82)

In the earlier stratum (Level VII) an Egyptian style residence, adjoining a migdol was identified. The published plan of this structure, showing superimposed walls, makes comparison with Amarna style buildings very difficult. The arrangement of rooms appears to be incomplete, as if certain interior walls were missing and secondary ones had been constructed.[1] The central hall, such a standard feature in Egyptian style houses, is unrecognizable. As excavated and published, this structure cannot be classified as an Amarna style residency. Indeed, Weinstein describes it as a building with a 'courtyard along one side ... and rows of long and short rooms occupying the rest of the structure except for connecting corridors' (1981: 18), comparable to the buildings at Aphek, Tel Mor and Tell esh-Sheri'a. Clearly, the Stratum 9 building at Tell esh-Sheri'a and Building 1104 at Aphek (see above) shared certain characteristics and differed from the Beth Shan (Level VI) and Tell el-Far'ah (S) residencies; nevertheless, it is not clear to me how Weinstein arrived at his interpretation.

Other Sites

Several other sites are mentioned in the discussion of Amarna style houses in Palestine. These include the Amman Airport structure, the house at Tananir on Mount Gerizim, and the fortress at Tel Mor.

---

1. It is not uncommon for a wall to be built across a pillared room to support a sagging second storey. However, it remains difficult to ascertain whether this was primarily a structural necessity or a redesign of interior space; cf. the Amman Airport Building.

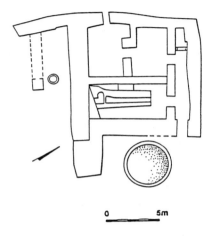

0 _____ 5m

Figure 82. *Beth Shan Level VII, after Rowe 1930: Fig. 2*

'Amman (Map Reference 238/151)

The ancient site of Rabbath Ammon, reinhabited in 1876 as the modern city of 'Amman, is located in the Jordanian highlands, 40 km
northeast of the Dead Sea. On the grounds of the civilian airport to
the east of the city, a square structure, first discovered in 1955, was
identified by G.L. Harding as the 'Amman Temple. Excavations were
carried out in 1966 by J. B. Hennessy on behalf of the British School
of Archaeology in Jerusalem, and in 1976 by L.G. Herr and
L.T. Geraty (Herr 1983: 1).

The 'temple', which measured c. 15 × 15 m, had a very regular
plan (Fig. 83). A square, central room is surrounded on all sides by
rectangular rooms parallel to the exterior walls. These walls were
1.95–2.00 m thick while the interior walls were 1.2 m. Although this
building has certain construction techniques in common with other
Late Bronze Age Amarna style buildings, there are also significant
differences. For example, the Stratum II Residency at Tell el-Far'ah
(S) had 2 m thick exterior walls, but this structure was c. 23 ×
23 m and had at least 17 rooms, whereas the 'Amman building at
15 × 15 m had only 7 rooms. This means that the size, shape, and

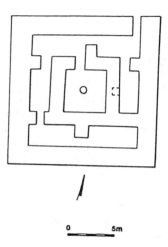

Figure 83. *'Amman Airport Building, after Avi-Yonah 1978: 990*

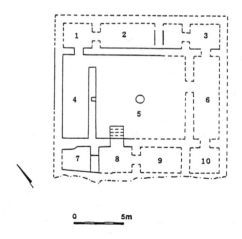

Figure 84. *Tananir, after Boling 1981: Fig. 2*

arrangement of rooms was considerably different in the Residency. There were, of course, many houses at Tell el-Amarna (e.g., K51.1, 15 × 17.5 m) smaller than the 'Amman building. In such houses, the rooms were proportionately smaller, and the walls were less thick (c. 55 cm). In fact, comparison with these small houses is inappropriate because the thickness of the exterior walls of the 'Amman temple (2 m) places it in the category of high status buildings. At the same time, it does not include any of the other high status features of the Amarna style houses, such as the shrine or niche, the dais or divan, and the lustration slab in the central hall (Crocker 1983: 53). In addition, the second most characteristic room of Egyptian houses, the Loggia, is missing.

Subsequent excavation in the area of the 'Amman building by Geraty and Herr, uncovered a structured rock pile which included signs of burning and a large number (1127) of human bones. The suggestion of the excavators that this locale served as a cremation pyre must be seriously considered (Herr 1983: 23, 25). The results of these excavations strengthen the view that the 'Amman building may have been used for certain rituals, although their exact nature remains uncertain.[1]

Tananir (Map Reference 176/179)

Tananir is the site of a structure located on the lower slopes of Mount Gerizim, c. 300 m from ancient Shechem. Originally excavated by G. Welter in 1931 as part of the German and Dutch excavations at Shechem, the site was re-excavated by R. Boling in 1968 for the American Schools of Oriental Research (Boling 1975: 33).

Building A (Fig. 84), which was partially exposed by Welter and unpublished except for a few paragraphs (1932: 314), was the second phase of occupation at this site.[2] Boling dated Building A, as well as

---

1. The numerous finds of jewellery in the fill beneath the floors of the 'Amman building may be the result of a one-time event whereby these items were deliberately buried. There is no irrefutable evidence to associate the burial of the jewellery with whatever ceremonies may have occurred on the structured stone pile to the north of the building. It is hard to imagine how so much gold and jewellery would accumulate otherwise in fill dirt when there was so little evidence of occupation on the south and east sides of the building (Herr 1983: 11).

2. This sequence does not include the Early Bronze activity in this area

the earlier phase, to the Middle Bronze Age, MB IIC (1975: 48). Due to the fact that the site had been previously excavated, few artefacts were found *in situ* (Table 4.79). However the finds published from the ASOR excavation do indicate a variety of domestic activities, especially food preparation, cooking and storage, textile production, agriculture, and lighting (Boling 1975: 69-83). The tool kit for L. 110, when compared to the food preparation and consumption paradigm, has a similarity coefficient of 166 or 83%, a very strong comparison for this study.

It is disappointing that all specifically cultic objects, which formed the basis for Welter's identification of the Tananir building as a temple, have been lost. It is not clear to me why Boling thought that the presence of a needle and an alabaster vessel was support for a cultic interpretation (1975: 56). Indeed, the very small bowls (Boling 1975: Pl. 1: 5, 9, 10) are a better indicator of cultic activity, which Boling admits (1969: 101), although they could have been used in a domestic cult rather than in a public ritual.[1]

The plastered floors and walls, the central pillar base and the large rooms all point to an important building. While not the size of a 'palace', Building A was an exceptionally fine structure with a possible total size of c. 18 × 18 m (not including Building B to the northeast). It is this final phase, Building A, that Boling compared to the 'Amman Temple.

Although there are many points of comparison, there are also many noticeable differences that must be seriously considered. While the 'Amman building at 15 × 15 m is almost as large as Building A at Tananir, the interior room sizes are very different. This is due primarily to the very thick walls (c. 2 m) of the 'Amman structure. The result is that the square, central room is only one quarter the size of Room 5 at Tananir. In addition, the niche opposite the central pillar at 'Amman does not open into the central room but into a side room (Fig. 83). Another important difference is the fact that there was only one doorway into the central room in the 'Amman building whereas two doorways into Room 5 at Tananir were documented and others

represented by a small amount of pottery sherds and flint tools (Boling 1975: 66-68). That Building C, consisting only of the square central room in its earliest phase, was contemporary with the nearby rooms of Building B is a working hypothesis on the part of Boling (1969: 101).

1. For a study of the domestic cult in a later period, see Holladay 1987: 249-99.

were suggested (Fig. 84). This serious difference in traffic patterns and communication between rooms has been pointed out by V. Fritz who understood the 'Amman building as a tower (1971: 151). As Herr has noted, this view does not allow for the large amount of pottery recovered from the excavations of Harding and Hennessy and for the concomitant lack of occupational debris surrounding the structure (1983: 27).[1]

It seems safe to say at this point that the 'Amman structure was not originally designed as a domestic building regardless of the large amount of ceramic remains. Secondly, there is insufficient similarity between this building and the structure at Tananir to determine the function of the one by comparison with the other. Thirdly, because of the loss of the original artefacts and excavation details from Tananir, the functional identification of this structure must remain tentative. The building at Tananir may have been a large residence in the Egyptian style. It is clear from the excavations at Amarna that some houses were square while others were somewhat rectangular because of additional rooms. However, on the basis of the type of analysis employed in this study, no firm identification of activity areas can be formulated that would conclusively support the view that the Tananir building was a private house.

Table 4.79. *Tananir—Finds and Functional Classes*

Locus	Finds	Functional Class
110	4 bowls	food preparation/consumption
	2 cooking pots	food preparation
	1 juglet	multipurpose
	1 lamp	lighting

The similarity coefficient for L. 110 is 166 or 83% when compared to the food preparation and consumption paradigm.

| 308 | 1 whorl | textile production |

1. V. Hankey interpreted the function of the 'Amman building as that of storehouse, accounting in this way for the large amount of pottery vessels found in the debris (1974: 168). However, there should have been evidence for nearby occupation that went with the construction of such an impressive storehouse.

Tel Mor (Map Reference 117/136)

The site of Tel Mor is located on the north bank of Nahal Lachish (Wadi Sukreir), 7 km northwest of Ashdod. This small mound, covering only 0.6 hectares, was probably associated with the port of Ashdod (Avi-Yonah 1977: III, 889). The first Late Bronze Age level which was sufficiently exposed to reveal a complete building was Stratum 9. No plan of the the main building has been published although it has been described briefly and identified as a storehouse (Avi-Yonah 1977: III, 889).

The main building of Strata 8–7 was a heavy-walled structure that measured c. 23 × 23 m (Fig. 85). The exterior walls (2.0–2.5 m thick) were characterized by inset-offset construction. The plan, which shows some similarities to that of Building 906 at Tell esh-Sheri'a in that it has no central room, seems to have been the basement level of a multistoried building. Because the finds have not been published, no functional analysis can be attempted. However, it is clear that this building was not a typical Residency, at least on the basis of the ground floor plan.

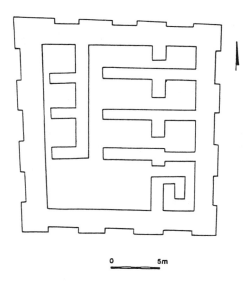

0   5m

Figure 85. *Tel Mor Fortress, after Dothan 1977: 888*

Summary

In this study of the Egyptian style buildings in Canaan during the Late Bronze Age, three types of structure have been identified: the Residency (Beth Shan, Tell el-Far'ah [S] and possibly Tananir), the 'administrative' building (Tell esh-Sheri'a, Tell el-Hesi, Khirbet el-Meshash, Aphek), and the possible fortress (Tel Mor) or tower (?) ('Amman). Because the finds from these buildings have not been adequate for a detailed functional analysis, this assessment of function is based primarily on the differences in room size, shape and arrangement. Only in certain instances have the contents of a room reflected the activities that were carried out there.

Because the function of so many rooms remains unknown, it is not clear, in many cases, whether or not the ground floor served as living quarters. Those houses described in this study as Residencies of the Amarna style were, indeed, patterned on their Egyptian prototypes with the reception rooms and living quarters on the ground floor. While there may have been additional sleeping and working areas on the roof or on the upper storey, the ground floor plan clearly reflects the same room arrangement as the houses at Tell el-Amarna.

The buildings designated as 'administrative' structures did not exhibit the customary features of Late Bronze Age Palestinian houses, such as food preparation areas, small storerooms, ovens, bins and silos. Long, rectangular storerooms, stairways to the second storey, stone-paved floors and pillared halls characterize these buildings. Some of these same features were found in the building at Tel Mor, but the thickness of its exterior walls and the inset-offset construction suggests that this building served a defensive purpose. The 'Amman building seems to be an anomaly among these structures. Complete publication of recent excavations is urgently needed to sharpen these distinctions.

Chapter 5

ACTIVITY AREAS AND SIMILARITY COEFFICIENTS

In this study I have been able to identify various functional tool kits representative of domestic activity areas in second millennium Palestinian houses on the basis of the finds recovered in archaeological excavations. In order to establish a consistent methodology for dealing with the archaeological record, all reported ceramic vessels and artefacts were organized in locus groups and these groups were compared to paradigms designed as models of specific functional tool kits. The model tool kits were constructed to test for areas of food preparation and consumption, storage, pottery production, textile manufacture, weaving, personal adornment, economic affairs, and animal care and management.

Altogether, 22 sites with Middle Bronze and/or Late Bronze Age structures were analysed. From these sites, 26 occupation levels[1] yielded 97 locus groups with a sufficient number of vessels and artefacts for comparison with the functional paradigms. These groups fell into the five categories: food preparation and consumption, storage, pottery production, textile manufacture and weaving (Table 5.1).

1. Occupation levels with tool kits comparable to the functional paradigms are: Hazor 3, 2, 1B, 1A, 1; Megiddo XI, X, VIII, VIIB, VIIA; T. Mevorakh XV, XIV, XIII, XII; Beth Shan VI; Ashdod 2; T. Batash; Tell Beit Mirsim E, D; Kh. el-Meshash Area E; Beth Shemesh V, IVA, IVB, IVC; T. el-'Ajjul lower city, upper city.

Table 5.1. *Locus Groups Successfully Compared to the Functional Paradigms*

Sites	Food Preparation/ Consumption	Storage	Pottery Making	Textile Industry	Weaving
Hazor	18	7	1		
Megiddo	11			5	1
T. Mevorakh	8	2			
Beth Shan	3	3			
Tananir	2				
Ashdod	1				
T. Batash	2	2			
Beth Shemesh	8	3			
T. Beit Mirsim	3	2			
Kh. el-Meshash	1	1			
T. el-'Ajjul	7	3			
T. esh-Sheri'a	1				
T. el-Far'ah (S)	2				
TOTAL	67	23	1	5	1
Percentage	69%	24%	1%	5%	1%

No assemblages of finds representative of Personal Adornment, Economic Affairs, or Animal Care and Management had sufficient numbers for successful comparison with the functional paradigms using Robinson's coefficient of similarity.

On the basis of our successful comparison of 84 locus groups with the functional paradigms, it is clear that the two most important domestic activities for which enough evidence remains in the archaeological record were food preparation and/or consumption and storage. While this is not surprising in itself, there are other activities, integral to the domestic space, that occupy much of daily life but which are poorly represented by nonperishable material artefacts, such as social interactions of various kinds and sleeping. All perishable articles, such as clothing, bedding, interior decoration and natural products, such as wood, leather, straw, and the like, have disintegrated except in rare instances.

The comparison of my results with other kinds of domestic assemblages, chosen from sites differing culturally and chronologically from this sample, could be useful in assessing the reliability of the functional paradigms as a tool to identify artefact assemblages[1]. For

1. According to Seymour and Schiffer, 'few ethnoarchaeologists have obtained systemic inventories and subjected them to detailed analysis and rarely are complete

this purpose, assemblages from non-urban domestic contexts have been chosen. One such assemblage, enumerated in sufficient quantitative detail to be useful, was presented by Brooks and Yellen. In their study of 16 seasonal camps of African forager groups, artefacts related to food procurement, processing and consumption dominated: 150 items from the camps represented 76% of the total finds. Other categories represented in the assemblage were hunting 12%,[1] textile manufacture and adornment 5%, toys 5% and other activities 1% (Brooks and Yellen 1987: Table 2.2).

A closer similarity might be expected when comparing the results to finds from other, more permanent, domestic structures. As an example, the assemblage of finds from House 6G:3 at Snaketown, Arizona, contained 2 bowls, 3 jars, 1 scoop, 1 handstone and a hearth, along with a cache of shell material (in a distinct locus). When compared to our food preparation and consumption paradigm, the similarity coefficient for this assemblage is 116 or 58%. A second house, 9E:2 (also known as 2:9E—Haury 1976: 65), contained items representing two or more activities. Food preparation and consumption is evident by the presence of 8 bowls (Haury 1976: 65, and Figs. 12.50, 12.51), 2 jars, 2 hearths, 1 mano and charred maize kernels. Other activities are represented by a spindle whorl, smoothers, polishers, axes, (Seymour and Schiffer 1987: Fig. 12.3) and choppers (Haury 1976: 65). Comparison of the complete assemblage with the food preparation and consumption paradigm yielded a similarity coefficient of 108 or 54%. Further refinement is not possible due to the fact that the finds were scattered throughout the house, whereas the paradigms used in the present study were designed to deal with smaller loci.

An unusual example of detailed reporting from a Near Eastern site is that of R. Dornemann (1981) in his preliminary study of Late

household inventories described in ethnographies' (1987: 551). Neither Kramer or Watson compiled such inventories on a house by house, or room by room, basis. In view of the difficulty of finding useful household assemblages in ethnographic studies, I have chosen archaeological assemblages which have no connection with the ancient Near East in order to avoid a circular argument.

1. The names of the artefact categories used by Brooks and Yellen have been adjusted to correspond to those used in this study; hunting (unchanged), gathering and food processing (food preparation), manufacture of clothing/ornaments (textile manufacture and adornment), toys (unchanged), other (other activities).

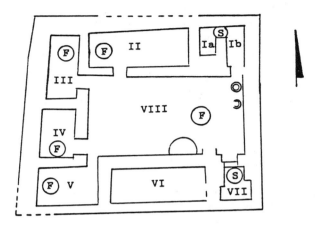

Figure 86. *Tablet House at Tell Hadidi, after Dornemann 1981: Fig. 2*

Bronze Age pottery from Tell Hadidi, with special reference to the
finds from the Tablet House (Fig. 86). In his article, Dornemann
specifies that the ceramic forms drawn in his Figures 3, 4 and 5–10
represent more than half of the vessels found in the Tablet House.
This statement is accompanied by a table (his Table 1) which enumerates the types and quantity of vessels for each type by room (1981: 31,
32). In order to see whether such reporting allows for more complete
functional/spatial analysis, this assemblage will be analysed using the
same format and statistical evaluation employed throughout this study
(Table 5.2; Charts 5.1, 5.2).

The assemblage presented for the Tablet House at Tell Hadidi consists primarily of ceramic vessels.[1] Few objects, aside from tablets and
grinders, are mentioned. Unfortunately, it is not clear that these finds
constitute the total artefact assemblage. In spite of this, the building

1. It is unfortunate that there are so many typographical errors in this article. For
example, the names of the ware forms in Table 1 are poorly positioned; from
'Pitchers' on, the names are above the wrong numbers; Figs. 3:1 and 2 are misspel-
led; Fig. 7 has no item numbers. Secondly, Table 1 lists one cooking pot for Room
IV, whereas the text mentions two, and locates the pots for Room 1a on the line for
1b, and vice versa (1981: 33).

yielded 127 complete or restorable vessels, not to mention the numerous sherds, reported as a group, from Room II and the melted vessels in Room V (Dornemann 1981: 32, 33). Only one room had less than 4 items while the average was 16. These statistics are comparable to those from Hazor and Tel Batash but stand in marked contrast to such sites as Ashdod (2 vessels reported for all rooms in Stratum 3 and 36 items reported for Stratum 2), Beth Shemesh and Tell el-'Ajjul (2–5 items per room).[1]

Table 5.2. *Tablet House Finds and Functional Classes*

Locus	Finds	Functional Class
Ia	4 pithoi	dry storage
Ib	2(?) jars	storage
	3 jugs	food preparation/storage

The similarity coefficient for L. Ia and Ib is 171 or 85.5% when compared to the storage paradigm.

II	3 bowls	food preparation/consumption
	1 goblet	food consumption
	3 kraters	food preparation/consumption
	3 cooking pots	food preparation
	1 jar	storage
	4 pithoi	dry storage
	1 flask	liquid storage

The similarity coefficient for L. II is 163.1 or 81.5% when compared to the food preparation and consumption paradigm.

III	3 bowls	food preparation/consumption
	12 goblets	food consumption
	7 kraters	food preparation/consumption
	5 cooking pots	food preparation
	1 jar	storage
	3 pithoi	dry storage
	1 jug	food preparation/storage
	2 flasks	liquid storage
	jar and tablets	business
	1 jar stand	storage
	grinding stones	food preparation
	3 jar lids	storage

1. Certain site publications, such as Megiddo, reported many more objects than ceramic vessels presumably due to the respective value placed on these items. At the same time, few finds of any kind were reported for certain strata, such as Megiddo Stratum XII and Stratum XI where the reported finds were widely scattered among the excavated structures.

Table 5.2—*Continued*

Locus	Finds	Functional Class
	grain	food storage

The similarity coefficient for L. III is 173.6 or 86.8% when compared to the food preparation and consumption paradigm.

IV	2 bowls	food preparation/consumption
	1 goblet	food consumption
	2 cooking pots	food preparation
	1 jar	storage
	4 pithoi	dry storage
	1 jug	food preparation/storage
	2 jar stands	storage
	1 zoomorphic vessel	special

The similarity coefficient for L. IV is 132.9 or 66.4% when compared to the food preparation and consumption paradigm, and 133.6 or 66.8% when compared to the storage paradigm.

V	5 kraters	food preparation/consumption
	1 cooking pot	food preparation
	2 jars	storage
	3 jugs	food preparation/storage
	1 juglet	multipurpose
	1 lid	storage

The similarity coefficient for L. V is 167.4 or 83.7% when compared to the food preparation and consumption paradigm.

VI	1 krater with hole	unknown
	burial in jar	infant burial
	stone pavement	unknown
VII	carbonized grain	food storage
VIII	4 bowls	food preparation/consumption
	4 goblets	food consumption
	6 kraters	food preparation/consumption
	3 cooking pots	food preparation
	2 jars	storage
	5 pithoi	dry storage
	2 jugs	food preparation/consumption
	baking tray?	food preparation
	tablets	business
	strainer	food preparation
	3 lids	storage
	2 ovens	cooking
	seated statue	special/cultic

The similarity coefficient for L. VIII is 173 or 86.5% when compared to the food preparation and consumption paradigm.

The number of finds reported for this building (133) is outstanding when we remember that at Tell Beit Mirsim Albright reported only 59 items for the Patrician House. Needless to say, the amount of recoverable items depends on the state of the house at the moment of abandonment and the cause of its destruction. Evidently, the Tablet House suffered a sudden and unexpected end in which most of the items were preserved *in situ*. This means that the room assemblages should reflect the range and location of the activities which occurred repeatedly in that house.

That careful recovery and detailed reporting makes it easier to understand the activities carried out in this particular house is quickly seen when the assemblages are compared to the functional paradigms. The similarity coefficients are, on the whole, somewhat higher than those for a house of comparable size competently reported in my sources, such as House 6063 at Hazor, Area C (Chart 5.1). In the Tablet House, 4 rooms can be compared with the food preparation and consumption paradigm with the following results: Room II = 163.1 or 81.5%, Room III = 173.6 or 86.8%, Room V = 167.4 or 83.7%, and Room VIII = 173 or 86.5%. One room, L. IV, compared equally well with the food preparation and consumption paradigm (132.9 or 66.4%) and the storage paradigm (133.6 or 66.8%). Twin Rooms Ia and Ib compared well to the paradigm for storage (Chart 5.2) with a similarity coefficient of 171 or 85.5%. Room VII contained no ceramic vessels (Fig. 86). Instead, the floor was covered with carbonized grain indicating considerable investment in space used for storage. In comparison to the storage paradigm, this room can be given the artificial similarity coefficient of 199 or 99.5%. Room VII at Hadidi may serve as a model for understanding the function of small, empty rooms in other houses, such as Room 6237 of Hazor House 6063[1] (see also, L. 15 at Beth Shemesh).

The fact that so many room assemblages could be compared to the food preparation and consumption paradigm is surprising in view of the large number of storage vessels in each room of the Tablet House (39% of all ceramic ware forms) and of large kraters and vats (18%), although the distinct function of the latter is not entirely clear on archaeological grounds alone. Certain pithoi and vats had perforated

---

1. At Hazor, Room 6042 in House 6101 (Area C) was also found empty, as was Room 8029 of House 8039 (Area F). In neither case, however, was there mention of botanical remains.

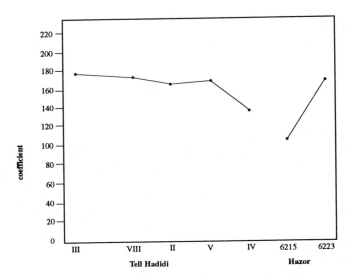

Chart 5.1. *Similarity Coefficients: Food Preparation and Consumption in House 6063 at Hazor and the Tablet House at Tell Hadidi*

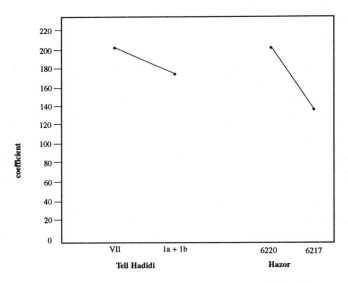

Chart 5.2. *Similarity Coefficients: Storage in House 6063 at Hazor and the Tablet House at Tell Hadidi*

bases which makes their function of storing liquids for a long time problematic (Figs. 3: 1-3; 7: 4; 8: 1-4; however, see Gates below). The number of cooking pots from the Tablet House that were identified and illustrated (13 = 10.2% of the total assemblage) bears witness to greater care in archaeological field methods and changes in theoretical concerns during the past 50 years. The recovery of these ordinary local wares at Hadidi, and at other contemporary excavations, contrasts sharply with the results from Area CC at Megiddo where 1 cooking pot was reported out of a total of 316 items (0.3%). On the other hand, this discrepancy in numbers, along with the vats and large amounts of grain, could point not only to improved excavation methods but also to specialized functions carried out in the Tablet House. As we have already seen at Tel Batash, especially in Room 467 (14 cooking pots and 30 jars, jugs and juglets), cooking pots, when they were not in use, seem to have been kept in storerooms. I have already argued this in regard to potters' wheels during the off season; see Hazor, Area C, L. 6217.

However, another interpretation is also possible. Gates's study of the tablets from this building shows that the vats and grain were associated in the production of beer (1988: 66-68). It is probable that some of the cooking pots, especially those found in storerooms, were also associated with this industry and were used at some stage in the production process.

Because a room assemblage of pottery and artefacts may be disturbed in its final moments or sometime thereafter, the location of the finds may not represent their usual functional place. An example of a badly disturbed room is described by Dornemann (L. II). Here, a cooking pot, which contained the remains of food, was found among pithoi and kraters in what was obviously a storeroom. Was the cooking pot put in the room temporarily when danger or fire threatened? No oven or cooking area was reported for Room II so that it must be assumed that all cooking was performed in L. VIII where ovens are drawn on the plan (Dornemann 1981: Fig. 2). Indeed, clear evidence of cooking was found in Room VIII where 2 cooking pots were found *in situ* in the southernmost oven (Dornemann 1981: 33). This oven was associated with a raised pavement, possibly a feature connected with the cooking process or for parching grain. The function of a plastered, semicircular feature in the same area is less well understood.[1]

The simultaneous publication of objects, with their locus numbers, is also necessary if the complete story of artefact distribution and activity areas is to be told. We do not yet have all the objects from Tell Hadidi.[2] However, with the publication of the tablets from the Tablet House, we now know that beer production and grain storage took place in this house along with the daily tasks of food preparation. This industrial activity located in a house extends the repertory of domestic activities that are suggested in this study of Palestinian houses, where the range of posited non-food related activities included textile production, pottery manufacture on a small scale, personal adornment, tool manufacture, storage of tools and weapons, economic transactions and recreation.

These three examples of artefact groups from domestic sites representing widely different cultures and periods demonstrate that the archaeological record typically preserves evidence of tool kits associated with food preparation and consumption and storage, the same activities which tested well in this study of Palestinian houses. The weakest parallel was that of the African forager assemblage. Here 88% of all finds, distributed over the entire site, were related to food procurement and preparation, whereas in the Palestinian locus groups successfully compared to the functional paradigms, 69% were related to food preparation and consumption. A closer parallel was found in the assemblages from the Hohokam houses at Snaketown, Arizona (6G:2 and 9E:2), with similarity coefficients of 116 and 108 respectively when compared to the food preparation and consumption paradigm. The range for Palestinian houses was 101 to an artificially high 199. Other domestic activities, such as textile manufacture and shell working, were also in evidence in the Hohokam houses. As it appears from Charts 5.1 and 5.2, the strongest parallel was the Tablet House at Tell Hadidi which dated to the second millennium BC and shared certain similarities, in terms of object and vessel types, with the Palestinian houses analysed above (Chapters 3, 4). These similarities derived from the fact that Hadidi was geographically contiguous with

---

1. A similar feature, also located in a food preparation area, was uncovered at Tell el-'Umeiri, L. 5K96.21, in 1987 (Daviau, in press).

2. Objects which have not been mentioned in the text can be seen in photographs published in the earlier report (Dornemann 1979: Fig. 33).

ancient Palestine and shared comparable modes of production and levels of urbanism.

Despite unavoidable differences, the methodology employed in this study receives further support from the work done at Grasshopper Pueblo by Richard Ciolek-Torrello (1984). This breakthrough in New World archaeology moved the discussion of Pueblo room function from dependence upon architectural variation to an analysis of activity areas based on the spatial, quantitative and associational attributes of artefact groups or 'toolkits' within architectural constraints (Ciolek-Torrello 1984: 130).[1]

At Grasshopper Pueblo, the loci chosen for analysis were specifically first-storey rooms; all 'second-story rooms and the lower floors in a superimposed sequence of floors' were excluded (Ciolek-Torrello 1984: 135). A second stage of selection eliminated all rooms with more than 200 sherds m-2. Although such a selective approach could not be used in studying second millennium Palestinian houses, Ciolek-Torrello's classification of room functions corresponds well with the types of activity areas recognized in this study.

Ciolek-Torrello was able to distinguish 6 room types: (1) Limited Activity rooms, (2) Habitation rooms, (3) Domestic Storage rooms, (4) Multifunctional Habitation rooms, (5) Manufacturing rooms, and (6) Storage/Manufacturing rooms. Type 1 has affinities with those rooms from Palestinian houses where remains proved insufficient for a full comparison with the functional paradigms. Type 2 corresponds to the rooms that compared positively to the food preparation and consumption paradigm. Type 3 is similar to those rooms we classified as storage rooms. Type 4 corresponds to those rooms in our corpus, whose tool kits indicated several activities, and which may have served as living rooms. On the other hand, Type 5 does not compare well with Palestinian houses, where, insofar as our data goes, manufacturing activities usually took place in the same rooms as other domestic activities. Type 6 corresponds reasonably well to our rooms where manufacturing equipment was temporarily in storage.

Given that my study of Palestinian houses used a considerably simpler statistical method, and was based on previously published

---

1. The functional identification of each artefact and ceramic vessel type was based on 'reasonable functional interpretation' and 'intuitive appraisals of formal and associational characteristics' commonly in use among southwest archaeologists (1984: 136).

reports, the degree of similarity between my results and those obtained by Ciolek-Torrello seems all the more significant. This is a serious confirmation of the usefulness of Robinson's similarity coefficient and of ethnographic analogy in analysing activity areas at Palestinian sites.

Chapter 6

DISTRIBUTION OF DOMESTIC ACTIVITIES

At those sites where functional tool kits have been identified, a further investigation into the relationship of the various activities to their location in the architectural space, and to each other, can be undertaken. Such a study assumes that recognizable tool kits represent the activities that occurred repeatedly in a particular house just before the time of its destruction or abandonment. The meaningful organization of these activity patterns within architectural space can demonstrate the way in which ancient domestic architecture functioned to provide a suitable environment for each of the routine activities of daily life.

Food Preparation

Food preparation and storage are the two most common domestic activities that I was able to localize. The areas apparently associated with food preparation and consumption usually exhibited certain architectural features, such as ovens/hearths, benches/shelves, bins and pits, that were otherwise associated, in my ethnographic survey, with activities typical of a kitchen and/or living room area. My study of these features, where they were reported or illustrated, shows that the number (Chart 6.1) and location (Chart 6.2) of ovens varied considerably from house to house. In 38.5% of the cases, two or more ovens seemed to be associated with the same house, for example, Hazor Stratum 3 House 6205 (Fig. 3) and Megiddo Stratum XI (Fig. 11). Tell en-Nagila (Fig. 38) and Ashdod (Stratum 3 and Stratum 2) (Figs. 57, 58) are two sites where three or more ovens were reported for the same structure. Much more common, 62.5% of all occurrences, was the identification of one oven per domestic unit, for example, Tell Beit Mirsim Stratum D (Fig. 27). In certain cases, both types of distribution were evidenced, for example, Hazor Area C and Area F

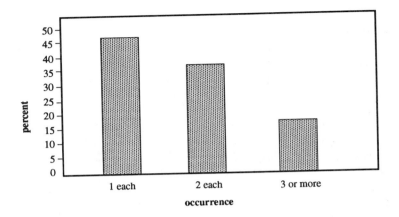

Chart 6.1. *Ovens per House*

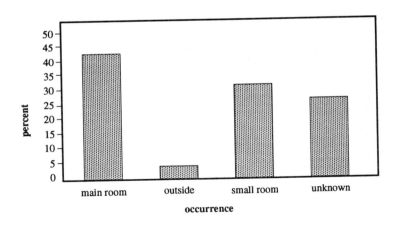

Chart 6.2. *Location of Ovens*

Stratum 1B (Figs. 40, 43) where the plans show some houses with one oven and others with two.

The location of the oven seemed to follow several well defined patterns. The first was that of an oven located in a large room,[1] for example, Hazor Stratum 3 House 6205 (Fig. 3), Hazor Area F Stratum 1B (Fig. 43), Ashdod Stratum 3 and Stratum 2 (Figs. 57, 58), Tel Mevorakh Stratum XIII (Fig. 23), see also Tell Hadidi (Fig. 86). In other instances, the oven was located in a small entry way, sometimes separated by a partition wall, for example, Hazor Stratum 3 House 6205 (Fig. 3), Tell Beit Mirsim East House Stratum D (Fig. 27), Tell el-'Ajjul Area G (Fig. 35), Hazor Area C Stratum 2 (Fig. 39), Hazor Area F Stratum 1B (Fig. 43), Megiddo CC Stratum 7A (Fig. 51a) and Beth Shemesh Stratum 4 (Fig. 65b). Such a pattern clearly indicates that cooking was not carried out exclusively in courtyards during the Middle and Late Bronze period in Palestine. In fact, only 3.2% of all ovens could definitely be located outside the house. What cannot yet be determined is whether the location of cooking changed with the seasons.

While the cooking of food and the baking of bread obviously were associated with the oven,[2] other food preparation activities such as grinding and mixing of food products clearly could and did take place in other rooms of the house. This can be seen by the cluster of food preparation assemblages in rooms surrounding the locus where the oven is found, for example, at Beth Shemesh Stratum 4a (Fig. 61), Tel Halif Stratum 9 (Fig. 70), Hazor Area C Stratum 1B (Fig. 41) and Hazor Area F Stratum 1B (Fig. 44), all in all in 89% of the successfully identified activity areas. Not surprisingly, food preparation seems to have taken place near the oven in other cases (11% of identified areas), for example, at Hazor Stratum 2 (Fig. 39). What is significant is that so many rooms in the same structure were devoted to or included evidence of food preparation and consumption. In certain instances, almost every room contained some items, ceramic vessels or artefacts, that could be associated with these activities.

Living room areas, where food consumption took place apart from food preparation or cooking, could not be identified with certainty.

---

1. By their very nature, ovens were situated near a wall, behind a partition wall, or in a corner to be out of the way of drafts (see the plans in this volume, *passim*).

2. The small number of possible hearths (8?) identified in this study (Figs. 3, 26, 40, 61, 62b, 63, 65b, 66) are not included in the count of ovens.

Part of the reason for this is the fact that the same vessels, in all probability, were used for both purposes. It can also be assumed, when there is no evidence to the contrary, that both cooking and eating may have taken place in the same room, especially when that room was the largest in the house.

Storage

Food storage was also associated with food preparation. Storejars, jugs, juglets, bowls and cooking pots were found both in storerooms and in food preparation areas (see Tables for individual examples). The small number (19) of discrete storerooms identified in this study may reflect the problems of recording and reporting as well as the fact that storerooms were not static areas. Items other than jars containing food stuffs seem to have been put in storage,[1] such as weapons, tools, ceramic vessels, loom weights and potter's wheels. And the amount of food storage probably fluctuated with the seasons and the location of the site in relation to agricultural produce. On the other hand, large pithoi were certainly left in one place and functioned much like granaries, or in-ground silos, that were filled and emptied without being moved. This is also true of the flour bins observed by Watson and Kramer (see above, Chapter 2).

The location of the storerooms in the domestic space seemed to be fairly consistent. Storerooms typically were small, roofed rooms that opened onto the larger hall or courtyard. Usually, there was no traffic through these rooms, in contrast to the major food preparation area, for example, the blocked doorways in the storerooms of House 6215 at Hazor (Area C) (Fig. 41). The association of shelves, grain pits and bins with storage activities is more difficult to confirm because of the lack of information concerning the use of these features and their multi-purpose character; shelves could serve as benches, pits for refuse and bins as mangers. As we have seen above, only one grain room, comparable to that at Tell Hadidi, was identifiable among the buildings under consideration here, Room 15 of Stratum IV at Beth Shemesh.

---

1. Watson mentions a variety of items stored in wall niches and suspended from the walls of the typical living room (1979: 124-5), such as small tools, vessels, lamps, and pots and pans.

Textile Production and Weaving

On the basis of ethnographic observation and ancient iconography, it could be expected that evidence of textile production would be located in the main room in association with food preparation. In this study, the largest distribution of tools and equipment used in textile production was reported 'for Megiddo Area CC Stratum 7A (29 loci). Unfortunately, only five textile production tool kits were large enough to compare successfully with the paradigm, Megiddo L. 1813, 1820 and 1835N. Although less well excavated, Stratum 7B also yielded two concentrations of artefacts related to the preparation of yarn and the production of textiles: Megiddo L. 1831E and 1833N. Because of the limited evidence for this activity, no certain pattern of spatial distribution can be determined. What is clear is that textile production occurred in houses along with a variety of other domestic activities. While it is not surprising that no separate spinning area was identified, the spinning probably being done as a casual activity in a great many social and solitary settings, the fact that only one weaving area could be located was unexpected and may point toward a favoured location somewhere other than the ground floor.

Pottery Production

Only limited evidence of pottery production in the domestic space was discovered, namely Hazor Area C Stratum 1B. The two instances reported for that site (Fig. 41) indicate that certain types (or levels) of pottery production could occur in the same building along with food preparation (L. 6225) and cooking (L. 6063). The third direct witness to pottery making, in Hazor L. 6217, seems to represent a potter's wheel in storage rather than in current use. Because no other major facilities seemed to be present, such as a kiln, it seems reasonable to assume, pending further excavation, that pottery production in these houses was on a limited scale and probably was directly related to the presence of Shrine 6136. Yadin judged this to be the case based on the evidence from Area H where a kiln and workshop were located in the Temple area (1972: 76, 82). In view of this limited attestation of pottery manufacture in a domestic setting, it can be assumed that production for the domestic market was carried out elsewhere on a larger scale (see the pottery production equipment from the caves at Megiddo listed by Wood 1985: Pl. 2).[1] As a result, the inclusion of a pottery production area cannot be assumed to be part of the typical domestic activity areas in Late Bronze Age houses nor even to be located within the main occupational areas of the tell proper.

Business, Personal Adornment and Recreation

Artefacts pertaining to ancient business transactions, such as weights and seals, both of cylinder and scarab style, were numerous in both Middle and Late Bronze Age houses, especially at sites in the south, such as Tell el-'Ajjul (Tables 4.56, 4.58, 4.59) and Tell el-Far'ah (S). At Megiddo as well, seals (Table 7.1), amulets, jewellery, status goods and cosmetic items were numerous (Tables 4.17, 4.20, 4.21). By analogy with the results of ethnographic observation, it could be expected that entertainment and business took place in the living room (see above, Chapter 2). So too, this study has not been able to document any discrete activity areas that were used exclusively as an office where men's personal possessions and tools were kept, or as a bed/workroom where women's or children's personal objects would be stored. Instead, all such objects were found seemingly at random along with items associated with other functional tool kits. Indeed, it was possible to isolate few tool kits clearly representative of business, adornment, cosmetic use or recreation.

Two suggestions can be drawn from such results: the first is that activities such as business transactions, the use of cosmetics and jewellery, and recreation were carried out in the main room along with food preparation and consumption. This is no serious departure from the ethnographic observations reported by Kramer and Watson although it is at some variance with evidence taken from ancient iconographic sources, which distinguished the reception and sleeping rooms from the food preparation areas (see Fig. 1). The second suggestion, more in line with ancient iconography, is that reception rooms and sleeping areas (if these were indeed separate) were on an upper storey. As we have already seen, Albright argued for such a solution in his study of the Middle Bronze Age houses at Tell Beit Mirsim, especially the Patrician House of Stratum D. The evidence

---

1. For an Iron Age example of a pottery workshop area, see Ashdod Area D (Dothan 1971).

analysed in this study does not support either suggestion strongly. However, the existence in some houses of rooms without doorways on the ground floor does argue for an upper storey devoted to domestic activities that gave only limited access to these lower rooms, which, by this interpretation, could have served as storerooms. This configuration is most clearly seen at Hazor Areas C and F Stratum 1B, especially in House 6063 (see also Tables 3.60–63, and discussion of wall thickness).

Other Activities

Evidence for a number of activities not performed in the houses themselves was also suggested in the artefact assemblages. This evidence included tools of various kinds, weapons, some agricultural equipment and debris from certain industries, such as metallurgy, for example Hazor Area F Stratum 1B (Fig. 44), and Beth Shemesh Stratum 4c (Fig. 63). While these objects may have been in storage or 'at rest', the tools and weapons could just as easily have been in secondary usage, although the artefact assemblages, as reported and analysed in this study, did not shed much light on this possibility. Further comparison with assemblages excavated in more controlled circumstances could be useful in extending our understanding of other common activity sets, such as those used in carpentry and building construction, agriculture, war and local defence.

Animals and Stables

Neither the analysis of Late Bronze Age houses nor the study of Middle Bronze structures were successful in identifying areas of animal management. While courtyards were apparent in some houses, I could identify no clear evidence of mangers in such settings. Bins, which may have served, in other circumstances, as mangers, seem in all cases to have been firmly associated with food preparation and storage activities in such a way that the presence of animals seems to be counter-indicated. Bins were commonly located in corners surrounded by ovens and food preparation equipment, or in basement rooms, for example, Hazor Stratum 2 (Fig. 39) and Hazor Area C Stratum 1B (Fig. 41), and possibly Megiddo BB Stratum X (Fig. 13). While other houses, such as those in Megiddo BB Stratum VIII

(Fig. 48), contained bins, these structures were not well enough preserved to evaluate their function with certainty. The only notable exceptions are the instances of bins located against the outside wall of a house, as at Hazor Area C, L. 6212 (Fig. 3), L. 6100 (Fig. 40), Area F, L. 8016) and the basin at the entrance of the building at Aphek (Fig. 80).

Despite the awkwardness of the admission, I can document no other positive evidence for the presence of animals. As was shown above (Table 3.64), the typical 'courtyard' in Palestinian urban houses was very small in size when compared to those observed in rural Iran where animals entered the courtyard and were then housed in underground stables. One possible suggestion may be that animals were cared for outside the walls of second millennium towns. It is possible that few herd or draft animals were kept in the walled towns and that their extramural holding pens have not yet been recognized in the archaeological record. Further surface survey and the excavation of farmsteads and villages, along with continued faunal analysis, may shed additional light on this problem.

Chapter 7

RECLAIMING AN INCOMPLETE ARCHAEOLOGICAL RECORD

Earlier in this study, the artefacts and ceramic vessels from certain strata of four particular sites eluded comparison with our functional paradigms. The most common difficulties preventing this operation were the incomplete character of the archaeological record, or the use of early excavation, recording and publication methods that did not allow for the restoration of adequate locus groups (see Chapters 3 and 4 for specific sites).

Nevertheless, the finds recorded for these particular strata at Hazor, Megiddo, Beth Shemesh and Tell el-'Ajjul can be assembled and assigned to various functional classes. The percentages of finds assigned to each functional class are given below (Table 7.1).

The results of this compilation show ceramic and artefactual evidence pertaining to several functional tool kits, such as personal adornment, economic affairs, use of tools and weapons, possession of special or status items, and cultic activities. My tabulation makes it clear that one of the factors involved in the failure of the data/paradigm comparison is the small amount of ceramic material included among the reported finds, especially at Megiddo, Beth Shemesh, and Tell el-'Ajjul. This can be seen most clearly when comparing the degree of occurrence of food preparation and consumption items at the problematic sites with the degree found at locus groups that tested positive (38.4% Mean, Table 7.1 versus 69%, Table 5.1).

A significant difference can also be seen when contrasting the occurrence of storage items with the locus groups compared to the storage functional paradigm (1.3% Mean, Table 7.1 versus 24%, Table 5.1). The only activity where representation is fairly close between these two groups is textile manufacture. In this case, the mean for all finds from the four sites considered here was 9.7% (Table 7.1), whereas the mean for the locus groups was 5% for textile production and 1% for weaving (Table 5.1).

Table 7.1. *Finds and Functional Classes per Stratum*

Classes	Hazor Stratum 2	Megiddo BB XIIIB(SE)	XIIIB(NW)	XIIIB(N)	XIIIA(NW)
Food Preparation/ Consumption	87.0%	60.0%	25.0%		50.0%
Storage					
Pottery					
Textiles				60.0%	22.2%
Adornment		10.0%			
Economics				10.0%	
Tools/Weapons			31.5%		
Special/Status					14.8%
Cultic			12.5%		
Other/Mixed	13.0%	30.0%	31.0%	30.0%	13.0%
TOTAL	100%	100%	100%	100%	100%

Classes	Megiddo BB XII(SE)	XII(NW)	XI(SE)	XI(NW)	X(SE)
Food Preparation/ Consumption	56.2%		50.0%	33.3%	46.3%
Storage					
Pottery					
Textiles			2.5%		24.3%
Adornment		40.0%	10.0%	16.6%	7.7%
Economics	25.0%		10.0%		3.8%
Tools/Weapons	12.5%		10.0%	8.3%	4.6%
Special/Status				41.5%	7.7%
Cultic			10.0%		
Other/Mixed	6.3%	60.0%	7.5%	0.3%	5.6%
TOTAL	100%	100%	100%	100%	100%

Classes	Megiddo BB X(NW)	Megiddo AA XIII	AA XII	AA XI	Megiddo CC VIIB
Food Preparation/ Consumption	53.2%	66.6%		61.0%	24.0%
Storage					
Pottery					
Textiles	22.8%			9.4%	16.6%
Adornment	3.8%		42.6%		15.0%
Economics	3.8%			9.4%	9.4%
Tools/Weapons	3.8%				12.0%

Table 7.1—*Continued*

Classes	Megiddo BB X(NW)	Megiddo AA XIII	AA XII	AA XI	Megiddo CC VIIB
Special/Status					
Cultic	11.4%				
Other/Mixed	1.2%	33.4%	55.4%	20.2%	23.0%
TOTAL	100%	100%	100%	100%	100%

Classes	Beth Shemesh V	IVB	IVC	T. el-'Ajjul Area GCC	GCD
Food Preparation/ Consumption	50.0%	75.0%	71.4%		
Storage				40.0%	
Pottery					
Textiles	2.5%				37.5%
Adornment	10.0%				
Economics	10.0%				37.5%
Tools/Weapons	10.0%				
Special/Status				60.0%	
Cultic	10.0%				
Other/Mixed	7.5%	25.0%	28.6%		25.0%
TOTAL	100%	100%	100%	100%	100%

Classes	T. el-'Ajjul Area GCD–GDT	GDG–GDY	Mean
Food Preparation/ Consumption	15.4%	21.0%	38.4%
Storage			1.3%
Pottery			
Textiles	15.4%		9.7%
Adornment		21.0%	8.0%
Economics	30.8%	7.0%	6.9%
Tools/Weapons	23.0%	14.0%	6.3%
Special/Status	15.4%	21.0%	7.3%
Cultic			2.0%
Other/Mixed		16.0%	20.5%
TOTAL	100%	100%	100.3%

In order to determine whether the degrees of occurrence for the functional classes identified in Table 7.1 are meaningful, I will compare them with a 10% random sample of the homes studied by

Patty Jo Watson at Hasanabad (see above, Chapter 2). The Hasanabad houses chosen for comparison are Houses 4, 19, 29 and 37.[1] Because not all houses were illustrated (only 24 out of 44) and some illustrations showed only the living room and not the complete house (Houses 27 and 37), the sample shares one of the classic elements of the archaeological record, namely partial preservation. In addition, the listing of household items is not complete in terms of quantification[2] or specific functional identification. These factors make it impossible to assemble locus groups that could be compared with my functional paradigms. However, it is possible to classify functionally most of the objects and features in the Hasanabad houses and determine their degree of occurrence. The mean for the various functional classes of finds from the Hasanabad houses (Table 7.2) could then be compared with the mean for each activity from the four Palestinian sites (Table 7.3) documented below (Table 7.1).

Table 7.2: *Hasanabad Houses—Finds and Functional Classes*

Classes	House 4	19	29	37	Mean	S.D.
Food Preparation/ Consumption	34.8%	41.1%	21.7%	50.0%	36.9%	11.9%
Storage Pottery	30.4%	17.6%	17.4%	35.0%	25.1%	9.0%
Textiles Adornment			21.7%		5.4%	10.85%
Economics			24.1%		6.0%	12.05%
Tools/Weapons Special/Status	9.0%				2.2%	4.5%
Animal Care	17.4%	29.5%	4.3%		12.8%	13.3%
Other/Mixed	9.0%	11.8%	8.7%	15.0%	11.1%	2.9%
					99.5%	

Within this small sample of Hasanabad houses, the level of consistency in materials relating to food preparation or consumption (S.D. 11.9%) and storage (S.D. 9.0%) is noteworthy.

1. Finds and features are listed in Watson 1979: Figs. 5.3, 5.15, 5.21 and 37.
2. In certain cases, Watson indicates plural items without specific quantities. Based on her discussion in the text, estimates have been made regarding the number of items in order to make her data useful for this study.

Table 7.3. *Mean Percentages from Hasanabad Houses and Hazor, Stratum 2, Megiddo, Beth Shemesh and T. el-'Ajjul*

Classes	Hasanabad Houses	Palestinian Sites	Normalized[1] Palestinian Data
Food Preparation/ Consumption	36.9%	38.4%	44.2%
Storage	25.1%	1.3%	1.6%
Pottery			
Textiles	5.6%	9.7%	12.4%
Adornment		8.0%	
Economics	6.0%	6.9%	8.8%
Tools/Weapons	2.2%	6.3%	8.1%
Special/Status		7.3%	
Cultic		2.0%	
Animal Care	12.8%		
Other/Mixed	11.1%	20.5%	26.3%
TOTAL	99.7%	100.3%	101.4%

Clear differences are apparent in this comparison due to the recovery of numerous items of personal adornment and status from the Palestinian houses. Such items were not enumerated by Watson on a house by house basis or even as a total number for the whole town. Nevertheless, the close comparison in terms of food preparation and consumption items, evidence of family business activities and textile manufacture clearly demonstrates that the archaeological indicators appear to measure the same range of activities in the same relative proportions as those represented in an ethnographically observed village society that occupies a somewhat similar environmental area, employs similar production modes, and operates at a comparable technological level as second millennium urban residents of Palestine. In itself, these results are not insignificant, when one considers the caveats concerning the archaeological record and the ways in which it is reported and published, already mentioned in this study, that imply that archaeological reconstruction of ancient life ways is either subjective or extremely difficult. For the categories under consideration, it would appear that our resources are considerably better than might

1. The percentage of occurrence of items in various functional classes from Palestinian sites has been normalized to reflect only the categories of data inventoried at Hasanabad. This means that the categories of adornment, special/status items and cultic objects have been omitted from consideration.

otherwise have been imagined. What is somewhat surprising is the consistently high proportion of items involved in food preparation/ consumption and storage: taken together, 62% of the ethnographic sample from Hasanabad, and 45.8% of the normalized archaeological sample.

One obvious omission from the ancient Palestinian houses is evidence of animal care and management. This activity, as represented in two households and two living rooms, constituted 12.8% of items in the material culture of the inhabitants of the houses sampled from Hasanabad. This omission was also noticed in the locus groups that were comparable with the functional paradigms; not even a single assemblage could be compared to the animal care and management paradigm (see Table 5.1). Thus the primary distinction between the material culture of Hasanabad and the second millennium sites presented in this study may well be one of rural versus urban life styles rather than one of time period (London 1989: 47-48).

Domestic Economy

At most sites, the activities identified in this study are what can be expected as typical of behaviour patterns located within domestic structures. However, when certain activities that are not typical, or at least not highly visible at most sites, are perceived to be highly represented at a few selected sites, their respective artefact assemblages suggest that the residents of these sites were involved in specialist crafts, industries, and/or commercial enterprises on scales not witnessed at the 'average' site. In some cases, the evidence for these activities can be demonstrated even when precise activity areas cannot be located within specific houses.

Three sites warrant our attention: Tell el-'Ajjul, Megiddo and Beth Shan.

Tell el-'Ajjul

The inhabitants of Tell el-'Ajjul were certainly involved in extensive commercial activity at a very different scale than most of their neighbours. This is evident from the large numbers of seals from both the Middle and Late Bronze Age strata (155). That this number is significant can be seen by comparison with items related to storage and

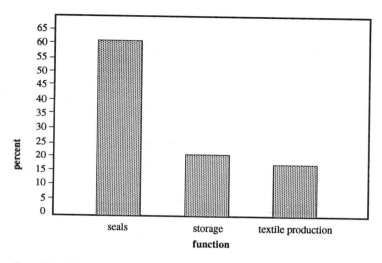

Chart 7.1. *Relative Proportion of Seals and Items Related to Storage and Textile Manufacture at Tell el-'Ajjul Strata 2–3*

textile production, two typical domestic activities (Chart 7.1). While the exact nature of this commercial activity cannot be determined by the methodologies employed in this study, the location of the site in the southern Coastal Plain between Egypt and the rest of Canaan and Syria to the north, as well as the fact that the majority of the seals were scarabs (see above, Chapter 3, Excursus) strongly suggests that this site served as a major port and entrepôt for Egyptian trade. The presence of status items among the reported artefacts, especially alabaster and faience objects, were probably related to this trade (Tables 3.51–54, 4.57–60).

Megiddo

In this study of domestic behaviour, I have assumed that most ancient peoples were regularly involved in the production of clothing and textiles. However, at Megiddo, the percentages of artefacts and tools that were utilized in these tasks are significantly higher than those for storage related items and show a significant increase from Stratum XI

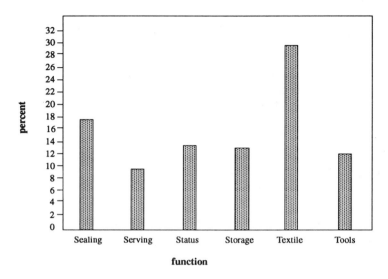

Chart 7.2. *Relative Proportion of Activity Related Artefacts from Megiddo in all Strata*

to Stratum VIIA (Charts 7.2, 7.3). The rate of occurrence of textile related artefacts at Megiddo was more than twice the mean for that activity at other sites (11.2 versus 5.4). Such evidence points to a town where textile production was carried out on a large scale and from which, in all likelihood, textiles were then exported. Activities related to this industry, such as sheep herding, shearing, washing and dyeing of wool, may have taken place outside of the walled town and, in most cases, would have left few remains in the archaeological record. Nevertheless, the fact that textile production tool kits are easily recognizable as highly visible in the material culture in relation to other artefact groupings, especially in Area CC, demonstrates clearly the importance of textile production to the economy of Megiddo (Table 4.19–20).

Additional support for this interpretation of the data may be gathered from the number of seals reported from domestic loci (49, 17.8%; Chart 7.2). These seals, and the fact that Megiddo was located along a major overland trade route to Syria and Mesopotamia, strongly suggest considerable commercial and administrative activities at Megiddo.

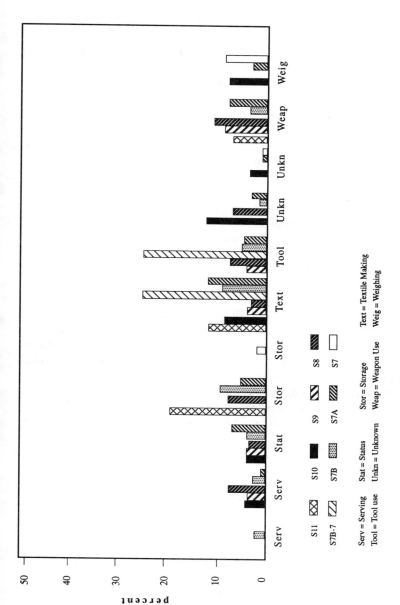

Chart 7.3. *Percentage of Activity Related Finds from Megiddo by Stratum*

Beth Shan

The Level VI houses at Beth Shan were located around a temple and its courtyard. In view of the proximity of these structures to the religious building, it is not surprising that several cult-related artefacts were found in the houses (see Table 4.34). While Beth Shan is not unique in the relationship of religious architecture to domestic buildings (see Hazor Areas C and F, Megiddo Area BB), it is interesting to note the number of religiously affective artefacts found there in comparison with those related to food preparation and consumption (Chart 7.4). Other finds classified as status items and found in these same houses may also have been related to cultic activity. Such finds suggest that these houses may have belonged to the priestly class or may represent the remains of an extensive domestic cult. However, it is likely that the model loaves of bread, found in domestic loci, were used in the temple cult rather than in private devotion at home.

The preceding examples clearly demonstrate that the archaeological record, although in its published form with all the inherent limitations mentioned above, preserves evidence sufficient for reconstructing distinct patterns of craft specialization, commercial and administrative functions and cultic activity across a large sample of second millennium Palestinian cities and/or city quarters. These interpretations have been based on the identification of the functional characteristics of ancient artefacts and ceramic vessels reported from domestic loci and their correlation to discrete behaviour patterns. In these recent examples, viewing the archaeological remains over an entire stratum has made it possible to distinguish activities which were carried out in a domestic setting even when I was not able to establish the precise location of these activities on a room by room basis. With more complete recording and publication of locus groups, it is reasonable to suggest that the archaeological record could be used to study the economic activities of individual families and of city quarters as well as increasing our ability to infer these activities on a community-wide basis. This capability would enhance the usefulness of archaeology as a major resource of socio-economic data, a role filled by epigraphic materials which are conspicuous by their small numbers in Palestinian sites.

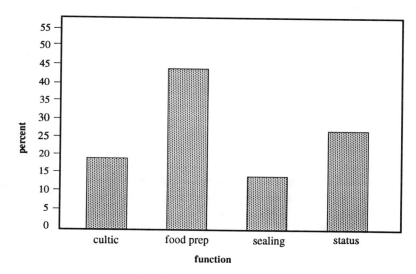

Chart 7.4. *Relative Proportion of Cultic Artefacts, Items Related to Food Preparation/Consumption, Seals and Status Items from Beth Shan Level VI*

Chapter 8

CONCLUSIONS

The essential purpose of this study of second millennium Palestinian houses was to identify the various domestic activities represented in the archaeological record and determine their respective location in the domestic space. Toward this end, I designed a group of ideal artefact assemblages called functional paradigms, drawn from ethnographic observation of traditional communities and from the iconography of a contemporary and related culture.

These paradigms served as a standard against which we could compare the artefact assemblages or locus groups derived from the archaeological record. The specific statistical formula employed for this comparison was Robinson's coefficient of agreement (also termed, within the text, as Robinson's 'similarity coefficient').

My expectations in this regard were constrained by several factors: (1) the degree of preservation of the archaeological record; (2) the limited exposure of Middle and Late Bronze Age levels; and (3) the incomplete nature of the published record. These factors are directly related to developments in the methods of excavation and recording that have occurred over the past 50 years and the impact of different theoretical constructs on the work of the archaeologist.

Nevertheless, I have been able to accomplish some of my goals, especially with respect to activities concerned with eating and storage. In some cases, individual steps in the food preparation process could be recognized and assigned to a definite area in the domestic space; it emerged, for instance, that ovens were usually located in large rooms, or in small rooms situated at or near the entrance of houses.

At those sites where, because of deficiencies in the published record, I was unable to identify particular activity areas in domestic structures, I was able to demonstrate instead the presence and dominance of certain activities at various sites within domestic areas. These activities included trade, textile manufacture and religious activities. While some of these activities were suggested in the published reports (Beth Shan, James 1966: 16), others were not (Megiddo, Loud 1948: 113), and in no case was the demonstration made that these interpretations were anything other than an informed guess.

One important result of this study is the clear evidence of the urban nature of the Middle Bronze and Late Bronze Age towns under consideration. This urban life style was characterized most clearly by the lack of artefacts and features associated with animal care and management. On the basis of this one activity we can posit a fundamental difference between the basic economy of the Late Bronze and that of the Iron Age where evidence for the care of animals within the domestic space is evident in the ground floor area of the '4-room' house (e.g., Braemer 1982: 259).

Such results are encouraging and allow us to expect a good deal from additional activity area studies which are now only beginning (Seymour and Schiffer 1987: 550). Such studies will undoubtedly suggest new ways of looking at the archaeological record and its witness to human behaviour patterns. Not only should we be able to identify what activities were carried out in the domestic space but also how that space was managed. This is crucial for an accurate evaluation of the material correlates of domestic behaviour because these correlates may be confused when various stages of a patterned activity may be preserved simultaneously, such as the activities in process, at rest (not currently in process), or undergoing a change in location or style of execution (Seymour and Schiffer 1987: 551). Recognition of such refinements in the analysis of the formation of the archaeological record should lead to more detailed recording and publishing, involving especially the issuing of tables or other instruments for presenting complete inventories. Concern for artefact distribution should also move the excavator to look at things in a new way, ask new questions and develop new strategies for the recovery of more complete activity sets, including floral and faunal remains, along with detailed studies of the functional values of ceramic vessels, artefacts, and associated architectural features.

A concern for activity area studies, considerably heightened by the research embodied in this study, has already had an impact on my own field excavations in Jordan. I am currently involved in the large-scale Madaba Plains Project which is excavating a series of sites using a uniform recording method and stressing a food systems approach. This approach involves, among other things, the recognition and identification of activity sets (associated artefacts, vessels and architectural elements), and gives special importance to those sets pertaining to the production, distribution, preparation, consumption, storage and disposal of food. All ceramic vessels and objects are photographed *in situ* at several stages during excavation to facilitate a closer observation of the processes of deposition and the patterns of association.

New methods of reporting the functional classification and spatial distribution of finds and their association in functionally specific locus groups are also being developed. Inclusion of all these associations in computer data management systems may soon make possible a quantum leap in comprehensiveness of publication and dissemination of basic excavation records in machine readable form, for example on laser disk, for comparative study by other scholars.

In short, the emergence of activity area studies opens up new paths for our exploration of the life ways and behaviour patterns of ancient peoples.

BIBLIOGRAPHY

Ahlström, G.W.
1979   The House of Wisdom. *SEÅ*. 44: 74-76.
1984   The Early Iron Age Settlers at Hirbet el-Masas (Tel Masos). *ZDPV* 100: 35-52.
Albright, W.F.
1932   *The Excavation of Tell Beit Mirsim in Palestine. I. The Pottery of the First Three Campaigns*. AASOR 12. New Haven: American Schools of Oriental Research.
1933   *The Excavation of Tell Beit Mirsim. IA. The Bronze Age Pottery of the Fourth Campaign*. AASOR 13. New Haven: American Schools of Oriental Research.
1938   *The Excavation of Tell Beit Mirsim. II. The Bronze Age*. AASOR 17. New Haven: American Schools of Oriental Research.
1943   *The Excavation of Tell Beit Mirsim. III. The Iron Age*. AASOR 21-22. New Haven: American Schools of Oriental Research.
1960   *The Archaeology of Palestine*. Gloucester, MA: Peter Smith.
1974   The Chronology of the South Palestinian City, Tell el-'Ajjul. In J.R. Stewart, *Tell el-'Ajjul: The Middle Bronze Age Remains*, 64-75. SIMA 38. Repr. Göteborg: P. Åströms Förlag.
Amiran, R.
1965   A Canaanite-Hyksos City at Tell Nagila. In *Archaeological Discoveries in the Holy Land*, 41-48. Compiled by the Archaeological Institute of America. New York: Bonanza Books.
1969   *The Ancient Pottery of the Holy Land: From its Beginnings in the Neolithic Period to the End of the Iron Age*. Jerusalem: Masada Press.
1976   Tel Hesi. In Avi-Yonah 1976: II, 514-20.
1978   *Early Arad: The Chalcolithic Settlement and Early Bronze City*. Judean Desert Studies. Jerusalem: The Israel Exploration Society.
Anderson, A.
1984   *Interpreting Pottery*. London: B.T. Batsford.
Anati, E.
1975   Tell Abu Hawâm. In Avi-Yonah 1975: I, 9-12.
Assaad, H.A.
1983   The House of Thutnefer and Egyptian Architectural Drawings. *The Ancient World* 6.1-4: 3-20.
1977   *Dictionnaire illustré multilingue de l'architecture du Proche Orient ancien*. CMO 3, Archéologie 2. Lyon: Maison de l'Orient.

1981   *La maison orientale: L'architecture du Proche- Orient des origines au milieu du quatrième millénaire*. 3 vols. Institut français du Proche-Orient. Bibliothèque archéologique et historique 109. Paris: Librairie Orientaliste Paul Geuthner.

Aurenche, O., and P. Desfarges

1983   Travaux d'ethnoarchéologie en Syrie et en Jordanie: Rapports préliminaires. *Syria* 60: 147-85.

Avi-Yonah, M., ed.

1975–1978   *Encyclopedia of Archaeological Excavations in the Holy Land*. 4 vols. Jerusalem: Israel Exploration Society and Masada Press.

Badawy, A.

1966a   *Architecture in Ancient Egypt and the Near East*. Cambridge, MA: The MIT Press.

1966b   *A History of Egyptian Architecture*. II. *The First Intermediate Period, the Middle Kingdom, and the Second Intermediate Period*. Berkeley: University of California Press.

1968   *A History of Egyptian Architecture*. III. *The Empire*. Berkeley: University of California Press.

Balensi, J.

1985   Revising Tell Abu Hawam. *BASOR* 257: 65-74.

Balensi, J., and M.-D. Herrera

1985   Tell Abu Hawam 1983–1984: Rapport préliminaire. *RB* 92: 82-128.

Beck, P.

1975   The Pottery of the Middle Bronze Age IIA at Tel Aphek. *Tel Aviv* 2: 45-84.

Beck, P., and M. Kochavi

1985   A Dated Assemblage of the Late 13th Century B.C.E. from the Egyptian Residency at Aphek. *Tel Aviv* 12: 29-42.

Beebe, H.K.

1968   Ancient Palestinian Dwellings. *BA* 31: 38-58.

Bienkowski, P.

1987   The Role of Hazor in the Late Bronze Age. *PEQ* 119: 50-61.

Binford, L.R., ed.

1967   Smudge Pits and Hide Smoking: The Use of Analogy in Archaeological Reasoning. *American Antiquity* 32: 1-12.

1972   Archaeological Systematics and the Study of Culture Process. In *Contemporary Archaeology*, 125-32. Ed. M.P. Leone. Carbondale: Southern Illinois University Press.

1977   *For Theory Building in Archaeology*. Ed. S. Struever. Studies in Archeology. New York: Academic Press.

1983   *Working at Archaeology*. New York: Academic Press.

Biran, A.

1975   Tel Dan. In Avi-Yonah 1975: I, 313-21.

1982   News and Notes: Tel Dan. *IEJ* 32: 138-39.

Birket-Smith, K.

1965   *The Paths of Culture: A General Ethnology*. Madison: The University of Wisconsin Press.

Bliss, F.J.
1894   *A Mound of Many Cities or Tell el Hesy Excavated.* London: Committee
               of the Palestine Exploration Fund.
Boling, R.G.
1981   Excavations at Tananir 1968. In *Report on Archaeological Work at
               Suwwanet eth- Thaniya, Tananir, and Khirbet Minha (Munhata),* 25-
               85. Ed. G.M. Landes. BASORSup 21. Missoula, MT: Scholars Press.
Borchardt, L., and H. Ricke
1980   *Die Wohnhäuser in Tell el-Amarna.* Berlin: Gebr. Mann Verlag.
Braemer, F.
1982   *L'architecture domestique du Levant à l'âge du fer.* Proto-histoire du
               Levant. Paris: Editions recherche sur les civilisations.
Breasted, J.H., Jr
1948   *Egyptian Servant Statues.* New York: Pantheon Books.
Brooks, A., and J. Yellen
1987   The Preservation of Activity Areas in the Archaeological Record: Etho-
               archaeological and Archaeological Work in Northwest Ngamiland,
               Botswana. In *Method and Theory for Activity Area Research,* 63-106.
               Ed. S. Kent. New York: Columbia University Press.
Burn, A.R., and M. Burn
1980   *The Living Past of Greece.* Boston: Little, Brown & Co.
Callot, O.
1983   *Une maison à ougarit: Etude d'architecture domestique.* Ras Shamra-
               Ougarit I. Paris: Editions Recherche sur les Civilisations.
1984   Rôle et méthodes des constructeurs de maisons à Ras Shamra-Ougarit.
               In *Le dessin d'architecture dans les sociétés antiques,* 19-28. Actes du
               colloque de Strasbourg, 26-28 janvier 1984. Leiden: Brill.
Campbell, E.F. Jr, and J.F. Ross
1963   The excavation of Shechem and the Biblical Tradition. *BA* 26: 1-27.
Campbell, E.F., Jr, J.F. Ross and L.E. Toombs
1971   The Eighth Campaign at Balatah (Shechem). *BASOR* 204: 2-17, 40.
Chadwick, J.
1961   *The Decipherment of Linear B.* Harmondsworth: Penguin Books.
Ciolek-Torrello, R.
1984   An Alternative Model of Room Function from Grasshopper Pueblo,
               Arizona. In *Intrasite Spatial Analysis in Archaeology,* 127-53. Ed.
               H.J. Hietala. Cambridge: Cambridge University Press.
Clarke, D.L.
1968   *Analytical Archaeology.* London: Methuen.
Clarke, D.L., ed.
1977   *Spatial Archaeology.* New York: Academic Press.
Cole, D.P.
1984   *Shechem I: The Middle Bronze IIB Pottery.* American Schools of
               Oriental Research Excavation Reports. Winona Lake, IN: American
               Schools of Oriental Research.
Collon, D.
1975   *The Seal Impressions from Tell Atchana/Alalakh.* AOAT 27.
               Neukirchen: Verlag Butzon & Bercker Kevelaer.

Cowgill, G.L.
1982   Clusters of Objects and Associations between Variables: Two
            Approaches to Archaeological Classification. In *Essays in Archaeo-
            logical Typology*, 30-35. Ed. R. Whallon and J.A. Brown. Evanston, IL:
            Center for American Archeology.
Crocker, P.T.
1983   Status Symbols in the Architecture of el-'Amarna. *JEA* 71: 52-65.
Crown, A.
1971   Some Factors Relating to Settlement and Urbanization in Ancient
            Canaan in the Second and First Millennia B.C. *Abr-Nahrain* 11: 22-41.
Cummer, W.W., and E. Schofield
1984   *Keos 3. Ayia Irini: House A.* Mainz: Philipp von Zabern.
Dalman, G.
1928–1937   *Arbeit und Sitte in Palästina.* Schriften des Deutschen Palästina-
            Instituts. Gütersloh: C. Bertelsmann. I-V.
1964   *Arbeit und Sitte in Palästina.* Schriften des Deutschen Palästina-
            Insituts. Hildesheim: Georg Olms. VI-VII.
Daviau, P. M. Michèle
1991   Field D: The Lower Southern Terrace. In Herr *at al.* 1991: 87-155.
in preparation Hinterland Excavations at Tell Jawa. In L.T. Geraty *et al.*, *The Madaba
            Plains Project, 1989.* Berrien Springs, MI: Andrews University Press.
Davies, G.I., ed.
1986   *Megiddo: Cities of the Biblical World.* Cambridge: Lutterworth Press.
            Grand Rapids: Eerdmans.
Davies, Nina de Garis
1933   *The Tombs of Menkheperrasonb, Amenmose and Another (Nos. 86, 112,
            42, 226).* The Theban Tomb Series 5. London: The Egypt Exploration
            Society.
1963   *Scenes from Some Theban Tombs (Nos. 38, 66, 162, with excerpts
            from 81).* Private Tombs at Thebes 4. Oxford: Oxford University Press.
Davies, Norman de Garis
1903   *The Rock Tombs of el Amarne 1.* London: Egypt Exploration Society.
1927   *Two Ramesside Tombs at Thebes.* New York: Metropolitan Museum
            of Art.
1929   The Town House in Ancient Egypt. *Metropolitan Museum Studies* 1:
            233-55.
Davies, N.M., and A.H. Gardiner
1936   *Ancient Egyptian Paintings.* Chicago: Univeristy of Chicago Press.
Deetz, J.
1967   *Invitation to Archaeology.* Garden City, NY: The Natural History
            Press.
1977   *In Small Things Forgotten: The Archaeology of Early American Life.*
            Garden City, NY: Anchor Press.
Dever, W.G.
1974   The MB IIC Stratification in the Northwest Gate Area at Shechem.
            BASOR 216: 31-52.
1976a   The Beginning of the Middle Bronze Age in Syria-Palestine. In

Magnalia Dei: The Mighty Acts of God, 3-38. Ed. F.M. Cross *et al.* Garden City, NY: Doubleday.

1976b   Gezer. In Avi-Yonah 1976: II, 428-43.

1980a   New Vistas on the EB IV ('MB I') Horizon in Syria-Palestine. *BASOR* 237: 35-64.

1980b   Archaeological Method in Israel: A Continuing Revolution. *BA* 43: 40-48.

1981   The Impact of the 'New Archaeology' on Syro-Palestinian Archaeology. *BASOR* 242: 15-29.

1982   Retrospects and Prospects in Biblical and Syro- Palestinian Archaeology. *BA* 45: 103-107.

1985   Village Planning at Be'er Resisim and Socio-economic Structure in Early Bronze Age IV Palestine. *Eretz Israel* 18: 18*-28*.

1987   The Middle Bronze Age: The Zenith of the Urban Canaanite Era. *BA* 50: 148-77.

Dever, W.G., *et al.*

1970   *Gezer I: Preliminary Report of the 1964-66 Seasons.* Jerusalem: Hebrew Union College Biblical and Archaeological School.

1974   *Gezer II: Report of the 1967-70 Seasons in Fields I and II.* Jerusalem: Annual of the Hebrew Union College-Nelson Glueck School of Biblical Archaeology.

1986   *Gezer IV: The 1969-1971 Seasons in Field VI, the 'Acropolis'.* Jerusalem: Annual of the Nelson Glueck School of Biblical Archaeology.

Dever, W.G., and S. Richard

1977   A Reevaluation of Tell Beit Mirsim Stratum J. *BASOR* 226: 1-14.

Dickens, P.

1977   An Analysis of Historical House-Plans: A Study of the Structural Level (Micro). In *Spatial Archaeology*, 33-45. Ed. D.L. Clarke. New York: Academic Press.

Dixon, D.M.

1972   The Disposal of Certain Personal, Household and Town Waste in Ancient Egypt. In *Man, Settlement and Urbanism*, 647-50. Ed. P.J. Ucko, R. Tringham and G.W. Dimbleby. London: Gerald Duckworth.

Doran, J.E., and F.R. Hodson

1975   *Mathematics and Computers in Archaeology.* Edinburgh: Edinburgh University Press.

Dornemann, R.H.

1979   Tell Hadidi: A Millennium of Bronze Age City Occupation. In *Archeological Reports from the Tabqa Dam Project—Euphrates Valley, Syria*, 113-51. Ed. D.N. Freedman. AASOR 44. Cambridge, MA: American Schools of Oriental Research.

1981   The Late Bronze Age Pottery Tradition at Tell Hadidi, Syria. *BASOR* 241: 29-47.

Dothan, M.

1976a   Ashdod I-II: The Second and Third Seasons of Excavations, 1963, 1965. *'Atiqot* 9-10 (English Series).

1976b   Akko: Interim Excavation Report, First Season, 1973/4. *BASOR* 224: 1-48.
1977   Tel Mor. In Avi-Yonah 1977: III, 888-90.
Dothan, M., and D.N. Freedman
1967   Ashdod I: The First Season of Excavations, 1962. *'Atiqot* 7 (English Series).
Dothan, M., and Y. Porath
1982   Ashdod IV: Excavation of Area M. The Fortifications of the Lower City. *'Atiqot* 15 (English Series).
Eitan, A.
1972   Tell Beit Mirsim G-F—The Middle Bronze IIA Settlement. *BASOR* 208: 19-24.
Ellison, R.
1984   The Uses of Pottery. *Iraq* 46: 63-68.
Erman, A.
1894   *Life in Ancient Egypt*. Trans. H.M. Tirard. London: Macmillan. Repr. New York: Dover Publications 1971.
Evans, J.D.
1973   Sherd Weights and Sherd Counts—A Contribution to the Problem of Quantifying Pottery Studies. In *Archaeological Theory and Practice*, 131-49. Ed. D.E. Strong. London: Seminar Press.
Falconer, S.E., and B. Magness-Gardiner
1984   Preliminary Report of the First Season of the Tell el-Hayyat Project. *BASOR* 255: 49-74.
Fathy, H.
1986   *Natural Energy and Vernacular Architecture*. Chicago: University of Chicago Press.
Flannery, K.V.
1972   Culture History v. Cultural Process: A Debate in American Archaeology. In *Contemporary Archaeology*, 102-107. Ed. M.P. Leone. Carbondale: Southern Illinois University Press.
Fletcher, R.
1977   Settlement Studies (Micro and Semi-Micro). In *Spatial Archaeology*, 47-162. Ed. D.L. Clarke. New York: Academic Press.
Franken, H.J.
1961   The Excavations at Deir 'Allâ in Jordan. *VT* 11: 361-72.
1969   *Excavations at Tell Deir 'Allâ I: A Stratigraphical and Analytical Study of the Early Iron Age Pottery*. Documenta et Monumenta Orientis Antiqui. Leiden: Brill.
Franken, H.J., and M.M. Ibrahim
1978   Two Seasons of Excavations at Tell Deir 'Allâ, 1976-1978. *ADAJ* 22: 57-80.
Frankfort, H.
1950   Town Planning in Ancient Mesopotamia. *The Town Planning Review* 21: 98-115.
Frankfort, H., and J.D.S. Pendlebury
1933   *The City of Akhenaten II: The North Suburb and the Desert Altars*. Memoir 40. London: Egypt Exploration Society.

Fritz, V.
1983   Paläste während der Bronze- und Eisenzeit in Palästina. *ZDPV* 99: 1-42.

Fritz, V., and A. Kempinski
1983   *Ergebnisse der Ausgrabungen auf der Hirbet el-Msas (Tel Masos) 1972-1975.* 2 vols. Abhandlungen des Deutschen Palästinavereins. Wiesbaden: Otto Harrassowitz.

Gardin, J.-C.
1980   *Archaeological Constructs: An Aspect of Theoretical Archaeology.* Cambridge: Cambridge University Press.

Gates, M.-H.
1988   Dialogue between Ancient Near Eastern Texts and the Archaeological Record: Test Cases from Bronze Age Syria. *BASOR* 270: 62-91.

Geraty, L.T., *et al.*
1986   Madaba Plains Project: Preliminary Report of the 1984 Season at Tell el-'Umeiri and Vicinity. In *Preliminary Reports of American Schools of Oriental Research-Sponsored Excavations 1980-1984,* 117-414. Ed. W.E. Rast. BASORSup 24. Winona Lake, IN: Eisenbrauns.

Gerstenblith, P.
1980   A Reassessment of the Beginning of the Middle Bronze Age in Syria-Palestine. *BASOR* 237: 65-84.

1983   *The Levant at the Beginning of the Middle Bronze Age.* Dissertation Series 5. Cambridge, MA: American Schools of Oriental Research.

Gibbon, G.
1984   *Anthropological Archaeology.* New York: Columbia University Press.

Gilead, I.
1987   A New Look at Chalcolithic Beer-Sheba. *BA* 50: 110-17.

Glock, A.E.
1983   The Use of Ethnography in an Archaeological Research Design. In *The Quest for the Kingdom of God: Studies in Honor of George E. Mendenhall,* 171-79. Ed. H.B. Huffmon. Winona Lake, IN: Eisenbrauns.

Gonen, R.
1984   Urban Canaan in the Late Bronze Period. *BASOR* 253: 61-73.
1987   Megiddo in the Late Bronze Age: Another Reassessment. *Levant* 19: 83-100.

Gophna, R.
1979   A Middle Bronze Age II Village in the Jordan Valley. *Tel Aviv* 6: 28-33.

1984   The Settlement Landscape of Palestine in the Early Bronze Age II-III and Middle Bronze Age II. *IEJ* 34: 24-31.

Gopnik, H.
1984   Social Stratification in Middle Bronze Age Palestine. Unpublished paper, University of Toronto.

Gould, R.A.
1980   *Living Archaeology.* New Studies in Archaeology. Cambridge: Cambridge University Press.

Grant, E.
1929   *Beth Shemesh (Palestine): Progress of the Haverford Archaeological
            Expedition.* Biblical and Kindred Studies. Haverford: Haverford
            College.
1932   *Ain Shems Excavations. 1928, 1929, 1930, 1931.* Biblical and Kindred
            Studies 4. Haverford: Haverford College, II.
1934   *Rumeileh being Ain Shems Excavations.* Biblical and Kindred Studies 5.
            Haverford: Haverford College, III.
Grant, E., and G.E. Wright
1938   *Ain Shems Excavations. IV. The Pottery.* Biblical and Kindred Studies 7.
            Haverford: Haverford College.
1939   *Ain Shems Excavations. V. Text.* Biblical and Kindred Studies 8.
            Haverford: Haverford College.
Hamilton, R.W.
1935   Excavations at Tell Abu Hawâm. *QDAP* 4: 1-69.
Hammond, M.
1972   *The City in the Ancient World.* Cambridge, MA: Harvard University
            Press.
Hankey, V.
1970–1971   Mycenaean Trade with the South-Eastern Mediterranean. *Mélanges de
            l'Université Saint-Joseph* 46: 11-30.
Harif, A.
1974   A Mycenaean Building at Tell Abu Hawâm in Palestine. *PEQ* 106:
            83-90.
Haury, E.W.
1976   *The Hohokam: Desert Farmers and Craftsmen.* Tucson: The University
            of Arizona Press.
Hayden, B.J.
1984   Late Bronze Age Tylissos: House Plans and Cult Centers. *Expedition*
            26.3: 37-46.
Hayes, W.C.
1959   *The Scepter of Egypt.* Cambridge, MA: Harvard University Press, II.
Henrickson, E.F.
1981   Non Religious Residential Settlement Patterning in the Late Early
            Dynastic of the Diyala Region. *Mesopotamia* 16: 43-139.
1982   Functional Analysis of Elite Residences in the Late Early Dynastic of
            the Diyala Region. *Mesopotamia* 17: 5-33.
Henrickson, E.F., and M.M.A. McDonald
1983   Ceramic Form and Function: An Ethnographic Search and an
            Archaeological Application. *American Anthropologist* 85: 630-43.
Herr, L.G., ed.
1983   *The Amman Airport Excavations, 1976.* AASOR 48. Philadelphia:
            American Schools of Oriental Research.
Herr, L.G., *et al.* eds.
1991   *Madaba Plains Project. II. The 1987 Season at Tell el-'Umeiri and
            Vicinity and Subsequent Studies.* Berrien Springs, MI: Andrews
            University Press.

Herzog, Z.
1980   A Functional Interpretation of the Broadroom and Longroom House Types. *Tel Aviv* 7: 82-9.

Hodder, I.
1982   *The Present Past: An Introduction to Anthropology for Archaeologists*. London: B.T. Batsford.

Hodder, I., ed.
1978   *The Spatial Organization of Culture*. New Approaches in Archaeology. London: Gerald Duckworth.

Hodder, I., and C. Orton
1976   *Spatial Analysis in Archaeology*. Cambridge: Cambridge University Press.

Hodson, F.R.
1982   Some Aspects of Archaeological Classification. In *Essays in Archaeological Typology*, 20-29. Ed. R. Whallon and J.A. Brown. Evanston, IL: Center for American Archeology.

Holladay, J.S., Jr
1984   *New Dimensions in Ceramic Analysis*. Paper read at the ASOR Annual Conference, Chicago.
1987   Religion in Israel and Judah under the Monarchy: An Explicitly Archaeological Approach. In *Ancient Israelite Religion*, 249-99. Ed. P.D. Miller, P.D. Hanson and S.D. McBride. Philadelphia: Fortress Press.

Horne, L.
1983   Recycling an Iranian Village: Ethnoarchaeology in Baghestan. *Archaeology* 36.4: 16-21.

Hunter-Anderson, R.L.
1977   A Theoretical Approach to the Study of House Form. In *For Theory Building in Archaeology*, 287-315. Ed. L.R. Binford. New York: Academic Press.

Ibach, R.D., Jr
1987   *Archaeological Survey of the Heshbon Region: A Summary and a Catalogue of Sites with Descriptions of each*. Hesban 5. Berrien Springs: Andrews University Press.

Jacobs, L.
1979   Tell-i Nun: Archaeological Implications of a Village in Transition. In *Ethnoarchaeology*, 175-91. Ed. C. Kramer. New York: Columbia University Press.

Jacobs, P.F.
1985   Tell Halif/Lahav: 1983 Season. *ASOR Newsletter* 36.4-5: 4-5.
1987   Tel Halif: Prosperity in a Late Bronze Age City on the Edge of the Negev. In *Archaeology and Biblical Interpretation. Essays in Memory of D. Glenn Rose*, 67-86. Ed. L.G. Perdue, L.E. Toombs and G.L. Johnson. Atlanta: John Knox.

James, F.W.
1966   *The Iron Age at Beth Shan: A Study of Levels VI-IV*. Philadelphia: The University Museum.

Johnson, J.H.
1977   Private Name Seals of the Middle Kingdom. In *Seals and Sealings in*

the Ancient Near East, 141-45. Ed. McG. Gibson and R.D. Biggs. Bibliotheca Mesopotamica 6. Malibu: Undena Publications.

Johnston, R.H.
1974a   The Biblical Potter. *BA* 37: 86-106.
1974b   The Cypriot Potter. In *American Expedition to Idalion, Cyprus: First Preliminary Report: Seasons of 1971 and 1972*, 131-39. BASORSup 18. Cambridge, MA: American Schools of Oriental Research.

Kamp, K.A., and N. Yoffee
1980   Ethnicity in Ancient Western Asia During the Early Second Millennium BC: Archaeological Assessments and Ethnoarchaeological Prospectives. *BASOR* 237: 85-104.

Kaplan, J.
1975   Further Aspects of the Middle Bronze Age II Fortifications in Palestine. *ZDPV* 91: 1-17.

Kassis, H.E.
1973   The Beginning of the Late Bronze Age at Megiddo: A Re-examination of Stratum X. *Berytus* 22: 5-22.

Kelm, G., and A. Mazar
1982   Three Seasons of Excavations at Tel Batash—Biblical Timnah. *BASOR* 248: 1-36.
1984   Timnah: A Biblical City in the Sorek Valley. *Archaeology* 37.3: 58-59, 78-79.
1985   Tel Batash (Timnah) Excavations: Second Preliminary Report (1981–1982). In *Preliminary Reports of ASOR-Sponsored Excavations 1981–1983*, 93-120. Ed. W.E. Rast. BASORSup 23. Winona Lake, IN: Eisenbrauns.

Kelso, J.L.
1968   *The Excavations of Bethel (1934–1960)*. AASOR 39. Cambridge, MA: American Schools of Oriental Research.

Kempinski, A.
1978   Tel Masos, its Importance in Relation to the Settlement of the Tribes of Israel in the Northern Negev. *Expedition*. 20.4: 29-37.

Kempinski, A., and V. Fritz
1977   Excavations at Tel Masos (Khirbet el-Meshash): Preliminary Report of the Third Season, 1975. *Tel Aviv* 4: 136-58.

Kent, S.
1984   *Analyzing Activity Areas: An Ethnoarchaeological Study of the Use of Space*. Albuquerque: University of New Mexico Press.

Kenyon, K.M.
1969   The Middle and Late Bronze Age Strata at Megiddo. *Levant* 1: 25-60.
1970   *Archaeology in the Holy Land*. 3rd edn. New York: Praeger.
1980a   Palestine in the Middle Bronze Age. CAH 3rd edn. 2.1: 77-116.
1980b   Palestine in the Time of the Eighteenth Dynasty. CAH 3rd edn. 2.1: 526-56.
1980c   Syria and Palestine c. 2160-1780 BC: The Archaeological Sites. CAH 3rd edn. 1.2: 567-94.
1981   *Excavations at Jericho*. III. *The Architecture and Stratigraphy of the Tell*. London: British School of Archaeology in Jerusalem.

Kenyon, K.M., and T.A. Holland
1982   *Excavations at Jericho. IV. The Pottery Type Series and Other Finds.*
            London: British School of Archaeology in Jerusalem.
Khammash, A.
1986   *Notes on Village Architecture in Jordan.* Lafayette, LA: University Art
            Museum.
King, P.J.
1983   *American Archaeology in the Mideast.* Philadelphia: American Schools
            of Oriental Research.
Kochavi, M.
1975   The First Two Seasons of Excavations at Aphek-Antipatris: Preliminary
            Report. *Tel Aviv* 2: 17-42.
1978   Canaanite Aphek: Its Acropolis and Inscriptions. *Expedition* 20.4:
            12-17.
1981   The History and Archaeology of Aphek-Antipatris: A Biblical City in
            the Sharon Plain. *BA* 44: 75-86.
Kochavi, M., P. Beck and R. Gophna
1979   Aphek-Antipatris, Tel Poleg, Tel Zeror and Tel Burga: Four Fortified
            Sites of the Middle Bronze IIA in the Sharon Plain. *ZDPV* 95: 121-65.
Kramer, C.
1979   An Archaeological View of a Contemporary Kurdish Village: Domestic
            Architecture, Household Size, and Wealth. In *Ethnoarchaeology*, 139-
            63. Ed. C. Kramer. New York: Columbia University Press.
1982   *Village Ethnoarchaeology.* New York: Academic Press.
Lacovara, P.
1981   The Hearst Excavations at Deir el-Ballas: The Eighteenth Dynasty
            Town. In *Studies in Ancient Egypt, the Aegean and the Sudan. Essays
            in Honor of Daws Dunham*, 120-24. Ed. W. Kelly Simpson and
            W.M. Davis. Boston: Museum of Fine Arts.
1983   Preliminary Report on the Deir el-Ballas Expedition, 1983. *ARCE
            Newsletter* 123: 5-10.
1985   Archaeological Survey and Excavation at Deir el-Ballas 1985. *ARCE
            Newsletter* 125: 17-20.
Lapp, P.W.
1967   Taanach by the Waters of Megiddo. *BA* 30: 2-27.
1969   The 1968 Excavations at Tell Ta'annek. *BASOR* 195: 2-49.
Leone, M.P.
1972   Issues in Anthropological Archaeology. In *Contemporary Archaeology*,
            14-27. Ed. M.P. Leone. Carbondale: Southern Illinois University Press.
London, G.
1989   A Comparison of Two Contemporaneous Lifestyles of the Late
            Second Millennium BC. *BASOR* 273: 37-55.
1990   *Traditional Potters of Cyprus.* Mainz: Jacob von Zabern.
London, G., and M. Sinclair
1991   An Ethnoarchaeological Survey of Potters in Jordan. In Herr *et al.*
            1991: 420-26.
Loud, Gordon
1948   *Megiddo II: Seasons of 1935–1939.* Chicago: Chicago University Press.

Macdonald, E., J.L. Starkey and L. Harding
1932   *Beth-pelet II*. BSAE Publication 52. London: Bernard Quaritch.
McEnroe, J.
1979   Minoan House and Town Arrangement. Unpublished dissertation, University of Toronto.
1982   A Typology of Minoan Neopalatial Houses. *AJA* 86: 3-19.
McGovern, P.E.
1986   *Late Bronze Palestinian Pendants: Innovation in a Cosmopolitan Age.* American Schools of Oriental Research Monographs 1. Winona Lake, IN: Eisenbrauns.
Mackay, E.J.H., W.M.F. Petrie and M.A. Murray
1952   *City of Shepherd Kings and Ancient Gaza V*. BSAE Publication 64. London: Bernard Quaritch.
Margueron, Jean
1976   'Marquettes' architecturales de Meskene-Emar. *Syria* 53: 193-232.
1985   Notes d'archéologie et d'architecture orientales. 4. Propos sur le sillon destructeur (étude de cas). *Syria* 62: 1-20.
1986   Notes d'archéologie and d'architecture orientales. 5. Stratigraphie et architecture de terre. *Syria* 64: 257-71.
Merrillees, R.S
1974   *Trade and Transcendence in the Bronze Age Levant*. SIMA 39. Göteborg: Paul Åström.
Muhly, P.M.
1984   Minoan Hearths. *AJA* 88: 107-22.
Mumford, L.
1961   *The City in History: Its Origins, its Transformations and its Prospects.* New York: Harcourt, Brace & World.
Museum of Fine Arts
1982   *Egypt's Golden Age: The Art of Living in the New Kingdom 1558–1085 BC*. Boston: Museum of Fine Arts.
Nicholas, I.M.
1980   *A Spatial/Functional Analysis of Late Fourth Millennium Occupation at the TUV Mound, Tel-e Malyan, Iran.* Unpublished dissertation, University of Pennsylvania.
Oren, E.
1982   Ziklag: A Biblical City on the Edge of the Negev. *BA* 45: 155-66.
1984   'Governors' Residencies' in Canaan under the New Kingdom: A Case Study of Egyptian Administration. *JSSEA* 14: 37-56.
Orton, C.
1980   *Mathematics in Archaeology*. Cambridge: Cambridge University Press.
Peck, W.H., and J.G. Ross
1978   *Egyptian Drawings*. New York: E.P. Dutton.
Peet, T.E., and C.L. Woolley
1923   *The City of Akhenaten I: Excavations of 1921 and 1922 at el-Amarneh.* Egypt Exploration Society Memoir 38. London: Egypt Exploration Society.
Pendlebury, J.D.S.
1951   *The City of Akhenaten III: The Central City and the Official Quarters.*

2 vols. Egypt Exploration Society Memoir 44. London: Oxford University Press.

Petrie, W.M.F.

1894   *Tell el Amarna*. London: Methuen.

1930   *Beth-pelet I*. British School of Archaeology in Egypt Publication 48. London: Bernard Quaritch.

1931–1934   *Ancient Gaza I-IV: Tell el-'Ajjul*. British School of Archaeology in Egypt Publications 53, 54, 55, 56. London: Bernard Quaritch.

Prag, K.

1974   The Intermediate Early Bronze–Middle Bronze Age: An Interpretation of the Evidence from Transjordan, Syria and Lebanon. *Levant* 6: 69-116.

Redman, C.L., ed.

1973   *Research and Theory in Current Archaeology*. New York: John Wiley & Sons.

Renfrew, C.

1973   *Social Archaeology*. Southampton: University of Southampton.

1984   *Approaches to Social Archaeology*. Edinburgh: Edinburgh University Press.

Renfrew, C., M.J. Rowlands and B.A. Segraves

1982   *Theory and Explanation in Archaeology: The Southampton Conference*. New York: Academic Press.

Richard, S.

1980   Toward a Consensus of Opinion on the End of the Early Bronze Age in Palestine-Transjordan. *BASOR* 237: 5-34.

Ricke, H.

1932   *Der Grundriss des Amarna-Wohnhäuses*. Ausgrabungen der deutschen Orient-Gesellschaft in Tell el-Amarna 4. Repr. Osnabrück: Otto Zeller, 1967.

Robinson, W.S.

1951   A Method for Chronologically Ordering Archaeological Deposits. *American Antiquity* 16: 293-301

Rogers, M.E.

1862   *Domestic Life in Palestine*. London: Bell & Daldy.

Rosen, A.M.

1986   *Cities of Clay: The Geoarchaeology of Tells*. Prehistoric Archaeology and Ecology. Chicago: University of Chicago Press.

Rothman, M.S.

1983   Two Ethnoarchaeological Studies and the Questions they Raise. Review Article. *BASOR* 252: 73-77.

Rowe, A.

1930   *The Topography and History of Beth-Shan*. Publications of the Palestine Section of the University Museum 1. Philadelphia: University of Pennsylvania.

1940   *The Four Canaanite Temples of Beth-Shan. 1930–1940*. Publications of the Palestine Section of the University Museum II. Philadelphia: University of Pennsylvania Press.

Saadé, G.
1979   *Ougarit: Métropole cananéenne*. Beirut: Imprimerie Catholique.
Sarcina, A.
1978–1979   A Statistical Assessment of House Patterns at Mohenjo-Daro.
                Mesopotamia 13-14: 155-99.
Schaar, K.W.
1983   An Analysis of House Form at Tarsus and Alambra. Unpublished paper
                read at American Schools of Oriental Research Annual Meeting, Dallas.
1985   House Form at Tarsus, Alambra, and Lemba. Report of the
                Department of Antiquities Cyprus: 37-44.
Schaeffer, C.F.A.
1939   *Ugaritica I: Mission de Ras Shamra*. Paris: Librairie Orientaliste Paul
                Geuthner.
Schiffer, M.B.
1987   *Formation Processes of the Archaeological Record*. Albuquerque:
                University of New Mexico Press.
Schliemann, H.
1881   *Ilios the City and Country of the Trojans*. Repr. New York: Arno Press,
                1976.
Schoenauer, N.
1981   *6,000 Years of Housing. I. The Pre-Urban House. II. The Oriental
                Urban House*. New York: Garland STPM Press.
Schroer, S.
1985   Der Mann in Wulstsaummantel: Ein Motiv der Mittelbronze-Zeit II aus
                Palästina. In O. Keel and S. Schroer, *Studien zu den Stempel-Siegeln
                in Israel*, I, 49-115. Orbis Biblicus et Orientalis 67. Fribourg: Presses
                Universitaires.
Seger, J.D.
1972   Shechem, Field XIII, 1969. *BASOR* 205: 20-35.
1981   Lahav Research Project: Excavations at Tell Halif, 1980. *BA* 44:
                183-86.
1983   Investigations at Tell Halif, Israel, 1976–1980. *BASOR* 252: 1-23.
Seger, K., ed.
1981   *Portrait of a Palestinian Village*. London: The Third World Center for
                Research and Publishing.
Sellin, E.
1904   *Tell Ta'anek*. Denkschriften der kaiserlichen Akademie der Wissen-
                schaften, Phil.-hist. Klasse, L. Vienna.
Seymour, D., and M. Schiffer
1987   A Preliminary Analysis of Pithouse Assemblages from Snaketown,
                Arizona. In *Method and Theory for Activity Area Research*, 549-603.
                Ed. S. Kent. New York: Columbia University Press.
Shear, I.M.
1968   *Mycenaean Domestic Architecture. I-III*. Unpublished dissertation,
                Bryn Mawr College, Bryn Mawr, PA.
Shipman, P.
1986   The Recent Life of an Ancient Dinosaur. *Discover* 7.10: 94-102.

Smith, S., and L. Woolley
1949   *The Statue of Idrimi.* London. British Institute of Archaeology in Ankara.
Spaulding, A.C.
1982   Structure in Archaeological Data: Nominal Variables. In *Essays in Archaeological Typology*, 1-20. Ed. R. Whallon and J.A. Brown. Evanston, IL: Center for American Archeology.
Stern, E.
1977   Tel Mevorakh. In Avi-Yonah 1977: III, 868-69.
1984   *Excavations at Tel Mevorakh (1973–1976). Part Two: The Bronze Age.* Qedem 18. Jerusalem: Hebrew Univerisity.
Stewart, J.R.
1974   *Tell el-Ajjul: The Middle Bronze Age Remains.* SIMA 38. Göteborg: Paul Åstrom.
Toombs, L.E.
1982   The Development of Palestinian Archeology as a Discipline. *BA* 45: 89-91.
Tringham, R.
1978   Experimentation, Ethnoarchaeology, and the Leapfrogs in Archaeological Methodology. In *Explorations in Ethnoarchaeology*, 169-99. Ed. R.A. Gould. Albuquerque: University of New Mexico Press.
Tubb, J.N.
1983   The MB IIA Period in Palestine: Its Relationship with Syria and its Origin. *Levant* 15: 49-62.
Tufnell, O., *et al.*
1953   *Lachish III: The Iron Age.* London: Oxford University Press.
1958   *Lachish IV: The Bronze Age.* London: Oxford University Press.
Vandier, J.
1952–1964   *Manuel d'archéologie égyptienne.* Paris: Editions A. et J. Picard, I-IV.
Wace, A.J.B.
1955   Preliminary Report on the Excavations of 1954: Mycenae 1939–1954. *Annual of the British School at Athens* 50: 175-89.
Watson, P.J.
1979   *Archaeological Ethnography in Western Iran.* Viking Fund Publications in Anthropology 57. Tucson: University of Arizona Press.
Watson, P.J., S.A. LeBlanc and C.L. Redman
1971   *Explanation in Archaeology: An Explicitly Scientific Approach.* New York: Columbia University Press.
Weinstein, J.M.
1975   Egyptian Relations with Palestine in the Middle Kingdom. *BASOR* 217: 1-16.
1980   Was Tell Abu-Hawam a 19th-Century (*sic*) Egyptian Naval Base? *BASOR* 238: 43-6.
1981   The Egyptian Empire in Palestine: A Reassessment. *BASOR* 241: 1-28.
Welter, G.
1932   Stand der Ausgrabungen in Sichem. *Archäologischer Anzeiger zum Jahrbuch des archäologischen Instituts.* II/IV: cols. 313-14.

Williams, D.P.
1973   Preliminary Report of the Environmental Archaeological Survey of
             Tell Fara, 1972. In *Archaeological Theory and Practice*, 193-216. Ed.
             D.E. Strong. New York: Seminar Press.
Winlock, H.E.
1955   *Models of Daily Life in Ancient Egypt from the Tomb of Meket-re' at
             Thebes*. Cambridge, MA: Harvard University Press.
Woolley, Sir L., and Sir M. Mallowan
1976   *Ur Excavations VII: The Old Babylonian Period*. Publications of the
             Joint Expedition of the British Museum and of the Museum of the
             University of Pennsylvania to Mesopotamia. London: British Museum
             Publications.
Wood, B.G.
1985   *Palestinian Pottery of the Late Bronze Age: An Investigation of the
             Terminal LBIIB Phase*. 2 vols. Unpublished PhD thesis, University of
             Toronto.
1990   *The Sociology of Pottery in Ancient Palestine*. JSOT/ASOR
             Monograph 4. Sheffield: JSOT Press.
Wright, G.E.
1967   Shechem. In *Archaeology and Old Testament Study*, 355-70. Ed.
             D.W. Thomas. Oxford: Clarendon Press.
1974   'The Tell: Basic Unit for Reconstructing Complex Societies of the Near
             East. In *Reconstructing Complex Societies*, 123-40. Ed. C.B. Moore,
             BASORSup 20. Cambridge, MA: American Schools of Oriental
             Research.
Wright, G.H.R.
1985   *Ancient Building in South Syria and Palestine*. Leiden: Brill.
Yadin, Y.
1972   *Hazor: The Head of all those Kingdoms*. The Schweich Lectures.
             London: Oxford University Press
1978   The Nature of the Settlements During the Middle Bronze IIA Period in
             Israel and the Problem of the Aphek Fortifications. *ZDPV* 94: 1-23.
Yadin, Y., *et al.*
1958-1961   *Hazor 1-4*. Jerusalem: Hebrew University and Magnes Press.
Yassine, K.N.
1974a   City Planning of Tell el 'Ajjul, Reconstructed Plan. *ADAJ* 19: 129-33.
1974b   *Domestic Architecture in the Second Millennium in Palestine*.
             Unpublished PhD dissertation, University of Chicago.
Yellen, J.E.
1977   *Archaeological Approaches to the present: Models for reconstructing
             the past*. 2 vols. Studies in Archaeology. New York: Academic Press.
Yon, M.
1981   *Dictionnaire illustré multilingue de la céramique du Proche-Orient
             ancien*. IFAPO, CMO 10, série archéologique, 7. Lyon: Maison de
             l'Orient Méditerranéen.
Yon, M.
1985   La ville d'Ougarit au XIIIe siècle av. J.-C. *CRAIBL* 1985: 705-23.

Sources unavailable for this study

Balensi, J.
1980   *Les fouilles de R. W. Hamilton à Tell Abu Hawam, effectuées en 1932–1933 pour le compte du Dpt. des Antiquitiés de la Palestine sous mandat britannique, niveau IV et V: Dossier sur l'histoire d'un port méditerranéen durant les ages du bronze et du fer (?1600–950 environ av. J.C.).* Unpublished PhD thesis, University of Strasbourg.

INDEX